A Man on Fire

ALSO BY DOUGLAS R. EGERTON

Heirs of an Honored Name: The Decline of the Adams Family and the Rise of Modern America

Thunder at the Gates: The Black Civil War Regiments That Redeemed America

The Wars of Reconstruction: The Brief, Violent History of America's Most Progressive Era

Year of Meteors: Stephen Douglas, Abraham Lincoln, and the Election That Brought on the Civil War

Death or Liberty: African Americans and Revolutionary America

Rebels, Reformers, and Revolutionaries: Collected Essays and Second Thoughts

He Shall Go Out Free: The Lives of Denmark Vesey

Gabriel's Rebellion: The Virginia Slave Conspiracies of 1800 and 1802

Charles Fenton Mercer and the Trial of National Conservatism

The Denmark Vesey Affair: A Documentary History
(with Robert L. Paquette)

The Atlantic World: A History, 1400–1888
(with Alison Games, Kris Lane, and Donald R. Wright)

A Man on Fire

The Worlds of Thomas Wentworth Higginson

DOUGLAS R. EGERTON

Oxford University Press is a department of the University of Oxford. It furthers
the University's objective of excellence in research, scholarship, and education
by publishing worldwide. Oxford is a registered trade mark of Oxford University
Press in the UK and certain other countries.

Published in the United States of America by Oxford University Press
198 Madison Avenue, New York, NY 10016, United States of America.

© Douglas R. Egerton 2024

All rights reserved. No part of this publication may be reproduced, stored in
a retrieval system, or transmitted, in any form or by any means, without the
prior permission in writing of Oxford University Press, or as expressly permitted
by law, by license, or under terms agreed with the appropriate reproduction
rights organization. Inquiries concerning reproduction outside the scope of the
above should be sent to the Rights Department, Oxford University Press, at the
address above.

You must not circulate this work in any other form
and you must impose this same condition on any acquirer.

Library of Congress Cataloging-in-Publication Data
Names: Egerton, Douglas R., author.
Title: A man on fire / Douglas R. Egerton.
Description: New York, NY : Oxford University Press, [2024] |
Includes index.
Identifiers: LCCN 2024032978 (print) | LCCN 2024032979 (ebook) |
ISBN 9780197554050 (hardback) | ISBN 9780197554074 (epub)
Subjects: LCSH: Higginson, Thomas Wentworth, 1823–1911. |
Abolitionists—Massachusetts—Biography. |
Social reformers—Massachusetts—Biography. |
Politicians—Massachusetts—Biography. |
United States—Armed Forces—Officers—Biography. |
United States. Army. South Carolina Volunteers, 1st (1862–1864)—Biography. |
United States—History—Civil War, 1861–1865—Biography. |
Poets—Massachusetts—Biography. |
Massachusetts—History—19th century. |
Massachusetts—Biography.
Classification: LCC F69.H62 E54 2024 (print) | LCC F69.H62 (ebook) |
DDC 973.7/114092 [B]—dc23/eng/20240926
LC record available at https://lccn.loc.gov/2024032978
LC ebook record available at https://lccn.loc.gov/2024032979

DOI: 10.1093/oso/9780197554050.001.0001

Printed by Sheridan Books, Inc., United States of America

*As a women's rights man and the father of daughters,
Higginson would surely approve.*

*For the women:
Evie
Hannah
Kearney
Leigh
Margot*

The Soul unto itself
Is an imperial friend —
Or the most agonizing Spy —
An Enemy — could send —

Secure against its own —
No treason it can fear —
Itself — its Sovereign — of itself
The Soul should be in Awe —
    —Emily Dickinson, 1863, sent to Thomas Wentworth
                   Higginson in South Carolina

The land our fathers left to us,
    Is foul with hateful sin:
When shall, O Lord, this sorrow end,
    And hope and joy begin?

What good, though growing wealth and strength,
    Shall stretch from shore to shore,
If thus the fatal poison-taint,
    Be only spread the more?

Wipe out, O God, the Nation's guilt—
    Then swell the Nation's power,
But build not high our yearning hopes,
    To wither in an hour!

No outward show, nor fancied strength,
    From thy stern justice saves;
There is no liberty for them,
    Who make their brethren slaves!
        —T. W. Higginson, National Anti-Slavery Hymn,
        July 4, 1846, published in *Liberator*, July 14, 1846

Contents

Introduction	1
1. "Launched upon the world": 1823–1841	11
2. "The rearing of a reformer": 1841–1849	33
3. "We all need action": 1849–1854	57
4. "War always educates men to itself": 1855–1857	85
5. "Always ready to invest in treason": 1857–1859	114
6. "Is there no such thing as *honor* among Confederates?": 1859–1860	136
7. "A fighting parson": 1861–1862	158
8. "Path of duty is the way to glory": 1862–1865	178
9. "The women's hour": 1865–1877	216
10. "The happiest day of my life": 1877–1888	247
11. "The crowning years": 1889–1911	274
Acknowledgments	297
Notes	301
Index	331

Introduction

"Colonel Higginson was a man on fire," read one obituary. "He had convictions and lived up to them in the fullest degree." The obituary added that he had "led the first negro regiment, contributed to the literature of America, and left an imprint upon history too deep to be obliterated." Thomas Wentworth Higginson would have been pleased to have been referred to as "colonel." He was proud of his military service and happily used the title for many decades after the end of the Civil War and up to his death in May 1911 at the age of eighty-seven.

Nonetheless, his time in the army was just one of many things for which he hoped to be remembered. "I never shall have a biographer, I suppose," he mused to his diary in 1881. Just in case somebody took up the challenge, however, he wished to provide a hint about his career. "If I do" find a chronicler, he wrote, "the key to my life is easily to be found in this, that what I longed for from childhood was not to be eminent in this or that way, but to lead a whole life, develop all my powers, & do well in whatever came in my way to do."[1]

It was a life marked by numerous struggles for social justice and progressive causes, from abolitionism to women's rights, from religious tolerance to socialism, and from physical fitness for both genders to temperance. Yet almost alone among his contemporaries and reform-minded friends, Higginson refused to devote himself to a single crusade. Even as a young man, he warned his mother that his "greatest intellectual difficulty has been having too many irons in the fire." Some of his colleagues disapproved of this, having dedicated all their efforts to ending slavery or advancing women's social and political rights. Then there were disputes about tactics. Some relied on the pen or the spoken word to garner support for their chosen cause. Abolitionists who followed the lead of Boston publisher William Lloyd Garrison, for example, typically declined to vote and believed that moral suasion and Christian pacifism would bring about an end to slavery. Frederick Douglass argued that violent means might be necessary to liberate four million enslaved Americans, of which he had once been one. John Brown went further still and urged his supporters to take the fight into the contested territories of the Midwest or even the South, which the government of Abraham Lincoln effectively did in late 1862, when the War Department authorized a regiment of contraband soldiers on the Carolina coast.

At one point or another, Higginson embraced all of these causes, which he dubbed the interconnected "Sisterhood of Reforms," and employed all of these tactics to advance them, using the written page, his eloquent voice, his Sharps rifle, and, on one occasion, even a makeshift battering ram.[2]

Higginson's dedication to a wide variety of reform causes, almost none of which benefited him personally and in fact often diminished the power of men of his race and class, makes his story resonate today, especially among those who desire a more just world for its own sake. As a white male born into privilege—although not wealth, thanks to his father's commercial ill-fortune and inattention to his financial affairs—Higginson might easily have spent his early years in cultivating the company of other men of his class or in rebuilding his family's lost wealth in business or industry. He instead devoted his life to assisting those less fortunate than himself, on occasion to the detriment of his own health. He was a man of action. But he also never turned his back on New England society and its literary culture, maintaining lifelong friendships with Emily Dickinson, Henry David Thoreau, and Samuel Clemens—and gravitated easily between worlds. Some call such reformers "bridge" activists, as they developed bonds between emerging organizations, contacted recruits and like-minded campaigners, and forged links between the political and social spheres. Many of the men and women Higginson labored beside possessed a single-minded belief that their methods were the *only* possible way to achieve their ends. When Douglass broke with pacifism and endorsed the Liberty Party, for example, Garrison was unforgiving. Ever pragmatic when it came to tactics, Higginson instead built bridges. He spanned worlds. Apart from one instance, he successfully maneuvered around Garrisonian pacifism while also running for office. He sipped tea with Elizabeth Cady Stanton before catching the train for Kansas to dispatch guns to Free Soil settlers, and he took time to comment on Dickinson's draft poems before steaming up Carolina's rivers at the head of a Black regiment. Higginson was ever the ally, a privileged descendant of New England's first white settlers always ready to cast his lot with the persecuted and oppressed.[3]

Far more than other Brahmin reformers, Higginson was always ready to put his life on the line. He was also the most optimistic of warriors, and even in the grimmest moments of the first two years of the war, when many abolitionists believed their cause was lost, he never lost faith that the nation could be salvaged. Speaking to Boston's Radical Club in 1871, Higginson argued "that this is a remarkably good world, and there are remarkably good people in it." There was hard experience behind this bland-sounding generalization. When he accepted the position of colonel of the South Carolina 1st Infantry in December 1862, some warned him that his recruits had been too brutalized by enslavement to make effective soldiers. That was not his experience. He "had never found a really degraded man among them," Higginson later observed, or encountered "one in whom great feeling might not be aroused in a flash." That sense of optimism drove his reform efforts. Even as a young man, he assured his mother that while life might be easier "with neither passions nor feelings to interrupt" him, that was not to be his fate. "Either a cloud that will pursue me—or sunbeam that I must pursue" would be his life's calling. "I sometimes sigh to see that I do not become calmer as I grow older." His lifelong buoyancy, as he often acknowledged in his journal, convinced even his most despairing ally that their cause would ultimately prevail. "Colonel Higginson is an enthusiast," one Boston friend wrote as he prepared to sail for South Carolina in late 1862, "but I do not see that he exaggerates or states anything but facts."[4]

Higginson's sense of duty and attendant *noblesse oblige* grew from deep familial roots in Puritan New England history, in his case stretching back to the day in 1629 when his ancestor, the Reverend Francis Higginson, waded ashore to help, as he put it, "raise a bulwarke against the kingdom of the Antichrist." Like a number of his ancestors, Higginson initially thought of a career in the Unitarian Church—and was ordained in 1947—telling his friend James Russell Lowell that the "actual experience has thus far enlarged and not diminished my view of what the pulpit may be & do." Francis Higginson had regarded Jesuits as the Anti-Christ, but Thomas Wentworth found dark forces at work among Southern slaveholders and really anyone who declined to join him at abolitionist and women's rights meetings. Never "let one Sunday pass in the professed preaching of Christianity," he railed at his Newburyport congregation in 1848, "and leave the name of SLAVERY unmentioned." When wealthy, business-minded Whig parishioners began to boycott his sermons, the church elders demanded that he resign his ministerial post, a decision that upset the more militant young women of his congregation. His temporary abandonment of the pulpit, however, only permitted him the leisure to devote himself more fully to his various causes. "I have the most intense dread of ennui," he once admitted to Mary Channing, his first wife. "When I look forward & see a space of time wh[ich] I cannot fully use to advantage, it gives me a sort of suffocating sensation."[5]

All this did nothing to persuade Higginson to change course or moderate his tone. Dedicated reformers, he believed, should be nonconformists who raised the ire of the complacent, even at the risk of being denounced as dangerously irrational. True agitators, "thought really sane, are content to be called crazy," he observed to the philanthropist Gerrit Smith. Never a mainstream New England Protestant, Higginson embraced the principles of Transcendentalism, with its core ideals of the goodness of all people, battled state-mandated Sunday concert bans, and fought to allow Catholic children to read in school from the Bible of their choice. In a lecture titled "Merchants," delivered in Newburyport's Washington Hall shortly after his 1849 dismissal from the church, Higginson condemned what he saw as his city's too secular view of employment and labor: "Life is taken up in obtaining, by hook or crook, the means to support life." Too many of his fellows believed that "'to make a living' is the only object of labor—and what is the end of it—only the body lives after all—and all the higher faculties of the soul, love, honor, integrity, courage—these sink, decay, and only *make a dying*."[6]

What set Higginson's spirituality apart, particularly from that of most other Transcendentalists like Emerson or of the Unitarian minister Theodore Parker, was his emphasis on the body. A lifelong physical fitness enthusiast, Higginson believed that training one's body through constant exercise was as important to spiritual enlightenment as improving one's mind. He believed national reform might require physical courage and perhaps even warrior prowess. In "Saints and Their Bodies," an 1858 essay published in the *Atlantic Monthly*, he attacked the common conception that "physical vigor and spiritual sanctity are incompatible." Observing that even Martin Luther derided physical fitness as a pagan ideal, Higginson fretted that this long-standing Christian "moral and physical" anemia, that is, bloodlessness, had infected most New England Transcendentalists. "My severe discipline in this life has come through the heart & the will, not through the intellect and the spirit," he reassured a friend in 1851. "Faith & reason have never given me any trouble." This ideal of muscular spirituality, originally devised by clergy for young men, Higginson recommended for both genders. He encouraged women reformers to undertake strenuous exercise in the cause of reforming the world. "We all need action," he once recorded in his journal. "This is shown by the way it transforms us."[7]

Higginson was never reluctant to put his theories into practice. When his friend Theodore Parker—thirteen years Higginson's senior and in failing health—issued the call for young men to fight for Free Soil in Kansas, Higginson took up the challenge, and as historian George Frederickson observed, "became the first Transcendentalist in arms." Armed only with his "Sharps rifle, [his] revolvers, or those failing, [his] own ingenuity and ready wit," as he put it in a letter home, Higginson found the dangers he encountered there a "delightful sensation," so much so that he escalated the peril he already faced in the territory by traveling east up the Kansas River to the Slave-Soil capital of Lecompton. Striking up a conversation with several "border ruffians," Higginson was amused to hear one say that "there's a preacher going about here preaching politics." He assured the group that he would let them know if he spied any ministers. "For a clergyman of such natural energy and intense self-righteousness," Frederickson marveled, "nothing was more enjoyable than armed combat against the forces of evil."[8]

It was this emphasis on physical force and his acceptance of violence that carried young Higginson away from his flirtation with Garrisonian abolitionism. In 1846, the twenty-three-year-old Higginson penned a brief "Sonnet to W. L. Garrison" in *The Liberty Bell*, an annual abolitionist gift book edited by Boston abolitionist Maria Weston Chapman. Late in life Higginson again paid tribute to Garrison, writing that it was to him "more than to any other man, that the great ultimate result" of abolition was due. Garrison's own grandson Oswald Villard was far closer to the mark when he observed that Higginson, with his "unbounded physical and moral courage, sympathized not at all with the Garrison school of non-resistant Abolitionists." Closer to the present, Emily Dickinson biographer Brenda Wineapple agrees: Higginson "was far more radical than William Lloyd Garrison, if, that is, radicalism is measured by a willingness to entertain violence for the social good."[9]

Such was Higginson's passion that even those reformers and Transcendentalists who did not share his aggressive tactics grudgingly praised them when used in the cause of freedom. In 1854, Higginson joined a handful of Black activists in an unsuccessful attempt to liberate runaway Anthony Burns. Ralph Waldo Emerson, who arrived in Boston only after the attack to deliver a sermon on the affair, conceded that "liberty is aggressive." Referring specifically to Higginson, who had suffered a sword cut to his chin, Emerson added that "it is only they who save others, that can themselves be saved." Massachusetts attorney and Free Soil politician Richard Henry

Dana Jr. agreed, but expressed surprise at Higginson's actions, given his genteel background. "I knew his ardor & courage," Dana later remarked in his memoirs, "but I hardly expected a married man, a clergyman, and a man of education to lead the mob." Higginson placidly waited to be arrested for his role in the affair, and when asked by a journalist to defend his exploits, simply replied, "I enjoy danger." Higginson was, Emerson mused, "the only Harvard Phi Beta Kappa, Unitarian minister, and master of seven languages who has led a storming party against a federal bastion with a battering ram in his hands."[10]

When not actually engaged himself in fighting, Higginson publicly endorsed it in others. When in 1856, John Brown and his followers murdered five proslavery settlers at Pottawatomie Creek, Kansas, mainstream Free Soilers and politicians in the process of switching their affiliation to Republican fell silent or denounced both sides for the rising ride of violence in the territory. Higginson instead joined Theodore Parker and Frederick Douglass in defending "righteous violence." The blood spilled in Pottawatomie, he insisted, put an "immediate check to the armed aggression of the Missourians." As one of the so-called Secret Six, Higginson would go on to raise funds for Brown's later ventures, and he briefly hoped to lead an expedition into western Virginia to free Brown and his men, who were arrested in Harpers Ferry in October 1859. "Higginson was perhaps the most radical man in America," concluded Brown biographer David Reynolds. "He, more than anyone else, carried forward John Brown's Abolitionist spirit." When in late 1862, Higginson was offered the commission to lead Black men of the First South Carolina Volunteers into battle, he reflected that he had "been an abolitionist too long, and had known and loved John Brown too well, not to feel a thrill of joy at last on finding myself in the position where he only wished to be."[11]

Ever the accomplished wordsmith, Higginson helped to fashion what historian Benjamin Quarles once described as a "radical vocabulary that was [as] equally unsettling" as was his willingness to resort to the sword. "Loud language," Higginson once asserted, was necessary to reach those whose ears were stuffed "with southern cotton." While Republican orators were far more likely to condemn the sin of slavery than reproach the sinner, Higginson and other abolitionists hurled epithets at what they regarded as Southern domination in Washington and dubbed the "Slave Power": "man-thief, child-seller, and woman-whipper." In the wake of the presidential election of 1856, which carried with it rumors of vast unrest among enslaved people across the South, the *Washington Union* compiled a list of inflammatory statements issued by leading abolitionists. Of the five men listed, four—Frederick Douglass, Robert Purvis, William Wells Brown, and Henry Highland Garnett—were Black. Only one was not. "The Rev. T. Higginson, of Massachusetts (white), declared: 'All the learning in the world is not worth so much as the *poorest pistol-shot* which any slave ever gave his master.'" With good reason, Higginson, after Brown, was the white reformer Southerners most wanted to see dragged before a court. True to form, when the Harpers Ferry raid collapsed, Higginson patiently waited to be arrested as an accessory and alone among the Secret Six refused to flee the country or seek asylum.[12]

White Southerners and Northern Democrats who were appalled by Higginson's language failed to note that he never endorsed random violence. He supported violence for a purpose. Like the failed revolutionary leader Denmark Vesey, about whom Higginson wrote in 1861, Higginson refused to denounce enslaved people who rose in revolt against their owners. Like Douglass, he posed no objections to inflicting bodily harm on slave catchers and even on federal marshals who came north in search of runaways. When Higginson joined Black activist Lewis Hayden in attacking the Boston courthouse, he was not merely challenging slavery but implicitly, as one historian observes, helping "Northern communities to overcome racial division and stand against the violence of mastery." However, when federal marshal Asa Butman arrived in Worcester to arrest him and was set upon by a mob, it was Higginson who rescued him and drove him to the train station and safety. As colonel of the First Carolina Volunteers, despite allegations by Southern editors, Higginson always kept his men focused on enemy combatants and never on civilians.[13]

Higginson's lifelong refusal to tether himself to a single issue has today kept him from fame by association with one. Scholars, whether of antislavery or literary or gender studies, tend to tell only part of Higginson's story. That also meant that he understood his need for activism had no endpoint. When the Thirteenth Amendment was ratified in December 1865, Garrison set the type of his final *Liberator* with his own hands, and then he was done. As historian Stacey Robertson observes, Higginson, together with Parker Pillsbury and Elizur Wright, was among the few old-line abolitionists to fully turn their energies to women's rights rather than abandon reform. As the son of a strong-minded mother, Higginson had grown up believing that women deserved full equality in all things as a natural right. While many antifeminists insisted that women's superior moral qualities made them unsuitable for the tawdry worlds of politics and business, and many of his female associates argued that it was precisely those attributes that would allow women to purify America, Higginson charted his own middle course. "It is a plausible and tempting argument, to claim suffrage for women on the ground that she is an angel," he wrote in 1862, "but I think it prove wiser, in the end, to claim it for her as being human." He believed, however, that women should always be in the forefront of their own crusade. One historian describes Higginson as being among the "first-wave pro-feminist men" as he supported women's involvement in the public sphere merely as an extension of individual rights. A literary scholar adds that when it came to poets and writers such as Dickinson and Julia Ward Howe, Higginson's "assistance enabled women of his acquaintance to aspire to be heard, seen, and read as had only begun to seem respectable or even conceivable." Women's "political education will not merely help men, but it will help herself," Higginson wrote. "The demand in her behalf is that she shall have the opportunity to make mistakes, since it is by this means she must become wise."[14]

Reformism did not pay the bills, of course, and for that Higginson turned to his pen and the lyceum lecture circuit. Even before a group of New England Brahmins founded the *Atlantic Monthly* in 1857, Higginson had already published dozens of short essays and poems, mostly in the antislavery press. But the *Atlantic* became his home, and by the time he published his last piece with them in 1905 he had submitted an even hundred essays. Although a careful man with a dollar—and like many an author, he quarreled with his editors over every penny—his output reflected his refusal to specialize. His essays ranged from meditations on quiet walks in the woods to pioneering essays on Vesey and Nat Turner. His fellow *Atlantic* authors, Higginson believed, "were teachers, educators, and bringers of the light with a deep and affectionate feeling of obligation toward the young republic their fathers had brought into being." The idea that "New England was appointed to guide the nation, to civilize it, to humanize, none of them doubted," Higginson claimed, and he certainly did not. Henry James later judged Higginson, that "conspicuous figure in almost all the many New England reforms and radicalisms," to be the quintessential *Atlantic* author. "Colonel Higginson has the interesting quality of having reflected almost everything that was in the New England air," both in his refined prose and in his subject matter, wrote James in an essay published in 1898. "I can scarce perhaps express discreetly how the pleasantest ring of Boston is in his tone—of the Boston that involved a Harvard [at] the birth-time of the *Atlantic*, the storm and stress of the war, the agitations on behalf of everything, almost, but especially of the Negroes and the ladies."[15]

Higginson's fondness for and support of the ladies, as James put it, came naturally. Throughout his life, he was molded and supported by women. His father, Stephen, whom Higginson remembered as a distant and feckless figure, died when he was only nine; it fell to his mother, Louisa Storrow, Stephen's second wife and sixteen years his junior, to raise her last child. To help manage their home, Louisa invited her eighteen-year-old sister, Anne "Nancy" Storrow, to live with them. Anne never married, and Louisa, despite still being young, never remarried. Until their deaths Higginson wrote to them nearly every day. After their deaths, Higginson did the same with his unmarried sisters, Susan Louisa and Ann Storrow. Late in life, when rereading his Harvard diaries, Higginson mocked his many youthful "desperate love-affairs," but as an adult, he was an attentive son, brother, husband, and father. "When his biography comes to be written," a Memphis editor said of Higginson in 1885, "in addition to his record as a gallant soldier, a brilliant writer and a ripe scholar, he should be named and honored for his marital nobility." Higginson's first wife, Mary Channing, the journalist noted, spent "most of her life confined to her room, and most of the time to her bed," yet Higginson "never wearied of his attention and kindness to her." That reads like faint praise to modern eyes, yet the reporter was correct in observing that "his friends often remarked" on how "divinely good [he was] to his afflicted spouse." In truth, many of his friends found Mary caustic and difficult, and his longtime ally Lucy Stone uncharitably hinted that Mary's issues were psychosomatic and worsened in proportion to her husband's increasing absences at distant reform conventions. "To the second Mrs. Higginson," the editor concluded—referring to Mary Potter Thatcher, whom he married in 1879—"he has been a most affectionate father to the two little girls that have been born to them." Indeed, the public was so fascinated by the notion of the colonel as a late-in-life father that when he attached a second seat on his velocipede for his young daughter Margaret, it made national news.[16]

Although today Higginson earns extensive cameos in studies of abolitionism, feminism, education, temperance, Victorian fiction, and even in films about Dickinson and in novels and books about Harriet Tubman, he is now best remembered as the colonel who led the First South Carolina Volunteers, the first Black regiment to be approved by the War Department. When published in 1870, his memoir about it, called *Army Life in a*

Black Regiment, was both a commercial and a critical success. Higginson downplayed his own heroism while extolling the courage of his men. He had an ear for language and was fascinated by the Lowcountry dialect of those in his regiment, some of whom were the sons or grandsons of Africans. As the musician and scholar Johari Jabir notes, *Army Life* is today "one of the most widely cited sources in nineteenth-century African American history, music, and culture." The book may be found in any number of bibliographies, as it "fits a number of genres: military, memoir, cultural criticism, and Black music studies." Because the Harvard-educated "Colonel Higgie," as his men called him, understood himself to be a cultural outsider in his own unit, Jabir adds, the volume also amounts to "travelogue writing."[17]

Higginson kept fiddling with the text, and in 1899 he revised *Army Life* one final time. In a dedication to General Rufus Saxton, who had offered him command of the First, the seventy-six-year-old Higginson wrote that Black military service in his war, and more recently in Cuba, was "a guarantee of that ultimate civil equality which [we] may not live to see, but for which we who knew these men in military service can never doubt their fitness." When Americans again went to war in 1917, six years after Higginson's death, President Woodrow Wilson had little use for Black soldiers, and *Army Life* fell out of print. In 1963, for the centennial of Black military service in the Civil War, the *Washington Evening Star* ran a full-page spread on "the Civil War as reported by the *Star* 100 years ago." The story featured images of the First and a portrait of Higginson, together with paragraphs and letters taken from *Army Life*. Collier Books immediately brought the volume back into print as a ninety-five-cent paperback. Today there are seven different editions of *Army Life* in print.

Higginson's wartime experience is worthy of the attention, and the colonel was proud of his service. But it covered only four years of his extraordinary eighty-seven-year life. We need to hear the rest of his story.[18]

1

"Launched upon the world"

1823–1841

He was born into history, and born to make history. Thomas Wentworth Higginson—"Wentworth" to friends and family—first opened his eyes on December 22, 1823. His mother, thirty-seven-year-old Louisa Storrow, had previously given birth to nine children and had buried four. Wentworth, who was to be her last, was born in the Cambridge, Massachusetts, home constructed five years before by his father, fifty-three-year-old Stephen Higginson, who had now sired fifteen children; two daughters and a son born to his first wife, the late Martha Sewall Salisbury, were interred in Boston. The three-story, wood-frame house on what was then Professors' Row (later renamed Kirkland Street) sat near Harvard College, where Stephen worked as a steward, collecting rents from students and procuring books and firewood for them. The street had witnessed the march of militiamen heading toward Bunker Hill in 1775; the soldiers had briefly stopped for a prayer at a nearby gabled-roof home, where Wentworth's friend Oliver Wendell Holmes Sr. was born in 1809. For the surviving children, the Higginson family's legacy as one of the region's oldest families posed a challenge. If they could not all achieve greatness, they were expected, as Louisa once counseled Wentworth, to settle, at least, "on a course that will lead to perfection."[1]

Wentworth's generation was the eighth to reside in Massachusetts, and he hailed from a long "line of Puritan clergymen, officials, militia officers, and East India merchants," as he wrote in later years, "all dating back to the Rev. Francis Higginson, who landed at Salem in 1629." Born in 1586 and raised in a staid Anglican household, Francis received his divinity degree from St. John's College, Cambridge University. He accepted the pulpit of a small church in Belgrave Village, quite near the market town of Leicester, but increasingly he was drawn to Calvinism, and in 1627 he announced himself a Puritan. Francis's nonconformist sermons attracted the ire of several of his powerful parishioners—a fate that was later to befall Wentworth—as well as the censure of Bishop William Laud, whose diocese included Leicester.

Expecting to be called before the High Commission Court and facing possible imprisonment, Higginson, like many Calvinists, began to consider emigration to the Americas. In his pamphlet, *Generall Considerations for the Plantation in New England*, Francis laid out his reasons for abandoning the fight against Anglicanism in the old country. He might be useful, he mused, in helping to "raise a bulwarke against the kingdom of the Antichrist which the Jesuits" allegedly sought to impose. As did most Puritans, he regarded the Anglican Church as Catholic in all but name and despised King Charles I for marrying a French Catholic princess. "It may be justly feared that the like judgment is coming upon us," he fretted, while Plymouth Colony might "be a refuge for many whom [God] meanes to save out of the general destruction." Like many radicals who thought nobles sinful for possessing too much land, Francis also worried about the disposed "poore, [who were] counted the greatest burdens" by the government, but who, "if things were right," deserved "the highest earthly blessings."[2]

On April 9, 1629, Francis signed an agreement with the Massachusetts Bay Company; the *Mayflower* had reached American shores only nine years before. For a minister with so-called "Leveller" tendencies—a Puritanical political movement that emphasized equality before the law and a natural right to property—Francis drove a hard bargain. In exchange for acting as vicar for the new town of Salem, he would receive 30£ "toward the charges of fitting himself with apparel, another 10£ for books, and an annual salary of 30£." He was also promised a manservant who would care for him and his thirteen-year-old son, John, and "catch him fish and foule." His wife, Ann Herbert, and daughter Mary were guaranteed "two maid servants." Six younger children also sailed with the family. And in a report that still made news more than two centuries later, Francis imported the first horses into the colony.[3]

The Higginsons and roughly one hundred other settlers sailed later that April from Gravesend aboard the *Talbot*. As land grew distant, Francis called his flock to gather on the stern. "We will not say, as the Separatists are wont to say at their leaving of England, Farewell, Babylon! Farewell, Rome!" he prayed. "We do not go to New England, as separatists from the Church of England; though we cannot but separate from the corruptions in it." The minister's fellow passengers, Wentworth later wrote, regarded him as "a grave man, and of worthy commendations," and the initial reports of Salem sent back to England prompted another three hundred Calvinists to join them. But their first winter was unforgiving, and of the sixty horses Francis imported, only twelve survived into the spring. He himself did not live much longer. As Governor John Winthrop reported to his wife in September 1630, the "good Mr. Higginson" was dead, as were "many others," from a variety of diseases. Wentworth admired his ancestor's courage and tenacity, if not his religious intolerance, enough to write a short biography of him in 1891. And as one friendly editor wrote after reading one of Wentworth's much earlier antislavery sermons, "one would be ready to believe that the spirit of his freedom loving Puritan ancestor, the minister of Salem, had spoken through him in tone and temper."[4]

Unusual for the time, all eight of Francis's children survived him, as did Ann, for another decade. In 1636, at the age of twenty, his oldest son, John, was ordained as chaplain at the fort in Saybrook, in the new colony of Connecticut. John also taught school until 1653, when he became the pastor of a Guilford church. Two years later, he was invited back to lead his father's Salem church, a position he held for fifty-three years until his death in 1708 at the age of ninety-two. His residency in Salem caught the attention of Wentworth, if perhaps in a less admiring way. After John's daughter Ann was abandoned by her husband, William Dolliver, who took to the sea, John allowed Ann and her child to return to his home, but he publicly complained that she was ruled "by overbearing melancholy, [and] crazed in her understanding." That was also his view of many of the women and girls in Salem. Together with his son John Jr., born in the colony in 1646 and an Essex County magistrate, the Reverend John Higginson examined several of those suffering from what he described as "dreadfull fitts" in the 1692 witchcraft hysteria. Although he was later to dabble in spiritualism, as did many fellow Transcendentalists, Wentworth chose to say almost nothing about his ancestor's involvement in the trials in his history of the early Higginsons, published a year before his death in 1911.[5]

Another generation passed, and Magistrate John's son Stephen, a Salem merchant, and his wife, Elizabeth Cabot, raised seven children, one of them Stephen Jr., born in 1743. As was tragically common in the eighteenth century given medical practices associated with childbirth, Stephen buried three wives—two of them sisters—but not before they bore him ten children and left him with their considerable dowries. His first wife was the daughter of a British merchant then residing in Boston, and the union both explained Stephen's royalist politics and provided him with business contacts abroad. But when the Revolution came, Stephen sided with the colonies. Relocating to Boston, he converted his shipping fleet into privateers and netted a small fortune. In 1778, he formed a trading partnership with his kinsman Jonathan

Jackson; election to the Massachusetts legislature followed, and as the war wound down Stephen was elevated to Congress in October 1782. A staunch nationalist, he was critical of the Articles of Confederation, the loosely framed terms by which the new republic was guided, and urged Virginia delegate James Madison to call a convention for its revision. When selected by Massachusetts to serve as a delegate at the Constitutional Convention in Philadelphia, however, Stephen begged off, insisting that he had to attend to rebuilding his transatlantic business and to caring for his children, including his son Stephen III, who was off at Harvard College.[6]

In later years, Wentworth wrote the second Stephen's biography, too, particularly interested in his grandfather's involvement in slavery. While rummaging through his grandfather's papers, he came across a 1787 runaway slave advertisement, placed by Thomas Smith, a business associate of Stephen and Jackson's. Smith was searching for his pregnant "Negro Wench named Beth," who had fled his Boston home with her husband and had sought work in Manhattan. Smith offered a sizable reward to anybody who would "take Charge" of Beth and return her either to him or to "Messrs. Jackson and Higginson." No clipping or letter revealed the end of that story, and Wentworth admitted he would "take an extreme interest in knowing precisely what reply was made." He prayed, however, that he might "doubt whether a cooperation between them in slave-hunting would have been altogether harmonious." Slavery had perished in Massachusetts over the course of the 1780s due to suits brought by Quock Walker, an enslaved man who ran away from a brutal owner in 1781 and won his freedom in 1791, and Elizabeth Freeman, so at least Wentworth could take solace in the fact that the first federal census of 1790 revealed only "free white persons" in Stephen's Boston household.[7]

"My father's whole fortune went when Jefferson's embargo [of 1807, against importation British goods] came," Wentworth remembered, as "his numerous vessels were captured or worthless." He was now referring to his grandfather's shipping business, in which his father was employed. Two years later, Congress amended the Embargo Act with the Non-Intercourse Act, which lifted restrictions on American ships except those bound for ports controlled by either the French or the British. The act proved to be a smuggler's dream, but even so, in February 1810 the State Department reported the capture of a "forged sea letter, of the ship Arno, of Boston, signed Stephen Higginson and company." Caught once, his grandfather was more careful thereafter. Even after Congress amended the act yet again that May with legislation that further reopened the sea lanes, Stephen publicly warned Captain William Kempton of the *Arno* to "do nothing to violate the laws" of the United States or any European "belligerents" and only imported hemp and iron from Portugal.[8]

The June 1812 declaration of war forced Stephen to shutter his company. On September 23, 1812, the *Boston Commercial Gazette* formally announced its dissolution. "All persons having demands against the said firm of S. Higginson & Co." were instructed to contact the business's main creditors, Samuel Perkins and Edward Newton. In 1814, Stephen rented out his Boston mansion and retreated twenty-five miles inland to the town of Bolton. Victory in an 1817 court case brought by one creditor provided no relief. Sued for $50,000, Stephen and his younger brother Henry won only a judgment stating they were not personally liable for the debt of the company. In any case, Stephen would have been unable to pay, and by 1820 the bankrupt widower was living with his nephew James Higginson in Brookline. "Formerly a very eminent merchant," as one charitable newspaper obituary put it, Stephen died on November 22, 1828, at the age of eighty-five.[9]

Wentworth recalled meeting his grandfather only once, but it was a vivid memory. Just before turning five, he traveled with his parents to Brookline "in a yellow and creaking chaise." Stephen still dressed the part of the elegant Revolutionary-era gentleman in the "small-clothes" of other days and carried a gold-headed cane that would be passed down to Wentworth. He wore all black, with ruffled cuffs and "tightly buttoned gaiters or buckled shoes below." A white cravat provided the only variety. His gray hair was pulled back in a queue and powdered and topped with a broad-brimmed hat. "His imposing figure, air, and manner filled me with ever new admiration," Wentworth remembered. "So, as all boys are wont to fancy, my grandfather appeared to me the peer of the noblest. And still more stately and elegant was he to my imagination when attired in full costume to receive his guests at dinner or evening parties in his own house." The fastidious dress, the adult Wentworth hastened to add, was in no "degree ostentatious." Just months away from death, Stephen, wrote Wentworth, "simply felt that it was a part of self-respect, as of mutual respect, to be scrupulously neat, refined, and elegant. In truth, my grandfather was a singularly manly, energetic, sensible, well-balanced, sagacious man of business, prudent and practical, prompt and energetic, full of enterprise yet conscientious and cautious." High praise indeed, and admiration that spanned the decades.[10]

* * *

Although only ten at the time of his father's death in 1834, Wentworth provided a far more detailed portrait of his grandfather, a man he met only once, than of his own father, who was relegated to less than three pages in his memoirs. Although Wentworth published two biographies of his illustrious ancestors and wished his readers to know that his grandfather had been "singularly successful until the difficulties between Great Britain and France," his own father earned but a cameo in his autobiography and appeared kind and decent but ultimately feckless—an improvident failure who outlived his own father by only six years.[11]

Born in Salem on the eve of the Revolution in 1770, the third Higginson to bear the name of Stephen was raised in luxury, the horrors of war mitigated by his father's lucrative privateering ventures. As the fourth child and second son, Stephen joined his father's firm after graduating Harvard College. He purchased a house on fashionable Mount Vernon Street in Cambridge and pursued "all the habits of affluence," Wentworth later reported. In 1794 he wed Martha Sewall Salisbury, the wealthy daughter of two old New England families; ten months later, Martha bore him a daughter, Elizabeth, who died less than a year later. Four other children quickly followed, including a second Elizabeth, but two of them, including Stephen IV, died young. Stephen's August 1803 birth must have been difficult, as Martha followed him to the grave only one month later, in September. She had only recently turned thirty-two.[12]

"My mother's early life was like a chapter in a romance," Wentworth later wrote of Louisa Storrow. But if her early years read like fiction, it was hardly a novel with a satisfactory finale. Her father, Captain Thomas Storrow, was an English officer. Captured during the Revolution, he was imprisoned in Portsmouth, New Hampshire, where he met and fell in love with seventeen-year-old Anne Appleton. After the war, the young couple resided first in Britain, then in Nova Scotia, and finally in Jamaica. In 1795 he resigned his commission with the intention of going into the shipping business in Boston, but he perished at sea. His daughter Louisa, born in Canada in 1786, was nine. Storrow's young widow opened a school for girls in Hingham, twenty miles outside of Boston, which briefly provided an educational foundation for Louisa. But Anne died within two years, in August 1796. Orphaned at the age of ten, Louisa accepted a position in the household of Stephen Higginson, helping to care for his two young daughters and a wife already described as an "invalid."[13]

During this period, around the age of sixteen, Louisa became engaged to Edward Cabot, a young mariner, but before the wedding could take place, Cabot, too, was lost at sea. After the death of her employer's wife, Louisa had no close relations and nowhere to go, and Stephen invited her to remain in his household as a governess and—here Wentworth, a careful wordsmith, chose a curious term—"an adopted daughter." In February 1805, seventeen months after Anne's death, Louisa agreed to become Stephen's second wife. He "was then in the prime of his beauty," she remembered in later years, "full of youthful ardor and flushed with success." She was nineteen and he thirty-five, an age difference that was only slightly unusual for the time and far from atypical for wealthy widowers and penniless young women.[14]

Fifteen months later, Louisa gave birth to Francis John, the first of her ten children. Stephen, named for his deceased half-brother, followed in 1808, and just less than two years later came Ann Storrow (Anna to friends and family). Louisa's first three children would grow to outlive her, but her fourth child, Edward Cabot, died in 1814 at just less than two years old. Two months after Edward's death, Louisa gave birth to Waldo, who would be the sibling closest to Wentworth, his youngest brother. Susan Louisa, born in 1816, lived to adulthood, as did Samuel Thatcher. But Mary Lee, Louisa's eighth, died in 1826 at the age of six, and yet another Edward Cabot died at the age of three in April 1824. Only four months after she and her husband buried the second Edward, Louisa gave birth to Thomas Wentworth, her tenth and last child (Figure 1.1). He appeared sickly and Louisa held out little hope for his survival.[15]

What this meant for Wentworth was that he was quite nearly raised an only child. His oldest surviving half-sister, Elizabeth, was twenty-five years his senior, and when Wentworth was eight, she married Reuel Keith, a Virginia minister, and relocated to Alexandria. That same year, Francis John married Susan Channing and set up his medical practice in Brattleboro, Vermont. Wentworth was but three when Mary Lee died. Waldo, Susan, and Samuel Thatcher were nine, seven, and five years older, respectively, and at a young age the two boys lived part of the year in a nearby boys' boarding school run by William Wells on Brattle Street. All of his siblings and stepsisters left Cambridge, and only Waldo, Anna, and Susan Louisa appeared often in the adult Wentworth's correspondence. His 1898 autobiography was typical

BIRTHPLACE OF THOMAS WENTWORTH HIGGINSON, KIRKLAND ST., CAMBRIDGE

Figure 1.1 The Higginson family's fortunes had already declined due to Thomas Jefferson's commercial warfare when Stephen Higginson's spendthrift ways forced him to take a job as a steward at Harvard College, his alma mater. It was here in this house on what was then known as Professors' Row that Wentworth was born on December 22, 1823. Courtesy of the Library of Congress.

of its day, in that it largely told of his life as a public man, and most of the reformers and radicals and feminists who filled its pages were national figures. Harriet Beecher Stowe earned six references, William Lloyd Garrison nine, and Wendell Phillips eighteen. But even so, Wentworth mentioned his brother Stephen, a Boston merchant, only three times; Waldo and Susan Louisa but once; and his other siblings not at all, despite the fact that five of them lived to adulthood. Because they were not a part of his youth, neither were they a part of his adulthood.[16]

In the same way, while Louisa's diary never truly criticized her husband, neither did she ever praise him, especially after her father-in-law's firm went bankrupt. Marriages at the time were as much relationships of necessity as of affection. With luck, fondness and even love might follow, but Louisa, who had been almost continuously pregnant for the first seventeen years of her marriage, reserved such sentiments for her children. "On Saturday, the 8th April, 1815, we left our home, endeared to us by a long and happy residence and by the society of many dear friends," she confided to her journal, "to make trial of new scenes, new cares, and new duties" in Cambridge, where her husband's friends had secured him a position as steward at Harvard College. Stephen's annual salary of $1,250 allowed a comfortable enough living, but his spending habits and fondness for entertaining did not reflect his new circumstances. "His hospitality was inconveniently unbounded," Wentworth later observed, and when Francis John, his eldest son, graduated from Harvard, Stephen celebrated with a dinner party of sixty guests. For her part, as a woman not born to privilege, Louisa was less comfortable hosting her husband's Harvard colleagues. She was particularly horrified by his habit of reading their private correspondence at dinner parties. After he invited two couples to spend a Sunday with them, Louisa, to her "utter dismay," found upon "entering the room that he was reading these letters [a]loud to them, and all of the things the very part referencing" her friend Nancy Thane. Louisa routinely begged Stephen to stop doing so, but he stubbornly believed that their personal missives "must be interesting to everybody."[17]

As a former Harvard man himself, Stephen was popular with faculty and students alike. He was especially fond of the divinity students and devoted a good number of hours to acquiring textbooks from abroad for the shelves of Divinity Hall. One colleague found it amusing that Stephen planned to return a box of Hebrew Bibles, thinking them misbound, as the title page appeared at the end of the book. Wentworth inherited his father's cheerful disposition but learned from his irresponsible spending habits. One Harvard friend remembered Stephen fondly, as a man always "glowing with benevolent sunshine, manners so genuinely those of a finished gentleman," but most of all, one of "charity" who was ever "kindly in substance." Another colleague agreed, praising Stephen as "an open fund for every cause and every person that needed and deserved his aid." Several years later, an obituary gushed that Stephen was "a man who despised money for any object or purposes other than for the means it afforded him of doing good with it to others." In short, Stephen practiced the sort of kind benevolence that impressed friends, alarmed his wife, and infuriated his creditors.[18]

Louisa played favorites with her children. Francis John, she once observed, dressed as "quite a man of fashion" and attended "all the parties great and small," but she wondered to what end. Unlike his buoyant father, her eldest son behaved "more like a person condemned to be hung than a gay beau." Although Francis John did marry, in 1831, while still in his twenties, Louisa fretted that "nothing can be more dismally gloomy than his aspect and demeanor." She tried to engage with him about his plans to be a physician but found it "rare to get a word out of him, and if you get an answer when you speak to him you may think yourself lucky." As for her two older sons, she judged Waldo to be superior in talents to Samuel Thatcher and so "always expected more of him." Although she thought him "sensible, correct and refined in feeling and character," she rather doubted that either would accomplish "anything interesting or commendable."[19]

Louisa's diary entries about her youngest could not have been more different. "My dear little baby grows better every day and is nothing but a pleasure to me," she assured a friend when the initially sickly Wentworth grew robust as he turned one. Everything he did she found charming. Wentworth was "so good and pleasant," she recorded around the time of his third birthday. "He got all the little chairs and crickets tied together" to resemble a carriage "and amused himself the greater part of time talking with his horses and going about from one to the other as happy as could be—he is the sweetest and most docile thing in the world and a constant delight to me." Page after page of her journal was devoted to his cheeriness and brilliance. While she sewed his clothes, Louisa remarked in December 1827, Wentworth, age six, her "comfort and delight," sat by her "side, reading or playing." He enjoyed reading Anna Barbauld's *Lessons for Children*, a British conversational primer, and "considering he is not yet 4 years old," Louisa marveled, he was "doing very well." Like all boys, the increasingly athletic Wentworth also delighted in fishing, "firing his bow and arrow and bouncing his ball," all of which Louisa thought enchanting.[20]

Shortly after his third birthday, Louisa enrolled "Little Tommy," as she sometimes called him, in a morning school. He took "great joy" in the program, according to his mother. Afternoons were spent at play, but as the evening approached, the two cuddled together by the fireplace to read. "Nothing takes him from his books and he has been reading to me tonight a whole chapter from Mrs. Barbauld's Lessons without missing a word," she wrote on a typical occasion. Wentworth also enjoyed poring over atlases and studying the Atlantic coast "round Cape Horn, up the Pacific to Valparaiso," she wrote to her son Stephen, who had taken a job with a shipping firm in Rio de Janeiro. He picked "up a little more geography every day and is the quickest little thing at learning that I ever saw." Presumably, Louisa saw little reason to hide from the child her admiration for his intellectual abilities, and if the adult Wentworth inherited his habitual cheerfulness from his father, his enormous sense of self-confidence was surely the gift of his mother.[21]

Having lost three children, Louisa was nearly frantic about Wentworth's health. Even the slightest hint of a cold prompted her to keep him home from school and dose him with castor oil. "I feel it necessary to use greater precautions with him than I should with any other child," she admitted in her diary. "It is bad to have such an anxiety on our mind for I can never feel safe." She continued to mourn the 1824 death of the second Edward Cabot, and Wentworth was "as a sweet solace [to her] in the anguish of bereavement and has continued a source of consolation and hope and joy in the dark hours of affliction." With each spring, however, Wentworth always appeared "much improved," and on those days Louisa complained only about his "incessant" demands for her attention. But as the boy was "the smartest little thing" she had ever seen, with his "uncommon combination of quickness and perseverance, with a power of attention and abstraction," she always forgave "the young gentleman."[22]

Louisa was soon to desperately need Wentworth's love and companionship. In late 1826, a man named Nathaniel Bowditch was elected to Harvard's Committee of Corporation, as its board of trustees was then known. A self-educated mathematician and ship's navigator, he set out to scrutinize all of Harvard's books and quickly discovered shortfalls in the accounts of college treasurer John Davis and steward Stephen Higginson. After Stephen collected rents from students, he passed the money along to Davis, but Bowditch found the records of both men incomplete and calculated that they owed the college $6,859.79. Although Stephen was not technically forced to resign his position, the Corporation sought to prod him into doing so, reducing his salary to $1,000 while increasing his hours and responsibilities. When Stephen told his wife that he had decided to quit, she "was opposed to his giving it up," a stoic Louisa recorded in her diary, but at length she agreed that as his new duties "would be a constant disturbance and irritation to him," he should "take his final leave of the College." Stephen was fifty-seven, and as the news of his dismissal appeared in papers in both Massachusetts and Rhode Island it was unclear to Louisa who might be willing to employ him. "I had a great deal to do in the house this morning," Louisa observed in her journal on November 16, 1827, as "I thought it necessary to reduce our household and in the first place discharge our cook, Eliza." To help manage their home, Louisa invited her eighteen-year-old sister, Anne "Nancy" Storrow, to live with them in exchange for providing her with "the chance of making her an efficient housewife."[23]

The family abandoned the three-story house on Professors' Row, taking up residence in a modest brick home facing the Cambridge commons. The death of the elder Stephen Higginson provided a small inheritance, and Francis John, now with an established medical practice, sent occasional gifts of money, as did his brother Stephen from Brazil. Waldo took a job with a preparatory academy as he prepared for a career in the law, and one Harvard colleague who believed Stephen had been unfairly treated "offered to assist in educating the children," Louisa wrote. Stephen's debts continued to grow, however, and Louisa realized that they would never be able to get out from under their burgeoning liabilities. "I am tired to death and long for the rest to mind and body," she confessed to her diary in March 1828.[24]

"He died when I was nine-years old," Wentworth simply noted in his memoirs, although he had turned ten two months earlier. "Died, at his residence in Cambridge, on the 20th of February, 1834, aged 63," reported the Boston *Christian Examiner*. Most of the obituaries were generous. One New Hampshire newspaper remarked on his "warmth, tenderness, disinterested, [and] cordial attachments." A Manhattan editor conceded that "his destinies in life led him through some of its darkest spots" but insisted that he always "held his head high above the poison of those withering vapours." Several pointed to the commercial warfare with Britain as the cause of his family's penury, and none, remembering the old maxim regarding speaking ill of the dead, commented on his spendthrift habits and the incompetent bookkeeping that had cost him his job with Harvard. It fell to Francis John to serve as executor of his father's will and to promise that he would "exert to his utmost endeavours" to pay off his father's debts. That single line, from his autobiography, was Wentworth's last reference to his father. "My main training came, consequently, from my mother and my aunt Miss Anne Storrow," who remained single her entire life. Aunt Nancy, as he called her, "was to my mother like a second self in the rearing of her children." And like Louisa, Anne believed young Wentworth could do no wrong.[25]

While still in his early teens, Wentworth began to learn about what would become the greatest cause of his life, antislavery. William Lloyd Garrison had begun publication of his uncompromising *Liberator* in 1831, but Wentworth's "own strongest impulse," he wrote in his memoirs, "came incidentally from my mother." While a steward, his father had befriended a good number of Southern students, as well as their parents, and chose to ignore the source of their wealth. As always, Louisa saw things differently. Shortly after the 1831 marriage of her stepdaughter Elizabeth to the Reverend Keith,

Louisa and her husband paid the young couple a brief visit. While taking a carriage ride through the western part of Virginia, the Higginsons fell into a conversation with the enslaved coach driver. "The colored people are poorly off here," the driver bluntly assured the two, as he understood they were from New England. Foolishly, Louisa suggested that he had "a good master who takes care of you," guessing that he was "better off than if you were free." "Missus," he replied, "free breath is good." He went on to tell of his wife and children, who had been sold to the lower South. "I was very much struck with this," Louisa wrote in her journal, "and could not answer him." Wentworth remembered the story and included it in his memoirs.[26]

* * *

In terms of his education, Thomas Wentworth Higginson followed the path of his brothers, enrolling in William Wells's preparatory academy at the age of eight. Among the pupils there was the older James Russell Lowell, later to share Higginson's passion for poetry and antislavery. The school, which was infamous among Cambridge boys for the brutality of its headmaster, emphasized Greek, Latin, and mathematics, skills that would earn them entrance into Harvard. Higginson's work ethic and growing size—at the age of thirteen, he stood just above six feet—kept Wells's switch off his back. After five years of study, Higginson judged himself ready for Harvard's grueling entrance exams.[27]

On August 28, 1837, beginning at six in the morning, the applicants were separated into two groups. Stretching over several days, the tests began with languages. "We were given English to be turned into Latin," Higginson wrote, "being called up at intervals" to be examined on a one-to-one basis. "I was asked the significance of a deponent verb," he added, and "what tenses of them corresponded to the active voice." The Latin exercises took all morning, and after a break the group shifted to Greek. Another recess ensued at two o'clock, after which the applicants "were sent into the north room and had algebraical (and afterwards arithmetical) sums given us." After that, the boys were called up one at a time and grilled on geography, a topic at which Higginson excelled given his childhood love of atlases. After twelve hours of tests, he returned home.[28]

A similar routine began the following morning. First, they were asked to translate Latin prose and poetry. As before the boys were called to the front to be examined individually in Latin prose. Greek followed, and Higginson translated ten lines from the *Iliad*. The exams stopped at two o'clock. The applicants were told to return in ninety minutes to discover whether or not they had been admitted. After standing in a long line, Higginson's group was finally called in. President Josiah Quincy III sat at the head of a long table, at which also sat all the faculty. Quincy called them up one by one. "The president addressed me and gave me my [admission] papers first," Higginson recalled, "and I came out." Although not yet fourteen, he was the only applicant not required to retake any of the exams. He was given the black coat donned by all Harvard students, and proudly wore his coat for the first time as he walked to Boston to buy a cap to go with his gown. The "commencement day" ceremony ended with Higginson returning his certificate of admission to President Quincy, who directed him to sign his name into a book, recognizing that he was one of the forty-five students in Harvard's freshman class.[29]

There was a reason that Wells had drilled three subjects into his pupils' skulls. Not only were they the keys to the entrance exam, but they were the main topics of study during the first year of college. Not until Higginson's second academic year, 1838, did Harvard diversify its basic curriculum, adding history, chemistry, modern languages, natural history, and geography, a subject at which he excelled. Later in life, Higginson complained that he acquired a "rather shallow reading knowledge of six languages" during his Harvard days, but even so, he took classes in English (grammar), French, Spanish, Italian, Latin, and Greek. Tutors taught most of the classes; professors were there primarily to judge students' performance. Rankings were on a "Scale of Merit," and even after the reforms of Higginson's sophomore year, students were penalized for taking "electives" by awarding them only half the scores earned in taking the old core classes. "No attempt was made to interest us in our studies," one dissatisfied student remembered. "We were expected to wade through Homer as though the Iliad were a bog."[30]

To mark the new stage in his life, Higginson followed the tradition set by his mother and generations of New Englanders and resolved to keep a diary, a promise he kept for decades until old age robbed him of even that day's memory. "Begun on my entering College," he wrote on March 29, 1849, this "volume will now be my confidant & companion." "*Resolution*," the resolute youth wrote, twice underlining the word, "To set down my thoughts and opinions here more than I have." His journal mentioned his favorite professors, including Henry Wadsworth Longfellow, who taught him French literature and language and treated his students "as if they belonged to his own circle of polished gentlemen." There was also mathematician Benjamin

Peirce and Jones Very, his deeply religious Greek tutor who frequently dined at the Higginson home on Sundays. Most of all, Higginson and his fellows were nearly obsessed with grades and spoke often of "class rank." At a lengthy gathering toward the end of his second year, Higginson and his friends ranked themselves and one another. Higginson placed himself fifth in the entire class, two seats behind Francis Parker. Born to an old New Hampshire family, Frank, too, had lost his father at a young age, and the bright but socially awkward Wentworth was immediately drawn to him. "*Parker* is I think the finest fellow in the class," he wrote in his diary, "moral [and] honorable." Although the industrious Higginson suspected that Parker had "not quite kept up" with his work enough to sustain the "great reputation" he had arrived with, he was "a noble fellow and [a] most intimate friend."[31]

As a Harvard student and even as a young divinity student, Higginson tended to form deep attachments to his older peers, especially those who were charismatic and self-confident. Quite often, those friendships were far stronger on Higginson's part than on that of the others. Such connections, then known as "bosom friendships," were common in the early nineteenth century, particularly among sons of the educated elite who, in their dress, comportment, and appearance, modeled their behavior on the genteel classes. Quite possibly, the absence of male role models in his life made his desire for close friendships all the more acute. With Parker, however, Higginson took his search for approbation too far and read the former's journal. Higginson scribbled into his diary in May 1839 that Parker "speaks of me thus in his journal, 'I like Wentworth rather quite well. He is now young but a good scholar—tolerable looking—awkward.'" A deeply gratified Higginson finished transcribing these words with three exclamation marks. Nowhere on that day's entry or after did he ever remark on the impropriety of reading through someone else's journal. Wisely, however, he neglected to inform his mother that he had done so, given her horror of her husband's similar breaches of privacy.[32]

References to Parker abound in Higginson's diary. "[Went with Parker] to the Botanic Garden," read a typical entry in late May 1839. "Walking with Parker & at his room." Parker stood out, though in truth any older student who praised Higginson's intellectual abilities won praise in his diary. When one of his fellows assured him that he was "3d in the class," that reference earned another three exclamation marks. Then, curiously, after several mundane early June entries, Higginson wrote, "Destroyed preceding journal, vol. iv." The entries began again on July 1 in his "Journal Vol 5." References such as "at Parker's eating gingerbread" or walking with him in the evenings soon returned to its pages. Parker comforted his friend after his application for membership in the college's Natural History Society was rejected, a rebuff that prompted Higginson to walk to the Cambridge cemetery to visit his father's grave. But never was there any explanation as to why portions of a journal Higginson presumed nobody but himself would ever read were not just crossed out but "destroyed."[33]

Higginson was mainly preoccupied with his class ranking and, like so many college students, complained about his grades. Upon receiving a low mark in his Latin reading, he fumed that he "deserved 18 rather than that 12 which is the lowest I have had since I've been in college!!!" He also fretted over his social awkwardness. As it had in his father's day, Harvard attracted a good many Southern students, and as Higginson remarked years later in his memoirs, they "usually had charming manners, social aptitudes, plenty of money," and were "graceful dancers." In short, they were everything that young Higginson was not. In January 1840, midway through his third year, he began to make references to clothing and young women. "Talked & danced with my cursed little cousin Lucy," he reported in one characteristically conflicted entry. Before the evening was over, he had danced with five other women, the last of them the "beautiful" Hannah Adam, the daughter of William Adam, Harvard's professor of Oriental languages. He then enjoyed "a glorious flirtation" with Hannah's sister Phoebe. Phoebe "was lame & couldn't dance," and so the two sat and played backgammon and checkers. But William Story, a law student and the son of Supreme Court Justice Joseph Story, paid "too much attention to Phoebe for my tastes." Thoroughly "in love with both" Hannah and Phoebe, as he noted in his diary, Higginson called on the Adam household the next afternoon. But despite his best efforts to be charming, he was clearly more enamored with the two than they with him. "They noticed every person who passed the window!" he complained.[34]

After such uncomfortable moments, Higginson determined to cool his "suspicious temper" by spending less time courting indifferent society girls and focusing on his studies, especially as he was unable to decide which young woman he most cared for. "Miss Georgiana might *affect* me," he noted, "but for P[hoebe]." The early spring term of 1840, he pledged, "must be devoted to the acquisition of *FAME* for my next campaign." Should he be able to achieve the recognition he sought, "then love and _____!" leaving it to his diary's imagination to fill in the blank. Certainly, male companionship would not take up much of his time, "for alas! Parker is my only friend."[35]

By attaching himself to older and more popular students like Parker, Higginson held himself to standards of excellence that were difficult to match. "I am not so affable as Frank Minot, so gay and graceful as Kirk Booth, so amusing & witty & accomplished at William Story," Higginson wrote, almost audibly sighing, "& so elegant in my dress as Aspinwall or so handsome as Preble." Higginson had enough self-awareness, at least, to perceive his personal weaknesses, and his lifelong belief in perfectionism began early. "I wish I were not so susceptible. I go to a party & fall in love & think about that person till someone or something else drives her out of my head." With "Margaret Chadwick or Miss Town or the Adam [sisters] I always think they feel me a fool." Perhaps, he mused, he should simply focus on "striving after rank & and having evening talks with Parker." His central problem, he determined, "is that I think of myself too much." At least when it came to his drive and intellectual ambition, he judged himself far superior to the Southern students. For all of their personal charm, he thought, "they were often indolent, profligate, and quarrelsome." Over the coming decades, nobody would ever use such terms when describing Higginson.[36]

On a trip through New Hampshire during the 1840 summer break, however, Higginson paused in his self-recrimination long enough to observe the plight of those less fortunate. While in Dover, he walked down to the town's cotton mills. The "factories [were] immensely gloomy looking buildings." In the mill towns, it was common for factory owners to erect barracks-like housing for farmers' daughters and immigrant women, and Higginson strolled "around the women's houses," which struck him as "desolate looking places." Not content to merely observe the mills, he wished to speak with "a Factory Girl & saw many of them." Higginson never reflected on the fact that talking to working-class women was far easier than conversing with ladies of his class, but then the conversations seemed to focus on conditions and wages rather than romance. At least "they looked neat & modest though not refined."[37]

Back in Cambridge by August for his final year at Harvard, Higginson located inexpensive rooms near the campus. Given his family's financial straits, living at home with his mother and Aunt Nancy would have been more sensible, but few Harvard men resided with their families, and, concerned about standing and reputation, Higginson had no desire to appear a charity case. Louisa not only paid her son's tuition but provided funds for his modest rental and the few items he required to live comfortably. Accordingly, he sent along a list of necessities: "3 chairs, 1 Washstand, 1 Bedstead, 1 [set of] Bedding of a uniform [and] pleasing pattern, [and] 1 Bureau." Lest she regard those requests as too extravagant, Higginson assured her that currently he "sits on the floor, sleeps on the sofa, and wash[es] in a tin cup." A few students were less concerned about appearances, evidently, as Louisa took in Harvard pupil Henry Cleveland as a border, and his rent allowed her to pay her son's "Term bills, as well as [her] Butcher bill and the Stewards bill."[38]

That winter, during a break in classes, Higginson journeyed south to visit relations in northern Virginia. His half-sister Elizabeth had died in December 1840, but his brother-in-law Reuel Keith was a professor at the Protestant Episcopal Seminar in Alexandria. On the way, he paused in Philadelphia and was unimpressed—"the City of Brotherly Love did not long contain" him. Washington, however, was altogether a different matter, at least when it came to its buildings, if not its people. Like all tourists, he gaped at the "historical paintings" in the Capitol rotunda, the "Congress Libr'y," then in the Capitol, and thought it "not large, but [a] good many valuable books." Higginson strolled past "the Presi't house, a beautiful building & around the garden wall," as well as the nearby "Treasury Dep't, [which was] also a grand building." While downstairs in the Capitol, Higginson stepped into the Supreme Court and discovered that Congressman John Quincy Adams was speaking, part of his two-day summation in the case of "the Amistad negroes." Higginson caught only part of Adams's lengthy oration, but what he heard struck him as "undignified & decidedly dull," and from what he could see, the justices were equally indifferent and "inattentive," and his rival William's father, Judge Story, "was almost contemptuous." While in the Senate gallery, Higginson watched Kentucky senator Henry Clay argue with his Democratic colleagues. "Mr C. not the superior looking man I conceive— quite old looking," and "the debate was uninteresting." Higginson soon left for neighboring Alexandria.[39]

Although the future militant abolitionist scorned his Southern classmates as dissolute, during his 1841 visit he found almost nothing about Southern culture to condemn. Higginson was there only briefly and resided with his brother-in-law in a seminary on the outskirts of Washington City, rather than in one of the large plantations below Richmond. But even so, he chided Frank Parker for his friend's "partial & prejudicial impressions of the South." "You imagine me, I doubt not, spending my time in indolent luxury," he wrote to Parker that February, "conversing languidly with languid Southern ladies, or lulled to a siesta by vast quantities of fans, agitated in the perfumed air by the hands of fair damsels." Only "the colour of the domestics (a man, a boy, and an antiquated chambermaid),″ he protested, reminded him that he was "south of the Potomac." Higginson had only turned seventeen the previous November and was easily swayed by the words of Reverend Keith, who was in his late forties. It was to take Higginson several more years to absorb what he had witnessed in Washington and Virginia and to understand that what made Keith's domestics different from New Hampshire mill girls was not merely their race but their status as unwaged chattel. Even so, when he reflected on a trip that he made in 1844, three years later, he noted only that it reinforced his earlier views that Southern culture was based upon "indolence [and was] full of vaporized laziness." The crime, he would only later realize, was not how slavery degraded white industry, but rather what it did to Black bodies and their right to their own industry.[40]

While Higginson toured the Washington region, his mother worried about her youngest child's welfare. "I have been waiting rather impatiently for ten days past to hear from you," Louisa wrote in mid-February. Higginson had made the mistake shortly after his departure in telling her that he was suffering from a slight cold, "which in the absence of news" she had "magnified into a fever." Young men of Higginson's age and physique thought themselves indestructible, but Louisa had buried too many children not to know the ever-present threat of death. "When you are more acquainted with the fair sex, you will understand the force and fervor of their imaginations, and perhaps the superior wisdom of the *Stronger* vessel may condescend to temper it by allowing less food for it than one of the Lords of Creation now think fit to do." Just in case Wentworth somehow missed her vehemence, she underlined her experience. "*I have an unlucky habit of caring about my children*," she reminded the son who had known so few siblings, "one that prevents me from feeling quite easy unless I know they are doing well."[41]

Increasingly irritated by her son's silence, Louisa fired off a second missive three days later. As the wife of a bankrupt, she fretted that Wentworth was about to graduate armed only with Greek and Latin in his coming battle with the real world. "I never have been satisfied with the smattering which is got in College," she wrote. She thought that the four years spent on campus was "only an Introduction to Science and learning—the beginning and not the completion of their education." She prayed that her son agreed, and as the child for whom she had pinned the highest hopes, she believed he "may become a real Scholar." Louisa had every expectation that Wentworth would rise to the occasion. "You would do injustice to your talents and opportunities if you did not determine to avail yourself of all means just put into your hands

MRS. STEPHEN HIGGINSON (LOUISA STORROW)

Figure 1.2 Before his mother's death in 1864, Higginson wrote to her nearly every day. Mary Thatcher Higginson never met her late mother-in-law, but perhaps intimidated by their close connection even in death, she mentioned Louisa only nine times in her biography of her husband. See her *Thomas Wentworth Higginson: The Story of His Life* (Boston, 1914). From the author's collection.

and persevere steadily in a course which will lead to perfection." She softened her conclusion, if only a bit: "I do not know what your particular taste would lead you to but there is no doubt someone strictly in which you might excel, and whatever that is you would find your account in devoting yourself to."[42]

Perhaps inspired by his mother's words, in the late spring of 1841 Higginson determined to teach for several years and then turn to the study of law. Graduation was set for the coming August, and as he would still be four months shy of his eighteenth birthday, he believed he had ample time "to pursue general study" and possibly even to revise his "choice of study." That June, Higginson secured a position with Samuel Weld, a wealthy thirty-five-year-old descendant of several generations of clergymen, who ran a school for boys in the Jamaica Plain neighborhood of Boston. Weld agreed to pay him $600 per year, and as he told Parker, he "succeeded in getting a good room for $25 the year and board from $3 to $4" each month. Higginson briefly returned to Cambridge for his graduation ceremonies and then hired a wagon to carry his "various luggage" and pieces of furniture to his boardinghouse. "I was launched upon the world at last alone! Tragic!"[43]

Teaching days began early at half-past six in the morning with breakfast and a prayer and continued until eleven. Although Higginson towered over the boys, he was just slightly older than those preparing for college, and so initially discipline was a problem. To assert his authority, he dragged his pupils on a long march through the "pouring rain and furious cold gale," and after that, he "came off victorious." He also added boxing to the curriculum, an activity that gave the lanky Higginson and his long arms an advantage, but an endeavor Weld frowned upon. To get around Weld's objections, Higginson moved the lessons "to the hours before school." One pupil, Higginson was pleased to report, "boxed very scientifically," while another "strikes like lightning." Otherwise, the days were consumed with the standard Harvard preliminary courses of "Geography, Latin reader, Greek reader & Grammar, History & Philosophy." The boys were uniformly "studious, several interested & bright, & almost all good natured, but talked noisily." Most days also included an evening session from seven to eight o'clock, which Higginson described as "cursed" as it interfered with the young bachelor's social schedule.[44]

Now a Harvard graduate with steady employment, a more confident Higginson turned his attention back to young women. He had begun to fill out, and the muscles he gained from his long walks and boxing matches added to his presence; his dark hair, which he wore long, offset his sapphire eyes. To mark his latest chapter in life, Higginson began a new journal, and, unsure which young lady to whom to dedicate his private musings, he selected three. Among his fellow boarders was a Miss Wetherly, "a slender pretty woman with red hair, very affable, though not first rate or brilliant."

When he could escape his pupils, Higginson called often on Sarah Bradley. On one occasion, he visited Maria Stone, who he was pleased to discover "seated [him] familiarly by her at the table and began to talk most cordially." The most popular ladies of his acquaintance, however, attracted other suitors. Higginson thought one such suitor "insufferable & affected," and he "enjoyed giving him some cuts which he hadn't gumption to repartee." Ever devoted to self-improvement, Higginson also learned to ride horses. Idle hands, as the old New England maxim preached, were the devil's workshop, and in any case, he did not intend to remain a tutor forever. Excellence in all aspects of life might prepare him for future endeavors. And of course, also please his mother.[45]

Larger issues were about to intrude upon Higginson's romantic pursuits. By the day of his graduation in August 1841, President William Henry Harrison had died, and power had passed to his militantly proslavery vice president, John Tyler of Virginia. Tyler was keenly interested in the annexation of the Republic of Texas, a drive that was to reopen old sectional wounds and return the nation's attention to the prospect of slavery's expansion westward. For Higginson, whose plans for a legal career were tentative at best, the coming decade was to force him to reconsider his charitable views of Southern life, reevaluate his responsibilities regarding the social ills all about him, and exchange the stewardship of a handful of boys for a far larger congregation.

2
"The rearing of a reformer"
1841–1849

Higginson had been, at thirteen, the youngest student in his Harvard class, and now, at seventeen, he was also the youngest of his friends to graduate. Even by antebellum standards, very few college graduates had not yet reached the age of eighteen. Yet both New England society and Louisa, who had sacrificed to make her son's education possible, expected Higginson to begin to make his way in the world. That included settling on a vocation and then starting a family, if perhaps not immediately as to the latter point, at least in Louisa's opinion. Over the next few years, Higginson would do both, but never in a conventional fashion. As he put away childish things, such as his early admiration for Southern folkways, and grew increasingly radical, his emerging political views and activities would endanger his livelihood and chosen profession. That was regrettable, in his view, but also inconsequential when it came to leading a life of purpose and morality. The coming years, as he remarked in his 1898 memoirs, were to witness the "rearing of a reformer."[1]

Higginson expected his tenure at Stephen Weld's preparatory academy to be temporary, and Weld's continuing disapproval of Higginson's belief that his young charges required physical fitness as well as Latin merely accelerated his decision to quit his position. After six months, he resigned and took another temporary job, this time as tutor to the three sons of his widowed cousin, Stephen Higginson Perkins. He moved to Brookline and took up residence in Perkins's self-designed "pretty cottage." The job paid $250 yearly—less than half of what Weld had paid him—but included room and board. The merchant, Higginson marveled, was a true Renaissance man, and the way he had prepared himself for a career in international trade fascinated the young teacher, reminding him of his mother's admonition that Harvard's emphasis on classical studies had inadequately qualified him for life. Perkins had traveled to Germany to study business, then returned to New England to read law under Edward Everett, then a congressman, before signing on as a crewman on ships bound for East Asia and the Caribbean. Although not wealthy, Perkins invested in art and owned the finest paintings Higginson had ever seen outside Harvard's collection. Perkins read both French and German and recommended authors for Higginson's improvement. Best of all, from Higginson's perspective, he refused to allow his sons to study more than four hours each day. After that, Higginson was encouraged to take the boys with him on his forest rambles. "It was a happy time," Higginson reflected.[2]

Under Perkins's tutelage, Higginson began to broaden his reading. Like most of his generation, he revered Ralph Waldo Emerson and, as he later admitted to the essayist himself, finished most days with his "usual dose of Emerson & to bed." Apart from Emerson, "the writer who most took possession" of Higginson was the late German romantic author Jean Paul Richter, whose humorous novels delighted New England's emerging Transcendentalist community. Higginson also devoured a number of German playwrights and novelists, especially works by Johann Wolfgang von Goethe and Friedrich Schiller. Initially, Higginson contented himself with translations of their work, but always adept at languages, he determined to teach himself German so he could appreciate their words directly. Richter's novels inspired Higginson to hope that he too might be able to pursue a "purely literary life" and earn his living with his pen. Higginson also worried that both the study and the practice of law would so consume his time that he would have no energy for other pursuits. "The objection to the study of the law is not that it is not interesting," his friend Dwight Foster warned him, as Higginson later recalled, "but that it fills your mind with knowledge which cannot be carried into another stage of existence." Never truly wedded to the idea of a life before the bar, Higginson used Foster's counsel to finalize his decision to find a profession that better suited his sense of self.[3]

Family matters intruded briefly, if tragically, when Higginson's brother Samuel Thatcher vanished at sea. Five years Wentworth's senior, Thatcher, as his mother called him, had obtained a job with the shipping company of Bullard and Lee in January 1841 and sailed for Rio de Janeiro aboard the brig *Luna*. But in March, on the return passage from Brazil, the ship disappeared in a storm. For Louisa, who had already suffered through the death of three of her children, the loss was profound, especially as there was no gravesite at which to mourn. She and her sister Anne had recently relocated to Brattleboro, Vermont, to be near her eldest son, Francis, who had established a medical practice there. Prior to sailing, Thatcher had granted Waldo, by now a lawyer, power of attorney over his affairs, and so it fell to him to manage Thatcher's modest estate, just as it fell to Louisa's favorite child to comfort her in her grieving.[4]

With his mother and Aunt Nancy in Vermont and Waldo in Boston, Higginson naturally socialized with Perkins's circle of family and friends. Among those he met in the spring of 1842 was Perkins's niece—and Higginson's second cousin—Mary Channing. Three years older than Higginson, Mary was the daughter of Dr. Walter Channing, who taught obstetrics at Harvard's medical school. Although already a bit frail at only twenty-two, having lost her mother at a young age, Mary endeared herself to Higginson. He admired her quick wit and strong sense of self. "Liked her better than I expected," he confided to his journal on May 9. The two took a long walk after tea and Higginson found her "very gay" and even a bit flirtatious. While possessed of a "seeming want of softness," as he put it, Mary had a "fine heart" and was "very independent in her opinions," which tended toward reformism. The more he saw Mary, Higginson assured Aunt Nancy, the more he appreciated her. She could be curt, but whatever her "faults of manner," he did "like her very much indeed & think she has substantially a fine mind & a fine character." Some men, Higginson mused, might regard Mary as too strong-willed, but that was the trait he most admired in his mother. "I don't think she's in the least appreciated," he marveled. But she was appreciated by him.[5]

Higginson's fondness for Mary prompted the young teacher to think more seriously about his future. As ever, Louisa was doing so as well. "I heard from Brattleboro a few days ago," he laughed to Aunt Nancy. "A page of advice from mother interspersed with compliment enough to ensure my reading it through" and "concluding finally with a slight moral." In response, in January 1843 he penned a lengthy explanation of his plans. "If I have any genius, I should have a fair chance to cherish it," he hoped. It was "not vanity," he insisted, that led him to believe it was within his "power to make [his] living as a *literary* man." Should that goal not be achieved immediately, he still had the ability to make money enough by teaching. Knowing that his mother would not appreciate the wisdom of his scheme, he promised her that his career plans were "not at all Utopian." Although he would assuredly earn a far better income as an attorney, he had "been brought up poor" and was "not afraid to continue so." While never particularly close to Thatcher, his brother's death reminded Higginson that life could be fleeting, and although he had turned nineteen only the month before, he knew himself well enough to know that he could accept being penniless, particularly "if it is a necessary accomplishment to a life spent as I wish to spend it." Should it prove necessary, Higginson thought, he could remain "sufficiently independent," a remark indicating that for all of his affection for Mary, he had no plans to wed anytime soon. "How far this will recommend itself to you I cannot judge," he concluded, and he expected "to be frowned at by many & laughed at by some." Either way, Higginson vowed, he had "entirely made up [his] mind" on the matter.6

To better prepare himself for a life of letters, or perhaps as training "for a professorship in literature or metaphysics," Higginson resolved to return to Cambridge in September 1843 for a period of intense study. At the time, Harvard had no graduate programs in those fields, so Higginson simply dubbed himself a "resident graduate" of the college. Before leaving Brookline, he and Mary reached an understanding about their future. Although she was of a marriageable age by New England standards of the day, her fiancé was still in his teens. There was also a distinction between achieving a modest income and what Louisa called her son's current "vow of poverty." Mary was content to wait. Higginson carted his small collection of furniture back to Cambridge and rented "the cheapest room [he] could find" in a boarding house near campus. "Never was I happier in my life than at that moment of transformation," he would write in *Cheerful Yesterdays*. "It was my flight into Egypt."7

His postgraduate days in Cambridge had an effect, and over the coming months, he found himself increasingly drawn to Unitarian philosophers and those German Transcendentalists steeped in biblical criticism. Higginson first became familiar with the writings of Theodore Parker, and then with the minister himself. Thirteen years Higginson's senior, the Unitarian theologian and abolitionist was critical of what he derided as "Old Testament miracles, prophecies, dreams, [and] miraculous births." In *The Transient and Permanent in Christianity*, published in 1841, he argued that Christians should experience the divine intuitively and base their beliefs on individual experience. Higginson quite agreed. He hoped to acquire "all the wisdom of the ages & sum it up in a deep wisdom [and] be wholly thought," he ambitiously announced to his fiancée (who was now his "own darling" in his missives). Established churches and staid theology repelled him, but revelation and personal knowledge might lead to greater truths and inspire his actions and activities in this world. After one visit to a traditional congregation, Higginson assured Mary he felt even more strongly his "doubts about the whole institution of the church & even of the sabbath." It occurred to him that he might follow Parker's path and find a congregation that welcomed nontraditional preachers, as a good number of Unitarian pulpits in New England sat empty, many because young theologians abandoned the physical church in search of greater spiritual nourishment. A minister's salary might also permit him to write and to marry, as Waldo, the only sibling Higginson was close to, was then preparing to do. But he was as yet far from confident that was to be his path. "One thing is plain that my even being a minister is far from certain," he promised Mary, "& that makes one's whole future entirely less certain."[8]

As his clashes with Stephen Weld over his charges' need to balance a life of the mind with physical vigor suggested, he was growing into a man who enjoyed a robust debate, and sometimes even a fight. Harvard's Divinity School was in the midst of a schism over Parker's increasingly unconventional sermons. At about the same time that Higginson was trying to decide upon a course of study, Parker delivered a series of lectures that questioned the perfection of Jesus. Conversative clergymen sought to ostracize Parker and close their churches to him, but a number of Divinity School students begged him to come and address them. Despite the fact that Parker was himself a Harvard graduate, the faculty formally voted to refuse him permission to speak. But suspecting that Harvard's students were in a position to make the school a force for Unitarianism, Higginson began to prepare for its three-year course of study, beginning in the fall of 1844.[9]

The student body in the Divinity School remained small, and not for several more decades would Harvard actually grant degrees in theology. But it was the principal seminary for New Englanders who aspired to the pulpit, and as one of thirty-eight new students Higginson joined the largest class yet. Divinity Hall housed a chapel on the second floor and featured an impressive library with four thousand volumes. A nearby caretaker's house had been renovated into a "Commons," which provided board for a reasonable $3.50 a week, and so Higginson abandoned his boarding house for a room on campus.[10]

Content to be back in a formal curriculum after a year of reading his own selections, Higginson threw himself into his coursework. By tradition, students composed hymns in preparation for December's Christmas services, and although he was unable to match the prodigious output of his classmate Samuel Longfellow—the younger brother of his undergraduate professor—the budding poet drafted "The past is dark with sin and shame," which Longfellow and fellow student Samuel Johnson published in an 1846 collection of hymns. Although hardly an indication of his later promise, the poem concluded with typical Higginson optimism: "'Tis dark around, 'tis dark above, But through the shadow streams the sun; We cannot doubt Thy certain love; And Man's true aim shall yet be won!"[11]

* * *

"There were always public meetings in Boston to be attended," Higginson later wrote. He particularly enjoyed hearing Theodore Parker and theologian and abolitionist James Freeman Clarke, the minister at Boston's King's Chapel. Both encouraged their congregations to apply Christian principles to the pressing social issues of the day, and their example reminded Higginson "that one might accomplish something and lead a manly life even in the pulpit." Most influential of all, there were Wendell Phillips and William Lloyd Garrison. Upon his return to Cambridge, Higginson had been disappointed to discover that the college and even the Divinity School remained strongly opposed to the abolition movement. Southern men continued to set the social tone for undergraduate life, and many faculty theologians wished to steer clear of the often acrimonious internal debates over merging spirituality with reform movements, hoping to keep their students focused on religious questions. Higginson, of course, naturally sided with those students who thought Parker's approach theologically sound. "It was in the direction of the anti-slavery reform," Higginson decided, that he "felt the most immediate pricking of conscience."[12]

Later, in explaining his enlightenment on the nature of slavery, Higginson credited Garrison, as well as "two books, both by women," Lydia Maria Child's *An Appeal for That Class of Americans Called Africans* and Harriet Martineau's *The Martyr Age in America*, both written in the decade following the initial publication of Garrison's 1831 newspaper, *The Liberator*, which uncompromisingly called for immediate emancipation and denounced colonization. But he also noted the influence of his mother and, to a lesser extent, his brother Francis John's 1834 pamphlet, *Remarks on Slavery and Emancipation*, which exhibited all of the optimism of the early abolitionist movement. As did Garrison, who thought slavery so self-evidently wrong that within several decades, Southern planters would see the error of their ways. Francis John presumed that even white Southerners agreed "that no human being has an abstract right to hold another in a state of perpetual bondage." Higginson noted, however, that when in 1700 Judge Samuel Sewell published *The Selling of Joseph*, the first antislavery pamphlet published in the mainland colonies, it was publicly endorsed by his ancestor John Higginson, the Salem minister. On other occasions, his family influenced his thinking, if only by disagreement. Higginson's uncle Samuel Perkins had lived in French Saint-Domingue at the time of the Haitian Revolution, and although his book on the bloody revolt would not be published until 1886, he was often insistent when debating the issue with his nephew that abolition "would lead to instant and formidable insurrection." Although Higginson admired his uncle for his "gentleness" and "sincerity," he regarded that view as "deluded" and thought it the same sort of reactionary belief that once led to Garrison's being attacked by a mob.[13]

Somewhat awestruck by their unbending opposition to slavery, Higginson, as he later admitted, "longed to be counted worthy of such companionship." To that end, he wrote a song, "National Anti-Slavery Hymn," to be sung at Dedham's July 4, 1846, "anti-slavery picnic," which Garrison dutifully published in the *Liberator*. Higginson also composed a brief "Sonnet to W. L. Garrison," which was published in the 1846 edition of *The Liberty Bell*, an annual abolitionist gift book edited by Maria Weston Chapman. The aspiring poet wrote that while "'tis not that deeds like thine need more poor praise," he wished it known just how much he admired "the true depth of that devoted heart/Where selfish hope or fear had never part/To swerve thee, with the crowd, from Truth's plane ways!" Years after, Higginson judged the poem—which called Garrison the "rugged Luther of these latter days"—to be rather "crude," but it caught the attention of New England's antislavery community, and the mere fact of its publication strengthened his hope that he might yet find a living as a literary man.[14]

By the time that Higginson became actively involved with abolitionism, Garrison had been publishing his *Liberator* for fifteen years, and Higginson was well aware of the bitter schism in the antislavery community between those who followed the pacifist Garrison's example and those, particularly among the Liberty Party, who wished to pursue antislavery within the political system. Higginson suspected that eradicating slavery might be "a comparatively easy thing" if the various antislavery factions could be "united." Yet even as a young man, he realized that he differed from both the Garrisonian wing and the politically minded Liberty Party activists. On one hand, he observed, the Garrisonians were generally "non-combatants of principle," and while Higginson's focus on the body and his fascination with athleticism—which he was soon to advocate for young women as well—was not unknown to abolitionists, neither was it something they emphasized. Higginson also understood that the Garrisonians' "non-resistant" position had its limits, and those "who believed in the physical rescue of fugitive slaves were nonetheless their pupils." Although Garrisonians, unlike the Liberal Party men, for the most part were non-voters, they were more consistent advocates of women's rights, including the right to vote. For Higginson, whose support for women's rights shared the same familial sources as his endorsement of antislavery, that fact mattered considerably. He concluded that while the abolitionist movement was too vast "to be held in any single hand," he still believed that "it was to Garrison more than to any other man, that the great ultimate result was remotely due."[15]

On the other hand, Higginson could not share Garrison's view that political action against slavery was contemptible. Garrison's devout belief in the power of ethical regeneration led him to advocate what he termed "moral-suasion," the theory that slaveholders could be persuaded of the wickedness of human bondage. A young man in a hurry, Higginson judged that policy to be unrealistic. What troubled him about those abolitionists who voted was their obedience to the law. Higginson sided with those writers, both ancient and modern, who believed in the right to resist unjust laws by any means necessary. The tutor who had taught his pupils to box had not done so merely in the name of physical fitness, but because he believed that his nation's greatest social ills could not be defeated with sermons and pamphlets alone. Long before Higginson was to take up arms against slavery, he had, as he later put it, "quite made up his mind to fight."[16]

While Liberty voters hoped to advance their cause through elections, Garrison's followers shared his view that decent Christians were morally tainted by residing in the same Union as slaveholders. Higginson the theology student agreed with that sentiment. On New Year's Day of 1846, he recorded in his diary his "final self-enrollment in the ranks of the American Non-Jurors or Disunion Abolitionists." Although he intended to cast a ballot for Liberty candidates in the fall of that year, he was determined not to vote for any nominee who agreed to take an "oath to support the U.S. Constitution" when it came to the questions of fugitive slaves or Northern disunion efforts. Higginson's disunionism would not peak for another decade, until after the elevation of James Buchanan to the presidency in 1856. Liberty candidates hoped to achieve victory within the American political system rather than dismantle it, but as early as 1846, Higginson the optimistic student confidently believed that the time was "coming which may expose to obloquy and danger even the most insignificant of the adherents to such a cause."[17]

After but two semesters in Divinity School, Higginson began to look ahead, perhaps because his relationship with Mary was growing ever more serious. He had his eye on one large church led by an aged minister, and that minister, Higginson somewhat callously informed his mother, "will certainly not preside over the spiritual destinies of this parish six months longer," after which his pulpit would be "a new 'berth' open for the graduating youths." He was not yet prepared to quit his studies, however; he judged his current level of education to be "imperfect," and that was a problem as "the Unitarians think they've got a highly educated clergy." For the time being, he planned to remain a "reading man"—as he put it to Louisa—during the spring 1845 term, as there were so "many things in history of which to study." Three times a week Higginson devoted himself to learning Hebrew and studying Immanuel Kant, Jean Paul Richter, Friedrich Schelling, George Hegel, and "Mohammedanism," as Western Christians routinely dubbed the Islamic faith. He read widely on the Protestant Reformation and on the impact of the French Revolution on that nation's Catholicism, a topic he hoped to write about for the *North American Review*. "I expect the future to do its own work," Higginson predicted to his mother, and while he anticipated one day landing in the pulpit, for the present he was content in "preparing himself for the general" as opposed to training for a "particular vocation."[18]

Louisa continued to pray that her son would settle upon a life in the church. His poetry, she assured him, had "great improved" over the course of a year. "I like Poetry to be an inspiration, not a forced matter," she added. But a literary life offered no guarantees of a steady income and should be crafted only to illuminate where "the spirit leads." Choosing to ignore his occasional hints that his time at the Divinity School might not lead to the pulpit, Louisa promised her son that she was thrilled by his decision to preach. She also simply assumed that Mary agreed with her sentiments and feared her son might waver in his plans without Mary's guidance. She was even pleased that he had "got hold of Mohammedism," as the topic of Islam had always fascinated her. "You are just now doing what I have always wanted you to do," she concluded, and she looked forward to hearing more news about both his engagement and his selection of a parish.[19]

Wishing to be precise about his plans and disinclined to allow his mother to decide for him, Higginson waited to respond to her letter until the fall of 1845, when he began his third term at Harvard Divinity. He noted that "Mistress Mary" had come to Cambridge to see him, adding that both he and his fiancée were still ambivalent about his career choice. Several of his closest friends had graduated the previous summer. "The school is not very lively," he complained to his mother, as "the spirit was taken out when the last class left." The new student class was small and "mediocre" and there was no one from Harvard College. Only two of the incoming students were of interest to him. One of them was a young man "named Hurlbut from Charleston, S.C."[20]

Higginson first encountered the new student as he was passing through the front doors of Divinity Hall. There stood a young man, he wrote in his journal, "so handsome in his dark beauty that he seemed like a picturesque Oriental." William Henry Hurlbut, a South Carolina native, was four years Higginson's junior. As he had been several years ago with Francis Parker, Higginson was immediately infatuated by Hurlbut's "slender, keen-eyed, raven haired" appearance. In his memoirs, Higginson wrote that Hurlbut "arrested the eye and the heart like some fascinating girl." But it was not merely Hurlbut's beauty that attracted Higginson, who judged him "the most variously gifted and accomplished man" he ever knew. Hurlbut's late father had been a Massachusetts Unitarian minister who had settled in South Carolina in 1812, and after his death in 1843, William fell under the tutelage of his much older brother, who had antislavery tendencies and urged his young sibling to leave the South and prepare for the ministry. As a result, despite his refined Carolina manners, Hurlbut was, as Higginson put it to his mother, "a true Southerner [of] the best sort."[21]

For a time, the two were inseparable. Hurlbut composed hymns in honor of his friend, gushing that they contained "holy thoughts with which you have constantly mingled." Higginson explained to his mother that he had two types of friends: those he was content to meet with "once in a while" and those "whom I should like to see every day," and that small cadre consisted only of Hurlbut and fellow student Samuel Johnson. Long after their ardent friendship had cooled (and Hurlbut had altered his surname to "Hurlbert" and abandoned the pulpit in favor of a career in journalism), Higginson confessed to a young correspondent that regarding "intimate" male friendships, he had "never loved *but* one male friend with passion," adding that "for him my love had no bounds [as] all that my natural fastidiousness and cautious reserve kept from others I poured on him." Later still, in his 1869 novel, *Malbone*, Higginson based his leading character on his former friend: "Malbone's self-poised easy grace was the same as ever; his chestnut-brown eyes were as winning, his features as handsome as in the decades past."[22]

Shortly after Higginson's death, Mary Thatcher Higginson, his second wife, described his relationship with Hurlbut as a "romantic attachment." Reading over their letters to one another, she thought their correspondence "more like those between man and woman than between two men." The precise nature of the relationship between Higginson and Hurlbut, or that of the earlier friendship between Higginson and Francis Parker, for that matter, remains a matter of speculation, but the letters that Mary Thatcher found "always brilliant, often affectionate, [and] sometimes full of rollicking fun" were typical of letters written by well-educated youths of her husband's day. Steeped in the romantic writings of George Gordon Byron and Alfred Tennyson, it was common for college men to adopt the language of sensibility and the emotional, even extravagant expressions found in their favorite poems and novels. Both young men had lost their fathers at an early age, and given their intellectual promise and the expectations placed upon them by family members, it was not surprising that the two divinity students thought of themselves as "friend & brother," as Hurlbut signed his correspondence, more than as classmates. In the academic world of Cambridge, where students took their class standing seriously, their friendship was also critical in navigating the pressures of graduate studies.[23]

Class also played a role in college friendships, although Higginson perhaps was not yet aware of that. Working-class men advanced an image of masculinity that prized physical prowess, open sexuality, and drinking, typically at public saloons. Upper-class men derided it as coarse and immoral. As a young man who valued physical fitness and took pride in his boxing prowess, Higginson bridged this cultural gulf, just as he was to later bridge the divides in so many social and reform movements. But like other educated young men who carried the burden of family expectations, Higginson and his classmates shared a hope that their circle of male friendships would sustain them as they began to make their way in the world.[24]

* * *

Higginson concluded his divinity studies in July 1847, and that meant making decisions as to his occupation and his relationship with Mary. He had known her for five years and they had been engaged for more than two. At twenty-four, Higginson was still a bit young to wed by New England standards, at least for men of his class, but at twenty-seven Mary

THOMAS WENTWORTH HIGGINSON, 1846

Figure 2.1 At the age of twenty-three, Higginson was about to graduate from divinity school, which meant that decisions regarding Mary Channing and a solid occupation could no longer be deferred. Perhaps as preparation for both, Higginson here sported a hairstyle known as the "side part," which was more popular among businessmen and professionals than the "gentleman's cut," a style favored by young aristocrats that featured shorter hair on the side but longer on the top and back. Courtesy of Massachusetts Historical Society.

was older than most women on their wedding day. He now had the equivalent of two Harvard degrees, and as he laughed to Aunt Nancy, residents of Cambridge "look at me with a kind of suspicious glance—'Are you *still* here? Is there no end to you?'" Resolved, Higginson set the date for his ordination for September 15, and he and Mary decided to marry four days prior to that. Two congregations, one in Walpole, New Hampshire, and another in Newburyport, a coastal city in Essex County thirty-five miles northeast of Boston, had vacant pulpits and expressed interest in the recent graduate. "I expect to come to the Free Church system in the end," Higginson told his classmate Samuel Johnson, referring to the more independent churches in which membership was open to anyone. These new, radical congregations experimented with a more democratic polity, with some designed to resemble "primitive" or early Christian meetings in which men and women joined together to discuss moral and even political questions. "Everything has gone most smoothly about the ordination, [and] all the persons invited have accepted," Higginson assured his aunt, adding that he had twice visited Newburyport, including once with Mary to look at houses. He confided to Johnson that he was increasingly sure that "the pulpit" was to be his "vocation," and as for Mary, Higginson had no doubts.[25]

Higginson's trial sermon at Walpole met with mixed results. Never wishing to hide his passion for reform, for his homily he chose "The Clergy and Reform," preaching that clergymen should take the lead in reform movements, and especially in abolitionism. Because ministers enjoyed "an established station" in society, they bore a "tremendous responsibility [for] guiding, reforming, and regenerating the world." The retiring minister showed the text to his wife, who judged it theologically sound and praised it as "a real [Theodore] Parker sermon!" Other congregants thought differently, and Higginson was disappointed at the small size of the gathering. "I should much prefer a larger centre of influence," he complained to Johnson. "I'm afraid I couldn't preach to a handful." As it turned out, Higginson need not have worried, as he never heard again from Walpole's elders. "I can't make up my mind," he wrote his mother, "whether my radicalism will be the ruin of me or not." Louisa attempted to be sympathetic, but her response made it clear that she feared it might be. "You don't want women to vote, do you, or be lawyers, or go to Congress!" In fact, Higginson did. In 1846 he purchased a copy of Scottish feminist Marion Reid's *A Plea for Women*, his first volume in a collection of books on women's rights that would over time grow to more than one thousand before being donated to the Boston Public Library.[26]

Higginson's visit to Newburyport's First Religious Society went far more smoothly, despite the fact that the prospective minister refused to moderate his tone. If anything, Higginson chose to speak more bluntly, selecting as his topic "Freedom of Speech" and tying that question to the ongoing war with Mexico. A good number of Whigs, even in New England, had begun to advance the name of General Zachary Taylor, a Louisiana slaveholder, for their party's 1848 presidential nomination, and preaching in what he called his "worst thunder," Higginson denounced the conflict with Mexico as a "slaveholder's war." Among those listening to the sermon was John Porter, a wealthy industrialist. Rather to Higginson's surprise, when the two spoke afterward Porter actually congratulated him on the verbal "whipping" he had given the church's more conservative members. Porter did, however, trot out "the old story" of how the abolitionists were responsible for hindering national unity and economic progress. Still, according to Higginson, Porter told him that "a minister who has not free [speech] was not worth hearing." Higginson suspected that Porter was not alone in desiring a more conventional minister, but he was pleased that the congregation had listened so attentively. He had been prepared to dislike the town's mills and rum distilleries, but "on the whole," he told Louisa, he was "not disappointed" in Newburyport.[27]

While he waited for a formal offer from the Society, Higginson prepared for his wedding day. In celebration of both his marriage and his impending ordination, Johnson and Hurlbut wrote hymns to mark their friend's "entrance into the world." Not yet finished with his own studies, Hurlbut intended to remain in Cambridge. "I feel very keenly how much I shall miss your presence in this place consecrated by so many memories," he promised. Hurlbut vowed to visit Higginson and Mary often. "Since you are soon to be united to one whom your Nature" was so perfectly matched, he believed, "you will be happy."[28]

The couple was married on September 11 in Brookline by the Reverend James Freeman Clarke, a fellow graduate of Harvard's Divinity School. The ceremony was a brief and simple one, attended by Mary's immediate family and Louisa, Aunt Nancy, and Waldo. Higginson was happier even than he had expected to be, gushing to Waldo that it was "strangely beautiful that one who has so little outward sunshine as she has, [and] so much inward darkness as I, should now have such childlike merriment as we at times do." By Mary having "so little outward sunshine," Higginson was referring not merely to her acerbic wit but to worries over her increasingly delicate health. Mary was already experiencing a shortage of breath and would later be diagnosed with rheumatoid arthritis, which affected her lungs as well as her bones and joints. Whether that was the reason the couple remained childless is unknown. As Higginson was to note in his journal within just two years, his only sorrow was "the absence of children to one whose passion for them is so rare and profound." Try as he might to "pass for a sober and respectable" clergyman, he admitted to himself that "there is really no sentimental school-girl whose demand for being loved is greater or more comprehensive than mine."[29]

Four days later, Higginson was ordained in the church that was to be his home for the next two years. Constructed in 1801 on the design of London's

St. Martin-in-the-Fields Church on Trafalgar Square, Newburyport's First Society, a pleased Higginson later remembered, was "a fine type of an earlier church architecture in its graceful steeple, its lofty pulpit, and its sounding-board." Higginson had invited his older cousin and fellow Harvard Divinity School graduate William Henry Channing to preach the day's main sermon, with theologian and abolitionist James Freeman Clarke following. For his homily, Channing chose the moderate topic "The Gospel of To-Day," which was printed for distribution and praised by one newspaper as "certainly brilliant, comprehensive, lofty [and] humane." Clarke's charge was far more pointed. Aware that Newburyport was home to a number of pro-Southern merchants, Clarke prayed Higginson would use his pulpit "to speak scathing words of rebuke against the sin of slavery." Higginson spoke last, and as the least famous and youngest speaker at his own ordination, his precise words were not recorded. The next morning's Newburyport *Herald* reported, however, that while Higginson was clearly "a young man of much intellectual and moral power, he seems tinctured with those radical and imaginative notions" with which reformers hoped to remake society against the plan that "God has seen fit to guide it ever since the dawn of creation." The church elders could not claim they had not been warned.[30]

Whatever doubts they may have had about the tone of their new minister's ordination ceremony, the First Society's leaders met all of Higginson's employment requests. They agreed to an annual salary of $1,000, promised him freedom of speech in his sermons, permitted him to invite guest ministers to speak, and allowed him to accept the occasional invitation to preach elsewhere. The couple rented a modest home on Essex Street, just two blocks from the First Society. Higginson initially considered hiring a maid to help Mary with housekeeping, as she easily tired, but the two concluded that they should practice economy, and that employing a live-in servant might "destroy real romance." "I am fairly settled here in a lovely house, with a noble-hearted wife & a marvelous parish," he wrote to Johnson. Although the city had a reputation for being hostile to abolitionism, Higginson was pleased to discover that Newburyport activists not only sponsored regular antislavery conventions, but that those activists favored disunion, as he did. "I do not fear the consequences" of attending such meetings, he assured Johnson. "I have a firm hold, I think." Despite his desire to find time to write, he quickly realized that drafting sermons, hosting his congregants, and attending welcoming teas consumed almost all of his hours and energy. As Higginson told another correspondent, his not writing more poetry "will be for want of time or skill, not of inclination."[31]

Newburyport was close enough to Cambridge that Hurlbut and Johnson were able to visit often. Marriage did not mark an end to intense male friendships but rather intensified them. The former classmates practiced their sermons on one another, and Hurlbut's words, Higginson enthused, "spoke much to my soul." Mary always welcomed the visits, but they also tested her health. "The Lady of the Manor," Higginson admitted to Waldo, suffered from the coming of winter and had "a tendency to close her eyes when the evening shades prevail." As to his clerical responsibilities, Higginson found that those tasks "may wear on me," but that he was happy with the work. His congregation was regularly attentive, "kind & literate," even if not "literary." As he wrote to his brother Waldo, he continued to believe that ministers should be a force for change. Some of them at least appeared "willing" to be. In the meantime, he was determined to enjoy "the pleasantness" of his new position.[32]

Higginson's residence in Newburyport allowed him to renew several old friendships, among them poet and abolitionist John Greenleaf Whitter, whom he had first met shortly after his graduation from Harvard. "He lives with an odd Quaker-dressed mother, who haunted the back room with knitting and spectacles," he reported to Waldo. Higginson enjoyed their many conversations, and the two "laughed a good deal," but although the pair were united in their abolitionism, Higginson could not abide what he saw as Whittier's limited views. As did some other New England abolitionists, Whittier endorsed annexing Mexico on the premise that its desert terrain and 1824 ban on slavery meant the entire region would become free soil. Whittier believed it wiser for the United States to fight on for that demand rather than doing it through acquiring territory. If nothing else, their long conversations helped the young minister to hone and articulate his opinions on antislavery and disunion.[33]

Higginson threw himself into local reform movements. From the pulpit, he denounced his state's rising tide of anti-Catholicism and anti-Irish immigration, particularly after a local nativist group smashed windows at a cathedral in nearby Charleston. Few of the immigrants could read English, and Higginson spent one night each week tutoring them. He initiated a night school for mill girls in Newburyport, dutifully recording their names and that of the factories where they worked. One of the more advanced pupils, Harriet Prescott, assisted in teaching the younger girls, and later in life she described Higginson as a "great archangel." For his older and more educated female congregants, Higginson organized evening poetry and Shakespeare readings. He also visited the city's public schools and volunteered to serve on Newburyport's school committee. "Coming into the humdrum life of the town," Prescott marveled, "he was like someone from another star."[34]

The church's elders expected Higginson to invite speakers working the traveling lyceum circuit to speak at the First Society, and for him and Mary to host those men and women at their home. Higginson was happy to do both. Transcendental essayist Ralph Waldo Emerson visited, as did Oliver Wendell Holmes Sr. "'Tis a nice way of seeing great people," Higginson wrote his mother. Such fairly conventional speakers the elders welcomed, but they were less pleased when Higginson invited Kentucky runaway William Wells Brown to speak at his church. Higginson was undeterred, however, and he was delighted to discover that Brown also supported women's suffrage, temperance, and antitobacco, all causes Higginson himself endorsed. The "actual experience" of running the First Religious Society, Higginson assured abolitionist James Russell Lowell, "has thus far enlarged and not diminished my view of what the pulpit may be & do."[35]

Higginson's growing belief that a life of spirituality could not be segregated from the larger world only grew stronger as 1848 dawned, and with it heightened debate over free labor and the possible extension of slavery into the American Southwest. For decades, prominent politicians had sought to avoid discussion of any sectional issues that divided the North from the South. In New England, the dominant Whig Party pursued a pro-business agenda, and the region's leading statesman, Senator Daniel Webster, had based his long career on the proposition that the federal government lacked the constitutional power to abolish slavery in the Southern states. But the February 1848 Treaty of Guadalupe Hidalgo, which brought an end to the war with Mexico—a conflict deeply unpopular in New England—also put an end to the ability of politicians to ignore the issue. The treaty brought 529,000 square miles of new land into the Union, all of it due west of the slaveholding states. Even the habitually timid Webster was forced to take a firm position. "Under no circumstances," he announced, would he "consent to the further extension of the area of slavery in the United States, or to the further increase of slave representation in the House of Representatives."[36]

As Higginson's thoughts and sermons increasingly turned toward politics, he sought, unsuccessfully, to reach a wider audience by having his Sunday homilies published. He found a publisher who foresaw their selling as an inexpensively bound volume at 6 cents each, but only if Higginson could secure a like-minded bookseller. "It's hardly worth offering [them] to a bookseller who is not a Free-Soiler," Higginson admitted to Johnson. As for the mounting pressure from church elders to avoid incendiary topics, Higginson was unrepentant. "The more clearly I see, the more fervently I surrender myself," he assured Johnson, to "the new dawning Age of Faith." Everywhere, he believed, he found "ground of discontent in all our existing religious and ecclesiastical forms." Any determination to divorce Christian theology and social justice, he added, was "of the past."[37]

As the presidential campaign of 1848 heated up, Higginson found it increasingly impossible to remain silent. After the Whig Party confirmed Higginson's fears and nominated war hero Taylor over Webster, now quite elderly, and formally refused to issue a platform statement on the western territories, a number of younger Whigs called for free soil advocates of both major parties to "unite the Anti-Slavery feelings of the Union." They began to plan for a massive "Free State Convention" to meet in Buffalo, New York, on August 9. As many as twenty thousand delegates arrived from fifteen Northern states and three Upper South states, and although the motivating principle was keeping the territories free, a number of abolitionists, including Frederick Douglass, attended as well. The result was a curious presidential ticket of former president Martin Van Buren, who had opposed the annexation of Texas, and Charles Francis Adams, the son of the recently deceased John Quincy Adams. The new party's two-page platform demanded that Congress move against slavery where it had the constitutional power to do so and championed, as Charles Francis Adams wrote in his diary, "the rights of Free Labor against the aggressions of the Slave Power."[38]

Although the Free Soil platform retreated from the 1844 abolitionist Liberty Party's promise to advance the cause of voting rights for free African Americans, Higginson had found his cause. In October, he lectured on the free soil ideology in Newburyport's largest Methodist church—his own congregation, he admitted to his brother Waldo, being less welcoming on that topic. At Higginson's urging, the church encouraged "ladies to attend." One week later, at nearby Haverhill, he addressed a large audience. Higginson spoke so often around the northeastern portion of Massachusetts that he grew accustomed to seeing his name on posters "at the Corners of the Streets." His growing fame brought abolitionists to his door for consultation, among them Boston attorney Charles Sumner, who, Mary marveled, "stretched his ponderous form of seven feet in length under our roof." Mary pronounced Sumner's manners "not very good" but regarded him as "a true *moral* reformer." Higginson enjoyed his newfound fame but began to fear that his frenetic speaking schedule was damaging his health.[39]

Higginson railed against the Democrats but reserved most of his condemnation for Taylor and those Whigs who planned to support their old party as the lesser of two evils. He also trained his fire, as one admiring journalist observed, on the followers of Garrison and "that portion of the anti-slavery community who reject political action." Most Liberty Party members favored fusion with the Free Soilers, but as the latter refused to commit to an immediate end to slavery, a few disgruntled Liberty voters backed the candidacy of New York's Gerrit Smith. Believing a unified movement was the most likely to result in the liberation of the more than three million enslaved Americans, even if that meant backing a morally imperfect party, Higginson took on that faction too, making his case "in favor of a choice of evils," one Newburyport paper reported, "as ever we heard from a Taylor man."[40]

Higginson's enthusiasm in the cause quickly ran into the hard realities of campaign financing. Free Soilers in Higginson's third district nominated Charles Knapp for Congress, but when Higginson applied for money to finance campaign speakers, including Wendell Phillips, Charles Francis Adams, the nominee, patiently explained that the district would never defeat the Whigs. Phillips, he suspected, would "find it next to impossible to do much, and nobody who agrees with us is any better situated." Knapp lacked supporters. "We need a man, but where is he to be found?" Adams recommended that the new party's limited resources be spent where it might have the greatest impact. In the meantime, he counseled, Higginson might continue to organize and contact disaffected Whigs and Democrats in hopes of forging "an independent organization" by 1850 that would "command the respect of all good men." As the son and grandson of presidents, Adams was shrewd enough to understand that the abolitionists did not expect to win that fall but were collecting "the elements for a future union," and perhaps searching for a stronger candidate in two years, advice that prompted Higginson to think about his own future.[41]

That year, American voters flocked to the polls on the same day, November 7—the first time that had ever happened. As expected, the Free Soil Party failed to carry even a single state, and Taylor captured the presidency. But in Massachusetts, thanks to the Adams name, the Free Soilers won 28 percent of the vote. Despite Higginson's efforts, however, and as Adams had predicted, his third district was easily taken by Whig candidate James Henry Duncan, who defeated Knapp and received 64 percent of the vote. "Free Soil doesn't prosper much just in this town," he grumbled about Newburyport to Waldo; "it will take longer than in most places." Worse yet, older members of his congregation let him know that they preferred him to remain in the pulpit rather than "stumping the district" in favor of what they regarded as "a very wrong side." But as Higginson assured his mother, he did "not repent anything he had done in the movement & wish[ed] it could have been more."[42]

When reflecting on his growing estrangement from his church's elders, Higginson later admitted that he had not been tactful toward what he called his old "sea-captains." But then neither did he believe that his growing roster of reforms necessitated tact. Just before the election, he published a short poem, "The Fugitives' Hymn," in *The Liberty Bell*, the abolitionist gift book sold at the National Anti-Slavery Bazaar (Figure 2.2). The ode was innocuous enough, and editor Maria Weston Chapman sought to appeal to genteel readers by adopting a milder tone than most antislavery publications. Higginson's brief paean simply saluted the courage of unnamed runaways who trusted in a God "who didst lead us forth with a mighty hand/To the country of the free!" But Higginson's dour parishioners frowned on the fact that their salaried minister donated his time and pen to a fundraiser organized by the Boston Female Anti-Slavery Society. Nor did it help that Higginson shared the volume with numerous firebrands, from English suffragette Harriet Martineau, a known critic of the state of women's education in America, to Garrison, and from William Wells Brown and Frederick Douglass to Parker Pillsbury, an abolitionist editor whose attacks on religion's complicity with slavery earned him the ire of mainstream ministers.[43]

During the height of the campaign, Higginson had preached quite rarely, turning his pulpit over to other ministers most Sundays. Then, almost as if he were seeking an excuse to quit his pulpit, on November 30 he delivered a "Thanksgiving Sermon" based on the Book of Matthew's injunction that "man shall not live by bread alone." Higginson began by observing that there were two ways to celebrate the day. The first was to show gratitude "for the giver of all goods" by demonstrating one's "love for man and unfailing service" to others. The second was in believing that "*temporal goods*" were the "one thing needful in life." Although New Englanders had long since abandoned ideas of predestination, earlier Calvinist notions that equated poverty with sin and idleness lived on, and the wealthy businessmen in Higginson's pews did not care to be

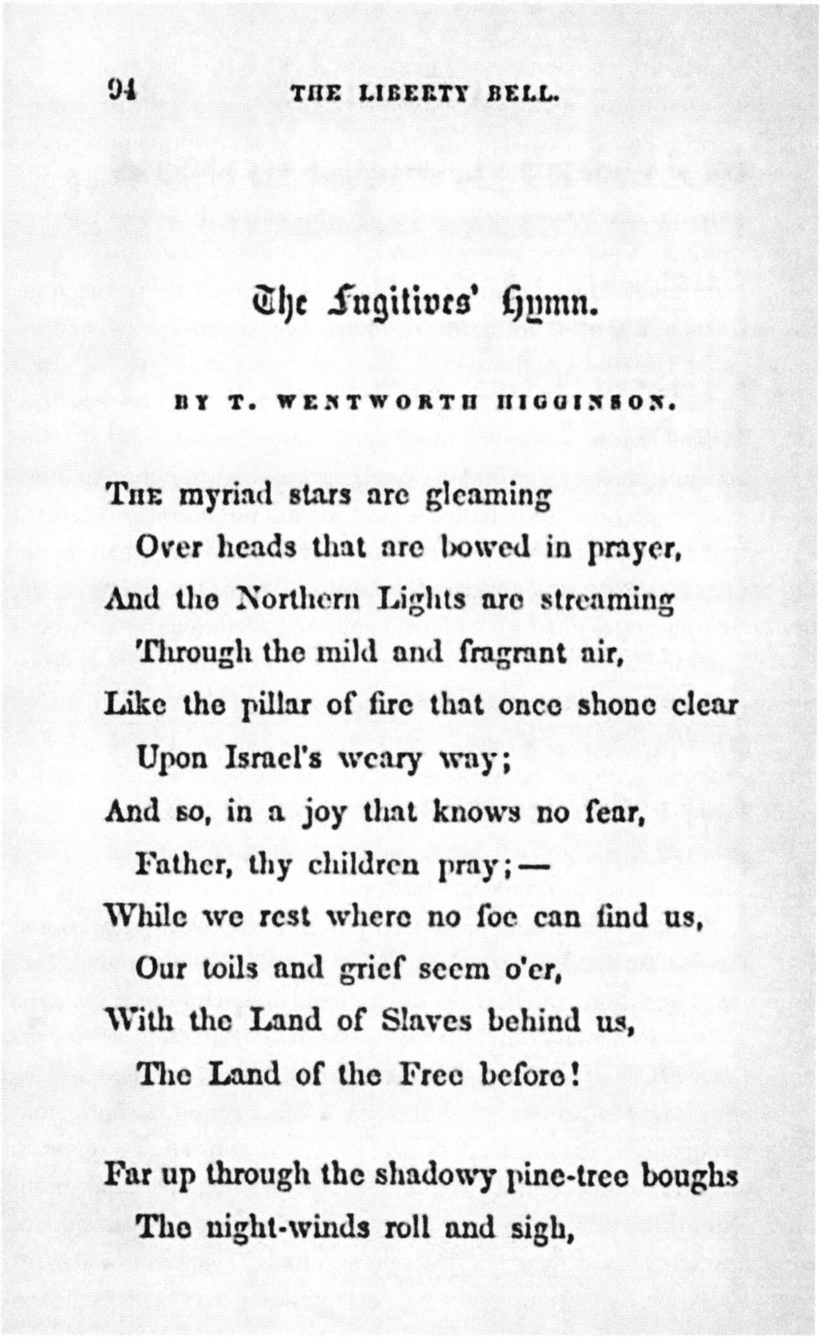

The Fugitives' Hymn.

BY T. WENTWORTH HIGGINSON.

The myriad stars are gleaming
   Over heads that are bowed in prayer,
And the Northern Lights are streaming
   Through the mild and fragrant air,
Like the pillar of fire that once shone clear
   Upon Israel's weary way;
And so, in a joy that knows no fear,
   Father, thy children pray;—
While we rest where no foe can find us,
   Our toils and grief seem o'er,
With the Land of Slaves behind us,
   The Land of the Free before!

Far up through the shadowy pine-tree boughs
   The night-winds roll and sigh,

Figure 2.2 Maria Weston Chapman began to publish *The Liberty Bell*, by Friends of Freedom, in 1839 as an annual giftbook sold at antislavery fairs and gatherings. Chapman and her sisters Caroline, Anne, and Deborah were all Garrisonian pacifists, and Higginson's prayerful poem reflected the views of the twenty-five-year-old minister who had not yet completed his transition to physical force abolitionism. From the author's collection.

reminded that no "classification" so readily "divided men, as that of *rich and poor*," or that too many of his congregants focused on this. Gazing out at parishioners who desired only a traditional Thanksgiving sermon, Higginson identified sinners by occupation. The merchant's temptation of "buying too cheap and selling too dear" was akin to the lawyer's "supporting bad causes and opposing good ones."[44]

Higginson devoted the remainder of his lengthy oration to the connections between his state's greed and "the Slave Power." Taylor's victory was "carried through, with the consent, the approbation, nay, the enthusiasm, of a majority of you." Because Whigs, Higginson charged, favored a protective tariff, they ignored the enslavement of Black Americans and chose "lives by bread alone." New Englanders, he reminded his congregation, had opposed the war with Mexico as "base and wicked," but just two years later cast their ballots for a general "who never could have been chosen had he not been both a Slaveholder and a Warrior." Well aware that this might be his last Thanksgiving sermon in Newburyport, Higginson admitted that it "would be pleasanter to bury all our sins, and only give thanks," but that would be dishonest. "I must speak what is in my soul or nothing," he vowed. "If God looks upon us to-day, he does not look upon us as a thought-loving, not as a freedom-loving people," he concluded, "but as a *money-loving* people, a people who 'live by bread alone.'" Proud of his thoughts, if hardly surprised by the stunned silence of his congregation, Higginson had the sermon published in both Newburyport and Boston.[45]

The homily garnered considerable attention in the abolitionist press and community, but some of the "Taylor brethren," meaning the president-elect's supporters, Higginson confessed to his mother, thought it went over the top and a few stayed away from future sermons of his. But a reporter for the Boston *Daily Republican* praised Higginson for his "manly boldness and independence" and his "scorching rebukes" to a congregation "composed almost entirely of rich Taylor men." So long as men such as Higginson lived, the unnamed reporter added, so would the Free Soil Party. In Ireland, abolitionist Richard D. Webb pronounced the sermon the "best piece of thunder I have late read or heard." Garrison himself reprinted the entire sermon in his paper's December 22 edition, somewhat naively adding that were Higginson "allowed to retain his present position, his congregation must indeed be a model one."[46]

One final episode in early 1849 brought Higginson's tenure in Newburyport to a close. He had recently been admitted to membership in the new

Town and Country Club, a private society of New England intellectuals and Transcendentalists founded by reformer and teacher Amos Bronson Alcott. Its circle of roughly ninety members included Emerson and Henry Wadsworth Longfellow, as well as Sumner and Garrison. Increasingly interested in a vocation outside the pulpit, Higginson encouraged Emerson to have the club launch a magazine, patterned after the Boston-based *Dial*, a journal dedicated to politics and literature. Several months before, Higginson had begun an essay on English poet Elizabeth Barrett Browning but was forced to set it aside until after the election. Had it not been for that magazine, Higginson assured Emerson, many a young man "felt themselves lonely and unsupported in the world." Emerson doubted the need for a second publication, but what ultimately divided them was Higginson's determination to admit women to the all-male club. Despite his reputation as an advocate of women's rights, Alcott was unsure of how the membership would react to the proposal, and he showed Emerson "the list of the names of the two ladies"— one of them abolitionist Abby Kelley Foster—submitted by Higginson. "On the instant I took a pen & scratched or blotted out the names," Emerson angrily wrote Higginson. The incident led to "a terrible fight," Anne Warren Weston reported, one that divided the club for some months, and in the end Higginson's resolution to amend the club's bylaws to add the word "women" was voted down.[47]

Following a brief vacation in the summer of 1849, Higginson realized that his only choices were to resign or be removed by his congregation. "The discontents of the parish, created last winter, slumbered through the summer," he wrote his disappointed mother on September 6, "but not, as I hoped, *dead*, have been blown into flames again by the necessity I was under of speaking my mind." His younger supporters, most of them women, felt "grave" as they counted the church's senior members abandoning Higginson one by one, leaving only a dozen or so "come-outers"—as religious abolitionists who dissented from church orthodoxy were called—"and one more in the pulpit" in the congregation. Ten days later, Higginson announced his resignation during a service. Somewhat sanctimoniously, he warned his congregation that they sinned not against him, but rather "against truth and light." As some of his younger parishioners wept openly, he reminded them again that people mattered more than Whiggish economic programs, and that he would never hold back from preaching "on a certain topic of practical morality." The Newburyport *Daily Evening Union* could not resist a jab at the city's pro-Southern merchant elite. Perhaps in the future, it editorialized, "a committee of the most opulent pew owners" should read over each sermon "in advance of its delivery and alter it to suit their pleasure."[48]

Higginson later admitted that he had "preached himself out of his pulpit," but searching for the bright side as ever, he realized also that the previous few months, though turbulent, had gone by "very fast." As a minister, he had largely channeled his reform impulses into words. Now he was free to put his thoughts into action. Unwilling to abandon the education of working-class women, he rented a nearby hall, where he taught nearly every evening. Higginson also announced he was joining the traveling lyceum circuit around eastern Massachusetts and promptly received twelve invitations to speak on every other Sunday evening. "It is pleasant to feel," he marveled, "that I have resumed my post of public scold." The public lectures would also have the virtue of keeping the young Free Soiler in the public eye, and by the next election cycle of 1850 he would be twenty-seven, old enough to serve in Congress.[49]

3

"We all need action"

1849–1854

Unemployed and three months shy of his twenty-sixth birthday, Higginson was unsure as to the next chapter of his life. He was never suited for inactivity. "We all need action," he scribbled into his diary. "This is shown by the way it transforms us." He did, however, assure his worried mother that he had "longed for this release from a life which did not content me." In the meantime, at the invitation of his cousin Mary Curzon, Higginson and his wife, Mary, moved six miles west of Newburyport to Artichoke Mills. Unmarried at twenty-five, Curzon and several siblings lived with their aged mother, Margaret Curzon, the widow of Higginson's uncle Henry, and she offered rooms in their home on the Merrimack River rent free to the couple. Higginson hoped that the occasional antislavery speech or essay would provide him and Mary with "as much money as laboring families live on," and it surely helped that sixteen-year-old Bridget Lynch, an Irish immigrant, aided in caring for the house and reduced the tasks of the increasingly immobile Mary. "We are safe on the moral side, safe on the material, and why not be contented and happy?" he reflected. "We are."[1]

Higginson's craving for intellectual and physical engagement was soon to be satisfied. His 1848 activism on behalf of the Free Soil Party sought to keep the new western territories free of slavery, and while all abolitionists judged that a noble effort, many New Englanders believed the Mexican cession territory generally inhospitable for cotton production. Within a short time of Higginson's resignation from the First Religious Society, however, Southerners in Congress were to achieve a number of victories that threatened Black freedom and white liberty in the North while opening up the Midwest for slavery. To the extent that unfree labor did not yet exist in the wide New Mexico Territory, Free Soil was a campaign for future freedom. But with the new Fugitive Slave Act, the slave power's tentacles reached into New England's towns and cities. "I think not now of the escaped slave, though he has all my sympathies," Higginson confided to a friend, "but of the free men and women who are destined to suffer for this act." Proud of his region and family's history and heritage, Higginson concluded that "the nation of which we have boasted was sunk in the dust forever, now that justice and humanity are gone." Here was a new challenge.[2]

In the first weeks following his forced retirement, Higginson took solitary walks along the river and absorbed the new rural life that succeeded "the storm" of Newburyport. In June 1850, after reading Henry David Thoreau's *A Week on the Merrimack and Concord Rivers*, Higginson determined to ride south to Concord and pay an unannounced visit to the author. He found Thoreau, six years his senior, at work with his father in their pencil-making shop. The family was welcoming, and Thoreau assured Higginson that Emerson had spoken of him. Thoreau's mother, "a gaunt and elder Abolitionist," had read and praised his Thanksgiving sermon. Higginson and Thoreau spoke for hours. "He talks sententiously and originally," Higginson mused, and although his manner of speaking resembled Emerson's, "his thoughts [were] quite his own." As he rode home, Higginson supposed that "nobody enjoys [Thoreau's] books as I do," although wisely he "did not tell him" so.[3]

At the same time, Higginson was busily riding the lyceum circuit, speaking on antislavery in public venues across the Northeast. By quitting his pulpit, he was liberated not merely from the conservative views of older Whigs but also from the pacifist, apolitical views of his younger Garrisonian parishioners. Speaking at one "Anti-Slavery Lyceum," Higginson condemned both the Democrats and the Whigs, "the two great parties of the day, as having sold themselves to slavery." For the first time, he hinted at the necessity of disunion, a position held by those abolitionists who felt themselves ethically tainted by living in a slaveholding republic. But first he believed it imperative that "the political power of freemen" should be brought to bear against slavery. Addressing the "non-voting" Garrisonians in his audience, Higginson praised the recent Buffalo Free Soil Convention as the best example "of the power of organization which a vital principle or truth could give." Aware that most of his abolitionist listeners not only disagreed with political antislavery but regarded Free Soilers as insufficiently militant, he delivered a point-by-point rebuttal, which one journalist thought "contained a strong argument against their favorite positions."[4]

Higginson's view that political activism was more effective than Garrisonian moral suasion was strengthened by the congressional debates of 1850 over the future of the Mexican cession territories. In an effort to force sectional reconciliation on the nation, Kentucky senator Henry Clay introduced a compromise package of bills. One bill allowed for the possibility of slavery's expansion into the vast Utah and New Mexico territories on the basis of popular sovereignty, while another, drafted by Virginia senator James Murray Mason, strengthened the 1793 Fugitive Slave Act by imposing crippling fines on those who assisted runaways and denying jury trials to alleged fugitives. When the final tally was taken on September 18, Whig congressman James Henry Duncan, who had defeated Charles Knapp, the Free Soil candidate in Higginson's district, was one of the 75 out of 183 members to cast a no vote on the Fugitive Slave Act. But in the name of national harmony, Duncan voted to organize the territories with the provision that they could later be elevated to statehood "with or without slavery, as their constitution may prescribe at the time of their admission." Abolitionists were unimpressed by Duncan's desire to placate the slave power, one editor charging that he had "voted to extend slavery and the slave trade over a large portion of New Mexico."[5]

To assist fugitives who had lived quietly in the North for years, as well as for those born free in New England but now denied the security of habeas corpus, Black communities and their allies formed vigilance committees. Determined to protect themselves and their neighbors, these committees proclaimed their readiness to disobey federal law, often arming themselves. Higginson joined the Newburyport committee and published an editorial promising that the people of Massachusetts "no more believe in the binding force" of the new law than earlier generations had believed "in the binding force of the Stamp Act." Should federal marshals appear in his town in search of fugitives, Higginson warned, they should remember that both the Bible and nature decreed "that they who take up the sword shall perish by the sword." In October he shared a Boston stage with Theodore Parker and Wendell Phillips, who had also come to embrace politics and the Liberty Party. Denouncing the fugitive law as "cruel and unrighteous," Higginson also contacted his old Harvard schoolmate Charles Devens, now a federal marshal. Wishing to appeal to Devens's decency, Higginson hoped they could agree that returning "to slavery a man guilty of no more crime but a colored skin" revealed that "justice and humanity" were vanishing from American life. Higginson was surely not surprised that he received no reply, but, undaunted, he republished "The Fugitive's Hymn" in Ohio's New-Lisbon *Anti-Slavery Bugle*.[6]

To better advance his views, Higginson began to publish columns in the Newburyport *Daily Evening Union*, a Democratic newspaper, though one friendlier to free soil ideas than the city's Whiggish *Herald*. Just days before speaking in Boston, he had published an editorial insisting that antislavery was the central issue of the age and that Massachusetts Free Soilers were "willing to stand, if need be, alone in political action." On October 13, Higginson appeared as a delegate to the Essex County Free Soil Convention, where he discovered that his words had an unintended impact. To stand against Whig incumbent Duncan in the November election, Higginson, like others, assumed that the nomination would go to his friend, the poet and Quaker abolitionist John Greenleaf Whittier. But although a Liberty Party stalwart, Whittier declined the nod and instead endorsed Higginson. The convention rose in applause, and taking the podium, Higginson accepted, promising, "If you want somebody to elect, you had better look elsewhere—but if you want somebody to stand and be shot at, let it be so." To his brother Waldo, Higginson reflected that he would not have begun his newspaper editorials had he "expected this nomination," but now that he had it there was "no thought of flinching."[7]

Louisa, who had never reconciled to her son's departure from the ministry, disapproved. But she was reasonably confident that the voters of his district would not send him to Washington. He was quite on "the unpopular side," she reminded him; "therefore I don't complain, only keep out of office and you may make as many speeches as you please." As expected, the Whigs again tapped Duncan, and although the Democrats nominated Alpheus Brown, the "Free Soilers and Locos"—antislavery Democrats—"united in several Counties." Conservative Whigs praised Duncan for supporting the Fugitive Slave Act. However, Garrison, referring to Higginson, "rejoiced that this young, eloquent and whole-souled man has been nominated for Congress." Garrison prayed that the friends of liberty would "make every effort to defeat Duncan and elect Mr. Higginson," whom he judged to be as far superior to Duncan "intellectually as he is above him in soundness of principle." As Duncan was thirty years older than Higginson, who barely met the minimum age requirement for Congress, the election was as much about generational change as ideology. But Garrison, himself forty-four, was enthusiastic. "The Free Soilers of the Third District have for a candidate a gifted, accomplished, and bold young man," he editorialized, "just the man to be supported by men who have principles to advance."[8]

Higginson had learned from his party's defeat two years before, and this time around he understood that righteous speeches alone did not win elections. Despite his praise of Higginson, Garrison's *Liberator* held fast to moral suasion, as did Frederick Douglass's Rochester-based *North Star*. What was needed, Higginson decided, was a newspaper that spoke for free soil. "I have never been a Whig," he needlessly assured Waldo, "& my sympathies are with the more radical portion of the party." Aware that many abolitionist voters feared that the Free Soil Party might not be as uncompromising about antislavery as was the Liberty Party, Higginson hoped to unite both factions more completely than had been done in 1848. Free Soil voters lacked the passion of more militant abolitionists, Higginson concluded, and an official organ could provide the party with "a strong intellectual & moral power" and give it "that unity & energy that it now lacks. "What he needed was a "leading scholar" to take it on.[9]

Who that "scholar" might be, and how he and the newspaper might be financed, was a question for which Higginson had no answer. Whittier publicly recommended Higginson for the task, and while Higginson was "quite encouraged" by his friend's confidence and privately thought his literary abilities adequate for the job, he understood that he lacked the name recognition necessary to attract the subscribers and donors required to keep a newspaper afloat. Douglass's *North Star*, which had begun publication in late 1847, barely turned a profit, and Garrison's loyal band of female disciples were not inclined to contribute to a political newspaper. The "difficulty of obtaining a suitable *Editor* so much better than I" was proving more difficult than expected, he complained to Waldo, and as any editor would also have to be the organ's chief fundraiser, the absence presented a problem "as to *means*."[10]

Desperate, Higginson turned to Charles Francis Adams. While still a Whig, Adams had in 1846 become the editor and co-owner of the Boston *Daily Whig*, a newspaper designed to speak for younger "Conscience Whigs" who hoped to convince their party to adopt a more militant antislavery stance. Thanks to his wife's properties, Adams paid his own salary, but at 2 cents per copy, the *Daily Whig* never turned a profit. Adams's reply was both more and less than Higginson hoped for. Adams agreed about the need for a newspaper but warned a disappointed Higginson that at present he preferred "to leave to others the greater part of the field, and to devote [himself] to different pursuits." Like Whittier, Adams suggested that Higginson assume the role of editor, but as to funds, Adams cautioned that the "Free Soil party as such is neither very rich nor very energetic." His unhappy experience as editor of the *Daily Whig*, Adams concluded, taught him that no "paper devoted to the free soil cause can go on successfully without the active cooperation of *all* its friends," and that prospect he thought unlikely.[11]

Undaunted, Higginson stumped his district, stopping especially in lyceums so that women could attend. He repeatedly charged that by voting for popular sovereignty in the Southwest, Duncan had "surrendered" the ideals of the Wilmot Proviso, the 1846 congressional resolution to ban unfree labor from any territories acquired from Mexico, a resolution that had never been passed. In a widely distributed pamphlet, Higginson's *Address to the Voters* recalled that in 1848, Free Soilers "were denounced as libelers whenever they dared hint" that Whig congressmen would never permit slavery's expansion. Yet in the final vote, Duncan "conceded to the new territories the right to establish slavery, should they wish."[12]

Most of Higginson's speeches, however, were reserved for the Fugitive Slave Act. Although he admitted that the Constitution did in fact allow for the recapture of fugitive slaves, he found nothing in its provisions that denied habeas corpus or legal protections to Black Americans accused of being runaways. "Instead of increasing" legal protections for suspects, "the new law *sweeps them all away* and makes the love of liberty a crime." If elected, Higginson promised, he would both "agitate" for the law's repeal and work toward an amendment to the Constitution that would overturn the clause—Article 4, Section 2—that supported the rendition of runaways. In the meantime, he thundered, what were New Englanders' responsibilities to "any law, even a Constitutional one," that required them "to assist or tolerate the enslavement of man by man?" The answer was clear: "TO DISOBEY IT!" By requiring his state's citizens to aid in the apprehension of those who sought freedom, Higginson concluded, the law had essentially nationalized slavery. "But if Massachusetts is not free, I know at least of one house that shall be." Should he ever close his door to "a hunted and guiltless man, or open it to his pursuers, then may the door of God's infinite mercy be closed forever against me." Higginson had no idea how prescient his words were.[13]

At first, rather to Higginson's surprise, the results appeared promising. Although Charles Sumner lost his bid for election to Congress from the First District, educational reformer and Free Soiler Horace Mann was "elected on anti-slavery grounds" in the Eighth. Initial reports in Washington's *National Era* held that Duncan ran well behind the Whig nominees for governor and lieutenant governor and was defeated. A Lowell newspaper crowed that the "Free-soil party has effectually controlled this election," adding that Duncan, "one of the traitors of the last session," had lost by a few hundred votes, "a just reward for his shuffling course of policy." But as more ballots were tallied, Duncan returned to the lead with 5,785 votes, besting Democrat Brown's

3,650 and Higginson's 2,431. Because Duncan's final count stood at 47 percent, and the state required a majority for election, the two vote leaders, Duncan and Brown, headed for a January runoff. Higginson's 21 percent represented slightly fewer than Knapp had received two years earlier, but his campaign clearly eroded Duncan's sizable 1848 majority; in some towns Higginson ran ahead of the Whig incumbent. In the end, the heavily Whig district returned Duncan to Washington by nearly 1,000 votes. Higginson lamented Sumner's loss but believed that as a backlash set in against the Fugitive Slave Law, more and more antislavery Democrats would join the Free Soil ranks. Taking his own loss in stride, he laughed that he "expected from Mr. Duncan a letter of congratulations on my happy release."[14]

On January 29, just days after reading of Duncan's victory, Higginson accepted an invitation to speak in Newburyport's Washington Hall, the town's major venue, and his choice of topics indicated he had no intention of moderating his positions in hopes of future political success. Higginson opened fire on Whig elder statesman Daniel Webster, recently appointed secretary of state but increasingly reviled in Massachusetts for supporting the compromise laws in his previous role as senator. In response to his abolitionist critics, Webster had delivered a speech in Manhattan in which he insisted that the intent of the framers of the Constitution was not to secure liberty but to "protect trade and commerce." In a blistering rebuttal, Higginson reminded his audience that during the peak of the Atlantic slave trade, "every plank of that bloody deck was defended, inch by inch, by merchants." Having been removed from his pulpit by Whig businessmen, Higginson saw little reason to avoid examining New England's complicity in marketing commodities to Southern planters or selling insurance policies to those involved in the internal slave trade. "The chain that commences in New Orleans or Texas, extends itself in unbroken continuity along the seaboard to Portland," he observed. "The interests of the slave-holder, and the interests of the merchant, the agent, and the manufacturer, are intimately blended." Many a parent in Massachusetts urged their sons to go into business, and Higginson endorsed that only so long as these young men pursued their "occupation so as to ennoble it." Perhaps remembering that his late father had been eulogized as a man "bred a merchant" but also one who donated his profits to those in need, Higginson urged all young men to take as their maxim that "the kingdom of God and his righteousness" should come before all else. "Dare to write this for the motto of your ledger, and then you may dare to be a Merchant." As his public lectures increasingly were, Higginson's speech was widely covered by the press and published in pamphlet form as *Merchants*. A few copies reached British shores, for when antislavery Unitarians met in a June 1851 convention in London, they condemned the Fugitive Slave Act and praised a handful of names—among them Higginson's and that of Boston minister and abolitionist Samuel May—for their labors on behalf of "their oppressed and suffering countrymen."[15]

Higginson was equally unrelenting several months later when a coalition of antislavery Democrats and Free Soilers wrested control of the Massachusetts Assembly from the Whigs. One of the state's senators in Washington, Democrat Robert Rantoul, was in ill health, prompting members of the legislature to consider a potential replacement. Although publicly opposed to any alliance with the Democrats, Sumner began to quietly lobby for the position. His old friend Charles Francis Adams, himself silently hopeful of a Senate seat, resisted any coalition, so Sumner instead turned to his old Free Soil allies, Higginson and former congressman Dr. John Gorham Palfrey. Palfrey readily endorsed the idea, hoping that he might capture the governor's chair, but, much to Sumner's shock, Higginson adamantly refused. "Will not Higginson see this matter in a practical light?" Sumner inquired of Whittier. "I respect him so much, & honor his principles so supremely, that I am pained to differ with him." Sumner then attempted to lobby Higginson, predicting that Massachusetts Democrats "will completely adopt our principles." But for Higginson, values were precisely the point. He welcomed the defeat of the Whigs, just as he hailed the defection of Democrats to Free Soil, but a partisan deal was far from a "triumph of a great principle." Free Soil members would have to concede too much in the alliance, and although he realized most antislavery men disagreed, he was proud to discover that he and Whittier stood "alone in the Free Soil Party in opposition to the coalition." Higginson was surprised, however, that Palfrey, recently opposed to any alliance, now emerged as its greatest advocate. "The Dr. & I are like the Christian and Mohammadan lovers who mutually converted each other & were then as far apart as ever," he wrote his mother.[16]

To better clarify his opposition, and especially after Sumner achieved election to the Senate and the editor of the *Essex County Freeman* began to reject his essays as likely to "distract the friends of freedom," Higginson published a lengthy explanation in the *Liberator*. Swearing that he hoped for the best from the successful coalition, he feared that antislavery voters were "deluded by too sanguine hopes of a sudden regeneration of the Democratic party." Had popular sovereignty advocate Lewis Cass won in 1848, "we should find the Democrats as pro-slavery as the Whigs," he observed. He predicted that were a Democratic president chosen in 1852 the party would again be openly proslavery. Repeating his willingness to accept penitent Democrats into the Free Soil fold, he noted that even the state party refused to write into their platform "the protection of Massachusetts citizens against unconstitutional invasion of their liberties." Aware that Garrison had little faith in either Free Soil or Democratic politicians, Higginson ended by admitting that he had gone with the Free Soil Party because it was the only one in which he could "speak the truth." Although a Liberty Party disciple in his heart, Higginson believed that a more moderate Free Soil Party not wedded to immediate abolition stood a far better chance of effecting change in the near future.[17]

* * *

Higginson soon had ample opportunity to demonstrate that he was willing to practice what he preached. On the morning of April 5, 1851, a messenger arrived at his door. "Another fugitive slave has been arrested in Boston," the note read, "and they wish you to come." Higginson arrived in Boston that afternoon and headed directly to Garrison's office. The runaway in question was twenty-three-year-old Thomas Sims, a Savannah bricklayer who had stowed away on a ship bound for Massachusetts. Sims had been living at 153 Ann Street in a boarding house for Black sailors and had unwisely written to his wife telling her that he was safe. Sims's owner, James Potter, sent an agent, John Bacon, to capture Sims. Bacon brought with him several policemen and a federal deputy marshal named Asa Butman. They succeeded in subduing Sims, but only after the desperate runaway stabbed Butman in the thigh. Because an 1843 Massachusetts law banned state authorities from assisting in the capture of runaways, Bacon and Butman housed their prisoner in the federal courthouse.[18]

Higginson was dismayed by the scene he found in the *Liberator*'s office. "It is impossible to conceive of a set of men, personally admirable, yet less fitted on the whole," he later wrote in his memoirs, than the Boston Vigilance Committee "to undertake any positive action." Garrison stood in the back, calmly drafting an editorial. The celebrated pacifist, Higginson concluded, was far less interested in "the rescue of an individual" than in "the purifying of a nation." A handful of Free Soilers and Liberty Party men were present, but they feared that any act of violence would injure them at the polls in the next election. Only Lewis Hayden, a Black member of the Vigilance Committee, struck Higginson as a fellow man of action. Himself a fugitive from Kentucky, Hayden had once been sold by his minister-owner for a pair of carriage horses, and he had no use for pacifism. When Higginson loudly suggested that at least Boston's Black community would "prove their mettle," Hayden promptly agreed. But then, drawing Higginson aside, Hayden admitted that many fugitives and even free Blacks had fled to Canada after the passage of the Fugitive Act. "What is to be done must be done without them," he concluded.[19]

Like Hayden, Higginson had no patience for moral suasion when a man's life was at stake. The teacher who had lost his position for tutoring his charges in the art of pugilism had not changed his mind about what he regarded as an artificial separation of body and mind. The previous year, when Georgia fugitives Helen and William Craft had been pursued through Boston before escaping to Great Britain, Higginson had declared that "the conflict with Slavery is not reform, it is revolution." Yet Boston's Vigilance Committee was little more than "a disorderly convention, each man having his own plan or theory" at a moment that demanded "the most unflinching unity in action." Too many of its members were Garrisonian "non-resistants, irresolute & hopeless visionaries" who lacked Hayden's practical grit.[20]

Inside the courthouse, six guards patrolled the halls outside the room where Sims was being held, while six more monitored their prisoner. To keep potential liberators at bay, the marshals encircled the entire building with a huge iron chain, a shackle that unintentionally symbolized the command the slave power wielded over Massachusetts. After the writs filed in Sims's behalf by antislavery lawyers were rejected by a state supreme court justice on the grounds that the U.S. Supreme Court had ruled nine years before that the 1793 Fugitive Act was constitutional, Higginson and Hayden took matters into their own hands. With the help of Reverend Leonard Grimes, a Black Baptist minister, Higginson managed to alert Sims to a plan in which he would leap from his third-floor window onto a stack of mattresses placed below, before escaping in a nearby carriage. Somehow the plan was betrayed, and just hours before the nighttime plan was to commence, Higginson gazed up to see workmen placing iron bars across the window. Just before dawn on April 12, federal marshals and nearly three hundred policemen and night watchmen marched Sims to the docks and bundled him aboard the *Acorn*, bound for Georgia. Upon his return to Savannah, Sims was publicly whipped before being sold to Mississippi. "It left me with the strongest impressions of the great want of preparation, on our part, for this revolutionary work," Higginson admitted, promising himself that would never happen again.[21]

Dismayed as well with the tepid response of Boston's white ministers, Higginson thought it unlikely he would ever return to the pulpit. He and Mary did not want to abandon their comfortable lives at the Mills, and despite "four or five calls or semi-calls," including one from a church in Salem, Higginson assured his Harvard Divinity School classmate Samuel Longfellow that there was "no chance at all over [his] ever taking a parish again." Just one year later, however, in March 1852, Higginson received an invitation to deliver a guest lecture in Worcester's Horticultural Hall. Reformers in the city were hoping to establish a church of a "reformatory character," as Higginson put it. Until they could formally create one, they invited "distinguished and liberal minded men to preach" on a visiting basis.[22]

Higginson thought so highly of both Worcester and his potential congregants that he almost immediately agreed to become the first pastor of what was to be called the Free Church. Two years before, in October 1850, he had attended the National Woman's Rights Convention in the city, so he knew of its progressive reputation. In the town of 130,000, there were "600 come-outers," that is, congregants who demanded their churches stand with liberty, "& a very thriving city & a clear Free Soil majority," he promised Mary. Despite that, Worcester seems to have "no one preaching anti-Slavery." Worried that her son would decline and having never come to terms with his departure from the First Religious Society, Louisa urged him to consider that a "fixed place" could provide him with "a sphere of enlarged opportunities for usefulness." She need not have worried. On May 3, the church's executive committee formally offered their pulpit to "the Rev. T. W. Higginson for one year," with a salary of $1,000, matching his former income at the Free Society.[23]

"Our household affairs proceed admirable," Higginson promised his sister, as he and Mary settled into their latest home, a modest house at 5 Chatham Street, exchanging the hospitality of former landlady Mary Curzon for an Irish housekeeper and cook also named Mary. "Fires are a sinecure & morning buckwheats an easy episode." Higginson's reputation as a man of action, secured by the Sims affair, meant that activists assisting Southern runaways routinely turned to him for support. On one occasion, Reverend May gave Higginson the responsibility of assisting a young woman and two children, all of them, apparently, white. On another, Higginson drove fugitives to the aptly named Liberty Farm, a safehouse owned by abolitionists Stephen and

Abby Kelley Foster on the outskirts of Worcester. Far from censuring him for his views and activities—actions that could have resulted in fines well in excess of his annual salary—the Free Church encouraged his antislavery sermons and unlike his former employer welcomed his invitations to guest lectures by Theodore Parker, editor Horace Greeley, and Harriet Beecher Stowe, whose *Uncle Tom's Cabin* was published in March 1852.[24]

Upon being named president of the Worcester Anti-Slavery Society, Higginson organized a series of lectures held in the City Hall. The speakers donated their time, but to cover costs Higginson charged 10 cents per lecture. During the 1853 and 1854 seasons, the roster of ten speakers included Ohio Free Soil congressman Joshua Giddings, Frederick Douglass, Wendell Phillips, and Reverend Antoinette Louisa Brown, the first American woman to be ordained as a Protestant minister. Higginson also hosted a number of antislavery meetings, featuring such notables as New York senator William Seward, Parker Pillsbury, and Gerrit Smith, the wealthy New York Free Soil congressman and philanthropist. Smith's renown for financing antislavery newspapers and causes would tie him and Higginson together over the course of the 1850s, as the Worcester minister grew ever more militant.[25]

As the most prominent abolitionist in central Massachusetts, Higginson also engaged in fundraising to purchase slaves, a practice denounced by Garrison, who believed the practice legitimized the ownership of one person by another and rewarded sin. Ever the pragmatist, Higginson thought theory less important than the individuals who were suffering. In one case, a New Englander who had settled in Georgia took one of his slaves as his mistress, and she bore him three daughters and a son. The unnamed man allegedly intended to return north and liberate his family but died before he could do so. The heir was willing to sell the family for $1,400, and after most of the funds had been raised, Higginson placed an advertisement in the *Worcester Spy* titled "A Chance for the Charitable" to obtain the remaining $200. His contact with the human face of slavery accelerated his movement away from moral suasion, just as his brief involvement with Sims convinced him of the necessity of illegal and even violent action to assist the enslaved. "It has been my privilege to live in the best society all my life—namely that of abolitionists and fugitives," Higginson remarked in his memoirs. "Nothing short of knowing them could be called a liberal education."[26]

Despite Higginson's growing disaffection with Garrison's principles, the normally dogmatic editor, who rarely tolerated dissension within the movement from his doctrines, invited Higginson to speak in the Boston

Melodeon—a spacious concert hall—at a ceremony commemorating the anniversary of Sims's return to bondage, and then again several months later in Framingham at a meeting celebrating the British Emancipation Act of 1833, where Higginson shared the stage with Parker Pillsbury, Massachusetts state senator Henry Wilson, and Black abolitionist Charles Lenox Remond. At the former, Higginson opened the day's events with a reading from scripture before turning the stage over to Theodore Parker. For the first time, the episode brought Higginson to the attention of the Southern press. The "reverend gentleman," charged the editor of the Raleigh *North-Carolina Standard*, was perhaps happier in having an enslaved martyr to venerate than he "would be if Brother Thomas [Sims] were starving and freezing to death in Canada."[27]

After the fall 1852 presidential contest resulted in the election of Democrat Franklin Pierce, a New Hampshire native but an unabashed defender of the Fugitive Slave Act, Higginson reluctantly concluded that the Free Soil Party was inadequate to the moment. John Hale, the party's nominee, captured only 4.9 percent of the popular vote, less than half of Van Buren's tally four years earlier. Invited to speak at the January 1853 Twenty-first Annual Meeting of the Massachusetts Anti-Slavery Society, Higginson adopted an uncompromisingly militant tone. "I say now, in this anti-slavery cause, or in any moral cause, there is no refuge from agitation but chains and dungeons," he shouted to "loud applause." If he used "warlike phrases," it was because the "conflict with sin is a perpetual death-grapple." As for his former party, "Free Soilers see that the disunion abolitionist"—and Higginson placed himself in that category—"goes in the right direction, even though, for them, he goes too far." Although he himself was a former Free Soil candidate, the party simply "does not go far enough." He had not given up on fighting slavery through political engagement, but he was open to other weapons. As "the Spirit of God [instructed] the old prophet," the task of "every man who has any remains of conscience in him [was] this only—overturn—and *overturn*—and Overturn. Amen."[28]

Despite its militant tone and embrace of Ezekiel 21:27, a verse that also promised that "the sword, the sword *is* drawn," Garrison pronounced Higginson's lengthy oration "excellent in manner, matter and spirit," and pledged to publish it in its entirety. Garrison remained wedded to moral suasion, but he rejected the Constitution as a proslavery document and accepted disunion from the South as the only way to live in a free republic not dominated by the slave power. When Higginson's speech was published on February 11, 1853, even the Progressive Friends of Pennsylvania, a Quaker society that advocated neither voting nor violence, wished to hear his words and invited him to address their yearly meeting. Higginson begged off due to his "wife's health and other engagements," but as he did on other occasions when he was unable to accept offers to speak, he mailed along statements "breathing the right spirit" to be read aloud.[29]

Other invitations he accepted. In November 1853, Higginson was approached by Francis Underwood, who together with John Jewett was planning to establish what they called "a Literary & Anti-Slavery Magazine" that was to become the *Atlantic Monthly*. Jewett had published *Uncle Tom's Cabin* the previous year, and the two were anxious to have Higginson as a contributor. Higginson responded the same day the letter arrived. For some months, he had been drafting an essay he called "The Romance of Slavery, or American Feudalism." Abolitionist authors had already drawn connections between "Hebrew & Roman Slavery" and the present, but of "Medieval serfdom," he told Underwood, little was "known & yet the analogy [was] more thorough." In its final form, the essay was a classic free-wage-labor exegesis, and, as many Free Soilers were to argue in coming years, viewed cotton slavery as "identifiable with feudalism, & the opposite of democracy, the American idea." As in the Middle Ages, an unfree worker in the South was not permitted to "take care of himself; he must be controlled by a master." Then, going beyond most free-wage-labor advocates, Higginson shifted his focus from race to class and anticipated by four years the 1857 theories of Virginia proslavery polemicist George Fitzhugh, who argued that it was "the duty of society to enslave the weak" regardless of race. The Constitution neither recognized nor permitted a fixed caste system, but hereditary slavery legalized "the superiority of class to class" by allowing only one "class to legislate." The American "idea of slavery, the [John C.] Calhoun kind," Higginson charged, implied not merely the inferiority of the Black race but also the inferiority of the white laboring class.[30]

Later that same month, Higginson was invited to speak in Philadelphia to mark the anniversary of the formation of the city's antislavery society. Once again, he begged off due to pressures from home, but he sent along a sermon he had planned to deliver in Worcester. His "Sermon on Satan," as he called it, garnered a great deal of attention in both the abolitionist and Southern press. Abolitionism was "*the moral school of this generation*," Higginson argued, even as the slave power was "gaining a larger and larger control of our National Government." When nations went into decline was the moment "*that individual virtue always shines brightest*." Evil stalked the land, but not in the "fictitious" way most supposed. It made little sense, Higginson lectured, to worry about "an obsolete devil with hoofs and horns" when the country wrestled with the "actual devils of War, intemperance, and Slavery!" Higginson identified no politician by name, but he insisted that wicked legislators, "acting through [an] institution of despotism," should be the reformers' "object of actual terror." As always, the ever-optimistic Higginson ended on a hopeful note. If "the immediate result" of reformers' labors were "uncertain, the distant result is sure."[31]

As the reference to intemperance in his "Sermon on Satan" revealed, Higginson had also become a devout adherent of the temperance movement, a crusade he later claimed he was "gradually drawn into" by family members, especially his mother. Both as a man who believed in the physical life and as a minister who subscribed to the perfectionist ideals widely shared by other reformers, Higginson advocated for a dry and tobacco-free Massachusetts almost as often as he spoke about the virtues of freedom. In 1851, Neal Dow, the mayor of Portland, Maine, had successfully pushed for a statewide law that banned the consumption of alcohol. At a temperance convention in Newburyport, Higginson was appointed chairman of his state's committee and tasked with obtaining information "relative to the operation of the Maine law." The State Central Committee begged him to give up his pulpit and serve as secretary for the organization at an annual salary slightly higher than what he was paid by the Free Church. Much to his mother's relief, Higginson assured her that he "of course declined," although he promised the committee that he would travel to Boston "after Christmas [and] speak on Temperance every Sunday for a few weeks."[32]

Higginson's support for temperance drew him more openly into a cause he had long endorsed but devoted little time to. In April 1853, Dow and Higginson issued an invitation to state and Canadian temperance committees to select delegates for the first "World Temperance Convention," to be held in Manhattan's Broadway Tabernacle on May 12. Below Dow's and Higginson's names appeared others, all of them male, despite the fact that women had long served as the driving force in the anti-alcohol crusade. Local affiliates selected women as delegates, among them Abby Kelley Foster, who traveled south with Higginson, and women's rights activist Lucy Stone, whom Higginson had recently heard speak on feminism. He found Stone's "entire argument for the equal political rights of the whole human race so simple and palpable," he reported in the *Liberator*, "that it is a mystery to me how any man with a clear head (to say nothing of a heart) can for a moment resist it."[33]

Upon arriving at the Tabernacle, Higginson was met by Stone, who "appealed to me in a way that called out all my chivalry," he told his mother, to nominate abolitionist and feminist Susan B. Anthony to the national committee then being formed by the convention. When Higginson did so, a Dr. Hewitt rose to say that he, for one, was not prepared to give to women that prominent a place. A Reverend Fowler from Utica agreed, begging that Higginson's motion "would not be pressed." When Higginson attempted to reply, he was met with cries of "Out of order," as was Stone when she sought to speak. Higginson took the floor long enough to announce that he was withdrawing his name from the national committee and recommending Stone take his place. "This 'World Convention' had disenfranchised half the world by excluding the women," he shouted, to "roars of laughter from the Bloomer side of the house," as one journalist put it. After one of the organizers angrily moved to delete their names from the proceedings, Higginson and Stone announced they planned to reconvene that afternoon in Dr. Richard Trall's Hydropathic Establishment "for a convention which would know no sex, color, sect or tongue." With that, Higginson, Stone, Anthony, "and other strong-minded women, with and without Bloomer pants," reported the *New York Herald*, marched out of the hall. "We kept our tempers so much better than our opponents," Higginson thought, "that we carried with us sympathy for many who did not go with us."[34]

When the seceders gathered again that afternoon, they were joined by Phillips and Garrison. The group pronounced itself the Whole World's Temperance Convention. But despite its position on women in leadership roles, Higginson was named president of the organization, with Anthony only as secretary. The group promised to return to Manhattan the following fall for a far larger temperance convention and adjourned after approving a statement drafted by Stone on women's rights within the movement. Those who remained behind in the Tabernacle also soon adjourned, one delegate grousing that Higginson and Stone could "not attend a temperance meeting without bringing in women's rights, slavery, and every other ism that has taken possession of their minds."[35]

Higginson and Stone formed a close friendship and professional relationship that was to last decades. She told allies that Higginson, together with Phillips and Unitarian minister William Ellery Channing, were three of the only men who best understood the wishes of American women. For his part,

Higginson praised Stone as "one of the noblest & gentlest persons" of his acquaintance, with her "lovely face & little Bloomerized-Quakerish person" who was yet "unshrinking and self-possessed as a loaded cannon." Together with Phillips and Quaker feminist Lucretia Mott, they crafted a statement, "To the Friends of the Cause of Women," on the four basic demands of women: equal opportunity of education, including in the "collegiate and professional institutions"; equal chances in the business sector; "wages paid to them, as compared with those of men"; and any employment they wished to pursue but do not, given "impediments in the way." Because Mott and Stone, Quakers both, were disdainful of electoral politics and believed parties harmful to individual rights, the statement said nothing about the ballot. Higginson obviously disagreed with that choice, but his willingness to follow Mott's lead in the statement suggests that he understood he could use his growing renown as a reformer to speak on *behalf* of women, but not *for* them.[36]

For Higginson, there was never a cause that was not worth fully committing to. As Massachusetts prepared to meet to revise its state constitution, he judged the time had arrived to press for voting rights for women. In *Women and Her Wishes*, a short pamphlet addressed to the convention's delegates, he elaborated upon the demands listed in "To the Friends of the Cause of Women" before swiftly moving into politics. Noting that French traveler Alexis de Tocqueville, in his 1840 *Democracy in America*, had observed that "*there is no class of persons* who do not exercise the elective franchise" in most New England states, Higginson observed that Tocqueville thus "fairly dropped [women] from the human race." Massachusetts residents recognized universal suffrage as an ideal but did not codify it. Half of the population had fewer rights than they would have under a monarchy. Higginson admitted that under English common law, the husband theoretically spoke for and protected the wife. But the economy in his region was changing rapidly, he remarked. In New England's cotton mills, there were no guarantees of protection. The pamphlet was widely distributed by Anthony and republished by Phillips in a collection titled *Women's Rights Tracts*. Poet and abolitionist James Russell Lowell judged it "the most compact of and telling statement on the woman question" he had read.[37]

Although, as one Manhattan editor charged, "there was not the slightest chance" the convention would accept their arguments, the gathering permitted both Higginson and Parker to speak on the question "Shall women be allowed to vote?" Higginson arrived armed with a petition from

Mary—who, despite her derision of Stone's bloomers, supported the cause—and forty-one other Worcester women demanding that all female adult citizens be permitted the franchise. In response to an earlier speaker who doubted that most women desired the vote, given that there were no protests, Higginson replied that the "same argument may be used concerning the black majority of South Carolina." Higginson also pointed out the irony that he was allowed to address the convention, while Stone—"the most eloquent vote in this community"—was not. To Higginson's disappointment, if not much to his surprise, the assembly referred the question to the Committee on Voters, where it quietly died. Hostile editors regarded the claims as amusing. "The Rev. Higginson is a man of great volubility," one journalist sneered, "though not much learning or talent."[38]

In early September 1853 Higginson returned to New York City for the Whole World's Temperance Convention, held in the Metropolitan Hall. As at the previous April's protest meeting, the conference named him president and Susan B. Anthony vice president. The speakers reflected Higginson's and Mott's view that women's rights were inseparable from other reform drives. Douglass, Parker, Phillips, and Garrison also spoke, as did temperance advocate and circus manager P. T. Barnum. Higginson remarked that "Lucy Stone spoke as only she can, & Lucretia Mott as only she can," and his cousin William Henry Channing thought Higginson presided "with great dignity, tact, and grace." As ever, Southern witnesses were less impressed. The fact that speakers comprised "a very nice assortment of free-soilers, abolitionists, and women's rights advocates," one Raleigh newspaperman dismissed, including "Douglass (a free negro)," should "deter any Southern Temperance man from having anything to do with it."[39]

The following month found Higginson in Cleveland for the October Women's Rights Convention. Unwilling to allow a good grudge to die, Garrison promptly introduced a resolution calling for the censure of the previous spring's temperance conference for its treatment of women, while Higginson inadvertently produced a second fracas by suggesting the conventioneers "take up a collection for the purpose of raising a fund to print the cheap tracts on Women's Rights." Abby Kelley Foster argued that any funds might be more wisely spent. Stone replied in "indignant terms" and carried the motion. When a group of young men, who sat in the gallery and mocked the proceedings, shouted that they would contribute if Stone would herself collect, she marched upstairs to confront the startled toughs, who contributed $50 to the collection plate. The convention added "another page to the disgraceful volume of the madness and folly of the Women of New England," sneered one New Orleans reporter.[40]

One year later, in October 1854, Higginson journeyed to Philadelphia to speak at the fifth National Women's Rights Convention. In preparation, he published an essay in the Boston *Una*, a women's rights journal. As did a good number of male reformers, Higginson judged the feminist movement to be "less immediately important than the antislavery movement," a position increasingly at odds with Anthony. But Higginson believed that the growing political antislavery crusade could soon eradicate slavery, while "the slavery of women lay deeper in the social system" and was "fixed more firmly in history." As a California newspaper reported, the "attendance was large and mostly composed of those who had social and political injuries to redress." This time the conference wisely selected a woman, Ernestine Rose, as president, while relegating Higginson and Mott to vice presidencies. Still convinced that the written word could be a formidable weapon, Higginson solicited documents and reports from various women's rights conventions to be bound "in many volumes, and deposited in different libraries."[41]

* * *

Earlier that year, Higginson's attentions had been forcibly returned to slavery and free soil by the May Kansas-Nebraska Act, legislation drafted by Illinois Democrat Stephen A. Douglas that overturned the 1820 Missouri Compromise, which had banned slavery in the portions of the Louisiana Purchase lands that had not yet been organized into territories. The repeal of the Compromise, demanded by Southern Democrats as the price of their support, permitted settlers to bring slaves into the Midwest under the auspices of "popular sovereignty." In protest, Higginson joined 3,500 New England clergymen in signing a petition condemning the bill as a "great moral wrong" that exposed the nation "to the righteous judgments of the *Almighty*." In a lengthy sermon delivered on the eve of the bill's passage and reprinted in the *Liberator*, however, Higginson focused less on the act's provisions than on castigating Northern moderates who had refused to endorse the Free Soil Party in 1848 but had supported the Compromise of 1850. "You called these *Peace Measures*," Higginson charged, "and called it treason when we vainly urged that there was no peace." What had their willingness to conciliate the South resulted in? "In 1850, the South demanded more, and more was given them." "Hear it again," Higginson concluded. "Never, never, never, will there be peace to this nation, until Slavery be destroyed."[42]

In his Kansas sermon, Higginson assured his congregation, "God himself cannot do without brave men." Three months later, he again had the opportunity to test his own courage. Near midnight on May 24, three federal marshals seized Anthony Burns, a thirty-year-old escapee from Virginia, and dragged him to Boston's federal courthouse. Among the officers was none other than Deputy Marshal Asa Butman, who had been stabbed three years before by Thomas Sims. The next morning, Wendell Phillips hurried to gather the city's vigilance committee members, and the Reverend Samuel May scribbled a quick note to Higginson: "Last night a man was arrested here as a fugitive. Come strong." The note arrived by messenger the following evening, and by then Amos Bronson Alcott had reached Higginson's door with word that a meeting had been called for the next night at Faneuil Hall. As it was too late to catch the train for Boston, Higginson sent messages to several Worcester activists, including Martin Stowell, who had earlier taken part in the rescue of a fugitive slave in Syracuse, New York. Higginson and his small band of allies boarded the morning train.[43]

Upon his arrival in Boston, Higginson discovered, quite to his dismay, that little had changed since the capture of Sims. A meeting of the Vigilance Committee was underway, but angry words hardly constituted practical solutions. "Most of the Garrisonian abolitionists were non-combatants on principle," an irritated Higginson grumbled, while Free Soilers hoped to impress moderates by "keeping within the law." Even his old friend Theodore Parker warned the council that those who hoped to rescue Burns should do so "only with the arms their mother gave them." Barely a half-dozen men at the gathering seemed inclined to put up a fight for Burns. In the end, all that came of the meeting was the appointment of an executive committee of seven men. "Napoleon said that there was but one thing worse for an army than a bad general, and that was two good generals," Higginson later remarked. "We had seven!" Although Higginson was still committed to antislavery ballots, when the slaveocracy used violent means to return men to bondage, he believed that violence was the proper response.[44]

After the meeting adjourned without any resolution, Higginson lingered behind to speak to Lewis Hayden and Stowell, both equally frustrated by the committee's indecision. Hayden suggested an attack on the courthouse after that night's meeting broke up, but Higginson cautioned that the marshals would expect such an assault. Stowell then proposed that the attack come during the meeting, after some "loud-voiced speaker" shouted from Faneuil's gallery that a mob of Black men was attacking the courthouse. That approach sounded appealing to Higginson, and both he and Stowell promised to round up five abolitionists ready to fight; Hayden vowed to be ready with ten more. Higginson then stopped at Gardner and Thayer on Liberty Square, sellers of "domestic hardware and cutlery," and purchased a dozen axes to be used against the courthouse doors, which he secreted around Court Square (Figure 3.1). Stowell hastened off to alert Parker to their plans. Parker evidently misunderstood the signal, and although Stowell looked for Phillips before the evening meeting began, he was unable to find him.[45]

Former state senator Samuel Sewall, one of the founders of the Massachusetts Anti-Slavery Society, called the meeting to order promptly at seven. It was the largest gathering that Higginson had ever witnessed at Faneuil, which was packed with protesters and curious spectators. As a member of the executive committee, Higginson was appointed a vice president, then quietly slipped out into the street and placed himself near one of his axes. Stowell and Higginson managed to extinguish the gas lamps that lit

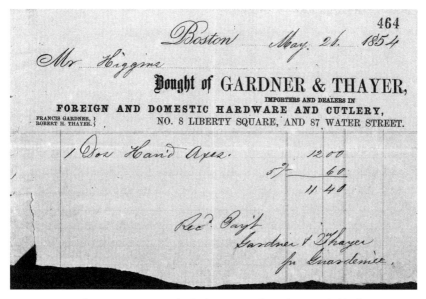

Figure 3.1 Before Higginson and Black activists found an available fourteen-foot beam to use as a battering ram, Higginson planned for a dozen men to use hand axes on the courthouse door, which he hid in strategic places around Liberty Square. Badly injured in the attempt, Higginson never retrieved the axes, but ever the precise accountant, he filed the bill away with his personal papers. Courtesy Houghton Library, Harvard University.

the Square and stood in darkness. Suddenly, around 9:30, "a wave" of perhaps five hundred surged toward the Square, running "pell-mell," but in vain Higginson scanned the throng for familiar faces. Still unaware of the plan, Phillips, inside the hall, urged calm and advised the audience against joining the mob. The packed stairways also prevented those near the front from reaching the streets. But Stowell was present, axe in hand, and shouted that Hayden had found a fourteen-foot wooden beam from a nearby construction site and was bringing it up as a battering ram. Higginson ran to the front and grabbed the beam, glancing over to see a Black man he knew only as "Pennington" opposite him. Running up the outside steps, the group smashed part of the courthouse's southwest door from its hinges, making only enough room for one man to enter at a time. Without hesitation, Hayden and Pennington sprang through, with Higginson close upon their heels.[46]

The small group found themselves confronted by "six or eight policemen," Higginson recalled, each brandishing a stout club. Upstairs, marshals frantically handed out pistols and stationed perhaps thirty more guards atop

NIGHT ATTACK ON THE COURT HOUSE.

Figure 3.2 Charles Emery Stevens was a Worcester neighbor of Higginson's, and evidently he traveled to Boston with Higginson upon hearing of Burns's arrest. His 1856 *Anthony Burns: A History* was the first book-length study of the affair. Although he did not take part in the attempt to free Burns, Stevens sat in on Burns's trial, was present in Faneuil Hall that evening, and witnessed the attack on the courthouse. From the author's collection.

stairwells. Although Higginson could not know it, Burns was in an impregnable cell with iron bars stretching from floor to ceiling and guarded by a half-dozen armed men. Higginson fell back on skills learned in his early boxing days, "but hands were powerless against clubs," he later admitted, and his "burly comrade wielded his lustily." Although he did not feel it in the moment, Higginson received a saber cut across his chin. A pistol shot, evidently fired by Stowell, hit guard James Batchelder in the groin, and another by Hayden caught Marshal Watson Freeman in the arm, just as a "large deportment of police" charged into the Square and began to make arrests. As the crowd outside the fractured door began to dissipate, Higginson shouted out, "Cowards, will you desert us now?" Stowell and Hayden fired more shots to cover their retreat. Guards carried the bleeding Batchelder to the basement, where he died later that night.[47]

Higginson eluded capture and somehow managed to make his way to William Ellery Channing's house, where his cut was bandaged up. Thereafter he bore the scar with pride. He awoke, he later recalled, "in a somewhat battered condition the next morning." He was well enough, however, to attend a midday protest meeting at the Tremont Temple, and then to speak that night, face bandaged and arm in a sling, to more than one thousand people at the City Hall. Federal marshals deputized the Bay State Artillery militia to help them escort Burns to the docks for return to Virginia. One of them, penitent in later years, confessed to Higginson that he "felt humiliated" as the thousands who lined the streets denounced them as "*Slave Hunters*, and *Slave Catchers*." At great financial cost, the federal government had succeeded in returning a single man to bondage, but the affair served to radicalize the city's often indifferent citizens. Even those Higginson had considered to be "very 'hunkerish,'" a pejorative term for conservative Democrats, were furious, "tenfold what it was on Friday morning."[48]

Given Stowell's arrest, Higginson's Boston friends warned him to return to Worcester. But those who advised him to lay low did not comprehend his growing radicalism and embrace of physical force. On June 4, Higginson delivered a sermon titled "Massachusetts in Mourning," a homily drenched in militancy. Some of his parishioners yet hoped for some peaceful resolution within the system, and indeed a petition calling for the repeal of the Fugitive Slave Act had in just days reached three thousand signatures. "For one, I am glad to be deceived no longer," Higginson countered. "I live under a despotism." The time had long since passed for Massachusetts Christians to have faith in Washington. "Let us speak the truth," he thundered. "Under the influence of Slavery, we are rapidly relapsing into that state of barbarism in which every man must rely on his own right hand for his protection." Federal marshals had not merely seized Anthony Burns; they had all but declared martial law in Boston. "May we gain iron in our souls," Higginson concluded. "Have soft hearts and hard wills, not as now, soft wills and hard hearts." Garrison and Douglass reprinted the address in full in their newspapers, the former praising it as a "valiant and effective Sermon." After it appeared in pamphlet form, the Washington *National Era* applauded its "calm and deliberate language" and asserted that Higginson had "resolutely made up his mind to resist oppression in the most direct manner, and by the use of such means as seems to him most effectual."[49]

Higginson would need to quickly summon a hard will. Within the week, word arrived from Boston that Asa Butman had warned Hayden that more arrests were imminent. Curiously, both the marshal and the Black activist were Freemasons, and Butman regarded it as his "duty" to notify Hayden, who then alerted both Channing and Higginson. Instead of taking flight, Higginson strolled to the station in Worcester and patiently awaited the arrival of Constable Frederick Ingalls; the two caught the evening train for Boston on June 10. The next morning, Higginson arrived at the city's Police Court, a state municipal court, accompanied by attorney and abolitionist Richard Henry Dana Jr. Because it remained unclear who had shot Batchelder, Higginson was charged only with "riot" and released after Channing posted $3,000 for his bail. No date for trial was set. The arrest was widely reported in the national newspapers, one paper in Baton Rouge pronouncing itself "very glad to see that one of the clerical rebels against the laws of the land has been arrested." Horace Greeley, the editor of the *New-York Tribune* and a founding member of the emerging Republican Party, saw it differently: "When kidnappers are the chief saviors of the Union, of course evangelists are rebels and rioters."[50]

Higginson returned to Worcester as authorities empaneled a grand jury to consider further charges. He dismissed the threat of prison, but his friends did not. John A. Andrew, an antislavery attorney, advised Higginson to lay low, and even Dana thought the evidence against his client strong enough to recommend that he should probably leave town. His family was more sanguine. His niece Louisa, daughter of his eldest brother, Francis, had come to stay with them to help with Mary; now Francis noted that "when we sent her off [to you], we did not think of aiding & abetting in any treason against the government." Higginson's mother wrote to assure him of her support, and even

Mary, never as cheerful as her husband, wondered only if the jailer would read their letters to one another while he was incarcerated. Louisa thought that unlikely. "Not if he writes them in his usual handwriting," she laughed.[51]

On July 15, the Boston municipal court's grand jury presented a bill containing four counts against eight men, including Higginson and Stowell. Hayden, despite having shot Freeman, escaped charges. The charges accused the eight of assembling "together in a manner that constituted a riot," an assault on federal marshals, an "attack upon the Court-house," and, thanks to their battering ram, of trying "to demolish the Court-house in an unlawful manner." The trial was set for the distant "first Monday of March" 1855. Wendell Phillips, a graduate of Harvard's law school, encouraged his friend to plead not guilty on the grounds that he owed allegiance to a "higher law" than that crafted by mere men. Should a jury acquit them, Phillips reasoned, he would not only assist antislavery "agitation by a trial, but by beating the government, a great point." Higginson agreed. "Each slave case teaches us something," he informed Garrison. "A few more such defeats as that before the Court House, and we shall have a victory."[52]

State charges did not satisfy President Franklin Pierce, however, who was determined to see the Fugitive Slave Law enforced across the North. The attempt to liberate Burns perfectly suited the law's threat of six months' prison time and $2,000 in civil and criminal fines for anybody who "knowingly and willingly obstructed" any federal officer or "claimant, his agent, or attorney" from recapturing fugitives from bondage. Pierce had recently appointed longtime Democratic activist Benjamin Hallett to be district attorney for the state of Massachusetts, and Hallett instructed the hapless Butman to journey to Worcester in search of evidence against Higginson. Somehow oblivious that the city was an antislavery stronghold with a large Black population—many of them surely themselves in danger of capture—the deputy marshal checked himself into the American House, the poshest hotel in Worcester, and made no effort to disguise the fact that he was armed.[53]

That evening, October 29, the city's Vigilance Committee held an emergency meeting, and by the next morning, one Worcester paper reported, "a large and excited crowd surrounded the hotel." The throng, largely Black, shouted accusations against Butman, "the notorious kidnapper of Thomas Sims and Anthony Burns." Foolishly believing he could intimidate the angry crowd, Butman appeared on the hotel's terrace, waving his pistol. Evidently prepared for just that, a Worcester policeman arrested the deputy marshal for carrying a concealed weapon and dragged him off to the "Police Court."

The crowd followed, and as Butman was being arraigned, William Dutton, a Black hospital orderly, rushed into the room and hit him on the head. Deputy Sheriff Lowell Baker then tried to arrest Dutton, who escaped through a window. Higginson was merely a spectator but thought it likely that the crowd outside the courthouse had a "strong disposition to lynch the man." George Frisbie Hoar, an antislavery attorney and former member of the state legislature, tried to pacify the mob by promising to broker an agreement in which Butman would immediately leave the city after posting a bond to return in two weeks for trial. As Hoar left the building with a cowed Butman, the mob of several hundred initially parted, but suddenly, Higginson observed, "a number of colored men fell upon him," one of them "planting a tremendous blow behind his left ear, which made him stagger." With that, Higginson, abolitionist Stephen Foster, and Stowell waded into the crowd, and together with Baker and Hoar, surrounded Butman as "rotten eggs and stones" rained down on them. Higginson hustled Butman into a nearby carriage and raced for the station. Too terrified to wait for the train, Butman begged to have the city marshal drive him to Boston. While they waited for the marshal, Higginson took the opportunity to give Butman a lecture "on the baseness of his whole career." As Butman boarded the coach, Higginson added that it might be wise for him never to return, and the bleeding deputy promised not to. "I never saw an image of more abject fear than that of the slave catcher," Higginson mused.[54]

The affair garnered almost as much press attention as the attempt to liberate Burns, but how newspapers reported it depended on the paper's location and political affiliation. Southern newspapers ran the story below the title "Abolitionist Riot." A Raleigh newspaper thought it "obvious that the people of Worcester and the people of the slaveholding States are deadly enemies." Another editorialized that "an ounce of lead suddenly injected into the calves of Free-soil patriots would have done them no harm." Even one Massachusetts Democratic journalist denounced the assault on Butman as "disgraceful to the community" and the work of "uneducated and unintelligent men." In response, the *Worcester Spy* observed that Butman owed "his life to the interposition of leading Free Soilers" and added that given his lack of gratitude, "he had better be left to his own resources for protection the next time he visits Worcester." Only the *New Orleans Daily Crescent* among Southern newspapers conceded that had it not been "for the interference of free soilers," the crowd "would undoubtedly have taken [Butman's] life."[55]

Despite Butman's inability to discover new evidence, Hallett, whom one Worcester editor dubbed "Pierce's slave-catching attorney," remained determined to obtain a federal conviction. On December 5, Higginson and Stowell were ordered to Boston to be charged with "committing acts of violence to obstruct the United States officers." Once again, Higginson had to post a bond, this time for $1,500, which his nephew James Higginson paid. Samuel Sewall rather than Dana stood before the dock as his attorney. Higginson much doubted, however, that any grand jury would indict so long as the charge was violating the despised Fugitive Slave Act. "There is an impression that they will drop the whole thing," he assured his mother, as rumor had it that the empaneled jurors were "disagreeing greatly about it." Higginson was correct, and as the *Spy* gleefully reported, the "Grand Jury, in the sound exercise of their legal discretion and rights, declined to find any bills." Amazingly, Hallett considered sending the unfortunate Butman back to Worcester "to wheedle or bully" yet another potential grand jury "into hunting in his pack." Prudently, Butman declined to do so.[56]

Despite Butman's disinclination to return to Worcester, Hallett made one final attempt, in March 1855, to convince a grand jury to indict on federal charges. Higginson reflected that if he had to face prison, he would rather do so for "violating the Fugitive Slave Act than for riotous behavior." The 1850 law, he believed, turned "honest Americans into conscientious law-breakers." Lucy Stone agreed, writing Higginson that it would best serve "the 'cause' if they should hang you." Hallett pushed for the indictment of Phillips and Parker, but Higginson judged "it absurd to suppose that a Massachusetts jury" would find the latter guilty. When the U.S. Circuit Court finally convened on April 3, Higginson's latest attorney, Free Soiler John Hale, moved to dismiss on the grounds that no grand jury had indicted and the marshal named in the suit had not been shot by any of the three men. The judge agreed, squashed the indictments, and discharged all three. Within days, state authorities too opted to drop all charges. The affair ended with one strange moment. While still in Boston, Higginson received word that Sarah Butman, the daughter of the deputy, wished to speak to him. By the time he was done dining with Hale, it was nine in the evening, and when he reached her house, all had "gone to bed, except an old woman with a candle." Whether she wished to berate him for his part in the rebellion or thank him for saving her father's life, he never discovered.[57]

Much later in life, Higginson reflected on following Hayden and Pennington into the Boston courthouse. "The experience was of inestimable value to me," he reminisced, "for it removed once and for all every doubt of the intrinsic courage of the blacks." It should not have, of course, especially as Higginson had often shared the stage with Douglass, who regaled audiences with the tale of his youthful fight with the infamous slave breaker Edward Covey. But the epiphany reflected a young reformer—Higginson had turned thirty-one only in December 1854 while awaiting trial—in transition from Brahmin minister to a direct-action, physical-force activist. Although Higginson had believed in the vigorous life from his earliest years, his increasing contact with both freemen and runaways willing to venture their lives in the name of Black liberty led him to understand that their hopes and dreams were not theoretical but all too real and in need of allies. So, too, had the ever-increasing demands of Southern planters taught the young man who had tentatively ventured into Free Soil politics in 1848 that even in his own New England home, a state that had abolished slavery in the 1780s, the danger of slave power was growing. As it spread its influence into the Midwestern territories, Higginson would soon extend his principles to a national canvas.[58]

4
"War always educates men to itself"
1855–1857

As a young man, Higginson thought of his life as falling into discrete chapters, and in many ways, his first three decades appeared to form precise episodes. When both state and federal charges against him were dropped in April 1855, for example, the Burns affair seemingly drew to a close and he could move on to something else. But many years later, Higginson came to appreciate how one chapter had seamlessly blended into the next. Gazing back at "the vast changes which every man of my time has seen," he wrote in 1898, and thinking of "those who created American literature" and served in the great abolition struggle that "freed millions of slaves," he understood that the individual threads of his long life were part of an intricate national tapestry.

In March 1855, one month before Judge Peleg Sprague agreed to dismiss all charges against Higginson, the Kansas Territory held elections for its first legislature. Taking advantage of the vague residency requirement for voting, proslavery Missourians rode across the border to pack the ballot boxes, resulting in thirty-seven of thirty-nine seats falling to Southern candidates. Having battled for freedom's cause in Massachusetts, Higginson assumed that the logical next step would be to fight for it in the Midwest. As the courthouse riot had garnered him national media fame—or infamy, depending on the journal's location—his allies and neighbors simply assumed the same.[1]

Even before his final court hearing, Higginson had already determined to take the great abolition struggle into the upper Midwest. Like other "very busy persons," he explained to his wife, Mary, he had "the most intense dread of ennui." When he gazed ahead at any "space of time" that he could not put "to advantage," it left him with "a sort of suffocating sensation." In early January 1855, Higginson boarded the train for points west, with the intention of speaking each evening—"extempore, of course," he assured his mother— on the need to resist the Fugitive Slave Act and on the threat of slavery's expansion into Kansas. He counted on the men and women he had shared antislavery and temperance stages with to organize his local arrangements, and he wrote ahead to Frederick Douglass, Syracuse minister Samuel Joseph May (cousin to the Boston abolitionist), Chandler Ford of Battle Creek, Michigan, and Reverend A. D. Mayo of Cleveland. Along the way, Higginson learned the "two arts of sleeping in cars & bathing all over in a basin of water." In Rochester, he reported home, his "lecture was *very* successful, though the audience not very large." There he housed with abolitionists Samuel and Susan Porter and dined with Douglass, although Higginson, who disliked almost nobody, thought Julie Griffiths, Douglass's business manager, "a not very agreeable Englishwoman." (In truth, Griffiths rubbed most people the wrong way.) But he was much impressed by Reverend Jermain Wesley Loguen of Syracuse, a Tennessee runaway who had joined Worcester activist Martin Stowell in breaking a fugitive slave out of that city's jail in 1851. After concluding his lecture in Detroit, Higginson was confronted by an audience member who stated, "Well, I should think they *would* have indicted you!" A smiling Higginson replied only that he thought that "a great compliment."[2]

Higginson, unlike almost all male abolitionists, refused to prioritize antislavery above all other crusades. Upon his return east he found time to publish several poems and brief essays on reform in the *North American Review*, *Putnam's Magazine*, and especially the new *Atlantic Monthly*, beginning a relationship with that journal that was to last for decades. Essays in the *Atlantic* led to an invitation to join Boston's Atlantic Club. Higginson was pleased at first, then quickly came to regard their dinners as tedious. Neither Ralph Waldo Emerson nor Henry Wadsworth Longfellow were "great talkers," he complained to his mother, and the general conversations, while "lively enough," tended to devolve into monologues by physician and poet Oliver Wendell Holmes Sr. More stimulating to Higginson were his efforts on Worcester's public school committee, where his crusade to allow Catholic students to read from the Bible preferred by their parents led to his removal from the board by "the Know Nothings"—the nickname given to the anti-immigration, anti-Catholic American Party. However, before his expulsion he had succeeded in abolishing Worcester's single segregated "colored school" and permitting Black students to be "admitted freely to all of the public schools of every grade."[3]

Higginson also continued to assist runaways, though he discovered that after taking his stand at the Boston courthouse, moving fugitives from safe house to safe house was not enough, that finding them a home was more important. In one instance, he placed an advertisement in the *Liberator* regarding "two colored boys, aged 11 and 8." He did not explain, of course, how they had arrived in Worcester, but he prayed that one of Garrison's readers might think it their "antislavery duty to provide for them." In another, Higginson briefly took in eight-year-old Mary Mildred Botts, the light-skinned daughter of Seth Botts, a Virginia fugitive. While Seth settled in Boston and changed his surname to Williams, Senator Charles Sumner took Mary on a tour of the eastern part of the state, in hopes of raising money for the family's purchase and because her white complexion made her useful to the antislavery movement. Mary was "so white," one journalist marveled, "that no one could detect the presence of negro blood." The childless Higginson was much taken with the girl, and while he surely understood her symbolic importance to the movement, he was outraged by how Sumner and antislavery attorney John A. Andrew "exhibited [her] to audiences as a curiosity." Higginson squired her back to Boston and "restored her" to her father.[4]

In a June 1855 speech at the Melodeon, Boston's popular concert hall, Higginson clarified the need to make it safe for fugitives to remain in Massachusetts. It was "degrading, dishonourable, [and] demoralizing" to have to usher refugees across the border with Canada. Free-state residents should instead "resolve that Boston is the terminus of the Underground Railroad henceforth." Although increasingly committed to the fight in Kansas, Higginson implored his listeners "not to dream of a land of freedom somewhere at the west, but to *make* a land of freedom here." There was "some honor," he added to loud cheers, in not sending "slaves to Canada, but to make Canada on the spot where we stand." The Massachusetts legislature was about to pass a law designed to secure a basic modicum of rights to accused runaways, but Higginson thought that insufficient. "We do not want 'Personal Liberty Bills,'" he shouted, "so much as we want a man with a backbone for Governor of Massachusetts." Ultimately, he concluded, it was up to the "people of Massachusetts" to commit themselves to oppose oppressive federal laws at every turn, as only then "shall we get anything under the name of freedom here that is worth the name."[5]

It was but a small step from the view that the federal government was the enemy of New England liberties to the idea that the time was rapidly approaching for the free states to leave the American Union behind. Speaking that November in Boston at a ceremony commemorating the twentieth anniversary of the 1835 anti-abolitionist riots that had reached even Boston and Philadelphia, Higginson wondered whether his state was "so changed, after all." After the repatriation of Sims and Burns, could any free-state resident truly believe in national progress? "The Union of 1855 is what the Union of 1835 was—a Union governed by slavery." New Jersey had been the last Northern state to pass legislation for gradual emancipation in 1804, yet it was a myth, Higginson thought, that unfree labor was relegated to the South. Their country was no longer one in which "slavery is national and freedom sectional," he warned, as the reality was "slavery is national, and freedom *nowhere*, for there is no foot, no square inch, even, of free soil in Massachusetts." While many Garrisonians believed themselves morally tainted by living in the same nation as slaveholders, however geographically distant, Higginson carried that argument to its logical conclusion by observing that because of the Fugitive Slave Act, slaveholders walked among them.[6]

Higginson returned to that theme a year later, at an August 1856 convention in Abington, Massachusetts. New England, he remarked, shared little with Southern states besides a common language. "There are no two nations in Europe whose antagonism of principles is at all comparable to the conflict of principles going on in this country," Higginson argued. The Crimean War had ended just months before, but Higginson thought it unlikely that there was the same degree of enmity between Britain and Russia as there was between Massachusetts and South Carolina. While liberty might be saved, he was less certain that the Union would be. As the growing chaos in Kansas indicated, it was not enough for Northern pioneers to wish to be allowed to settle in peace. The administration of Franklin Pierce clearly sided with Southern settlers, and the result was territorial restrictions on the rights of Northern settlers. "It is a new thing in history," Higginson charged, "a revolution not to escape from being slaves but to escape from holding slaves." Though he intended to vote in the fall election for the Liberty Party, which called for immediate abolition throughout the South, Higginson assured the party's perennial candidate, Gerrit Smith, that he had been a disunionist since 1846 and remained one yet.[7]

***

Higginson's activism and speaking tours sometimes interfered with his pastoral duties, but in one instance his ministerial responsibilities enhanced his national reputation, even as they sharpened the rancor of his critics. "Now for a great piece of news," Higginson wrote Mary from the road. "Lucy Stone *is* to be married." At age thirty-seven, Stone was well past the typical marrying age, yet Higginson joked that the ceremony would be "greater than Queen Victoria's." For the past two years, Stone had been courted by fellow abolitionist Henry Blackwell but had delayed marriage as she feared losing control over her life and finances. Stone had in fact put aside $6,000, and after Blackwell convinced her that theirs would be a relationship of equals, she agreed. Still, she placed the funds in the hands of trustees rather than allow state law to transform it into Blackwell's property. Higginson knew Blackwell only by reputation, and he confessed to his mother that he "groaned at first" upon hearing the news. Fellow reformers assured him that Blackwell was "a good man & person." Higginson nonetheless suspected that he was "by no means her equal." Higginson could not then know that Blackwell would in fact be unfaithful to his vow of fidelity, but as he told his mother, Stone "will be so beautiful in domestic life that I long to see her there, so I submit."[8]

The ceremony was set for May 1, with Higginson invited to officiate. The couple planned to be married in Stone's parents' home in West Brookfield, rather than in a church, to avoid any pomp or ostentation. Stone intended to retain her birth name, and while she traveled to Boston to buy a rose-colored dress, until the final moments she retained her doubts about the institution. "Henry says that I ought to be very thankful that a woman has this much freedom," she confided to Higginson, "but that is like telling a fugitive slave to be thankful there is a Canada, when he knows he ought to be free without going there." Mary accompanied her husband. Only a few family members attended. The group rose early that morning for the ceremony. Stone and Blackwell read their prepared "marriage protest," and in keeping with her instructions, Higginson asked Stone only to "love and honor (not obey)" her husband. "The heroic Lucy *cried* like any village bride," Higginson informed his mother. Caught up in the moment, Higginson even warmed up a bit to Blackwell, judging him "a man of tried worth, a leader in the Western Anti-Slavery movement." The small group then "plunged into" a hearty breakfast of steak, veal, and wedding cake, before Higginson and Mary departed for Worcester. "It was the most beautiful bridal [ceremony] I ever attended," Higginson mused.[9]

Upon returning home, Higginson sent a copy of the "protest"—as he called the ceremony text—to the *Worcester Spy*. "I never perform the marriage ceremony without a renewed sense of the inequity of our present system of laws, in respect to marriage," he told the editor before adding that he gave his "hearty concurrence" to the protest's six points. "I send it to you, that others may do likewise." The protest called upon "marriage partners [to] provide against the radical injustice of present laws by every means in their power" and was widely reprinted in both American and Canadian newspapers.

Significantly, however, even the Republican and antislavery press simply reprinted the statement and Higginson's endorsement without comment. Feminism and marriage equality were evidently even more radical than racial equality and abolitionism.[10]

Southern editors and Northern Democrats were far less inhibited. One Iowa journalist thought it preposterous that Stone kept her name and sneered that her "husband's maiden name was Henry Blackwell." A Louisiana editor insisted that Stone had "selected a female man" for her husband, one willing to "stay at home, and nurse the children, whilst the wife is permitted to go abroad and provide a living for the same." A Maine newspaper, though sympathetic to his views on slavery, trained its fire on Higginson. Since the Stone marriage was otherwise so unusual, the editor wondered, "why was it necessary to ask for [the] sanction" of a minister? Perhaps aware of Higginson's growing disunionist sentiment, the editor charged that it was hypocritical of Stone to obtain her license from "a town clerk who holds his office under a proslavery Constitution." Never one to back down from a fight, Higginson surely noted that his allies' silence on the issue meant the battle would not soon be won.[11]

Perhaps because of that, Higginson redoubled his efforts on behalf of women's rights. That fall, he agreed to speak at a number of women's rights conferences. In August, he joined Susan B. Anthony and other "strong-minded women" at Saratoga Springs, New York. September found him sharing Boston's Tremont Stage with Wendell Phillips and Stone, whom one Virginia editor insisted on calling "Mrs. Lucy Stone Blackwell." The largest convention was in Philadelphia in October. As always, newspaper editors tended to emphasize the male speakers, and Higginson did serve on the business committee at the Saratoga conclave. But Higginson saw it differently. "Lucy Stone of course was the real presiding genius" at the Philadelphia meeting, he assured his mother. "Lucretia Mott, the noble & beautiful mother-spirit of any reform in this nation," ran the meeting with her "powerful & firm-set mouth & the most brilliant eyes." In general, Higginson admired how organized and adept the women were. As he was coming to understand from his association with Black activist Lewis Hayden, he and Phillips might be valuable allies, but they should not *be* the movement.[12]

On occasion, Higginson's refusal to focus on a single reform movement— at a time when both women's rights advocates and abolitionists increasingly tended to concentrate on one issue—put his partnerships to the test. When Stone and Mott organized another multiday conference in New York City in the fall of 1856, Higginson proposed a resolution to extend sympathy to British suffragettes, exasperating those who believed that women's property rights in the United States were more important than wading into foreign suffrage disputes. Higginson also objected to the *New York Times'* ongoing coverage of the conference, claiming its stories were "as full as its criticisms on moral subjects are empty." Understanding the need to cultivate the friendship of powerful editors who could provide the movement with national exposure, Stone rose to speak and attempted to change the subject, while Blackwell politely chided Higginson by adding that the *Times* "was but a young journal" and might yet be won over to the cause. By the third day, when Higginson's scheduled oration "went rather extensively into the bleeding Kansas business," some of the delegates, one reporter observed, "listened with much impatience [as] the women evidently had enough of that hobby." Higginson was seemingly unaware of the discord, however, assuring his aunt that he "had a most pleasant time in New York & Lucretia Mott & Lucy Stone were never more noble."[13]

* * *

Less easily ignored were Mary's worsening health and Channing family troubles. Mary's brother, William Ellery Channing II, eked out a living as a poet, but he and his family mostly subsisted on an allowance from their father, Dr. Walter Channing. By the mid-1850s William's total annual income rarely exceeded $500, roughly half of Higginson's salary at the Free Church. William's wife, Ellen Fuller, found him increasingly difficult and moody and even began to fear for her safety and that of their children. By the fall of 1853 she determined to abandon their Concord home and live in Boston. Since the Higginsons had taken in their nine-year-old daughter, Margaret—named for her feminist aunt but nicknamed Greta—three years earlier, Ellen hoped they might house all of them until she could get settled. Higginson accepted the unhappy commission of driving a carriage to Concord to collect them all. William remained indoors. When Higginson attempted to call on him the next day, the aggrieved poet answered only with a curt note requesting Higginson "never call on [him] again."[14]

Despite their estrangement from Mary's brother, Higginson was thrilled to take in Greta. Quietly longing for the children Mary could not bear—an absence that perhaps tested his sense of his own manhood and masculinity—he regarded the girl as a daughter. "She is very sweet; full of talent & character," he told his mother, "very noble & truthful & deep in her feelings." Most mornings before breakfast, the two strolled about the town, and each night he told her a story. "I think with great satisfaction she is to be here so long." Yet even as Higginson consulted an attorney over what he presumed would be a court battle with William, Ellen reluctantly decided to attempt a reunion. To protect herself and her children, Ellen requested her brother, attorney Richard Fuller, create a trusteeship granting her half of her husband's income should they divorce. Hoping to soften the blow, Ellen assured Higginson that he was the "only being in the world on whose judgment" she relied and asked him to read over the document. A distraught Higginson agreed to do so, if only "for the children's sake." The reconciliation failed, however, and by 1855 Margaret and her three siblings were living with her mother in Dorchester. Five years later, Margaret, age sixteen, was again residing with the Higginsons and their housekeeper, Abby Eaton, in Worcester.[15]

On occasion, Mary's condition improved, though never for long. Rheumatoid arthritis affected her lungs as well as her bones and joints, and although only in her early thirties, she suffered from long bouts of coughing and colds, a condition not helped by the long New England winters. Quite often, her gnarled fingers could not hold a pen. "We have exhausted two homeopathic doctors & called in an Allopath," a new medical system that attempted to treat the symptoms rather than the underlying disease, Higginson had informed his mother in early 1853, "whose prescription is a wet sheet." With the onset of summer, Mary typically improved, and that August Higginson was pleased to see that she had "almost entirely given up her cane." Carrying Mary upstairs for bed, he reflected on how he had "almost forgotten how much she weighs." Unsurprisingly, Mary's deterioration took a toll on her outlook on life. Her kinsman William Channing Gannett once remarked that Mary was "a perfect mistress of the art of abuse, in wh[ich] she indulges frequently with peculiar zest & enthusiasm." By comparison to her husband, Gannett reflected, that most optimistic and charitable of men, Mary displayed "a very dry and cutting wit," although he grudgingly admitted she could also be "very amusing."[16]

Curiously, Higginson never considered relocating to a milder climate, although the South would not have been welcoming. Perhaps the vigorous Higginson held out hope of a cure, and he assured his mother that Mary was generally healthier in Worcester than near the coast. Even so, he left Mary at home for several weeks in September 1855 to join a group of friends in climbing and hiking around Maine. The group booked rooms in Hunt's Resort on the shores of Lake Minnewaska, where Higginson found it amusing that while writing his name in the hotel's ledger, a clerk responded, "Higginson! Why he's the Worcester abolitionist who had the scrape in the U.S. Court in Boston." So identified had he become with women's rights that local residents simply assumed "that Lucy Stone was coming" too and were "a little disappointed" by her absence.[17]

Upon returning to Worcester, either as part of an earlier agreement regarding his tour of Maine or because Mary's health had further deteriorated, Higginson requested leave of his pulpit for a winter trip to Fayal, one of the Azores, Portuguese islands 1,400 miles west of Lisbon. The couple sailed from Boston on October 30 aboard the three-masted barque *Agor*. Following a stormy beginning, the ship hit calm waters. "Even Mary admits that it is pleasant to sail today," Higginson scribbled into his diary. Although a strict temperance man himself, he permitted Mary to sip ale. "The ship is still, & Mary happy," he reported on November 5. "The deck is level & she can walk about & the ladies have their work out & all seems homelike." Upon landing Higginson was shocked by how the island was "all the South of Europe at once," a place "where not a person looks as any person ever looked in America." Or at least in his New England.[18]

The pair enjoyed Christmas season in these warmer lands, and the abolitionist took heart in the way that English and Portuguese families seemed to gather together so easily in the island's cathedral, "children light & dark, gazing and peering" at the church's holiday decorations. Higginson was also impressed by the egalitarian nature of the congregation, for while the cathedral had benches, they lacked the "locked pews as in Boston," where wealthy families purchased box seats toward the front of the church. Higginson took Portuguese-language lessons "from a charming & accomplished lady" and began work on a proposed book "on the religious aspects of the age." A year before, he had delivered a sermon he titled "Scripture Idolatry," which appeared in both pamphlet form and abbreviated in the *Liberator*, and he thought it might serve as an opening chapter. In the sermon, Higginson renewed his war on merchants, writing that he knew of "very profligate and worldly men who are 'mighty in the Scriptures,' and very pure and noble men who scarcely read them at all." As it turned out, he never finished the book that he tentatively titled *Return of Faith*, though he eventually published a single chapter in 1871 as "The Sympathy of Religions" in the journal *Radical*.[19]

Lethargy never became Higginson, though, and the language lessons and leisure to write were hardly sufficient to fill his days in the Azores. Perhaps, too, he worried about being too long away from his pulpit. He had hoped to return to Worcester by May 1, but the *Agor* sailed for Liverpool rather than Boston, so he warned one correspondent he would not "re-appear before June 1." As for his concerns about his position with the Free Church, he need not have fretted. One of the elders, Oramel Martin, assured Higginson's mother that there were "not more than three men that could keep the Free Church together." After all of "the very many able Sermons we have heard from your son," Martin added, those delivered by others "appear weak & stale and our people will not go to hear them."[20]

The Higginsons finally returned to Boston on the evening of June 7, "after a three week passage, rather a cold & rough one." As the tugboat arrived to escort the *Agor* to the docks, the pilot handed Higginson a newspaper, which, he told his mother, "sprung Sumner & Kansas upon me." The stories chronicled South Carolina congressman Preston Brooks's May 22 assault on Charles Sumner in Congress following the Massachusetts senator's fiery "Crime against Kansas" speech and the blockading of the Missouri River to prevent free soil settlers from reaching Kansas. Higginson hastened back to Worcester, where a public meeting cheered his arrival and resolved to assist the newly founded New England Emigrant Aid Company. The assault on Sumner, Higginson believed, "was the legitimate result of the general spirit of violence" then prevailing throughout the nation. Rather than seek to defuse Northern rage, Higginson thought it imperative "to arm any party of colonists more openly and thoroughly" than ever, and when a local committee was appointed to raise funds for settlers in Kansas, Higginson agreed to serve as Worcester's corresponding secretary with other local groups.[21]

Higginson's determination to purchase weapons for free soil settlers again uncovered one of the many fissures within the abolitionist movement. Chartered by the state legislature in April 1854, the Emigrant Aid Company was the brainchild of Eli Thayer, who ran Worcester's Oread Institute, a school for young women. Like many Republicans, Thayer's objection to slavery was based more on economic than moral grounds. As he observed in one promotional pamphlet, planting New England pioneers in the Midwest opened "commercial advantages to the commercial States" by creating a society "of free men who furnish a market to our manufactures and imports." For a capital investment that Thayer guessed would not exceed $5 million, a free and capitalist Kansas could benefit Massachusetts by establishing an economic connection between western farms and eastern ports and factories. And as an aspiring politician—Thayer would win election to Congress in

November 1856—he promised that all monies raised would be spent on food, clothing, and tools, not weapons. When informed that physical-force abolitionists like Higginson also expected to purchase rifles, Thayer assured one potential donor that his Society would "do nothing of this."[22]

Higginson generally believed that antislavery dollars and efforts were more wisely spent in fighting the Fugitive Slave Act and federal marshals in New England. The Republican emphasis on slavery's perceived economic failings, rather than its ethical sins, played no role in his thinking. "Where is the good," he wondered in one speech, "of emigrating to Nebraska if Nebraska is to be a transplanted Massachusetts, and the original Massachusetts has been tried and found wanting?" Thayer, however, saw no logic in that. "The argument of the reverend gentleman is this," he replied. "The best it is possible for you to do is to make another State which will be as bad as Massachusetts is, and therefore you had better do nothing at all," ignoring the fact that Higginson was proposing violent intervention in his home state. Thayer believed his Society and the Republican Party could achieve a free Kansas filled with "patriotic and law-abiding" farmers. He even suspected that Higginson quietly desired proslavery settlers to succeed in securing Kansas for the South, as that "might help to fire the Northern heart against the Union and make it more easy for disunionists to triumph."[23]

Though that charge was an exaggeration, Higginson refused to devote himself to a cause that did not merit his moral energies. Reading newspaper accounts of the troubles in Kansas was not sufficient, he decided, and that meant he had to visit the territory himself. Mary evidently did not want him to go, but Higginson explained that while he was "sorry" to leave her, a visit was "indeed indispensable." By late June 1856 his train reached Chicago, and one day later he arrived along the Mississippi River, where he booked passage on a steamboat for St. Louis, which, he assured Mary, was "a very safe place." At each stop he spoke with travelers, all of whom, he reported in a letter to the *Liberator*, testified to the "outrageous conduct of the Missourians, and the admirable conduct" of his fellow New Englanders. Free soil settlers returning north told Higginson that upon reaching Waverly, Illinois, they had been met by a small army of roughly three hundred armed proslavery men who disarmed the group and warned them to abandon the region. Having doubted Thayer's grit, such stories, together with the previous month's sacking of Lawrence, Kansas, by proslavery men, convinced Higginson of the need to respond quickly. He prayed that it would not require more outrages like the burning of Lawrence to "arouse the Eastern States to act."[24]

Higginson's letters to Garrison caught the eye of several Democratic editors, who accused him of "manufactur[ing] outrages" to incite "public opinion." This was the same reverend, the *Grand River Times* charged, "that figured in the Anthony Burns rescue attempt." The editor wondered "what denomination of the gospel of peace claims him," but as a man who knew his Bible, Higginson had few qualms about beating plowshares into swords. Neither did his feminist allies. Higginson was "looking after the interests of Kansas," Lucy Stone remarked to Susan B. Anthony. "God bless him too!"[25]

Higginson's determination was reinforced by what he witnessed in St. Louis. On July 2, shortly before returning home, he visited the offices and holding pens of several slave traders, including one owned by Corbin Thompson. Higginson thought Thompson "a good-natured looking man, not unlike a reputable stable keeper" in New England. Thompson happily offered to show Higginson his "stock," which turned out to be roughly twenty-four slaves, "the majority of them being children under fourteen." While there, a potential buyer appeared, hoping to purchase a companion for his daughter. "Please, Sir," a girl Higginson guessed to be eleven begged, unsuccessfully, "I wish I could stay with my mother." Most of the boys and men, Thompson explained, would be purchased by downriver planters. The "perfectly matter-of-fact character of the transaction, and the circumstance that those before me did not seem exceptionally cruel men," Higginson reflected, "made the whole thing more terrible." What he had witnessed was "a case, not of special outrage, but of every-day business, which was worse."[26]

Few white abolitionists had come face to face with the reality of slavery, let alone witnessed its cruelest component, the separation of families. Even during the Burns riot, the jailed fugitive remained more of a symbol of slave-power tyranny than any person Higginson had actually known. This time, Higginson spoke to an enslaved child he was powerless to help, just as he had conversed with perhaps the most callous man he had ever met. The incident—which he related again and again in various later publications—forced him to confront the enormity of his task. Higginson had never been an advocate of moral suasion, but Thompson's bland confidence that his business was like any other sort of commerce reinforced Higginson's belief that only by force could such a powerful and immoral institution be overturned. In coming weeks, the memory of the girl's separation from her mother prompted him to renew his efforts in Kansas, and in coming years it provoked him to return to his disunion campaign and work toward the separation of New England from a country that allowed slave traders to prosper.

* * *

Higginson had barely returned to Worcester before he was approached by his former critic Eli Thayer, who wished to hire him as a paid agent for his Emigrant Aid Company to oversee the shipment of goods and settlers to Kansas Territory. Mary's health had improved to the point that they could take "little walks & visits in the course of the evenings," and she evidently accepted the fact that her husband might have to return west. Although Higginson told his mother that Mary was "heroic & patient," Greta intended to return for an extended visit, and he hoped that Louisa might invite the two to stay at her home in Brattleboro. Higginson regretted that his trip would force him to miss the upcoming women's rights convention in Manhattan. Nonetheless he was wedded to the battle for Kansas. His "mission will not be a very warlike one," he vowed, surely no more dangerous than in "setting food on a ship." The habitually serene Higginson was annoyed when hearing his neighbors privately praise him for what he was doing and thought it "rather pathetic" that they were thanking him rather than doing something themselves.[27]

Higginson's old allies did not require confirmation that he had accepted Thayer's offer; they simply assumed from the start he would do so. From nearby Lexington, Martin Stowell wrote to say that he had raised a group of fifty-seven men, who had voted him "the military head of the party." B. B. Newton, encamped south of Boston near Mount Pleasant, reported that his recruits were busily "making bullets and exercising our skill in using them." Their use of martial language was revealing. Despite Thayer's public professions that he was merely raising money for clothing and food, one of Higginson's early tasks for the Emigrant Aid Company was to journey to Boston to purchase "twenty rifles and one box" of cartridges for $88 from William Read's "Guns, Sporting Apparatus, and Hardware Goods." Three days later he visited the shop of John Lovell, "Importer, Manufacturer, and Dealer in Guns," to acquire another twenty rifles for Vermont volunteers. To his worried mother, Higginson confided only that he had procured "a nice supply of boots & clothing." Together with a number of Worcester men, Higginson caught the September 1 train for Chicago, and from there "to Nebraska City & probably into the territory."[28]

Upon reaching Illinois, Higginson discovered a number of free soil pioneers who were reluctant to venture further west, among them Dr. Seth

Rogers, who was to serve beside Higginson during the Civil War. Most hailed from New England, though some families had been living in Indiana. "They are very glad to have me here," he wrote Louisa, "and are in need of efficient agents." Free-state organizers thought it wiser to "send arms [and] provisions" rather than more settlers, until Higginson could report back on conditions in the territory, and funds for that were "being raised faster than ever before," Concord-based abolitionist Franklin Sanborn reported. Aware that Mary and his mother feared for his safety, Higginson promised Louisa that his group had a mounted escort to protect them, and there was "probably not danger enough to make it exciting." The greatest hazard, he insisted, was the hot midwestern sun, but he wore a wide hat and coated his lips with "Sulphur pellets." In truth, once Higginson and his small band reached the Kansas border and proceeded on horseback, they were in danger of arrest by Governor John Geary, an appointee of President Pierce, or of assault by Missouri vigilantes. Hoping that numbers would protect him, Higginson joined a group of settlers led by James Redpath, an English-born journalist ten years his junior. Even so, their party soon encountered a squad of federal marshals and cavalrymen under the command of Captain William Walker, who startled Higginson by addressing him by name and demanding he meet with Geary. Following a brief meeting, the "pompous" governor released Higginson, who was pleased that in his absence, the marshals lacked the "wit to discover the Sharp's rifles and cannon" they had brought west. To better guard their arms, the group set up sentries. "Imagine me patrolling as one of the guard for an hour every night," Higginson finally admitted to Louisa, "in high boots among the dry grass, rifle in hand & revolver in belt."[29]

What Higginson found upon reaching Kansas was dispiriting. Although Geary, a Pennsylvania Democrat, was in fact attempting to be impartial when it came to armed settlers moving into his territory, like Pierce he believed the solution to sectional strife was to conciliate the South. As Higginson led twenty-eight wagons into Kansas, he encountered a train of nineteen returning north. "The Missourians could not conquer us," one defeated farmer informed Higginson, "but Governor Geary has." Another wrote to Higginson, telling of how his family had been driven out of their home by a "band of lawless ruffians." Had he known how dangerous Kansas was, he added, they would never have left New England. Even in Free Soil enclaves near Topeka, Higginson discovered "general poverty and privations of food." The home of Charles Robinson, a Thayer ally whom free soilers regarded as the rightful Kansas governor, had been burned, as had many bridges and mills. When free-staters attempted to defend their farms, Higginson charged, "the U.S. government steps in, & arrests their best and bravest." Despite all of this, Higginson held out hope that the very bleakness of the situation might change peaceable New Englanders into warriors. "What is most striking [is that] the same persons whom you saw a year ago in Boston, indolent and timid, are here transformed to heroes," he told one correspondent. Just as he had long believed that action rejuvenated him, it "was plain" to him "that the excitement had become a necessary stimulus to them."[30]

Higginson had to admit, however, how strange it felt for a New Englander to find himself utterly beyond civilization's pale and "outside the world of human law." Even when he disobeyed that law, as during the Burns riot, the courts had existed to "protect" him. In the chaos of bleeding Kansas, only his Sharps rifle and revolvers and, failing those, his "ingenuity and ready wit" would be his "protection." Oddly, Higginson thought it such a "delightful sensation" that he sought to escalate the danger by traveling east up the Kansas River to the slave-soil capital of Lecompton. Striking up a conversation with several "border ruffians," he was amused to hear one say that "there's a preacher going about here preaching politics." The others doubted any minister would be foolish enough to do so, but to Higginson's "dubious enjoyment," the first persisted: "He has his text and preaches religion, then he drops that and pitches into politics, and then drops that too, and begins about the sufferin' niggers." The speaker was sorry to admit he did not know the minister's name, but he assumed any short, timid New England clergyman would be easy to spot. Never suspecting who he was, the second Southerner bragged that "our boys" would enjoy "running him out of town." Shortly thereafter, though, one Democratic editor did identify Higginson by name. The man they searched for was "the same clergyman who had been indicted for breaking into the Boston courthouse where Batchelder was murdered." Those seeking Higginson, the editor added, should look for the scar on his chin, "which one of the officers gave him."[31]

As free-staters began to rebuild the burned town of Lawrence, its residents invited Higginson to preach. For his text, he chose the Book of Nehemiah, involving the rebuilding of the walls of Jericho after the Babylonian exile. The militant fourth chapter appeared especially pertinent, for the scripture described how an Israelite "had his sword strapped at his side while he built." Higginson remembered that Reverend John Martin had preached from the same text on the Sunday after the Battle of Bunker Hill, and his Lawrence sermon echoed both Nehemiah and Martin as he urged the weary pioneers to "fight for your brethren, your sons, and your daughters, your wives, and your houses." When the sermon was published in eastern newspapers, abolitionist Lydia Maria Child reflected, "[W]hat a convenient book that Old Testament [was], whenever there is any fighting to be done." Child's Garrisonian friends, nearly all of them pacifists, had been "greatly shocked by Higginson's course," but she disagreed. "If the heroes of '76 were praiseworthy, the heroes of Kansas will be more praiseworthy for maintaining their rights."[32]

Those settlers who had remained in the territory to rebuild Lawrence needed little persuasion. While still in the town, Higginson was quietly ushered into a house to interview a fugitive slave "who was being sheltered by a white man." The latter, a thin, clean-shaven individual, had been in Lawrence since September 7, when he had arrived to assist in preparing for the expected attack. Higginson promptly forgot the name the man gave him, writing later that the name "was certainly not Brown," referring to John Brown. Higginson soon discovered that the man was himself then "in hiding," and that as one of his sons had recently been shot by Missourians, he employed a variety of aliases. Several days later, Higginson was speaking to a woman when she dropped her workbasket, revealing a pistol. Just six months before, she told Higginson, she had "shut her eyes and screamed" when she first pulled the trigger. Now she kept her pistol handy and had practiced loading her husband's rifle should slave-state settlers return to Lawrence. "This easily is the transition effected," Higginson marveled, from genteel New England farmwife to antislavery soldier.[33]

Also among those Higginson encountered was James Henry Lane, a Mexican War veteran and former congressman from his native state of Indiana, who had organized a free-state militia company. A Democrat who had once voted for the Kansas-Nebraska Act, Lane had shifted political alliances with his move into the territory, and he now agreed with Higginson on the necessity of fighting. Lane, who had given himself the title of "general," handed Higginson "a crumpled piece of paper," appointing him to Lane's staff with the rank of brigadier general. The act won the approbation of both abolitionist and Republican editors, one praising Higginson for "putting on the whole armor" and laying "aside his clerical title." In a century when public men proudly wore any rank of military officer, Higginson gave it virtually no attention, never using the title and failing even to mention it in his memoirs. Still, he remembered Lane well enough six years on, when both became colonels in the first two Black Civil War regiments, Higginson at the invitation of the War Department, and Lane on his own initiative.[34]

On October 6, Higginson left Leavenworth, his last stop in Kansas, and began the journey home. His first few days of travel across Missouri were uneventful. But upon reaching Jefferson City and booking passage on the steamer *Cataract*, he and Miles Moore, a free-state activist whom proslavery settlers had threatened with lynching, found themselves amid a party of "drunken, gambling, quarrelsome boys," most from Virginia and South Carolina, who had been fighting in Kansas and wanted to spend their militia pay in St. Louis. They recognized Higginson and Moore. For each night of the four-day voyage, the two men barricaded themselves in a stateroom, "with our revolvers ready." But while the Southerners shouted the occasional threat at the locked door, they never attacked. Upon reaching St. Louis, Higginson unloaded his pistol and stored it in his trunk. After six weeks of danger, he felt as if "all of the vigor had suddenly" vanished from him, to be replaced by "a despicable effeminacy." Would he, the future colonel fretted, when danger next threatened, only "look meekly about for a policeman?" In an open letter to Greeley's *New-York Tribune*, he resolved that would not be the case: "War always educates men to itself, disciplines them, teaches them to bear its fatigue, anxiety, and danger, and actually to enjoy them."[35]

★ ★ ★

Upon returning to Massachusetts, Higginson found himself much in demand as a speaker. Both Susan B. Anthony and Lucretia Mott hoped to secure his services for the women's rights struggle, but the latter admitted to Lucy Stone that he was "full of Kansas." Invitations flooded in from Boston, Concord, Charlestown, and New Bedford, begging for him to address the "Kansas matter." Higginson accepted most of the requests, especially if they came from antislavery or Liberty Party groups, as he "*prefer[red]* not to speak at a Republican meeting." In the slave trader Corbin Thompson he had seen the enemy up close rather than through the pages of a novel. As he informed abolitionist Thaddeus Hyatt, it would be hard "not to say such things which the politicians prefer to leave unsaid."[36]

Rather to his audiences' dismay, Higginson's remarks were unrelentingly grim. In his speeches and in a series of letters published in the New-York *Tribune* on October 23, he described the "Free-State cause in Kansas" as never having "looked so gloomy." Many newspapers in the East reported a lessening of violence in the territory, but Higginson warned that Governor

Geary had imposed a ceasefire only "by disarming the Free-State people and leaving them at the mercy of their enemies." Although Geary had in fact attempted to disarm both sides and urged all settlers in the region to vote in the territorial elections, Higginson saw little point in doing so. As territorial authorities failed to enforce residency requirements—and there was no voter registration process—Higginson charged that "three-fourths of the vote given was thrown by Missourians" who simply rode across the border to cast a ballot and then returned home "the moment they had voted." In proslavery towns, poll watchers demanded "a fifty cent tax and repulsive test oaths," which Northern settlers refused to take. The only chance for a lasting peace, Higginson believed, was a complete victory for one side or the other. "The Missourians do not desire it," he observed about the chances for peace, until they achieve "the speedy introduction of Slavery," and Northern settlers refused to disarm if it meant "the daily arrest of their own men while Pro-Slavery men go free."[37]

Most of all, Higginson held out little hope in the November presidential election, where Republican candidate John C. Frémont faced Pennsylvania Democrat James Buchanan. Although Higginson admitted that the consequences of a Democratic victory would be terrible, he also told audiences of the racism he had encountered in Kansas from so many Northern pioneers. While it was clear to him that President Pierce, Governor Geary, and the Missouri "ruffians" were the villains, he had little faith in the Republican establishment. Founded in Free Soil politics, Republican candidates spoke only of the rights of free white laborers and refused to endorse Black voting rights in Northern states. When free-state settlers had created a rival government to oppose Geary's, they endorsed a series of discriminatory laws designed to dissuade free Blacks from moving into the territory. One Lawrence correspondent admitted that a member of the free-state convention scoffed that his "sister and wife" should receive voting rights if the ballot was extended to "negroes and Indians." He nonetheless assured Higginson that within twelve months a referendum on "the question of *free suffrage*" might pass. Higginson doubted that: "I predict that when the battle [is] fought, you will see this Kansas deny its own principles of liberty & equal rights, retaining its infamous black laws."[38]

Despite his pessimism, Higginson did not walk away from either the cause or the Emigrant Aid Company, in part thanks to the deluge of correspondence he received from dedicated New Englanders and desperate Midwestern settlers. Having read his dispatches in the *Tribune*, former Kentucky slaveholder turned Liberty Party presidential candidate James G. Birney wrote from his home in New Jersey, "What may be called the *skirmishes* of war have been a long time among us." Birney had freed his slaves after experiencing a religious conversion, yet if he regretted "that a civil war should rage," he doubted that "slavery [could] be exterminated without one—& I don't see how it can—I say let it come." Another abolitionist wrote from Amherst, commenting on Frémont's loss a few days before. "Buchanan's 'unconstitutional platform,'" he reasoned, "will allow us wider scope for operation in connection with Kansas." Franklin Sanborn concurred. "Submission for the next four years, or even for one year, seems to me out of the question." Three letters from besieged Lawrence echoed Birney's embrace of conflict. Samuel Tappan, a Worcester native and cousin to abolitionist financiers Arthur and Lewis Tappan, prayed they "never shall have peace in this country until the damn thing called slavery is exterminated." The second reported that Free Soil settlers were "burning with indignation and desirous of releasing their brothers from this bondage." The third reminded Higginson that the fight in Kansas had national implications. "When we strike the first blow," he promised, "that moment will be seized to give slavery its death blow in our country." Faced with so many pleas, Higginson put aside his doubts and redoubled his efforts.[39]

To raise funds for the free-staters, Higginson again took to the hustings. After he spoke in the town of Hartford, Vermont, eighteen young men stepped forward and promised to leave for Kansas. Others in the audience responded with cash, so much that it took Higginson a few days to count it all. "It is for Kansas, dear," he wrote Mary, "so you must be patient." Bostonians invited him to again speak, "having in view the collection of funds and supplies," and after hearing his lecture on Kansas, his cousin C. J. Higginson, a Boston banker, placed $30 in the collection plate. The "ladies" of Oakman, Massachusetts, "fitted out a box" of clothing and supplies for Higginson to ship to Kansas, Brattleboro contributed "*three* boxes of clothing," and the women of Concord raised $527 and set about making clothes to donate to Kansas. Any amount, no matter how small, was welcomed. A church in South Yarmouth raised $5; nearby North Bridgewater was more generous, with $399. Liberty Party perennial candidate Gerrit Smith, whose landholdings permitted him to finance a variety of reform measures, sent along funds enough to cover Higginson's traveling expenses.[40]

New England's wives and mothers sent socks and shirts, and even Mary, whatever reservations she and the church elders had about her husband's frequent absences, mailed a parcel of clothing to a widow Higginson had met while in Kansas. Their men preferred to purchase weapons. Young men in Boston formed a militia company, taking as their motto Higginson's slogan, "Peacefully if we can, forcibly if we must." John Wells of Chicopee looked into the purchase of sabers. One potential recruit wrote to Higginson asking whether he should "carry a revolver or a Gun or a Rifle" if he ventured west. Even Thayer came around and agreed to spend a large part of the contributions on weapons. Together with journalist Greeley and landscape designer Frederick Law Olmsted, minister Henry Ward Beecher, and Higginson, Thayer raised over $43,000 to buy Sharps rifles, "a mountain howitzer, fifty rounds of canister and shells with time fuses, five hand grenades, fifty rockets, and half a dozen swords." Each emigrant—as they were called—was also handed a Bible. After the cache of weapons arrived safely in Lawrence, Caleb Pratt wrote to Higginson, saying he could not "convey the feeling of our young men as they receive these evidences that their struggles are appreciated."[41]

Emboldened by the fundraising success, Higginson considered returning to Kansas for a third visit, this time as a soldier rather than an observer. The sacking of Lawrence, he told Gerrit Smith, was due to "the absence of leaders." At the very least, he intended to "start an organization of picked men" who could be ready to race to Kansas and take any opponent. Although his plan was approved, as he put it, "by all the best men" in Massachusetts, few wished to commit unless Higginson promised to lead the group. He begged the wealthy philanthropist to underwrite the venture. "I am commonly regarded as a pretty good business man, & fond of accurate accounts." While he awaited a reply, Higginson spoke again at Boston's Faneuil Hall in early 1857. By then, he had finally realized the identity of the man he met hiding in Lawrence. It was none other than "the Old Vermonter, Captain John Brown." Who would be a more worthy warrior than the man "who swallows a Missourian whole, and says grace after the meat?" Within months, Higginson, Brown, and Smith were all to meet again.[42]

If Eli Thayer reluctantly accepted Higginson's methods, he refused to embrace his goals. Perhaps naively, Thayer believed the rifles would be used only in defense, not to attack state or federal officials. In a fact-finding mission to Kansas in the weeks after Higginson had returned east, Thayer and newly elected Republican senator Henry Wilson of Massachusetts toured the territory. Again and again, free-state settlers asked the two what they should do if Buchanan captured the presidency and Geary's governorship continued.

Those who had heard Higginson or Lane speak "advocated resistance to the Government," but Wilson, who yet held out hopes for his party's victory, if perhaps not until 1860, was against this, as was Thayer. Thayer still suspected that Higginson and the "Garrisonian Abolitionists" cared little about the struggle in the Midwest and wished to "destroy, or even to impede, the work of the Emigrant Aid Company." Higginson, of course, desired no such thing and fully supported what was essentially Thayer's free-state militia. But unlike Senator Wilson, neither did he place any faith in moderate Republican politicians. For abolitionists, the eight years since the election of Zachary Taylor had been nothing less than a steady string of proslavery victories in Washington, from popular-sovereignty triumphs in the southwestern territories and Kansas to an oppressive fugitive slave law. If the Union remained in the hands of proslavery Democrats and their Northern allies, Higginson wanted no part of it.[43]

To that end, at the December 18 meeting of the Worcester antislavery society, Higginson rose to propose that a statewide "Disunion Convention" gather in their city on January 15, 1858. Buchanan's recent victory doomed the nation to four years more of a proslavery government, and believing the existing Union was "a failure," Higginson argued the time had arrived for Northern men to consider separating the free and slave states. Following a lengthy debate and vote, the society appointed a committee of correspondence to contact like-minded abolitionists across Massachusetts and begin preparations for the convention. Although women were present at the December meeting, because the question was considered political, only men, including Samuel May and Seth Rogers, signed off on the resolution. In all, sixty-five did so, but either because women were left out or because he thought disunion a step too far, the songwriter Stephen Foster, who had chaired the meeting to order, refused to sign.[44]

Garrisonians, who had long felt morally tainted by residing in the same country as slaveholders, responded with enthusiasm. Garrison and most of his pacifist disciples expected disunion to be peaceful. Upon returning to Boston, May rummaged through the membership books of the *Liberator* in search of allies to contact. "It is now sixteen years since I publicly talked & *preached* Disunion as a high moral & religious duty," he reminded Higginson. Another Bostonian wrote to endorse the movement as "the first audible step in a march to whose strong & steady tramp the land will tremble & its people awake." Hugh Forbes, a British soldier of fortune who had fought in the continental revolutions of 1848 and now edited *The European*, a German-language newspaper, assured Higginson the "voters of foreign birth in New Jersey, Pennsylvania & Illinois" supported the ideals of America more than in its current government and much opposed President-elect Buchanan. Republicans with Whiggish roots adhered to loose construction and federal power, Higginson observed to Smith, whereas abolitionists considered "the idea of Disunion" a practical solution and "not merely a technical sample about the construction of the Constitution." Both Garrison and Wendell Phillips, he added, believed "that the time [had] come for resisting the U.S. Government in Kansas, & sustaining such resistance everywhere else."[45]

Although Higginson thought it futile, some members of the Worcester group hoped they might entice a few Republicans into attending the convention. Beyond the still recovering Sumner, the man perceived to be the most radical Republican in the Senate was New York's William Henry Seward. Just before the new year, Higginson formally invited Seward to attend the January conference or to at least "communicate to us your sentiments on the topic." Higginson's blunt admission that he was "instructed by the Committee on Arrangements" to invite the senator suggested that he believed no Republican endorsed disunion, although he did add that most of the men who signed the resolution "were active supporters of Col. Frémont at the late election."[46]

Higginson was probably not surprised by Seward's rejection, but he may have been taken aback by the vehemency of his response. Already spoken of as the leading contender for his party's nomination in 1860, Seward increasingly sought to moderate both his tone and his positions. However, in a letter containing numerous partially scratched-out sentences, Seward observed that he believed "a dissolution of the American Union [to be] a calamity to be deplored." Nothing but "blind passion" led any man to "seek to destroy the present fabric of government." Understanding the gulf between Garrisonians and political Free Soilers like himself all too well, Seward expressed doubt that any recent Republican voter would support "a project to subvert the Union." He was right enough in thinking that few New England Republicans agreed with Higginson's course. However, his insistence that he had no "fears that the agitators of disunion either in free states or in slave states [might] carry out such desperate schemes" was, in Higginson's mind, the height of naiveté. Higginson simply filed the letter away and set to work on a holiday tableau. "I am deep in a Christmas Tree," he informed his mother. "In the intervals, I dissolve the Union & write letters to Kansas."[47]

Other Republicans also kept their distance, even if they did not respond with Seward's intensity. Henry Wilson and newly elected congressman Charles Francis Adams both declined to attend and pronounced the mere idea of a conference dangerous. "Impotent for good, this movement can only be productive of evil," Wilson responded. Adams, always more of a Free Soiler than an abolitionist, announced his willingness "to live indefinitely with slaveholders, even though some of them should tread a little on my rights." Higginson was a bit more surprised that Sumner, the Republican politician closest to militant abolitionists, also begged off. The two spoke in Boston, Sumner promising only to return to Washington to deliver a speech in the Senate so incendiary that it would be "as first proof brandy [is] to molasses and water." Most likely, Sumner added, it would get him shot. "Disunion is a not a desire, merely," Higginson replied, "it is the destiny of this nation."[48]

Even Louisa disagreed with her son's course. While he regretted that she differed with him, Higginson promised her he was "never more sure of being right." It was "written in the laws of nature two antagonist nations cannot remain together." Within a few short years, as Higginson later observed in his memoirs, he was fighting for the Union, while Seward and Adams were forced to accept the reality of disunion.[49]

A few local Republicans, especially those who sought only statewide office, were a bit more receptive. Francis William Bird, a former Free Soiler who had helped to organize the Republican Party in Massachusetts, promised to attend the conference and assured Higginson that he had "long been ready to meet the issue [of] Liberty or the Constitution if it must be." Higginson also paid a call on the elderly Josiah Quincy III, who had been president of Harvard when he was a student. Quincy confided that he had long thought the Union might be dissolved due to many causes, but if disunion came about because of slavery, that would be "by far the most *glorious* cause of separation." Old age, he added, "made him courageous." Most supporters, however, sprang from the abolitionist community. Phillips believed disunion "should be considered," and having gotten the word out in Boston, May labored to advertise the convention in Springfield, Lowell, and New Bedford, while Arnold Walker, a Black activist in North Brookfield, vowed that the "heart of the people [was] right on the subject." Politicians might wish to avoid the issue, Walker observed, but "the subject must be met, and will be, and the sooner the better." As if to prove Walker's point, the pro-Republican Newburyport *Daily Herald* attempted to trivialize the movement, sneering that as James Lane had bestowed the rank of general on Higginson, perhaps Kansas would make him a "Rev. General" and "president of the new republic."[50]

At 10:30 a.m. on January 15, 1857, in Worcester's City Hall, Higginson called the three-day convention to order. Freshly back from Kansas, journalist James Redpath covered the convention for the *New-York Tribune*. The assembly voted Bird the convention's president, with Garrison as one of the eight vice presidents and Higginson and Phillips chairing the business committee. Although Abby Kelley Foster and other "female notorieties," as one journalist put it, were in attendance, all of the offices again went only to men, and the conference attracted few African Americans. Before turning the podium over to Bird, Higginson introduced a series of resolutions he urged the conference to debate over the coming days. The "cardinal American principle is now, as always, Liberty," the first began, "while the prominent fact is now, as always, Slavery." The conflict between principle and fact "has been the whole history of the nation for fifty years." For a resolution, Higginson insisted, Northerners could not expect help from President-elect Buchanan nor from Roger Taney's Supreme Court—a prescient statement, coming as it did two months before the *Dred Scott* decision—nor even from those Republican leaders who looked ahead to 1860 while granting "the Slave Power" four more years to guide the nation's destiny. The difference between abolitionists and Republicans, Higginson argued, was that the latter had faith that the Union could be saved from within if only they could win more elections and capture the White House. Abolitionists, by comparison, believed that national unity "may be a blessing or a curse, and must be judged accordingly."[51]

In a lengthy speech on the second day, Higginson took issue both with Republicans who regarded the convention as nearly traitorous and with such fellow abolitionists as Frederick Douglass, who thought disunion would salve New England consciences while dooming four million enslaved Americans to unending bondage. As to the first, Higginson insisted that so long as the nation was governed by "this slave power, which calls itself a government," resistance to an unjust regime was the duty of all patriots. "Talk of treason!" Higginson shouted. "Why, I have been trying for ten years to get the opportunity to commit treason and have not found it yet." Sympathetic Republicans, he added, admitted that while the time might come when disunion is called for with each new Southern victory in Washington, they declined to say how many more "possible horrors and evils" would have "first to be endured." As to the latter, if the nation divided and the United States ceased to enforce the Fugitive Slave Law, slavery would collapse in the North, as thousands of bondspersons fled Maryland, northern Virginia, Delaware, and Kentucky for liberty in a truly free country.[52]

It was a testimony to Higginson's nearly unique place within the antislavery movement—a Garrisonian who both voted and accepted as necessary the use of violence, and an activist who refused to prioritize antislavery over women's rights, regarding the two as connected—that the convention was condemned by editors who disagreed with one another as to why the meeting was unwise. One Republican newspaper thought it unfortunate that Northern voices advocated a position previously "limited to the secession fire-eaters" of the South, while Douglass saw no logic in Higginson's theory that disunion would endanger slavery in the Upper South. "Will dissolution give the North any better right to interfere with slavery in the slave States," Douglass editorialized in his Rochester newspaper, "than they now have under the Union?" More aware of the depth of Northern racism than was Higginson, Douglass judged it likely that after disunion, Northern activists would turn their energies elsewhere. "Would the people of the free States feel any more kindly, or act any more justly, toward the colored people than before?" Confirmation of Douglass's fears came from a Boston Democratic editor. Fearing that Higginson's supposition was correct, should Maryland runaways reach the United States, he asked, "where are the self-emancipated negroes going to go?" If they crowded into Massachusetts, the state "should be obliged to re-enslave them to protect ourselves." Few readers surely thought that plausible, but most Democrats felt as did a Pittsfield, Massachusetts, editor, who described the conference as "a gathering of fanatics" unworthy of serious attention.[53]

An unrepentant Higginson regarded the Worcester convention as merely the start of a new movement, not as a lonely protest. He contacted James Shepherd Pike, the Washington correspondent for the *Tribune*, urging him to distribute their tracts in the capital. "All the laws of nature work for disunion," Higginson explained to Pike. As a final act, the conference urged abolitionists across the North to stage more regional conferences in preparation for a national conference to be held in Cleveland in October. One Ohio correspondent assured Higginson that in his state "large numbers" were in favor of dissolution. Samuel Joseph May of Syracuse warned Higginson that while he agreed that the "egregious wickedness" of slaveholders simply to keep the Union intact should be "fully exposed," most abolitionists in the region adhered to Smith's "interpretation" that the Constitution was in fact an antislavery document. Even in Boston, the Massachusetts Anti-Slavery Society had so little confidence in the movement's prospects that they declined to publish the convention's proceedings in pamphlet form, leaving it to Garrison to print the speeches in his *Liberator*. From Michigan, another supporter reported that local Republicans had given their constituents "a very imperfect idea of the Worcester convention."[54]

Before the fall arrived, Higginson had several opportunities to mend fences within the antislavery community. On March 6, Taney's Supreme Court handed down a 7–2 decision in *Dred Scott v. Sanford*. Abolitionists were furious with Taney's conclusion that Black Americans, even if born free, could not be citizens in the land of their birth, while Republicans were equally incensed that the Court ruled the 1820 prohibition on slavery in the upper Midwest to be unconstitutional. Although the Missouri Compromise had already been overturned by the Kansas-Nebraska Act, Republicans had vowed to restore the ban, and Taney had essentially ruled their core platform to be unconstitutional. Sharing a Manhattan stage in May with Garrison and Phillips, but also with Black activists Douglass, Robert Purvis, Charles Lenox Remond, and William Wells Brown, Higginson refused to moderate his disunionist stance. "We are not a nation," he insisted, "we are two nations, whom this frail paper bond has vainly tried to weld together into one." His habitual optimism and hope for the future was at its lowest point since visiting St. Louis. Yet, unlike some of the other speakers, who mocked Senator Wilson for his moderation, Higginson said that he had always cooperated with political abolitionists and told of recently talking with younger Republicans who had "begun to open their eyes to the grasp that slavery has taken upon the nation." In the wake of *Dred Scott*, no Northern voter could doubt the growing influence of slave power. Free Soil Republicans grew more radical by the day, he observed, and soon "the Henry Wilsons will cease to talk about hanging Disunionists, and will come back to their old opinion of the patriotism of the Garrisons."[55]

As Republican moderates grew more disaffected with Southern domination in Washington, Higginson became even more confident about the creation of a broad antislavery alliance. In June, Republicans held their state convention in Worcester, and Higginson and Garrison not only attended but, at the invitation of Congressman Joshua Giddings, an Ohio Free Soiler turned Republican, were invited to speak. The keynote was delivered by

Congressman Adams, a vocal critic of the disunion meeting. Like Higginson, Adams declined to alter his stance, remarking that although an antislavery politician, he did not regard slaveholders as "irredeemably wicked, any more than [he] did bankers, or hotel keepers, or liquor-sellers." Although a temperance man, Higginson believed Southern whites who owned Black Americans to be far more sinful than tavern owners. But the meeting lacked the usual rancor that the two sides had displayed at previous conferences, and whatever misgivings Garrison had about Republicans, he dutifully included Adams's speech in the convention's published proceedings, which his office sold in pamphlet form. Uncompromising as always, Higginson spoke in Boston two weeks later at a regional disunion convention. Once again, though, he spoke only words of conciliation to the handful of Republicans in the audience.[56]

Due both to this ceasefire between New England's Republicans and abolitionists and to President Buchanan's endorsement of the *Dred Scott* decision, the momentum for the October conference in Cleveland continued apace. Higginson, Bird, Garrison, and Phillips drafted a petition for general circulation, and by summer's end Garrison reported that it carried several thousand signatures. "It is evident that the mass of Republican voters are becoming more radically anti-slavery," the circular observed. "And nothing will do so much to promote that desirable change, as the fearless discussion we propose." That so many younger Republicans were at least willing to prepare for disunion, Higginson noted, alarmed moderate Republicans and Northern Democrats alike. Garrison published a lengthy editorial condemning the editor of Boston's pro-Republican *Evening Telegraph* for suggesting that the petition was actually a "trick" by Buchanan supporters "to create a reaction in their favor." In California, an editor similarly depicted the proposed Cleveland gathering—"a convention of slaves"—as a plot by "General Wentworth Higginson." This "arming of nigger worshippers" was aimed less at national disunion, the newspaper charged, than at the nullification of the Fugitive Slave Law. An Iowa editor, noting the attempt at creating a national movement by meeting outside of New England, thought Cleveland not far enough west. "We would suggest the locality be one hundred miles west of the Pacific coast, [and] one hundred feet below the surface."[57]

In early September, antislavery newspapers published details of the conference's final arrangements. Any interested American was invited to attend the October 28 and 29 gathering. The statement was signed by sixty men, representing six Northern states, not counting Higginson, Bird, Phillips, and

Garrison, and the notice mentioned that 4,200 voters and 1,833 "others," presumably women, hailed from seventeen Northern states. But the Cleveland conference was not to be. The sinking of a supply ship, the SS *Central America*, carrying gold (three tons of it) to Manhattan banks set off spirals of financial uncertainty (450 lives were also lost). The Ohio Life Insurance and Trust Company, one of the largest in the country, folded, prompting a sharp drop in the stock market. "In view of the earthquake shock" inflicted on even the wealthiest donors, the arrangements committee, Garrison explained to Samuel Joseph May, agreed to postpone their Northern convention "until a more auspicious time." Garrison understood that abolitionists in Ohio and Michigan would be hugely disappointed, and local groups continued to plan for regional disunion meetings. The most that Higginson and Garrison could promise was to send missives to those small conferences, with their thoughts on the Disunion question. Despite the setback, Higginson remained wedded to the dream, particularly now that the Supreme Court had denied "the right of Congress to establish freedom even in the territories." With only so many hours to spare and the necessity of spreading the gospel of secession, Higginson notified the Free Church's disappointed elders that after Sunday, October 3, he would preach only every other Sunday and never again speak at any two Sundays "in the same place."[58]

Smashing a battering ram through the Boston courthouse door had segued into packing a pistol in Kansas. Now his two missions into the Midwest launched Higginson's next crusade. "Nothing I saw in Kansas impressed me so deeply as this one thing," he told his parishioners, and that was the "absolute, total alienation between every man in Kansas who came from a free State, and every man who came from a slave state." But it was not merely that his travels convinced him of the correctness of disunion. Never completely won over by Garrisonian moral suasion, Higginson now had serious doubts that nonresistance could ever eradicate slavery. Even a Republican victory in 1860 might not liberate four million slaves. Republicans and abolitionists devoted far too much time to theoretical debates "upon the points of Constitutional interpretation," he said in a sermon, and when it came to "the practical solution of the slavery question," none of those discussions amounted to "a millionth part so much as the poorest shot that ever a fugitive slave fired at this master." His pistol and Sharps rifle, he concluded, would not stay packed away for long.[59]

"Some prophetic character must emerge as the new crisis culminates," Higginson suggested to Phillips after his second journey to Kansas. "Your life has been merely preliminary to the work that is coming for you." Although he could not then know it, Higginson might well have been confiding those thoughts to his own journal. In February 1857, abolitionist Franklin Sanborn wrote about "a *pretty good*" meeting he had organized the day before at the Boston statehouse. Among the speakers was the mysterious New Englander whom Higginson had met in Lawrence. "Can anything be done for the good old man in Worcester (or among your friends)," Sanborn wondered? Seven months later, in September, just as Higginson's plans for the Cleveland convention were collapsing, Sanborn wrote again. John Brown was back in Kansas and "as ready for a revolution as any other man," but he required money "and *active* support." Higginson, weary of debates over whether the Constitution was a pro- or antislavery document, welcomed Sanborn's suggestion that the militant Brown was "the best disunion champion you can find." With just his hundred men, Sanborn added, Brown could "do more to split the Union than a list of 50,000 names for your convention." Wholeheartedly, Higginson agreed.[60]

Later years brought further reflection. Like Douglass, Higginson never lost his admiration for Brown's courage and vision. However, also like Douglass, Higginson blamed himself for not grasping the fact that the passionate old warrior lacked the ability, and perhaps even the desire, to engage in carefully thought-out, "shrewd, pragmatic planning," and he blamed himself for what happened next.[61]

5

"Always ready to invest in treason"

1857–1859

"'Old Brown' of Kansas is now in Boston with one of his sons, looking for an object in which you heartily sympathize," Franklin Sanborn wrote Higginson on January 5, 1857, "raising and arming a company of men for the future protection of Kansas." Recently named secretary of the Massachusetts State Kansas Committee, Sanborn informed Higginson that the militant abolitionist hoped to raise $30,000 to form and arm a company. The plan sounded much like the one that Higginson had suggested to Gerrit Smith the previous fall, and he was intrigued. Sanborn admitted that he, too, was much impressed with John Brown, "and his deeds ought to bear witness for him." He urged Higginson to take the train to Boston as soon as possible, or to invite Brown to Worcester.[1]

Although committed to a disunionist conference in the coming weeks, Higginson reorganized his schedule and arrived at Sanborn's School Street office the next morning. He expected only to assist in raising funds for Kansas free-staters. Instead, he became embroiled in a far greater project to liberate Southern bondsmen, and perhaps even to incite a series of slave revolts that would render the *Dred Scott* decision null and void. Higginson's activities over the next few years increased his fame within the abolitionist community as well as his notoriety among white Southerners and Northern conservatives. His association with Brown, however, also helped to restore his habitual optimism and hope, both of which had taken a beating from what he had witnessed in Kansas. When, two years later, he emerged from the Harpers Ferry tragedy as Brown's most resolute defender, Higginson unintentionally positioned himself as the abolitionist most fit to carry out Brown's vision—along the Carolina coast rather than in western Virginia.

* * *

When Higginson and Brown met in that winter of 1857, they promptly recognized the other from their first encounter in Kansas. Despite their differences in education and temperament, Higginson immediately took to Brown, and Brown to Higginson. For the meeting, Brown had forsaken his frontier garb for urban dress, donning a brown broadcloth suit with a high leather collar. Sanborn described Brown as "tall, slender," possessing a "commanding figure," a determined soul whose "military bearing" combined "the soldier and the deacon." Sanborn's description might just as well have been of Higginson. For his part, Brown judged Higginson to be "both a true man and a true Abolitionist," as well as a man whose storied surname meant something in New England, especially when it came to raising funds.[2]

As enthralled as he was with Brown's dedication to the cause, Higginson wished to know more about his plans before turning over any of the $3,000 held by the Worcester County Kansas Committee. Rumors around Boston held that Brown was careless with money and negligent in maintaining precise financial records. Even Sanborn was hazy on Brown's plans, telling Higginson only that Brown intended some sort of operation along the Missouri-Iowa border, which might draw Free Soil settlers from those states into the Kansas fight. Brown mentioned nothing about liberating slaves in the South, repeating only that a return west required "200 Sharps rifles and $30,000," a grandiose request that concerned Higginson, who never forgot his own father's financial woes.[3]

It soon became apparent to Brown that militants such as Higginson were his only hope. Sanborn introduced Brown to a number of Boston abolitionists, but a meeting with Garrison proved disastrous. The two fell into a heated debate over whether Christianity permitted the use of violence, and shortly thereafter the editor continued the dispute in the pages of the *Liberator*. Would a free soil victory in Kansas be worth the effort, Garrison wondered, if antislavery settlers responded to proslavery brutality with cruelty? Unitarian minister and abolitionist Theodore Parker proved more receptive, as did Dr. Samuel Gridley Howe, who as a young man had traveled to Greece to serve as a surgeon in their revolution against the Ottomans. But for the time being, Brown focused on Higginson, peppering him with letters filled with a mixture of flattery and stridency, underscoring numerous phrases for emphasis. "My anxiety to secure *a mere outfit*; & to go off at once, is becoming extremely oppressive; & my heart grows sad in the fear of failure in the enterprise," he wrote in one. Higginson was hardly unreceptive, though he replied that his city had recently raised funds for New England settlers already in Kansas, and while he thought it necessary to provide arms to Free Soil pioneers, that was not the same as financing militiamen. The majority of Higginson's less militant benefactors, he confessed, did not support the latter.[4]

Despite his concerns about Brown's casual bookkeeping and ever-evolving schemes, Higginson continued their correspondence. Although the two were hardly conventional Transcendentalists, Brown was an evangelical who shared Higginson's disdain for mainstream politics and the legitimacy of any law that reformers thought unjust. All physical-force abolitionists countenanced the use of violence against those who would enslave others. However, not all shared Higginson's muscular activism; Brown did. He may not have heard of Higginson's involvement in the Burns affair prior to his arrival in Boston, but he clearly did shortly thereafter, and he rightly believed that it was but a short step from assisting fugitives and serving on vigilance committees to sponsoring slave rebellions. Many Republicans refused to condemn Southern planters as vicious men, preferring to couch their criticism in moderate tones of political economy. Not Brown or Higginson. As a radical abolitionist, Higginson remarked, Brown's "theology was Puritan, like his practice." Brown had come to devote his entire life to the cause. "The whole power of his mind had been given to the subject," Higginson marveled.[5]

Higginson was not alone among his associates in approving of Brown's motives and plans. Abolitionist and editor James Redpath, who had relocated to Boston after his time in Kansas, was one. Redpath had interviewed Brown in 1856 while in the territory, just days after Brown and his band murdered five proslavery settlers at Pottawatomie Creek. Although hardly a man of action, Ralph Waldo Emerson also publicly praised those who had attempted to liberate Anthony Burns, and he introduced Sanborn to the affluent abolitionist and Massachusetts industrialist George Luther Stearns. Higginson always assumed that New York philanthropist Gerrit Smith would be a reliable backer. Parker and Samuel Gridley Howe both lost their original reluctance to endorse—and help fund—any scheme Brown was concocting. Like Higginson, Parker regarded Brown's theology as hopelessly orthodox, and the relatively impoverished Brown resented begging from those who possessed the "wealth, luxury, and extravagance of this '*Heaven exalted*' people." They nonetheless shared a contempt for antislavery pacifism. Putting aside his earlier misgivings, Higginson assured Brown that he longed "to see you with adequate funds in your hands, set free from timid advisers, & able to act in your own way."[6]

The group was soon nicknamed "the secret six," though their identities and involvement with Brown hardly remained clandestine for long. As early as February 2, 1857, Ebenezer Cutler, the conservative pastor at Worcester's Union Church, published a denunciation of Higginson's association with Brown in the *Worcester Spy*. Higginson promised Redpath he would not be drawn into "newspaper conflicts." He also remained committed to acquiring equipment for young settlers who wished to relocate to Kansas, not yet seeing that as a separate project from Brown's. And so when the question of funding for prospective Kansas settlers came before the state legislature, Higginson turned to the normally friendly *Spy*, and at Stearns's urging drafted a letter encouraging a subsidy. Because of both his advocacy and his well-publicized early trips to the territory, Higginson was peppered with queries from potential free-staters. Some requests were easier to fill than others. One Reuben Randall, from Bolton, Massachusetts, wrote asking about weapons, and Higginson assured him "that a revolver was ready" as soon as he left for Kansas. Higginson also personally arranged passage for emigrés with the New England Aid Company, purchasing tickets for $20 each to carry them from Albany to St. Louis. Some, such as Daniel Foster, promised to join "Capt. John Brown's company in the next Kansas war" and perform "a baptism of blood" in the territory—but only if Higginson could send him "$300 to care for my wife and two little boys in comfortable circumstances" while he was absent. Smith quickly emerged as the group's principal funding source, but militant abolitionists recognized Higginson as the scheme's point man and organizer.[7]

Some requests tested Higginson's patience or placed him in an untenable position. From Iowa, an Elvira Pratt mailed three letters complaining that a Free Soil settler named "Wilson" had stolen her buggy, and she wished him "brought to justice." Pratt insisted that she too favored a free Kansas, acknowledging that "time is precious to one in your station," but she believed that heaven would reward him "in the knowledge that *wrong* is *righted*." Higginson ignored that request, but harder to disregard was Sanborn's message of late August informing him that Brown had returned to the Kansas border "with a quantity of supplies," though nothing like what he had hoped to acquire in "New England and New York." Sanborn remembered that Higginson had control of the $3,000 donated to his county's emigration committee and thought that there was "no reason why so much should be left on hand idle." Small donors had provided funds to support the emigration of Massachusetts farm boys, not to arm Brown's band of warriors. But when Sanborn reduced his request to "$1,000 or even $500" as being of "great service to the Captain," Higginson approved the transfer.[8]

Months passed with no word from Brown, and when Higginson finally learned his whereabouts in January 1858, Brown's plans had changed considerably. Kansas voters had rejected the proslavery Lecompton—the slave soil capital—constitution the previous month, President Buchanan and influential Southern Democrats in Congress endorsed it. Facing likely defeat in the Midwest, Brown began to consider the possibility of leading a series of raids into Virginia. He might assist slaves in reaching the North before returning south or set them up in fortified strongholds in the Alleghany Mountains, where they could join him in liberating others or serve as enticements for potential runaways.

The notion was not completely new within abolitionist circles, and Black activists in particular were well versed in the history of runaways and rebellions around the Atlantic world. Higginson, who would later write pioneering accounts of earlier conspiracies or rebellions led by Gabriel, Denmark Vesey, Nat Turner, and Caribbean maroons—colonies of runaways, derived from the Spanish *cimarrón*, or "wild"—was far from alone in believing such colonies of runaways could serve as staging grounds for later rebellions. As had "the maroons of Jamaica and Surinam," Higginson reasoned, these runaways could both provide refuge for fugitives and train them for the coming war over slavery. A few abolitionists, such as natural rights legal theorist Lysander Spooner, believed that such schemes required elaborate planning. Higginson thought otherwise. "In Revolutions the practical end always comes first and the theory afterwards," he mused.[9]

From the moment of their first encounter in Kansas, when Brown had been accompanied by a fugitive slave, Higginson had guessed that he was as dedicated to liberating slaves as he was to fighting for free soil. The news that the former objective had now wholly replaced the latter arrived in a letter from Worcester native Samuel Tappan, who was then in Lawrence. "I am happy to inform you that a certain Rail Road has been and is in full blast," he reported on January 24, 1858. "Several persons have taken advantage of it to visit their friends." Tappan's coded message alerted Higginson that Brown had been assisting runaways from Missouri and the Kansas Territory. The "project" was both dangerous and expensive, Tappan observed, and if Higginson knew of anybody "desirous of helping the cause," he should communicate with himself or "James Blood," Brown's latest pseudonym, in Lawrence. Blood, Tappan added, was soon to return east.[10]

Just days later, Brown stepped off the train in Rochester and appeared at the door of Frederick Douglass. Believing it unsafe to return home to

North Elba or even contact his family, Brown remained with the Douglass family for three weeks, paying $3 a week for food and lodging. While there, he began to put his Virginia plan into motion, mostly by writing to the "secret six" as well as to supporters in such places as Syracuse and Manhattan. Brown adopted yet another pseudonym and instructed his correspondents to write to him as "Nelson Hawkins," care of Douglass. He was "*perfecting by far* the most *important* undertaking of [his] whole life," Brown promised Higginson, and he required $500 to $800 "within the next sixty days." Brown hoped that Higginson might use his connections in Worcester and elsewhere to raise part of the amount. Higginson responded within the week, insisting that while he was "always ready to invest in treason," at present he had no money to give. Due to the lingering national recession, many of his allies were hurting financially, and what few funds he possessed had been donated specifically "for the Underground Railroad in Kansas." A distraught Brown immediately replied, "Rail Road business on a *somewhat extended scale* is the *identical* object for which I am trying to get means."[11]

Disheartened but not dissuaded, Brown next tried to convince his chief supporters to meet with him "for consultation" at Gerrit Smith's isolated Peterboro mansion. Details of Brown's participation in the Kansas murders were as yet vague in the East, though Brown himself feared arrest at the hands of federal marshals. "It would be almost impossible for me to pass through Albany, Springfield, or any of those parts, on my way to Boston," he told Sanborn, adding that when he left Kansas, he kept his departure secret even from his friends as he thought it safer to allow his enemies to believe he was "hiding somewhere in the Territory." Brown was "very anxious" to have Higginson attend the meeting, "*certain as I feel* that you will never regret having been one of the council." Sanborn agreed to attend and encouraged Higginson to rendezvous with Brown when his train passed through Worcester. He, too, however, wondered about Brown's evolving schemes. "I should not wonder if his plan contemplated an uprising of slaves," he wrote Higginson, "though he has not said as much to me." Sanborn was a bit concerned, he admitted, that his contacts in Kansas complained that Brown had "disappeared and has been of little service to them." A few warned Sanborn that Brown was "insane," but he dismissed those allegations. "Treason will not be treason that much longer, but patriotism," he wrote Higginson.[12]

Higginson was then busy with affairs in Worcester and unable to attend the meeting with Brown. Since the previous October, he had led services at the Free Church only every other week, and in late February he informed the disappointed elders that as of April 1, he was resigning his pastorate and devoting "his time to literary pursuits, and to miscellaneous lecturing and preaching," which he hoped would fund his modest life. Unstated was his desire to also devote himself to revolution.[13]

Still hoping to secure Higginson's aid, Brown traveled first to Brooklyn and then north to Boston's Hanover Street, taking a room at the grand American House on March 4. He promptly wrote to Higginson, imploring him to meet with him and Sanborn the next day. "Please enquire for Mr. Brown (*not Capt. Brown*) of New York," he instructed. Higginson arrived on Friday afternoon and was again impressed by Brown's demeanor. "His talk was calm, persuasive, and coherent," Higginson remembered, although he feared he saw in Brown's "thin, worn, resolute face signs of a fire which might wear him out." Parker attended the conclave as well.[14]

For the first time Brown offered details about his plans to liberate and arm Virginia bondsmen. Brown showed Sanborn a drawing with "rude outlines of his Virginia forts," the "maroon villages" he hoped to establish. The meeting ended to the satisfaction of all. Parker promised not to breathe a word of the proposal to Garrison or any of his pacificist supporters, and Sanborn enthusiastically assured Higginson that Brown finally had "a plan—the result of many years' careful study." For his part, Brown wrote to his son John—he had still not visited his family since returning to New York State—that his "call here has met with a most hearty response," so much so that he felt "assured of at least tolerable success."[15]

Stearns became the "Treasurer of the enterprise for N.E.," though the others were responsible for raising funds in their home regions. Only Smith, however, possessed ample resources of his own, and the effort revealed the difficulty of properly outfitting an abolitionist army by appealing to the purses of the antislavery community. Sanborn complained to Higginson that while Stearns promised a considerable sum, he also intended to "hold it back for a future emergency." Sanborn himself contributed only $25 of his own money, and while he begged his associates to participate, he had as yet been able to get "nothing else." On March 8, Brown left for Philadelphia in hopes of recruiting men there, telling Sanborn he hoped to pocket $1,000 upon his return. If the four poorest of the "secret six" could each raise $100, Sanborn calculated, Smith and Stearns might cover the rest. "Perhaps you cannot come up to that," Sanborn wrote Higginson, adding, "nor I possibly."[16]

In late April, the six again heard from "Mr. Hawkins," who was then in Chatham, Canada, a town east of Detroit that was home to a large number of runaways who had fled across the border after 1850. Once more writing in code, Sanborn—who took to signing his name only with initials—reported that Brown had recruited "a company of 12 to 20 shepherds," that is, soldiers, and was in need of supplies. Stearns had sent him $410. However, if Brown's plan was to go into operation by mid-May, he "wants more, and we must" provide it. Sanborn begged Higginson to raise $500 and then travel to Chatham himself to place it in Brown's hands. "Can you make it convenient to see him there?" Sanborn wondered. "It would be 'an interesting time,' he says."[17]

Adequate funding was far from the only concern. Although not one of the "secret six," British expatriate Hugh Forbes began to raise doubts about Brown's abilities. One year before, Brown had hired the former soldier, who had served with Italian revolutionary Giuseppe Garibaldi in 1848, to drill his recruits and train them in the use of arms. Brown had paid Forbes handsomely, but Forbes arrived in Kansas only months after the agreed-upon date. Despite this, Brown and Smith still had faith in his talents. Nonetheless, when Brown revealed his plan to Forbes in the spring of 1858, Forbes thought the notion of maroon fortresses ludicrous. Although a self-professed revolutionary, he lacked Brown's confidence in arming runaways, believing instead that well-trained white forces should invade plantations and then immediately usher the liberated Blacks northward. In early May, at which point Brown was in Chicago, Forbes wrote to Stearns, demanding that he be allowed to replace Brown as the unit's leader, threatening otherwise to expose the plot to the public. "It looks as if the project must, for the present, be deferred," Sanborn advised Higginson. Stearns and Parker agreed with him, he wrote, and as Forbes was then in Washington, he was in a position to "do great harm." Brown had hoped to begin operations soon, but Sanborn believed the plan should be postponed for at least a year. The only way for Brown and his men to succeed was by striking in a series of lightning raids. Forbes was in a position "to remove the terror of the thing by a complete exposure." Although Forbes was a professional soldier and the author of a much-praised pamphlet called *Duties of a Soldier*, Higginson was nearly as well read in the history of maroons and slave rebellions. He shared Brown's belief in the abilities of young runaways to master the basic art of war. Sanborn, for his part, thought Forbes either "a madman or a villain." He believed that "the matter must stop for the present."[18]

The majority of Brown's Eastern backers thought the wisest course was for Brown to retreat quietly to Kansas and renew the battle there. Higginson and Howe were the two resolute exceptions. In separate letters to Brown and Parker, Higginson argued against any delay. "*If the thing is postponed, it is postponed forever*," he warned Parker, adopting Brown's tendency to underline key points. If Forbes truly intended to reveal the plan unless handed Brown's generalship, he could "do as much harm next year as this." Once the plan was put into action, Higginson added, "who cares what he says?" Writing from Canada, Brown appeared inclined to accept Higginson's counsel, but with a caveat. He encouraged Higginson to warn his abolitionist allies "to keep clear of F[orbes] personally," but he also judged it a mistake to then "*decide* the course to be taken, while under an excitement." Brown's vacillation worried Higginson, who said that he and Howe "have seen no reason to be discouraged." He and his friends in Manhattan regarded Forbes as "more fool than knave." If Brown proceeded soon, Higginson promised he would redouble his efforts to raise more money, knowing such promises always appealed to Brown. In the meantime, Higginson wrote "to the others, strongly urging them not to give up the ship."[19]

Sanborn was equally confident that his view—holding off—was the correct one. Forbes had revealed the Virginia maroon plan to Republican senator Henry Wilson, Sanborn feared, and perhaps New York's William Seward, "and God knows how many more have heard about the plot." "To go on in the face of this is mere madness." On May 18, the same day that Sanborn wrote to Higginson, Higginson tried again to persuade Parker, who was skeptical. Forbes could "do no harm if we can steal a march on him," he argued, and in any case, "any betrayal *afterwards* will only *increase the panic*" among Virginia slaveholders, which was all to the good. Higginson had consulted with the journalist Charles Dana, who assured him that Forbes was "a blundering blockhead." It would be "disgraceful for us to be outmaneuvered by such a fellow," Higginson fumed. Parker responded politely, saying only, "I think I'm right in the matter."[20]

To settle the issue, Sanborn and Stearns urged Brown to return to Boston, hoping he and the four might convince Higginson that "holding off was for the best." Sanborn delayed informing Higginson that Brown had arrived in the city on May 20. Those urging delay met with Brown first, and not until May 31 did Sanborn write: "Hawkins is here at the American House, Room 86, can you not come down and see him." On June 1, Higginson met privately with Brown, who reported that Sanborn had promised to secure him his desired $3,000 provided he postponed his operation "till next winter or spring." According to detailed notes Higginson kept of the meeting, Brown admitted that he and his thirteen recruits in Canada "considered delay very discouraging." Higginson wondered aloud why the others did not agree, and "the old veteran"—as Higginson called him—bluntly replied that "they were not men of action." Brown thought Smith "a timid man," while Stearns and Parker did not "abound in courage." But as "they held the purse," Brown thought it imperative that "they not think him reckless." Six days later, Higginson called on Howe and discovered that the others had given Brown $500 in gold and a supply of arms, but only on the condition that he return to Kansas. Brown left Boston "in good spirits," Howe added, leaving Higginson to wonder if Brown intended to keep his promise.[21]

Rather to Higginson's surprise and disappointment, Brown kept his word to Sanborn and after a brief stop in North Elba, north of Albany, to visit his family, returned to Lawrence in mid-June. Having alienated Forbes, his most experienced soldier, Brown now exasperated perhaps his most valued supporter. Two of Brown's sons traveled with him, Sanborn informed an annoyed Higginson, with the intention of lying low for the fall and winter and then finally putting the Virginia plan into "action next spring." In the meantime, Brown was "desirous of getting someone to go to Canada and collect recruits for him among the fugitives." Hoping that Higginson was willing to ignore the fact that he did not approve of delay, Sanborn urged him to undertake the task, and perhaps bring Harriet Tubman with him. Higginson had met the Maryland runaway-turned-activist some years before and regarded her as "the greatest heroine of the age," and Sanborn hoped the idea would appeal to Higginson. "Now is the time to help in the movement, if ever," Sanborn added to an unsympathetic Higginson, who feared that the time to act had now passed.[22]

Apart from Higginson, the only person unhappy with the turn of events was Forbes, who contacted Higginson about his own funds. "I have been grossly defrauded in the name of Humanity & *Antislavery*," he fumed. Although Brown had compensated him for training recruits in Kansas, Forbes charged, "certain Committees" had promised him an additional monthly stipend for the support of his family in the East. "The New England promisers broke their engagements toward my family," he concluded. Weary of the entire affair and once again pessimistic about their cause, Higginson neither ventured to Canada nor responded to either man.[23]

***

Disillusioned with Brown and Sanford, Higginson turned his attention to other crusades. Personal matters also demanded their share of his time and attention. His youthful, intense friendship with William Henry Hurlbert had cooled over the years, although in 1848 Higginson took heart in the news that Hurlbert had visited Rome and been blessed by the pope. As late as 1853 Higginson had recommended his Harvard classmate to publisher Francis Underwood as "a young man of the most versatile talent" and a "universal scholar." Because of their long friendship and the affection he once held for a gifted young man he had regarded as a brother, Higginson was even willing to overlook the Southern-born journalist's support for the Democratic Party and Kansas-Nebraska author Stephen Douglas. But as the decade wore on, Hurlbert rarely answered Higginson's monthly letters, and the man who had once composed a hymn for Higginson's first installation failed to send congratulations about his appointment to the Free Church. Higginson chided his old friend—still "Willie Hurlbut" in his correspondence—for not having "written me one word about my Installation sermon when so many persons for whom I care nothing have written." But he promised that "out of the depths of my charity I still believe in you" and liked to imagine "that you are glad to know that I am well & useful here." To his diary, however, Higginson admitted that he gave "too much love to the dearest and fairest and oh! what sad dissatisfactions."[24]

Higginson was hardly alone in finding Hurlbert appealing. Kate Field, an established journalist roughly a decade younger than Hurlbert, characterized him as "a very handsome, fascinating, gifted, accomplished naughty fellow." For one moment in the summer of 1856, Higginson thought it likely that his friend was finally preparing to settle down and marry, but at the last moment Hurlbert broke off the engagement, which Higginson judged "a *real* tragedy." The misfortune deepened one year later, when Charles Strong, a Manhattan attorney, discovered a letter that Hurlbert had sent to his wife. It was "such a letter as a foolish man would write to his mistress in the first week of concubinage," Strong charged. The aggrieved husband demanded a separation and let it be known around town that Hurlbert was "an unprincipled adventurer." The scandal tarnished Hurtbert's "vast social reputation," as one former admirer put it. Even Hurlbert's employer, the *New York Times*, began to suspect that his troubles outweighed his talents. In hopes of escaping the "petty gossip" that engulfed him, Hurlbert sailed for London in the spring of 1858. Higginson considered their long relationship to at last be over.[25]

Other concerns were less worldly. Although attempts to contact deceased loved ones or to achieve a more perfect level of religious understanding had been common in parts of the North—particularly in New England and upstate New York—"spiritualism," as the movement was called, took on a new importance to reforms in the mid-1850s. In the spring of 1857, just as he was beginning to withdraw from his weekly duties at the Free Church, Higginson's curiosity prompted him to attend a "spiritual sitting" hosted by "medium" Nathaniel Willis, the son of a wealthy publisher, who recently had been expelled from Harvard Divinity School.[26]

As the meeting began, Higginson heard what sounded like a guitar playing under the table. Glancing beneath the tablecloth, he saw "with perfect distinctness the instrument, lying on its back untouched by anyone." A "faint flickering light" glowed above the strings, but Willis "was entirely out of its reach." As the stunned Higginson watched, the guitar "moved slowly along, by some force," until it was at his feet. A few of those in attendance suggested that Higginson sing to the tune, and as a sort of test he did. "Every song I sang was accompanied accurately and gracefully on the guitar," he reported. Afterward he rested his hands upon the table and experienced "a very peculiar electrical sensation," as did others at the sitting. Higginson never thought to question whether actual current explained the guitar music or the flickering light, but when asked to judge the "fraud or genuineness of these phenomena," he fell back on the maxim of scientist François Arago: "He is a rash man, who, outside of mathematics, pronounces the word 'impossible.'"[27]

If Higginson was naive in accepting what he had experienced, he was hardly alone. Fellow abolitionists Garrison, Parker Pillsbury, Amy Kirby Post, Joshua Giddings, and Harriet Beecher Stowe all embraced spiritualism, and, although few Black activists did, among those who were fascinated was William Nell. Unitarians were particularly drawn to the movement, as the adherents of both that faith and spiritualism rejected formalistic rigidity and sectarian disagreements in the name of discovering a more complete spiritual unity and harmony. While some evangelicals believed that a sudden conversion experience was necessary for salvation, spiritualists instead favored gradual growth toward perfection through the nurture of spiritual influence. For Higginson, whose sermons read like biblically influenced debaters' notes, revivalist ministers such as Charles Grandison Finney were too fiery and overzealous for his tastes. Most of all, spiritualists believed that otherworldly communion might be a vehicle for progress, and few who accepted spiritualism were not already devout believers in the next life or did not burn to reform the present world. The fact that many spiritualists were also interested in alternative healing helped to draw the Higginsons into the fold. Amy Post in particular sought cures in hydropathy, in which patients were treated with hot and cold baths and wet body wraps. For Higginson, spiritualism offered divine perfection for him and a possible cure for Mary.[28]

Higginson had been too young to be affected by the deaths of his siblings Mary Lee and Edward Cabot, but he was nineteen when his brother Samuel had disappeared at sea, and he was painfully aware of how often premature death had visited the Higginson family, just as it did so many families in antebellum America. In an era of profound religiosity, it was but a short leap from the certainty that one's loved ones watched from heaven to the hope that those who possessed special gifts might reunite the living and the dead. Two newspapers devoted to spiritualism, New York's *Spiritual Age* and Boston's *Banner of Light*, were already in print, and both were thrilled to welcome a reformer of Higginson's renown into the fold. When Higginson announced that he intended to deliver a series of speeches in the summer of 1857 on "the Rationale of Spiritualism," the editor of the *Spiritual Age* expressed his confidence "of his abilities to present the question of Spiritualism in a candid, rational, and convincing manner." Higginson's hope, he replied to the editor, was "to establish every main point which can be established" while drawing the distinction between "what is proved from [what] is merely probable." Although he had become convinced that "the mass of the 'manifestations' are solid and genuine," he admitted that spiritualism's "principles, canons of judgment are all yet to be settled." His scientific approach, he thought, might earn adherents among "those who deny the new phenomena" but also be of use to "those who accept them." The "most dogmatic is most likely to err," he warned.[29]

The occasional lectures on spiritualism continued into the early months of 1858, interrupted only by his second Boston meeting with Brown that March. Higginson's chance to enlarge his message came during the following fall, when Parker developed tuberculosis and had to step down from his Boston pulpit. Although an influential Transcendentalist, Parker had remained distant from the spiritualist community, so the opportunity to temporarily take over his congregation provided Higginson with a fresh audience. There, and again in December 1858 in a large venue in Manhattan, Higginson emphasized what he believed to be the unassailable "facts" behind the movement and how they reflected "the progressive tendencies of the age." He reminded any doubters in his audiences that what had become accepted science was once regarded with skepticism. Just as the discovery of "electricity and magnetism" had moved society from "brute muscle to steam," breakthroughs in "spiritual electricity" enabled "mind to act on mind and [brought] soul in contact with soul." To those who remained unconvinced, Higginson suggested they "consult the exposers of Spiritualism," who might uncover charlatans but find themselves unable to disprove the genuine. Concluding his speeches with an appeal to Transcendentalists in the seats, he drew links between the two ideas. "The world could not be reformed by truth," he insisted. "It is love, and not truth, life, and not light, which makes men really better."[30]

In the summer of 1859, as Parker prepared to depart for Florence, where he prayed that warmer weather might improve his health, he again invited Higginson to his pulpit for a number of sermons. This time Parker specifically requested Higginson to speak on spiritualism, having "never offered" to do so himself. Perhaps because of that endorsement, public interest in the lectures grew, and despite the size of the Boston Melodeon—a spacious concert hall—newspapers urged those interested "to go early to secure seats." As before, Higginson reminded his audiences that what was once questioned was now commonplace: "Even Isaac Newton was denounced and satirized in his time." But the former Unitarian minister in Higginson also remembered that God's wisdom and mysteries did not rely on scientific proof. "Improbable?" he asked. "God keeps in his provinces multitudes of grander instances, that are yet to come to our lower sphere and startle us with their mystery, and crush down the pride of human science." Some might scoff, Higginson concluded, but he found "it had brought new joys, new hopes, and imparted a new meaning and dignity to life." As was his custom, he spoke without notes, but following his spring and summer orations, Higginson took up his pen and published his thoughts in a pamphlet, *The Results of Spiritualism, A Discourse*.[31]

Just as his fame as a spiritualist was about to achieve new heights, Higginson's latest passion clashed with his greatest cause. The two leading spiritualist newspapers, he complained to Garrison, quietly requested that he keep the focus in his orations firmly on spiritualism and that he "say nothing about slavery." Higginson admitted that although endless references to his speeches and sermons appeared in both the *Banner* and the *Spiritual Age*, he "very seldom" read those papers. Yet upon doing so, he regretted that spiritualists avoided subjects that might dissuade anyone from joining their movement. Although Higginson hoped their failure to address what he regarded as the ultimate sin of his time was due to the moral failings of one or two editors rather than the readers of those newspapers, he could not separate the two crusades. Indeed, his embrace of spiritualism strengthened his belief that the world might be perfected for a just God. Yet his public lectures on spiritualism ceased as quickly as they had begun, and he returned his energies to antislavery and to the plight of women.[32]

* * *

Women's rights were never far from Higginson's thoughts. In February 1858 a group led by Caroline Wells Dall presented a petition to the Massachusetts legislature "protesting against being taxed while denied representation." The assembly had little interest in bringing the question to a vote, but they did permit a hearing on the issue. Dall spoke, as did Higginson and Wendell Phillips, and while the antislavery press expected little good to come of the effort, one abolitionist editor pronounced the "subject very able and thoroughly discussed."[33]

Three months later, Higginson and Phillips journeyed to Manhattan, where they attended the eighth annual Women's Rights Convention. Unlike in previous years, the conference chose not to publish their proceedings in pamphlet form, leaving it to James Gordon Bennett's *New York Herald* and the *Washington Union* to lampoon the conference attendees as "fanatical drones," and to the *Anti-Slavery Bugle* to praise them. Whereas men had dominated the testimony to the Massachusetts Assembly just months before, women ran the New York meeting and filled the majority of speaking slots. Susan B. Anthony served as president, assisted by a planning committee comprised of Dall, Lucy Stone, Antoinette Brown Blackwell, Frances Gage, and Ernestine Rose. Garrison and Higginson both spoke, and the *Bugle* was pleased to report that Black activists Douglass and Charles Lenox Remond were in attendance. The conference approved resolutions demanding "legislative action in the removal of the legal and political disabilities of women." Participants judged the meeting "eminently a success," although the unmarried Anthony was annoyed that Elizabeth Cady Stanton's growing family kept her tethered to her home in Seneca Falls. Stanton was "consoling herself that she is doing the work of rearing for the world six of Mr. Higginson's model saints," Anthony grumbled to Blackwell, a reference to Higginson's recent article in the *Atlantic Monthly* about the need for a robust physical culture among evangelicals.[34]

Over the course of the next year, Higginson routinely picked up his pen on behalf of his feminist allies. To friendly newspapers, he submitted a short piece on "dress reform," defending those like Stone who adopted less restrictive clothing. Higginson observed that the "peasant women" he had seen in Fayal wore "skirts heavier than those of our ladies, although shorter." He admitted that while he was no "judge" of women's clothing, he "certainly advocated the absolute right of all women to wear anything they wish to wear." To his friend James Russell Lowell, editor of the *Atlantic*, he submitted "Murder of the Innocents," which appeared in the magazine's September 1859 issue. In a Dickensian satire, Higginson imagined a "School for Young Ladies" called "Do-the-Girls Hall," in which school "committees" advocated "a vast machine for grinding down Young America." With no eye to gender or age, Higginson's dystopian school placed young women on "the tread-mill," providing them only with the basic knowledge they would require as wives or mothers, leaving "the poor remains of childish brains" unprepared to face a changing world and unwilling to challenge the conventional roles that society devised for them. Widely excerpted in the press, the essay was recommended by Northern papers, and even Southern newspapers such as the *Nashville Union and American* lauded it while being careful not to mention the author's name.[35]

Higginson expanded upon that theme in the same year's "Ought Women to Learn the Alphabet." In a lengthy essay that quoted authorities both ancient and modern, he argued that even though his century had witnessed more books written by women and about women than in any previous age, they had been published "under the shadow of intellectual contempt." Throughout the Western world, he charged, women were systematically encouraged, "from birth to death," to "acquiesce in their degradation." Young women were informed that as their adult destinies would be different from that of boys, their education should also be different, and that if they were taught the same subjects, society would "annul all differences between them." That, Higginson insisted, was a circular argument and one designed to deny adult women access to the professions. "There is the plain fact: women must be either a subject or an equal: there is no middle ground." Just as he believed that Black abolitionists should lead the antislavery movement, Higginson thought it proper that "the final adjustment" of both educational and societal inequality lay with women themselves. Ideas advanced in an essay penned by a male, he acknowledged, might change a few minds, but most men would not be swayed to confer rights and privileges upon women unless challenged by their wives and daughters. "In how many towns has the current popular prejudice against female orators been reversed by one winning speech from Lucy Stone," he wondered. The essay earned Higginson a good number of favorable notices, mostly in the Republican press, and he himself thought highly enough of it to include it as one the twelve reprinted in his 1882 *Atlantic Essays* anthology.[36]

Higginson parted ways with at least some of his women's rights partners, however, on the increasingly pressing issue of antislavery violence versus moral suasion, the latter being a position endorsed by Garrison's many female subscribers. Militancy, of course, implied masculinity, and while a handful of female abolitionists might endorse physical-force abolitionism—especially Black women such as Tubman—few white women anticipated assaulting Boston courthouses. The long-simmering disagreement flared up in Boston when the Massachusetts Anti-Slavery Society held its twenty-sixth annual meeting in January 1858. As did Brown and Douglass, Higginson believed that violence in Kansas and on the floor of the Senate—Charles Sumner's horrific beating—had changed the terms of the struggle. Speaking first, Higginson pronounced it a "defect" that the Society had "never found enough actual work for its members to engage in. He agreed that the "*moral position of this Society is the highest and noblest possible*," yet he also thought "their practical position does not take hold of the mind of the community," particularly the Northern Black community, which demanded bold action.[37]

Garrison seized the podium and responded "with great force." The Society's business, he insisted, was not to "construct a political platform" but to "speak the truth." Violence was sinful and political action invited immorality, he contended, and it was *not* his duty to "contrive ways for men in Union with slavery and determined to vote without regard to the moral character of their act, to carry out their low ideas." Abby Kelley Foster attempted to forge a middle ground, in part because her husband, Stephen, was more inclined to side with Higginson and his approach, suggesting that women could sway public opinion by "telling them truths which they were unwilling to hear," while men might "carry a ballot." But neither side much persuaded the other, and Higginson continued to believe that moral suasion alone had failed.[38]

Higginson continued to defend his position in coming months, repeatedly suggesting that if runaway slaves and Black abolitionists had come to embrace physical force and the Liberty Party, which advocated immediate abolition, white abolitionists had no right to condemn their methods. Speaking that March at a predominantly Black convention at Faneuil Hall, he reminded his audience that the first man through the courthouse door in the Burn riot was not himself, "contrary to general supposition," but Lewis Hayden, a Black man. Two months later, while addressing the New York Anti-Slavery Society at Manhattan's Mozart Hall, he elaborated on this theme: "We white Anglo-Saxon Abolitionists are too apt to assume the whole work is ours, and to ignore the great force of the victims of tyranny." He admitted, "For years I was disposed to think that salvation for the slave in this country was to be worked out not *by* him, but *for* him. My eyes have been opened, and I see it otherwise now." As with his women's rights partners, Higginson understood that he might be a vocal and valued supporter, but he could not be a leader. "Never in history was there an oppressed people who were set free by others," he concluded, "and it will not begin here and now." Garrison was again in the audience, but in a reminder to both as to who was the true enemy, a proslavery Richmond editor condemned the speech, sneering that the determined Higginson "thinks it a great pity that he did not create the world."[39]

That fall, as the off-year elections of 1858 approached, Higginson continued to promote both the Liberty Party and militant abolitionism in speeches across New England. Despite their ideological disputes, Garrison dutifully advertised his public talks. But Higginson also found leisure, as he had throughout the decade, to attend dinners at Boston's Atlantic Club, a private association limited to *Atlantic Monthly* authors. Emerson and Longfellow were also longtime members, and one visiting New Yorker found Higginson conversing with physician and writer Oliver Wendell Holmes Sr. and poet and abolitionist James Russell Lowell. "The food and the fun, the wit and the wine, were generous, juicy and sparkling," the charmed Manhattanite gushed.[40]

* * *

If the genteel conversations at his club provided Higginson with a respite from antislavery battles, reality intruded in early September 1858, when John Brown, who had seemingly vanished six months before, resurfaced, if initially only in rumors. The first whispers that Brown was finally prepared to act appeared in a letter from abolitionist Lysander Spooner to Wendell Phillips, requesting his endorsement for a scheme to assist runaways in forming insurgent maroon camps in western Virginia. This time the plan included the proviso that working-class whites might find common cause with the runaways. "Nearly all the non-slaveholders of the South would be with us," Spooner argued, and finding themselves outnumbered, terrified Southern planters would capitulate "without shedding a drop of blood." Spooner did not mention Brown by name, but most abolitionists understood who was behind the plot. Garrison promptly denounced the idea, but Stephen Foster and Higginson were delighted by the news.[41]

On September 11, Sanborn notified Higginson that Brown was "as ready for revolution as any other man," but as ever he needed funds. Correctly guessing that the habitual requests for money might convince a frustrated Higginson that Brown's visionary plans remained just that, Sanborn wrote again three days later to assure Higginson that "J. Smith"—the latest of Brown's many pseudonyms—had leased a farm to be used as a staging ground. Several weeks later, Sanborn wrote again to say that Franklin Jackson Meriam, an ally of James Redpath's, was off to join Brown's band. "He invests some money in the speculation," Sanborn reported, "and is an eager youth." Meriam promised to report back on Brown's progress to "the stockholders," as Sanborn dubbed Brown's six chief supporters. As Meriam planned to travel through Worcester on his way, Sanborn hoped Higginson might have a message for "the Shepherd," that is, Brown.[42]

Smith was increasingly unnerved about the potential violence in Brown's plan. The financier warned Sanborn that he preferred to be kept in the dark as to events in the South. "I do not wish to know Captain Brown's plans," he pleaded. "I hope he keeps them to himself." For his part, Higginson, who had been disturbed by Brown's disappearance, was gratified to hear that he was finally on the move. "I am rejoiced to find that you are not yet discouraged, and are still looking forward to the Enterprise," he wrote Brown on October 29, which "*ought* to have begun last spring." Hoping to prod Brown into continuing his activity, Higginson was open about how disappointed he had been by its postponement and hoped that it would not extend longer than the following spring. At present, his "purse" was empty, but he hoped to render Brown "some service, besides good wishes."[43]

The differences of opinion within the "secret six" reflected the larger divisions within the antislavery community. At about the same time that Higginson was finally reunited with his old friend Harriet Tubman, his ideological differences with Garrison again erupted, at the January 1859 annual Massachusetts Anti-Slavery Society meeting. There, Pillsbury, Abby Kelley and Stephen Foster, and Higginson all endorsed a resolution that denounced the Republican Party as "being more dangerous to the cause of freedom" than the Democrats due to their refusal to endorse Black political rights in the North. The Fosters argued that as an antislavery party that declined to endorse abolitionism, Republicans were "stealthily sucking the very blood from our veins." Despite his antipathy toward political action, Garrison rose to disagree, insisting that the backers of the resolution were "unduly despondent" and observing that the Republicans' success in the previous year's election indicated that more Americans were embracing antislavery. The debate grew heated, with Abby condemning Garrison's "premature self-congratulation." In hopes of dampening the ill-feelings, Garrison responded to his critics with weak attempts at humor, which only made matters worse.[44]

After the convention adjourned for the day, an enraged Higginson followed Garrison into the cloakroom, shouting that the editor had insulted him personally. Stephen Foster joined the fray, charging that Garrison's "pleasantries" actually contained hidden slights as to Abby Kelley Foster's personal appearance. The public never learned of the backstage bitterness, but the newspapers highlighted the growing division between Liberty Party advocates, most of whom favored the use of physical force against slaveholders, and moderate pacifists, many of whom regarded Republicans as potential allies. Even after the passage of several months, Garrison continued to complain that Higginson refused "to accept my explanation but left me in an inflamed mood of mind." For his part, Higginson never completely forgave Garrison.[45]

Higginson was equally annoyed with the elusive Brown. Sanborn wrote to Higginson just days after his spat with Garrison, assuring him that Brown had "begun the work in earnest." However, Sanborn admitted that he was still unsure as to Brown's current location, fretting that he might "fall into the hands of the United States or Missouri" officials. Two months later, in March 1859, and then again in April, Sanborn contacted Higginson about raising yet more funds for Brown. Brown swore he was "ready *with some new men* to set his mill in operation," Sanborn promised in the usual coded manner, "and seems to be coming East for that purpose." Smith had promised another $1,000, Sanborn assured a dubious Higginson. "Can you do nothing among the good people of Worcester?"[46]

Higginson declined to donate. He had not heard from Brown in nearly a year, and the whole project began to seem "rather chimerical." New England newspapers reported that Brown had ushered twelve Missouri runaways into Canada. Higginson wondered what that effort, laudable though it was, had to do with establishing maroon colonies in western Virginia. Finally, on May 1, Higginson wrote to Brown, telling him he planned to raise no more money for a venture that appeared destined never to happen. "My own loss of confidence," he admitted, was "also in the way [of] fundraising." Trying to soften the blow, he added that his loss of faith was "not in you, but in the others who are concerned in the measure." The plan should have commenced the year before, and "those who were so easily disheartened last spring may be deterred now." Should Brown set himself "free from timid advisers," Higginson promised, his current dismissive opinion would change dramatically. Rather than respond in writing, Brown journeyed to Boston, unsuccessfully begging Higginson to meet with him at the American House. "You ought to see him," Sanborn urged, "for now he is ready to begin."[47]

Weary of Brown's and Sanborn's promises and endless requests for money, Higginson instead devoted himself to his other reform issues. In late May, he spoke at the Yearly Meeting of Progressive Friends in Longwood, Pennsylvania, where a large crowd was treated to lectures on "sectarian oppression," the protection of runaways "on Pennsylvania soil," women's rights, the necessity of supporting "the most radical anti-slavery" tactics, land reform, and the avoidance of tobacco and "any manner of alcoholic drinks." One week later, on June 4, Sanborn wrote yet again, promising that Brown had finally "set out on his expedition." Then followed silence. In mid-August, Brown contacted the "secret six" once more, asking for an additional $300. Howe sent along $50, and Smith pledged another $100. Higginson again declined, and Sanborn was reluctantly obliged to inform Brown that the remainder of the request would "come more slowly." All Higginson knew was that Brown had written from West Andover, Ohio, and he guessed that if Brown was ever to get underway, "the foray would begin" somewhere due south, in western Pennsylvania. "Nobody mentioned Harpers Ferry," Higginson later remembered.[48]

"Ten days later the blow came," Higginson wrote. On the morning of October 18, he strolled into his local newspaper shop, where the proprietor remarked, "Old Osawatomie Brown has got himself into a tight place at last." Higginson grabbed a newspaper and read it before returning home. The initial reports, he supposed, resembled nothing like the truth. In reality, Brown and twenty-two men, seven of them Black, had briefly taken control of Harpers Ferry, Virginia, in hopes of seizing the U.S. Army's arsenal there and distributing the arms to nearby slaves. The *Richmond Enquirer* reported that "the insurgents numbered 200 whites and blacks" and were "led by a man named Anderson." The *Wheeling Daily Intelligencer* raised the number of "armed Abolitionists" to 250 whites, "with a gang of negroes [also] fighting." Before the day's end, the Richmond *Daily Dispatch* increased the tally yet again, claiming that "from 500 to 700 blacks and whites [were] engaged in the insurrection" and that "*many of the principal citizens of Harpers Ferry have been killed.*" One Baltimore paper ran their version below the headline "NEGRO INSURRECTION," while Greeley's *New-York Tribune* gave it the most favorable interpretation possible, claiming that the "riot" was orchestrated by white workers who had "grievances against the Railroad."[49]

By the next morning, the newspapers had published more accurate accounts, reporting that U.S. marines and soldiers commanded by Colonel Robert E. Lee had recaptured the arsenal and killed or captured the badly wounded Brown and most of his men. In a fit of remorse, Higginson reproved himself for being one of those "who had given him money and arms" but had "not actually been by his side." The endless postponements had convinced him, Higginson admitted, that the whole enterprise had grown "rather vague and dubious" in his mind. Much later, when he discovered that Frederick Douglass had declined to take part in the assault, warning Brown that he was walking into a geographical "trap," Higginson's guilt was somewhat assuaged. For the present, however, he found some solace in shipping a batch of newspaper accounts to the Brown family in Lake Placid, New York. Among the clippings was an interview with the jailed Brown, who declared himself merely an agent of Providence. "That sounds just like father," one of Brown's daughters replied to Higginson.[50]

Later years brought further reflection. Like Douglass, Higginson never lost his admiration for Brown's courage and vision. But also like Douglass, Higginson blamed himself for not grasping the fact that the "sly old veteran" lacked "the wit, the capacity, or the penchant for sane, shrewd, pragmatic planning," and in hindsight he regretted not having "acted to force the sane decision toward reasonableness and safety" upon Brown, since he "had not the ability to make it for himself." Yet in the moment, Higginson refused to repudiate him. When authorities discovered Brown's trunk of letters, implicating his supporters in his various plans and conspiracies, many of Brown's oldest supporters lost their nerve and went into hiding. Suspecting that he was far from done with either Brown's family or the cause in which they both served, Higginson alone among the "secret six" refused to flee, condemning "the extreme baseness" of those abolitionists who did.[51]

6
"Is there no such thing as *honor* among Confederates?"
1859–1860

As the grim news of the Harpers Ferry debacle was wired across the nation, Higginson and the other five chief backers of John Brown quickly grasped the implications for themselves. Newspaper editors, not all of them in the Southern states, called for the swift and severe punishment of Brown, his men, and his abolitionist supporters. Nervous Republicans were as anxious as Democrats to condemn the raid. Former congressman Abraham Lincoln, whose Senate campaign of the previous year had earned him national recognition, challenged Southern journalists to identify a single one of Brown's men who was a Republican. Higginson refused to panic, even as newspaper stories told of documents discovered at Brown's base camp in Maryland that revealed the extent of the conspiracy. Although not technically one of the "secret six," abolitionist James Redpath had been one of Brown's staunchest supporters, and he admitted to Higginson that he "could neither rest nor sleep" for days after reading of Brown's capture.[1]

Over the next months, Higginson's refusal to abandon Brown's cause, deny his own involvement in the affair, or flee the country would garner him renewed respect within the abolitionist community—even among those who refused to give up on pacifism—and revived animosity from Southern editors and politicians. After Brown, both friends and foes came to regard the Worcester crusader as the most radical white man in the country. To his admirers, Higginson combined Garrison's strong-minded dedication with Brown's fierce conviction that their guilty land could be cleansed only with blood. As always, however, Higginson refused to be categorized, and he continued to believe that activists like himself could forge bridges between the various reform communities and causes, even if that meant—reluctantly—endorsing a Republican free soiler for the presidency in 1860 and then fighting for a Union he had once tried so mightily to dissolve.

Within days of Brown's capture, abolitionists began to contact Higginson, urging him to take charge of fundraising for any legal defense. It fell to Higginson to be the central treasurer for the Kansas crusade, where his network of reformers and his fastidious bookkeeping skills—inspired by his father's insolvency—solidified his reputation as a careful man with funds. "Will you undertake the calling, &c. of such a meeting?" Boston minister Samuel May asked. Unsolicited, Samuel Blackwell of New York sent a contribution, as did Daniel Stickley of Maine, describing himself as a poor but dedicated abolitionist, who sent along $1. In Rochester, William Fall heard rumors that Higginson "had kindly consented to receive donations for the purpose of employing northern counsel for John Brown, the friend of the *Slave*." Fall sent a draft for $10, "with much esteem, tho' a *stranger*."[2]

To better coordinate the effort, Higginson caught the train for Boston in late October. In a circular dated November 2, he, Samuel Gridley Howe, abolitionist and attorney Samuel Sewall, and Ralph Waldo Emerson sought contributors "to aid in the defense of Capt. Brown." With money pouring in, the question was whom to hire. Wendell Phillips wrote to suggest that the four men approach attorney Montgomery Blair, who had defended Dred Scott, while William Ingersol Bowditch, a member of Boston's Vigilance Committee, contacted Higginson, proposing to act as Brown's junior counsel. George Sennott, a Boston abolitionist, advanced, somewhat curiously, Benjamin Butler, a celebrated criminal defense attorney but at that time a Democrat who had been publicly critical of antislavery men. Southern editors took a dim view of the effort. Radical abolitionists hoped to raise funds enough to successfully defend "Osawatamie Brown at his coming trial," one North Carolina paper reported, reminding readers of his connection to a violent 1856 skirmish in Kansas between pro- and antislavery forces. "Rev. T. W. Higginson acts as treasurer."[3]

Even before counsel could be hired, some of Brown's supporters, including Phillips, suggested presenting evidence of Brown's alleged "insanity" to Virginia governor Henry Wise. Higginson was appalled at the thought, as was Redpath, who believed the notion detracted from Brown's courage and heroism. Redpath, however, deemed any fundraising to be pointless. "I have not the faintest hope of his escape from martyrdom; have you?" he asked Higginson. Higginson too had his doubts, telling his mother that he, Howe, and Phillips had "done what we could for him by sending counsel," but that "beyond this no way seems open for anything." Were he a lawyer, Higginson assured his mother, he would have gone himself. While he was quite sure that any testimony he might provide at Brown's trial would only damage his case, when informed that Wise was considering summoning him and Sanborn as witnesses, Higginson pronounced himself "ready to go."[4]

At length, the state of Virginia assigned a number of attorneys to Brown, including the unfriendly Samuel Chilton, a native Virginian. Higginson's group was able, however, to hire George Hoyt, a young Massachusetts Republican. But as prosecutor Andrew Hunter, a Virginia slaveholder and Wise's personal attorney, began to compile evidence against Brown, it quickly became clear the state sought to indict more than just the old warrior and his men. In addition to the cache of letters discovered at Brown's rented Maryland farm, a check from Gerrit Smith for $100, drawn from the State Bank at Albany, was discovered in Brown's possession on the day of his capture. As Brown was facing charges of treason as well as murder, anyone who had assisted in his plans or helped fund them was in legal jeopardy of being an accessory to that crime. On October 29, the *New York Herald* reported that Wise intended to seek Smith's extradition. Wise also contacted President Buchanan, asking for the federal government's assistance in apprehending "Frederick Douglass, a negro man charged with murder, robbery, and inciting servile insurrection." Smith promptly began to destroy all of his correspondence with Brown, and he sent his son-in-law on a mission to the Brown family in hopes of securing any documents they might possess. Two weeks later, Franklin Sanborn assured Higginson that he had destroyed his letters, and indeed any letters "which might be used against [him in] any way." Sanborn was yet unclear as to what the Virginia prosecutors intended, but the "secret six," he believed, could thwart prosecution by disappearing evidence and refusing "any writ of Habeas Corpus."[5]

Five of the six scattered. Smith claimed that he was suffering from acute mania, "vertigo [and a] dyspeptic stomach," and checked himself into Utica's New York State Lunatic Asylum, where he was treated with cannabis and morphine. Howe published a letter in the *New-York Tribune*, insisting that he had no prior knowledge and that the "events at Harpers Ferry" were "unforeseen and unexpected by me." Theodore Parker had already left for Florence in hopes that warmer weather might cure his consumption. Douglass moved up the timetable for his already scheduled series of lectures in Britain. Unlike the dying Parker, Sanborn was perfectly healthy, but he wrote to Higginson from Maine, saying that on the advice of friends he planned to "try a change of air" for his "old complaint" in Quebec. "Burn this," Sanborn added.[6]

Higginson alone stood firm. Several of his friends encouraged him to follow Sanborn's example and retreat into Canada. He thought it "undesirable to do this." Having supported Brown's cause, even if he had never heard details about the Harpers raid, Higginson regarded it as the duty of the six backers "to stand our ground and give him our moral support." One thing he had learned from Henry Thoreau, he later reflected, was that civil disobedience meant being willing to suffer the consequence of one's actions—"whatever that might be." Initially, he refrained from commenting on the behavior of Brown's other backers, but when Sanborn urged him to issue no public statements about his own complicity, Higginson lost all patience. "Sanborn, is there no such thing as *honor* among Confederates?" he snapped. It was bad enough for Sanborn to flee the country, but to demand silence from others was worse. "Why, I had thought the poorest thief or conspirator w[oul]d feel the sense of shame" in turning against their fellows. Was this not an even greater wrong, as "the nobler man whom we have provoked on into danger is the scapegoat of that reprobation—& the gallows too?"[7]

Higginson was harder yet on Howe. "I thought it would be the extreme baseness in us to *deny* complicity with Capt. Brown's general scheme," he wrote. Several weeks earlier, Howe had suggested that as it would be foolish to incriminate themselves, the best course would be to make no statements. But then, in a lengthy letter to the *Tribune*, Higginson charged, Howe denied "all knowledge not merely of the time & place of Brown's great drama—but of the *enterprise itself*." While he had no wish to "judge," Higginson fumed, "Smith's insanity & your letter, are to me the only two sad results of the whole affair."[8]

Howe waited three months to reply, finally responding in mid-February 1860, that Higginson's missive "seemed to me, at the time, unkind and hard," and that it gave him "great pain." His public letter, Howe insisted, was not published so that he might escape punishment, but rather in hopes of showing that Brown had been a single "individual acting upon his own responsibility." Together with a plea of insanity, that fiction might have resulted in Brown's imprisonment rather than his execution. Even Sanborn refused to accept Howe's defense. He wrote Higginson that he too was "a little sorry" that Howe's initial statement had been published. Sanborn continued to maintain, however, that Higginson's public admissions of his own involvement threatened "to implicate others." Yet he, too, retreated into an improbable excuse, claiming that his two visits to Canada were not designed to "avoid arrest as a criminal" but rather because he did not want to be called to Virginia to appear as a witness. If summoned, he swore to Higginson, he planned to again disappear. Higginson had already promised to leave for Virginia if subpoenaed. Sanborn never changed his position, writing in later years that "Higginson desired even greater publicity for the truth than then seemed necessary."[9]

Even as Sanborn decamped for Quebec, Higginson took the stage at Worcester's Brinley Hall on October 25 to deliver a spirited defense of Brown's mission. He praised Brown as a brave champion of human freedom, saying that his only regret was that the raid "was not successful." Then, much to the dismay of any Republicans in the crowded hall that night, Higginson assured his audience that "nine out of ten of the Republicans of Worcester" agreed with his sentiments. Democratic editors pounced on the remark. Garrison, on the other hand, praised the speech, offering the hope that Higginson's rare admiration for Republican Free Soilers was correct. Higginson's solitary courage in the wake of Harpers Ferry was never forgotten by reformers, and decades later, when poet Stephen Vincent Benét penned his magisterial *John Brown's Body*, he observed, "Only the tough, swart-minded Higginson, Kept a grim decency, would not deny."[10]

As Higginson continued to collect legal funds that October and November 1859, he realized enough had been raised to assist Brown's family, who lived an impoverished existence in the Adirondacks near Lake Placid. Believing it unlikely that Brown would escape the noose, Higginson hoped to provide funds for the surviving raiders, especially Albert Hazlett and Aaron Dwight Stevens. With $1,721 in his possession, Higginson determined to visit Brown's family, both to get their permission to spend some of the money on the legal issues facing Brown's men and to see for himself how the family was faring. The journey was not an easy one. The village of North Elba was not on any rail line and sat 138 miles north of Albany. Much of the land had belonged to Smith, who hoped the town might become a community for former slaves, but situated at an elevation of nearly 2,000 feet it proved inhospitable to farming. On November 1, after several days of hard riding—and once having to chase after his runaway horse and wagon—Higginson reached the farm. Despite the onset of winter, he judged the mountainous region "a fit setting for the heroic family." Their standard of living was less so. "I found them poor, abstemious, patient, [and] unflinching," he noted. Mary Ann Brown, Brown's second wife and the mother of thirteen of his twenty-one children, came out to welcome him. "Tall, erect, stately, simple, kindly, slow, [and] sensible," Higginson told his mother, Mary immediately "won [his] heart pretty thoroughly."[11]

"The farm is a wild place, cold and bleak," Higginson recorded. It was too cold to plant corn, so the family raised sheep for the wool. Inside the modest, unpainted frame house, Higginson met Salmon Brown and his wife; twenty-three-year-old Salmon had taken part in the Kansas fighting, but weary of violence, he had refused to go to Harpers Ferry. Isabella, the wife of Watson Brown, who was mortally wounded in the raid, was there with her baby, as was the pregnant Martha, the wife of Oliver Brown, who had also died at Harpers Ferry. Mary Ann's three youngest daughters, Anne, Sarah, and five-year-old Ellen, completed the household. Brown's eldest daughter, Ruth, and her husband, Henry Thompson, and their children lived on a nearby farm. The family had yet to receive any letters from Brown himself, and newspapers and mail arrived at the remote hamlet but once a week, if that. Higginson brought the latest clippings and news with him, all of it bleak.[12]

The family already knew the worst of what had happened during the raid, if not the details. That night, as the women silently sewed, Martha showed Higginson their small collection of daguerreotypes. "This is Oliver, one of those who were killed at Harpers Ferry," Martha quietly added. Glancing up at her, "a wife at fifteen, a widow at sixteen," Higginson noticed that "not a muscle quivered, and her finger did not tremble as she drew the thread." He perceived that the Brown women, who largely occupied traditional roles, harbored different attitudes toward their father than did the Brown sons. Unlike Higginson or Douglass, Brown neither embraced women's rights nor promoted them in their own home. His expectations of his sons were equally conventional. As the evening wore on, Salmon admitted that "we boys felt a little pleased sometimes when father left the farm for a few days." Ruth spoke up "reproachfully," Higginson observed, insisting that "we girls *never* did."[13]

Sometime that evening, Mary Ann announced that she wished to travel to Virginia to see her husband one last time. She did not intend to endorse any insanity plea, and most likely she guessed that her husband was doomed. Higginson later said only that he offered to accompany her south, despite his own peril in doing so, and wrote that after spending a single night in North Elba, he "drove away with Mrs. Brown in the early frosty morning." Taking his wagon, the two rode south until they reached a rail junction and boarded a train for Boston. At one stop, Higginson purchased a newspaper that told of Brown's conviction and sentence. Placing the paper in her hands, Higginson watched as Mary Ann "bent her head for a few moments on the back of the seat" before them. At length she sat back up "and spoke calmly." She had "always prayed that her husband might be killed in fight rather than fall alive into the hands of slaveholders," she assured Higginson. But in view "of the noble words of freedom which it had been his privilege to utter" in his jailhouse interviews, she could "not regret it now." Upon arriving in Boston, the two took rooms at the American House, where so much of Brown's activities had been planned, and Mary Ann promptly telegraphed Governor Wise, requesting permission to visit her husband. Higginson's small act of kindness appeared in newspapers across the country, the Northern press praising his efforts and Virginia editors stunned by his willingness to venture into their jurisdiction.[14]

Three days later, as Mary and Higginson headed south for Maryland, a telegram from Brown's attorneys arrived. "Mr. Brown says for God's sakes don't let Mrs. Brown come," George Sennott cabled Higginson. Sennott was unsure precisely where the two were, but one of the cables finally reached them in Baltimore on the morning of November 8, just as they were preparing to board the train for Virginia. One day later, a letter from Brown addressed to Higginson arrived at Howe's home. As Howe explained to Higginson in a lengthy note, Brown "urges that his wife shall not go to him." To see him wounded and in jail, Brown feared, "would *only tend* to distract *her* mind *tenfold*; & would only add to my affliction; & *cannot possibly* do me *any good*." Brown was prepared to suffer a stoic martyr's death. "Mr. Brown fears your presence will undo the firm composure of his mind," yet another attorney warned, "& so agitate him as to unman & unfit him for the last great Sacrifice." Aware of how little the family had to survive on, Brown wanted Mary Ann not to waste any money on the trip, but to purchase "Bread & cheap but comfortable clothing, fuel, & for herself & children for the winter."[15]

After escorting Mary Ann back to North Elba, Higginson returned to Worcester, where he found a letter from Brown dated November 9. Brown repeated a number of the points made through his attorneys before remarking that Mary Ann could "receive a thousand times the consolation AT HOME that she can possibly find elsewhere." Mindful that his silence had worried both Mary and his children, Brown promised Higginson that he would "write her CONSTANTLY." He had been "quite cheerful" regarding his fate before he heard of her trip, and he begged Higginson to tell Mary Ann "to be calm and submissive." Just to make sure that Higginson understood his desires, Brown replaced his normal tendency of underlining words with capitalization. "I can certainly judge better in the matter than anyone ELSE," he warned, before softening his conclusion with his "warmest thanks to yourself and all other kind friends. God bless you all." As Brown requested,

Higginson forwarded the letter to Mary, who reassured Higginson that her husband's words were "a great comfort" and that her only thoughts were "thy will Oh Lord will be done."[16]

Brown's daughters also wrote in thanks to Higginson. "Before you came, all looked dark & dreary to us—we had not received one word of comfort from any source," Ruth observed. "*Never did my heart overflow with gratitude so much*, as it has the last week, since reading your soul cheering letters," she added, imitating her father's tendency to underline entire passages for emphasis. As it became clear that Brown's sentence of death would not be commuted, Ruth wrote again: "If there is no reprieve for our dear Father will the Virginians not allow us to have his body? Please do intercede for us, *dear friend in some way*."[17]

Governor Wise was, in fact, willing to return the hanged bodies to the family, and a relieved Annie, the most literate of the Brown daughters, told Higginson that they had received "two excellent letters from our poor dear Father," who did not want the family to feel "in the least degraded on his account." Annie assured Higginson that she felt quite "proud when I think that his blood runs in my veins."[18]

Perhaps realizing that his previous letter to Higginson had been less than gracious, Brown wrote again just before his death, this time expressing his "deep feelings of gratitude for your journey to visit & comfort my family as well as myself." Higginson had recently sent the family a stack of newspaper clippings, together with $25, and that meant a good deal to Brown, who had suffered numerous bankruptcies. "Truly you have proved yourself to be a 'friend indeed'; & *I feel* my many obligations for all your kind *attentions*." Brown was surely aware that Higginson had neither fled nor denied any involvement in the plot, and he wished Higginson to know that he was "very cheerful" and would "continue so 'to the end.'" "Yours for *God & the right*" were his last words to his fellow warrior.[19]

As December 2, the date set for Brown's execution, neared, abolitionists planned a series of events designed both to mourn Brown's death and to celebrate his memory and the cause for which he was about to die. Emerson said in a lecture that Brown would "make the gallows as glorious as the cross," and Garrison, speaking at Boston's Tremont Temple, abandoned his usual pacifism to wish "success to every slave insurrection at the South," insisting that he did not "stain his peace profession in making that declaration." In Worcester, one disapproving Louisiana editor reported, "there was something more of a demonstration." Higginson, described by the newspaper as "a captain in Kansas [and] the chief agitator on this occasion," spoke first. Boston-based abolitionist and women's rights activist Abby Folsom followed, only to be derided by the editor as "that garrulous Xantippe," referring to the supposedly ill-tempered wife of Socrates. As was the case across New England, Higginson asked that church bells toll for two hours at around the time of Brown's execution in Charlestown.[20]

Although similar ceremonies took place as far west as Ohio, with as many speakers as there were services, Higginson's words especially attracted the ire of Southern and Democratic editors, perhaps because of his involvement in the Burns affair and his role with the "secret six." The St. Paul *Weekly Pioneer and Democrat* charged that Lydia Maria Child's public letter to Brown was but an imitation of "the examples of [Henry Ward] Beecher and Higginson." James Gordon Bennett's reliably Democratic *New York Herald* editorialized that Higginson and Beecher should never "have been permitted to defile the pulpit." Such "violent, foul tongued men" managed to "disgust people with religion itself." The press inspired one unnamed resident of Tuscaloosa, Alabama, to write Higginson, warning that if he and other abolitionists attempted "any such work a little farther south, we will not await the action & sanction of the Government, but we will burn every mother's son of you as fast as we catch you." Death by burnings, the anonymous Southerner added, would "give you a foretaste of the [hellish] joys of that happy future for which you are so well preparing yourself." Never suspecting that within three years he would in fact be taking his antislavery activities "a little farther south" to the Carolina coast, Higginson simply filed the letter away.[21]

* * *

Having served first as treasurer for the "secret six" and then as chief fundraiser for Brown's defense, Higginson fell naturally into the role of Brown family supporter. Even before any public announcement could be made, sympathetic reformers simply assumed that he was the man to whom donations should be sent. "Do you still act upon the Committee for the relief of the families rendered needy by the Harpers Ferry affair?" one contributor wrote Higginson from New Bedford. "If so, will you please give me a statement of their needs?" Even before Higginson could respond, the man wrote again, suggesting that Higginson might have "a first-rate lithograph" of Brown drawn up "and sold for the benefit of his family." Higginson's Worcester neighbor H. W. Wayland posed a similar idea, recommending that he announce a dollar campaign. "Here is a dollar for myself, and & dollar for my wife," he wrote. "Who will give the next, & the next, until Worcester has given a thousand names & a thousand dollars." Despite the fact that leading Republicans stumbled over one another in their haste to dissociate themselves from the raid, one moderate party member urged Higginson to call a public meeting "in aid of John Brown's family [that] could be headed 'John Brown and Freedom.'" So many citizens might attend, this Republican hoped, that perhaps "a party would spring up under this name that would rule our country in 1860."[22]

Far more realistic was a topic that spoke to Higginson's humanity. Ruth Thompson's young son John had been living in Boston with his grandfather's supporters, and Higginson, ever desirous of a child to raise, promised the family that he would be thrilled to take the boy in, as he had "numerous friends [who] would be willing & glad to protect him." Family friend Francis Jackson, however, judged the boy to be "so wrought up, & over excited" about his grandfather's fate that he thought it wisest to send the child back to his parents or even "out of the Country." Should that be the case, Irish abolitionist Richard Webb wrote Higginson, he would be happy to take in and hide any of Brown's family or friends in Dublin.[23]

Still other correspondents wrote with related ideas. Mary Mann, the widow of educational reformer Horace Mann, sent a small sum to help commemorate "the memory of the brave colored men who went with Captain Brown to help their brethren out of slavery." Students at Oberlin College—the first school to admit women, including Lucy Stone—submitted $195.44 for the "Memorial Stone" that was being designed to sit atop Brown's grave and those of his family and fellows at North Elba. As in the past, to better coordinate fundraising, Samuel May asked Higginson to speak at a public meeting in Boston planned for February 16 of the new year. Brown's only living brother, Frederick, hoped that Higginson would speak, and obviously May expected a large crowd, as Black abolitionist Charles Lenox Remond believed that a modest admission fee of 10 cents would raise a considerable amount of money. From North Elba, Anne Brown wrote to Higginson in thanks for the continuing donations, though she hoped the money might equally be spent on the legal defense or even liberation of the raiders Stevens and Hazlett. The Richmond *Daily Dispatch* took a dim view of what they dubbed Boston's "Ovation to the 'Martyrs'" and declined to report on the gathering beyond saying that Garrison, Higginson, and former slave turned Boston minister J. Sella Martin had delivered speeches.[24]

Although Republican presidential hopeful Senator William Henry Seward had moderated his critiques of the South in recent months, some abolitionists hoped to capitalize on the widespread Northern denunciations of Brown's execution and prod the Republican Party into a more progressive stance regarding race relations. Abolitionist J. D. Fowler asked Higginson to return to Boston and lecture on "our present relations to Slavery [and] to consider what action should be taken." Neither major party had yet held its nominating convention, but the prevailing wisdom was that the Democrats were in danger of imploding along regional lines, and if so Fowler wondered whether it was wise to splinter the antislavery community by again advancing Smith's candidacy with the Liberty Party. Even Higginson, with his long-standing disdain of mainstream parties, replied that it might soon be necessary to fuse with Republicans: "I have long felt with you that we most need organization and I look at the movement you refer to as very important in that direction."[25]

* * *

On the day of Brown's execution, Governor Wise was taking no chances. Fearing that militant abolitionists might try to liberate Brown at the last minute, Wise spent $250,000 to protect the gallows, all but exhausting Virginia's cash reserve. Brown rode to the site atop his coffin, his arms "closely pinioned at the elbows," one observer noted. Roughly 1,500 cavalry and militiamen had been called up, among them the cadets at the Virginia Military Academy. The cadets were led by Professor Thomas J. Jackson, who was disappointed to see only "unflinching firmness" in Brown's demeanor. Sixty-five-year-old Virginia secessionist Edmund Ruffin, who had joined the cadets so that he could witness the execution, was equally disheartened to discover that Brown mounted the steps as though he were "a willing assistant, instead of a victim."[26]

To most Northerners who read reports of the hanging in their local newspapers, spending that much money to execute one man appeared absurd. But Wise was not naive. As early as October 28, James McKim, a Presbyterian minister and abolitionist, had rendezvoused with James Redpath in Philadelphia. Redpath was then going under the pseudonym of J. R. Cotton, and the two contacted Higginson, insisting that "everything possible or probable should be attempted" to liberate Brown: "No stone should be left unturned." Although the success of a rescue attempt from the heavily guarded gallows struck Higginson as improbable, he was willing to consider various proposals. For a time, at least, he did think it possible that a band of armed guerrillas could break Brown out of the Charlestown jail, and, as ever, he became the chief fundraiser for the effort. Nathan Cheney sent $300 from Boston, empowering Higginson to use the money in any "noble cause," whether for Brown's defense or deliverance. Despite their recent rift, Sanborn wrote to Higginson, urging him persuade Redpath to raise men as soon as possible. "Redpath must go to Ohio," he believed, "that is our only chance of rescuing Brown." Evidently feeling guilty that he had resisted marching on Harpers Ferry, Salmon Brown wrote to encourage the effort while begging off participating due to family responsibilities. "I wish to God that I were one of the 200 to make rescue of the prisoners," he assured Higginson two days before his father's execution. "Unless something of the kind is done, death is inevitable to all of those good men."[27]

The plot came to nothing. George Hoyt, one of Brown's attorneys, essentially served as a spy for the rescue efforts, going so far as to draw up a detailed sketch of the two-story, red brick jailhouse. But Brown himself, Hoyt reported, "positively refused to consent to any such plans" on the grounds that more men would die on his behalf. Not knowing of Brown's refusal, New York abolitionist John LeBarnes promised Higginson that he had enlisted fifteen to twenty-five men in Manhattan, all of them "ready and determined." But LeBarnes had heard nothing from Ohio, and he guessed they would need roughly one hundred men "to seize the houses of the Cavalry Companies" before moving on the jail itself. LeBarnes's recruits appeared to be more mercenaries than abolitionists, as they each demanded $100 for "expenses." Hoyt journeyed north to Ohio to see what he could do, but in mid-November he wrote to Sanborn with the news that "nothing [was] doing there." On November 28, LeBarnes cabled Higginson, "Project abandoned."[28]

Having served as the accountant for so many Brown ventures, it naturally became Higginson's lot to collect funds for the defense of the raiders who had been captured and awaited trial. Stevens had been shot at Harpers Ferry but survived, and Hazlett had escaped into Pennsylvania, then had been arrested in Carlisle and extradited to Charlestown. Rebecca Buffum Spring, a Quaker abolitionist and cofounder of the New England Anti-Slavery Society, informed Higginson that she was organizing a petition regarding Stevens to be sent to John Letcher, who succeeded Wise as Virginia's governor on January 1, 1860, "asking for this young man's life." Although Spring regarded any pardon as unlikely, she prayed "that Virginia vengeance is satisfied." Richard Hinton, an English-born journalist and abolitionist, wrote to suggest they hire two Southern attorneys for Hazlett, perhaps including a "Mr. Chilton of Wash. City to defend him, with Lawson Botts Esq. of Va." Even more so than Spring, Higginson judged the case lost, as one Harpers' resident had witnessed Hazlett "in the act of shooting a citizen," and he had done himself little favor by assuring Carlisle authorities that his name was William Harrison just before telling Virginians that he was actually William Harris.[29]

Several of Brown's associates went so far as to suggest kidnapping Governor Wise and bartering his life for Brown's. Higginson regarded such schemes as absurd, but he was willing to entertain the prospect of forcibly liberating the two raiders. Their trial was set to begin on February 1, and Higginson supposed that the two would not be as closely guarded as Brown had been. The thought appears to have originated with Charles Tidd, a Maine lumberman who had moved to Kansas, where he had first met both Brown and Higginson. Unlike the hapless Hazlett, Tidd had made good on his escape from Harpers Ferry, and on December 8 he wrote to Higginson that he was "ready to do whatever is in my power to render any assistance to Stevens." Either Hinton also heard from Tidd or simply came to the same conclusion, as just days later he contacted Higginson. "Count me in for one," he pledged. "Stevens & Hazlett *must be saved*."[30]

The question was who best to lead the task. Lucy Pomeroy, a Massachusetts native whose husband, Samuel, had served as agent for the Northeastern Aid Society of Kansas, wrote from the territory to warn Higginson that it was "dangerous to entrust any 'secret million'" to Hinton. "He is a good fellow, thoroughly Anti-Slavery, of the John Brown type," she advised, but "*not* [one] of those gifted with large secretiveness & caution." Although the two had never met during Higginson's time in Kansas, he instinctively thought of James Montgomery. The Ohio-born and Kentucky-raised Montgomery had gained fame in the East by settling in Kansas, where he raised and led a "self-protective company" of militiamen who sought to drive proslavery settlers out of the territory. While disappointed in Higginson's choice, Hinton set out for Kansas to persuade Montgomery to accept the challenge. Higginson also wrote to Montgomery, inviting him to travel east to Pennsylvania, where the two could better coordinate efforts. John LeBarnes joined in, telling Higginson that he had given Hinton $50 and asking that Higginson raise another $200 "for probable expenses."[31]

All of the conspirators, with the exception of Higginson, began to adopt pseudonyms in their correspondence. Charles Tidd signed his letters "C.P.," using his first and middle initials. Hinton signed with his three initials and suggested to Higginson that they "write either in some cypher or with iodine" that could be seen only when the letter was held over a flame. Rather more sensibly, Redpath warned Higginson that he had "reason to believe there are spies watching you" and that he should not mail any "letter that you are not" willing to trust to the post office. G. F. Warren, one of Montgomery's associates, confirmed that Higginson's letter had reached Montgomery, but remarked that "you must be very cautious how you send such letters." Undeterred, Higginson continued to sign all correspondence with his full name, confident in the righteousness of his cause and, as always, willing to face the consequences of his actions.[32]

Initially, Montgomery was reluctant, telling Higginson that he found himself "in a strait, impelled by two forces: duty to my family and creditors, and duty to the *cause*." Montgomery also believed that his efforts were better spent in Kansas. Nonetheless, he admitted that Higginson's plea had given him "a sleepless night." At length, he gave in. From Leavenworth, he cabled Higginson, "I have got eight machines," using a code term for soldiers and signing his name "Henry Martin." When Hinton, now going under the name of J. Reed, cabled that he and Montgomery and the eight militiamen had reached Pittsburgh, Higginson left Worcester and caught the train for Harrisburg. Upon arrival, Higginson went to the home of Dr. William Rutherford, an abolitionist he regarded as a "tower of strength." Just before departing, Higginson received another letter from LeBarnes, with the usual request that he raise "some *money*" and provide "*assurances* of provisions for families—in case of *accidents*," by which he meant deaths in the rescue attempt. But all of Higginson's concerns quickly vanished when he finally met Montgomery in Rutherford's parlor in mid-February. Tall, bearded, devout, and nine years Higginson's senior, Montgomery struck the younger abolitionist as his ideological twin. He was "one of the most charming men I ever saw," Higginson wrote to Mary on February 17, "and a man to follow anywhere." Other abolitionists thought Montgomery a bit too ready to resort to violence, but Higginson judged him "mild & sweet." From that moment on, Montgomery was his "master machinist."[33]

As with the previous schemes, the plan came to nothing. LeBarnes's contacts in New York informed him that they believed any rescue attempt "should be postponed until [his] appeal has been tried." More disheartening still, Rebecca Buffum Spring received word from Stevens that he was both "chained and guarded." Following an unsuccessful attempt to escape, his guards had fastened shackles around his ankles, the chains affording him just "room to take a half step." A sentinel stood watch "outside the view-bar door" and was relieved by a fresh guard every two hours. While the group was in Harrisburg, newspapers reported that both Stevens and Hazlett had been sentenced to die on February 14. Sitting down with Montgomery, Higginson drafted a "memorandum" on the possibility of rescue. The weather had turned unusually cold, and Higginson guessed his party would have to "traverse mountainous country at 10 miles a night, carrying arms, ammunition & blankets & provisions for a week." To build a fire might betray their camp's location, but to go without one would court death. Once in Charlestown, the nine or ten men would have to assault a building guarded by two sentinels, perhaps as many as twenty-five guards, "& a determined jailor." They must then "retreat with prisoners & wounded probably after daylight" through snowy terrain.[34]

Both Montgomery and Higginson had previously risked their lives in the cause. Still, neither was foolishly willing to do so in a hopeless struggle. Both had unwell spouses, and neither had the monetary resources to provide for their wives should they not return. "It is snowing hard today dearest," Higginson wrote Mary on February 18. "That makes our machinist feel badly." Higginson had long promised to lecture in Yellow Springs, Ohio, and Chicago, and he swore to Montgomery that he would return within the week. "If the ground is still covered with snow," he promised Mary, he would simply leave for home.[35]

The news that Higginson and Montgomery had definitely abandoned any rescue attempts set off another round of mourning in the North. Edward Spring, Rebecca's husband, told Higginson that the plan's cancelation "severed the last threat of hope" he had. Spring wished that his wife's petition might melt "the hard heart" of the new governor, even as he admitted that was "almost impossible." From North Elba, Mary Ann Brown assured Higginson that she felt "great satisfaction to think that there was some effort made to save the lives of those poor men." Just days before the two were hanged, Higginson wrote to Stevens. Like the former minister that he was, he offered Stevens the comfort that "death is only a step in life, & there is no more reason why we should fear to go from one world into another than from one room into another." After all, "the world where John Brown [now] is cannot be a bad one to live in." Higginson signed off by adding that his wife—"who would have been willing that I should risk my life to save yours, had that been possible"—also desired "to join with me in invoking upon you Heaven's best blessing." The two young men died together on March 16 and were buried in New Jersey. Years later, they were reinterred with eight other raiders in North Elba.[36]

* * *

By the dawn of 1860, many Americans feared that the nation was about to be sundered. That prospect held little terror for Higginson, as he had always believed himself morally tainted by residing in the same republic as slaveholders and had long advocated disunion. Just as he believed that justice required him to violate man-made law in attempting to rescue Stevens and Hazlett, he cared nothing about the very real possibility of being arrested as one of the "secret six." In Washington, Senator James Murray Mason, a proslavery Virginia Democrat, announced plans to hold hearings on Brown's raid and investigate his backers. The *New York Times* reported that Brown's cache of letters and documents found when he was captured proved beyond doubt that prominent men were complicit in the Harpers Ferry plot, while a Democratic Chicago newspaper claimed that the two "prominent gentlemen" most commonly referenced in captured papers were "the Rev. Theodore Parker and the Rev. T. W. Higginson." As one of the charges levied against Brown was treason, those who knew of his scheme were equally culpable, and both Parker and Higginson, the Chicago editor asserted, "were cognizant of Brown's plans."[37]

In hopes of securing legal protection, both Sanford and LeBarnes contacted Massachusetts assemblyman John A. Andrew, a Republican and abolitionist increasingly spoken of as a possible gubernatorial candidate. Andrew, who was a distant relative of Higginson, was already at work trying to amend the state's 1855 Personal Liberty Act, designed to provide a modicum of legal rights for accused runaway slaves and their allies. Otherwise, Andrew's advice was ominous. If called before Mason's Senate committee, he warned, Brown's backers were "not allowed to withhold evidence which incriminated" them, and if they tried to, they faced a year in prison and a fine of $1,000. Sanborn also spoke to Senator Henry Wilson, a moderate Republican, who provided similar counsel. "No help can be expected from him," Sanborn advised Higginson. But upon the advice of Andrew, Sanborn added, he had changed his mind and decided to go to Washington if called. Andrew had alerted Sanborn to an 1846 federal statute that permitted a U.S. judge to issue a warrant for arrest to force "a witness whose evidence is declared *material*" to appear before them. Should such a warrant be issued, Sanborn hinted, it could only be resisted "by tumult." Sanborn guessed Higginson to be protected by abolitionists in Worcester, just as he had been protected from Marshal Butman, but he judged Boston to be "rather precarious." Might "your Worcester people" be willing to "go down to Boston to take Dr. Howe or Mr. Phillips out of the marshal's hands?" he wondered.[38]

Evidently Higginson, too, contacted Andrew, as the attorney alerted him that he had five of his letters "that ought to be in your possession" given that they might have to be turned over to a judge if requested. The letters "are ready & subject to your order," he wrote Higginson, hinting that he was prepared to either return or destroy them. Sanborn changed his mind yet again; he and Howe finally resolved that while they would refuse to appear before Mason's committee, they would tell what they knew to a friendly Massachusetts court. As a devoted abolitionist and a friend of John Brown, Sanborn explained to Higginson, it could not "be safe in a city so near Virginia." Higginson refused to apologize for his activities. "I infer from your note that you intend to go [to Washington] if sent for," Senator Wilson wrote to Higginson. "You will have to testify even if your testimony tends to convict yourself." The senator noted that Higginson could not be tried for crimes "by the general government," but what the state of Virginia might do with his affidavit was another question altogether. The one saving grace, Wilson mused, was that Mason was less interested in trapping a handful of abolitionists than in casting "a drag-net over the North" and getting one of the "secret six" to reveal "a great plot and implicate several public men in it." In particular, Mason hoped to damage the presidential prospects of Senator Seward, whom the *New York Herald* had already charged to be "the arch agitator who is responsible for this insurrection." In reality, Seward had met Brown only once in his life, and Higginson regarded the moderate New York Republican as being as worthless as Wilson.[39]

On January 11, the Senate drafted summonses for Sanborn, Howe, and Smith, but chose to ignore Higginson. Higginson had previously agreed to lecture in Concord, and initially Sanborn offered Higginson a room in his house. By the time Higginson arrived, however, Sanborn had again fled to Canada, as had Howe. Higginson instead stayed with the Emersons, where a letter from Sanborn awaited him. Sanborn insisted that while he originally intended to remain in Massachusetts and refuse the summons, his family and many of his friends urged him to flee the state. Once again, Higginson was infuriated by Sanborn's behavior. "I do not pretend to understand your position or Howe's," he snapped. Were he called to testify, Higginson promised, he would never utter a word "that might inculpate you two." Although he declined to use it as an excuse, Higginson also had family responsibilities. The 1860 census described the thirty-six-year-old Higginson as a "literary man" whose personal estate of $1,000 provided for his wife, sixteen-year-old Margaret "Greta" Channing—who was again residing with the Higginsons—and Abby Eaton, a young "domestic" from Maine. "What you mean by offering to testify in Boston, I cannot conceive," Higginson continued. Wilson had assured him that Mason did "not desire the Massachusetts witnesses" to actually appear before his committee. Mason only wished to publicly announce "that he could not obtain the necessary information," Higginson guessed. Sanborn's cowardice was compounded, Higginson concluded, by the fact that Sanborn had always promised him— "openly stated"—that he would not go to Canada. If Higginson's earlier rebuke had damaged but not completely severed his relationships with Howe and Sanborn, this final missive did.[40]

Redpath, who also refused to hide, believed that he would be safe from subpoenas. "I shall stay at home and *fire* at the first intruder on my premises," he assured Higginson. "That the body of a U.S. Marshal is not impervious to a bullet well directed, is a lesson that I think now needs to be demonstrated." Redpath's friends took up his defiance and also wrote to Higginson, begging assistance from Worcester. "We are now fourteen in number who are willing to shoot or be shot at, at five minutes notice," William Handy insisted, in protection of "Redpath or any other man who represents the principles of right [and] liberty." As did Higginson, Handy thought it "dangerous" to rely on the legal system, and so it was incumbent upon physical force abolitionists to "resist an unjust, mean, barbarous, mandate imposed" upon Northern citizens "by the slave power." Although Higginson promised Mary that he had no right to risk his life "without strong reasons," protecting the lives of his allies was a sound enough cause. Together with Eli Thayer, his Worcester-area congressman and a partner in the Kansas emigration crusade, Higginson organized a "League of Freedom" to coordinate efforts to liberate Redpath should state courts permit federal marshals to arrest him as a potential witness for Mason's committee. But as he himself guessed he would be, Redpath was left alone.[41]

Proud of his actions, Higginson delivered a rousing speech in Concord in early April, urging that city's young men to "maintain the action" of other Massachusetts towns. The "well known abolitionist agitator," as the unfriendly *New York Herald* characterized Higginson, praised the "effective military organization in this town to carry out the principles of resistance to United States laws." He reminded his audience of the fate of the unfortunate Butman, and what had happened to him in Worcester. "To better coordinate future efforts, Higginson recommended that a "Committee to Resist" be created. The *Herald* ran the entire story under the headline "Violent

Measures Proposed." Higginson declined to characterize the story as particularly unfair.[42]

Although Brown's project had utterly failed, Higginson continued to buy and ship arms to Free Soil settlers in Kansas. He wrote to James Abbott in Lawrence that he had just shipped off a box by paid Express freight "containing *hardware*." He also quietly raised funds to assist Brown conspirator Tidd, his parents, and his sister in Brookline, Massachusetts. Tidd had been one of the raiders to flee Harpers Ferry and escape capture. He hid out in Warren County, Pennsylvania, where he and his sister Elizabeth begged for money enough to keep him safely concealed and assist their "destitute" parents, who were too "aged [and] too feeble" to join their son or relocate to the Midwest. The elusive Tidd was never captured but lost his life in 1862 fighting with Union forces in North Carolina.[43]

* * *

Ever since John Brown had proposed creating a series of maroon colonies in the Virginia hills for runaways, Higginson had been pondering the history of marronage in the Atlantic world, and what relevance it might hold for his own country. A visit to Harvard's library brought him into contact with two early nineteenth-century histories of the Jamaican maroons and an account, less sympathetic, of "the revolted negroes of Surinam" published by a British officer. In two *Atlantic Monthly* essays published in February and May 1860, he drew several parallels to Brown's raid. Well aware that those who had denounced Brown in life as a fanatic came to mourn and revere him in death, Higginson wrote of the "public indignation" over the way that runaways were treated by British authorities in what became the Second Maroon War of 1795. Britain's scorched earth tactics and use of "bloodhounds" forced Parliament to "send a severe reproof to the Colonial Government." Higginson was unable to calculate the cost of crushing the Harpers Ferry raid, but, in his essay on Surinam, he estimated that the British had expended "forty thousand pounds a year" in their efforts to dismantle the South American colonies. Neither essay actually mentioned Brown. Still, his occasional references to current affairs in the United States made the connection abundantly clear to his readers.[44]

By then the presidential contest of 1860 was well underway. With four major candidates in the field, the antislavery community faced a dilemma, one that it had so far been able to avoid. The Democratic Party, as predicted, had imploded, splintering into two national campaigns, with John C. Breckinridge, the current vice president, representing Southern

Democrats, while Illinois senator Stephen Douglas and his platform of popular sovereignty spoke for Northern Democrats. What remained of the defunct Whig Party nominated former Tennessee senator John Bell. To the surprise of most observers, Republicans abandoned frontrunner Seward in favor of the relatively unknown former congressman from Illinois, Abraham Lincoln. Both Democratic platforms endorsed the annexation of Spain's slave-powered Cuban colony, and Bell both owned and hired slaves to work his iron foundries. By comparison, Lincoln was a free soiler, and although not an abolitionist, he had built his reputation on hostility to slavery and was the most viable antislavery candidate since John Quincy Adams. Higginson's old ally Parker Pillsbury regarded Lincoln as too soft on the South and endorsed the candidacy of Liberty Party perennial Gerrit Smith. In voting for Republicans, Pillsbury insisted, "you as effectively vote for slavery as you would in voting for Stephen A. Douglas." Higginson was less sure and quipped that the Democratic Party resembled a badly cooked mince pie: "Very white and indigestible upon the top, very black and very indigestible at the bottom, with untold horrors between." The line was picked up in a dozen or so newspapers, including one in Baton Rouge.[45]

A small number of Liberty Party activists met in Boston and endorsed Smith. However, from the moment Smith had checked himself into a Utica asylum to escape possible extradition, Higginson had judged him a coward and a failed leader. The *New York Herald*, which endorsed Douglas, was enthusiastic about the prospect of resolute abolitionists supporting Smith and his "no quarter to slavery" platform, on the grounds that if enough Liberty voters remained loyal to their party, they might "spoil the calculations of the Republicans in one, two, three or four very important Northern States" and so cost Lincoln a majority in the Electoral College. Despite these reasonable fears, Smith announced himself healed of "dyspepsia, and over-working the brain" and prepared for his final campaign. Smith liked Lincoln personally, he assured one journalist, but believed he had not gone "far enough on the subject of abolition."[46]

Aware that four major party candidates and one minor party nominee might well deny any one of the aspirants an electoral majority and so throw the election into the House, where slaveholder Bell, who was being hailed as a centrist, might emerge as the consensus choice, Smith's candidacy worried more pragmatic abolitionists. Higginson was one of them, and Garrison another. Smith's followers were but an ineffectual "baker's dozen," Garrison dismissively wrote in the *Liberator*.[47]

Despite their ideological differences, Higginson admired a number of Republicans, most especially John Andrew and Senator Charles Sumner, who himself understood the critical role that militant abolitionists played in New England party politics. As Wendell Phillips once remarked to Sumner, "Our agitation, you know, helps keep yours alive in the [Republican] rank and file." At length, Garrison made his position clear, publishing a statement in which he praised Republicans for standing up to "the Slave Power." In actual policy, as opposed to pure dogma, Garrison editorialized, he could not see that the Radical Abolitionists differed materially from the Republicans. During his single term in Congress in the mid-1850s, Garrison added, Smith's actions were essentially the same as the majority of antislavery Republicans. Higginson agreed. As more Liberty voters defected to the Republicans, he argued, much of the "old bitterness" between abolitionists and former Free Soil Party moderates waned. Sumner and Senator Henry Wilson in particular, Higginson observed, "were in constant and hearty intercourse with the Garrisonian apostles."[48]

Other abolitionists followed. In Seneca Falls, New York, abolitionist Henry Stanton publicly endorsed the Republican ticket, despite the fact that his wife, Elizabeth Cady, was Smith's cousin. George Luther Stearns, an old ally of Higginson's from their Kansas emigration crusade, came around, as did Samuel Joseph May. Previously a Garrisonian nonvoter, May praised the Republicans as the party "the slaveholders most fear," and one moving in the right direction. At the September Worcester Anti-Slavery Convention, Higginson clarified his thinking on the matter. Better, he admitted, to elect an avowed abolitionist, "but before we could have [Stephen] Foster for President, however desirable that would be, we must have Lincoln." Lucy Stone backed her old friend and also lauded Garrison's editorial. Foster was furious. "I love my friend Higginson," he rose to say, "but if there is anything I loathe, it is his opinions." The two never agreed on the issue, though Foster's anger soon cooled, and Higginson was so fond of the anecdote that years later he included it in his essay "Anti-Slavery Days."[49]

During the last weeks of the campaign, all signs pointed to a Republican victory. On October 9, voters in Ohio, Pennsylvania, and Indiana flocked to the polls to select new governors. President Buchanan had carried his home state of Pennsylvania in 1856 by a comfortable margin. This time the Republican gubernatorial candidate won by thirty thousand votes. In Seneca Falls, abolitionists Henry and Elizabeth Cady Stanton delighted in the coming victory. Writing to her son just before the family's

Thanksgiving—then celebrated early in the month—Elizabeth thought it a blessing this would be "the last time we shall be compelled to insult the Good Father by thanking him that we are a slave holding Republic."[50]

Higginson agreed that the Southern states would secede should Lincoln win, and, like the Stantons, he was not frightened by the prospect. For years, he had championed disunion, although that of New England from the rest of a racist nation. The only question remaining was whether secession and Southern independence might be accomplished peacefully, and, should Southern whites begin to fire upon Northerners, whether he would have to take his old Sharps rifle out of its case.

7

"A fighting parson"

1861–1862

"Civil war has at last begun," trumpeted the *New York Herald* on April 13. "A terrible fight is at this moment going on between Fort Sumter and the fortifications by which it is surrounded." In Worcester, reports that Confederate shore batteries had fired upon a U.S. military installation "produced the greatest excitement." A "vast crowd," Higginson wrote his mother, gathered around the office of the *Worcester Spy*, waiting for the latest telegraphic updates from Washington and "discussing the news which is given them in extras." Massachusetts men, so bitterly divided along partisan lines only months before, announced themselves ready to support the Lincoln administration. "Never before" in Worcester, Higginson assured his mother, had he witnessed such "absolute unanimity on a single subject" as he did on the city's determination to protect the nation.[1]

As had many, Higginson had seen the dark clouds gathering ever since South Carolina's secession the previous December. Wealthy Massachusetts cotton industrialists hoped to avoid any conflict that might damage their profits, however, and endorsed various proposals designed to conciliate the South then before Congress. In that atmosphere, even Boston grew hostile to abolitionist voices. The uncompromising Wendell Phillips found it increasingly difficult to secure a stage, and, when he did, mobs in both the audience and the streets shouted him down and threatened his life. To protect Phillips and antislavery congregations after a crowd smashed the windows of a Black church on Joy Street, Higginson, Oliver Wendell Holmes Jr., and Norwood "Pen" Hallowell formed a band to guard speakers and protect abolitionist homes and churches. On one occasion at Boston's Music Hall, the guards smuggled Phillips onto the stage but were forced to retreat through a side entrance after being confronted by what Hallowell described as "a howling mob." The armed band formed ranks around Phillips and "fought" their way down a nearby alley, followed by "a great crowd, hooting and howling." The group got Phillips safely home, where the orator spent the remainder of the evening defending his house with a pike once owned by John Brown.[2]

Two weeks later, on January 24, hostility against abolitionists grew worse when the Massachusetts Anti-Slavery Society convened for their twenty-fourth annual meeting. Hoping to secure the legislature's protection, the Society requested the use of the statehouse, only to have the assembly deny the plea by a lopsided vote of 69 to 13. The Society then settled upon Boston's Tremont Temple. "I was again in service with the same body of followers already described to defend the meeting," Higginson later wrote. Suddenly a "body of men" crashed through the outer doors and rushed toward the stage. Higginson recalled that he had his hand on his revolver when he realized that the "invaders" were led by Mayor Joseph Wightman, who demanded that the Society vacate the hall. Phillips refused to leave the stage, so Wightman's group sought to drown him out. "Higginson made himself heard through the storm, and spoke in a very manly and effective style," Lydia Maria Child informed her friend, abolitionist Sarah Shaw. At length, Phillips was allowed to finish. Higginson spoke next, shouting that he would "take his stand upon the right of free speech." All of this "looked like a coming storm," Higginson remembered. "It was observable that men were beginning to use firearms more, even in New England."[3]

Higginson finally did gain entry into the state legislature the next afternoon as the assembly debated the repeal of the state's 1855 personal liberty law, which afforded accused runaways a modicum of legal protection. In hopes of appeasing the seceding states, a coalition of Democrats and moderate Republicans in Washington wished to repeal such Northern laws, which were passed in the wake of the Fugitive Slave Law. Higginson, Phillips, and Boston minister J. Sella Martin, once a fugitive from Alabama, arrived to "remonstrate against its repeal." To Higginson's surprise, one of the Republicans willing to revoke these protections was Senator William Seward. "I cannot agree with you and Mr. Seward about the Union," Higginson explained to one inquiring Republican, "because I think the Free States without the Slave will instantly command an influence [abroad], moral and material, which is denied us now." Democratic editors, who remembered Higginson's role in Harpers Ferry, saw it differently. "Higginson and several other niggers and Abolitionists appeared before the special Legislative Committee," one Iowa newspaper groused, but it was all in vain, as the personal liberty law "will undoubtedly be repealed."[4]

16   THE BALLAD OF THE

That the black body guard might as well keep away,
'Twas a waste of good money to give them their pay;
And Phillips might save his miserly pelf,
For he was a *black guard* entire of himself.

And there, too, sat the Reverend Higginson,
The Yankee Chadband, a regular Stiggins' son,—

Rev. T. W. Higginson, a model " no concession," " not an inch," ultra Republican.

Figure 7.1 Thirty-seven years Higginson's elder, Harvard graduate Lucius Sargent shared his passion for temperance, writing, and women's rights—his cousin was playwright and feminist Judith Sargent Murray. But he regarded abolitionists as a danger to the republic, and his *Ballad of the Abolition Blunderbuss* (Boston, 1861) attacked Higginson as a "Yankee Chadband," a hypocrite in Charles Dickens's *Bleak House*. From the author's collection.

Because of such conservative efforts, President Lincoln's call for seventy-five thousand volunteers to put down the rebellion and force the seceded states back into the Union left Higginson deeply troubled. Ever since his first trip to Kansas, Higginson, a confirmed disunionist, "never had doubted that a farther conflict of some sort was impending." As he had argued for years, a separation of the free and slave states would render the Fugitive Slave Act a nullity and dislocate slavery across the Upper South. The 1st Regiment of Artillery that was desperately manning Sumter was based in Fort Independence in Boston harbor, so those were Massachusetts men under fire. But despite his reluctant vote for Lincoln the previous November, Higginson guessed that the president's attempts to both subdue and placate white Southerners meant the conflict would not soon become a crusade against slavery. Garrison agreed, wondering in the pages of the *Liberator* whether "our troops" would be risking their lives in the cause of abolition or dying to restore a Constitution that protected slaveholders. Even so, Higginson took a new interest in what he called "military books," scribbled down "notes on fortifications," and began to study "the principles of attack and defense."[5]

If Higginson could not influence the policies of the War Department, he hoped to take advantage of the state-centered nature of the American military. Traditionally, recruits enlisted in state regiments, which were then folded into a U.S. Army brigade (of four or five regiments). Higginson contacted his old ally John A. Andrew, recently elected governor of Massachusetts, about the possibility of raising a regiment of militant abolitionists, including Salmon Brown, James Montgomery, and some of the latter's Kansas men. "The only way for anti-slavery men to share in the control is to share in the sacrifices," Higginson observed. "All I ask, now, is an opportunity to fight, *under orders*, carrying with me such men as I can raise." The nation's capital was as yet unprotected, and Higginson argued that if his unit moved into the mountains of western Virginia, that could fulfill John Brown's plan to liberate slaves while drawing rebel forces away from the capital.[6]

Word of the proposed regiment quickly spread through the antislavery community. John Bailey, a young bank clerk and Lincoln supporter from Milford, wrote to say that he was "anxious to act well" for the nation so long as some Americans remained enslaved. John Brown Jr., who shared his father's habit of underlining key words for emphasis, wrote from Ohio to say he was "not yet willing to again run the gantlets of *both* North and South." Yet he thought it wise to "*prepare*, and *act, when* the sympathies of the

North would sustain us." C. C. Chickering heard that Higginson was "getting up a band of picked men, of the John Brown stamp," and he and his friends were ready to enlist. One writer was so enthusiastic about the project that he wanted to equip them all, although his financial circumstances allowed him only to "offer to buy somebody a pair of shoes." Young attorney A. D. Jackson was ready to sign up, though preferring not to serve alongside "men who do not wish to introduce the Anti-Slavery element into the contest." Yet another wrote that "every Abolitionist feels more inclined [to] operate against Slavery than Secession." E. Y. White was all in as well. His fellows in a radical regiment would carry "the memory of John Brown *in their hearts*."[7]

Andrew assured Higginson that he was in favor of the project, although the fact that the governor also insisted that he could not fund Higginson's militia suggested his doubts about its feasibility. Abolitionist and industrialist George Luther Stearns promised Higginson $500. Samuel Gridley Howe wholeheartedly endorsed the idea and also promised to raise money for arms and wages. Higginson had learned to doubt Howe's promises, however, and so his next stop was the office of Pennsylvania governor Andrew Curtis. Like Andrew, however, Curtis pledged only words, though he would donate "a thousand dollars if John Brown could be brought back to life." Remembering that Brown's raiders included African Americans, Curtis warned Higginson that most people would not "yet tolerate a militia of color." By then, however, New York's Seventh Regiment—including Sarah Shaw's son, Captain Robert Gould Shaw—had arrived in Washington. Those reinforcements, Higginson believed, would protect the capital.[8]

With Higginson's hopes of creating an antislavery regiment every bit as militant, his uncertainty about the looming conflict once more occupied his thoughts. Andrew offered him the rank of major in the Fourth Battalion of Infantry. But Higginson declined, telling Andrew that he was not convinced the federal government was antislavery enough. Southern secession, Higginson reminded his mother, "simply fulfills the predictions made at our Disunion Convention four years ago" that so "horrified" Republicans like Seward. "We *are* two nations & not one nation," he insisted, and everyone could now see that. As did Garrison and the Stantons, Higginson had long thought himself morally tainted by being a citizen of a slave republic, and thanks to secession, he found his feelings justified. "There can never be a re-union with Slavery," he reasoned, because there is "a *reason* for the mutual antagonism" between the free and slave states. Even so, he could not resist writing a short editorial for the *Worcester Spy*, responding to Southern boasts of superior marksmanship. In Kansas, Higginson swore, "the Northern men proved decidedly superior to their opponents, not only in courage and endurance, but in marksmanship also."[9]

* * *

In the months before the war began in earnest in late July 1861 at Virginia's Bull Run Creek, Higginson focused his energies on writing for the *Atlantic Monthly*, churning out a number of small essays on the subjects that had long appealed to him, almost as if he guessed this would be his last chance to write on lighter subjects, given the looming crisis. In the same issues that carried war-related pieces by Charles Francis Adams Jr. and Harriet Beecher Stowe, Higginson returned to old themes, advocating the "Health of our Girls," and extolling the virtues of walking in quiet fields in "My Out-Door Study" and "April Days." His odes to solitude and nature, perhaps unconsciously, reflected his efforts to distance himself from a cause to which he could not devote his entire soul. The closest he came to sectional topics was his denunciation of tobacco use, "A New Counterblast," and his March 1861 essay "Gymnastics." Both pieces reflected his lifelong advocacy of exercise and physical health. Yet at a time when abolitionists routinely characterized the slaveholding South as savage, Higginson's belief that fitness allowed both men and women to tame their violent instincts resonated with his antislavery readers. "There is, or ought to be, in all of us a touch of the untamed gypsy nature," he lectured, "which should be trained, not crushed." Higginson never abandoned his habit of taking long walks, but gymnastics, he contended, trained athletes to learn the sort of discipline and control that forced "animal energy [into] its natural channel."[10]

Higginson was proud enough of his *Atlantic* essays to consider publishing them in book form. But, perhaps distracted by the preparations for war going on all about him, he set that idea aside—until 1882, in any case—and instead started research on a work of history he proposed to call "History of Slave Insurrections." Within months, he changed his mind yet again, deciding to publish a series of *Atlantic* essays on Denmark Vesey's 1822 plot and Nat Turner's 1831 revolt—the two largest antebellum slave rebellions—which might later become book chapters. Crafting nonfiction essays about men he had never met was a new experience for Higginson, but he set about the task with due diligence, writing to antislavery friends in hopes of obtaining memories or documents. William C. Nell loaned him his copy of Henry Bibb's 1849 pamphlet on slave rebelliousness, and Lydia Maria Child sent him the lengthy reminiscences of a free Black carpenter who had worked alongside Vesey in Charleston. Higginson also paid a visit to the Massachusetts Historical Society, where he discovered a series of pamphlets published by Charleston authorities and ministers about the Vesey conspiracy.[11]

Published in June 1861, Higginson's essay was the first to chronicle the nearly forgotten story of Vesey's life, while also reflecting his long-held view that the death of slavery should be brought about by enslaved and free Black Americans. A former slave who had purchased his freedom in 1799 with lottery winnings, Vesey planned for those still enslaved to seize Charleston before sailing for the republic of Haiti. The plot, Higginson argued, was "the most elaborate insurrectionary project ever formed by American slaves," and in "boldness of conception and thoroughness of organization there has been nothing to compare with it." His words echoed his admiration for John Brown, who, although never mentioned in the piece, influenced Higginson's characterization of Vesey's men. "He was remarkable, throughout his trial, for his great presence and composure of mind," Higginson wrote of Rolla Bennett, one of Vesey's closest friends and lieutenants, in a depiction that could easily have described Brown. Higginson also marveled at the refusal of Charleston's then-mayor to admit that slavery was the root cause of slave revolts. He "racked his brain to discover the special causes of the revolt, and never trusted himself to allude to the general one." To Higginson, however, there was little doubt as to why South Carolina had produced a Denmark Vesey, or why that state had been the first to secede after hearing news of Lincoln's election. South Carolinians had never forgotten what had happened, even decades later, he wrote in conclusion.[12]

Two months later, in August, Higginson published his second essay, this one focusing on Nat Turner's 1831 uprising in southern Virginia. Earlier in the decade, Higginson had been critical of Stowe's *Uncle Tom's Cabin* on the grounds that it had no real Black heroes in it. Uncle Tom, Higginson believed, should have resisted, as had Turner. Because whites had died in the revolt, the story was familiar to Northern audiences, and so after a brief description of the events, Higginson drew far more explicit connections to the Harpers Ferry raid and to the need for Black Southerners to rise up against the Confederacy. "John Brown invaded Virginia with nineteen men, and with the avowed resolution to take no life but in self-defense," Higginson argued. As a physical-force abolitionist who had himself packed firearms while in Kansas, he refused to shy away from the kind of revolutionary violence Turner had been willing to employ to liberate Black Virginians.

Brown's plans to move into the hills and Turner's hopes of retreating into the Great Dismal Swamp were each "practicable," had both leaders made better provisions for how to counter white retaliation in the days immediately after the violence began. After the initial bloodshed, Higginson believed, Turner and his men should have hastened to the town of Jerusalem, taken the arms and ammunition found there, and then fled into the Swamp, where Turner "might have sustained himself indefinitely against his pursuers."[13]

Higginson used a variety of Virginia newspapers to construct his narrative, and from them he pulled numerous stories of white vengeance. "The truth is," he wrote about the aftermath of the failed revolt, "it was a reign of Terror." Suspected rebels were murdered without trial, and Black men were "tortured to death, burned, maimed, and subjected to nameless atrocities." Higginson's essay implicitly praised Brown, declined to condemn Turner, and disparaged white vigilantism. The national press therefore took more interest in his Turner essay than in his Vesey piece. Predictably, the reaction broke along partisan lines. Greeley's *New-York Tribune* promoted Higginson's findings as a "timely article appertaining to the state of the country," while one Vermont newspaper thought they provided needed historical context to Stowe's 1856 novel, *Dred: A Tale of the Great Dismal Swamp*. The Democratic *New York Times*, however, perfectly understood Higginson's implicit policy recommendations of defeating the Confederacy by revolutionizing the South and despised him for it. Higginson was promoting "the John Brown method," it editorialized, advocating "blacks, free or slaves," to attack whites with "pikes, scythes, knives, and pitchforks," while "Wendell Phillips and Charles Sumner will sing 'Te Deum'" as the Confederate army "dissolves like the morning mist."[14]

It was clear by late July, however, that the Confederacy was far from dissolving. Newspapers brought word of the debacle at Bull Run. A fierce Confederate charge routed undertrained forces led by General Irvin McDowell, and the Union soldiers, who had expected an easy march into Richmond, instead retreated to Washington in disarray. Almost alone in his opinion, Higginson thought the news not "at all discouraging." Had McDowell's troops invaded deeply into Virginia, reunion might well take place with slavery intact. "But for this reverse," he assured his mother, "we should never have the law of Congress emancipating slaves used in rebellion," as the Confiscation Act of July 1861 allowed for. Although the carefully worded act did not explicitly liberate bondsmen who were being used by the Confederate military to build fortifications, it did establish a national policy of prohibiting the return of runaways, which border state officers had been inclined to do, provided their masters were Union loyalists. "Now for the first time it is a war of emancipation," Higginson mused. "I am satisfied that we are gravitating toward a bolder anti-slavery policy." He took solace also in the fact that thanks to Southern intransigence, Congress had not approved of any concessions designed to seduce the Lower South back into the Union, "which would have destroyed our consistency without strengthening our position."[15]

In early September, former Massachusetts state senator Benjamin Butler, now a U.S. Army general, spoke in Worcester. Just months before, while stationed at Fort Monroe, Virginia, Butler had permitted a handful of runaways into the garrison, suggesting to his War Department superiors that they should be regarded as "contraband of war," which helped produce the Confiscation Act. Butler told his audience that "wherever our armies went they must carry Freedom with them." After Bull Run, Higginson rethought his earlier view of service, concluding that "anti-slavery men were leaving the war altogether too much in the hands of Democrats." Mary's health, previously a consideration, had improved. When Governor Andrew announced that yet another state regiment was to be constituted, Higginson resolved to get involved. Without waiting for authorization from the governor, he opened a recruiting office in Worcester. Being so well known among the abolitionist community and particularly among the city's young men—"through the athletic clubs and drill clubs"—he had little difficulty in raising two companies of two hundred men.[16]

Authorization from the governor soon arrived. Rumor had it that Andrew would appoint Captain Rufus Saxton the unit's senior officer. Saxton was an antislavery man who had taken part in the November 1861 Battle of Port Royal, which had placed Beaufort, South Carolina, and many of the sea islands in Union hands. But the commission went to Higginson. "Mary has of course taken this with her usual courage," Higginson told his mother, regarding it as "a conviction of duty." He expected to serve as a desk captain somewhere in Massachusetts, but even so he made plans to leave Mary in the hands of her niece Greta and three others. "Fortunately, she is growing rather better," Higginson thought, although perhaps "not as well as when [he] went to Kansas." A gifted organizer once he put his mind to it, Higginson promptly wrote to James Freeman Clarke, offering him the position of regimental chaplain, and then began to drill his recruits. Having pored over a handful of army manuals, he was able to put his young charges through their paces. He was surprised to discover "how little all this militia training amounts to," although like many a commander in the coming years, Higginson would learn the difference between practicing maneuvers in camp and acting in the face of withering fire.[17]

Higginson continued to believe that the conflict would be of short duration. "I have not the slightest idea that the Free States will hold out three years," he wrote his mother, suspecting that the nation would fall apart before then. Not that he had any confidence that the Confederacy could sustain itself for even that long "for want of money." This made it imperative, he thought, to hasten the drive to transform the war into an abolition conflict. In a speech widely reprinted, at least in the Republican press, Higginson pronounced it "absurd to attempt to carry on the war without striking at slavery." This would be like an attempt to storm hell "without interfering with the personal comfort of Satan." As he had prophesied for well over a decade, so long as slavery existed, there could be no sectional peace.[18]

* * *

Just as Higginson's efforts neared fruition, his as-yet-unnumbered regiment fell victim to a power struggle between Governor Andrew and General Butler over who ultimately controlled the Department of New England, a district of six states created in October 1861. When outgoing secretary of war Simon Cameron took Butler's part in the dispute in early February 1862, the governor instructed Higginson to cease his efforts, and "the whole affair," Higginson later wrote, "proved abortive." Having thrown himself into the project, Higginson found the disappointment painful. He promptly returned to his writing. Although Thoreau had published *Walden* in 1854, Higginson had evidently never read it; when Thoreau sent him a copy, he thought it very fine—"rising into sublimity at the last." Higginson had complained to *Atlantic Monthly* editor James Fields that his entire family regarded the most recent issue as "a decidedly poor number," weak in content and lacking anything on the war or emancipation. Believing it incumbent upon himself to rectify that problem, he mailed Fields several essays. "Snow" and "Midwinter" were typical Higginson essays, both describing long walks on a wintry day. Somewhat different was his "Letter to a Young Contributor."[19]

Although Higginson had managed to make a good living with his pen, and Fields cheerfully accepted anything Higginson sent his way, he also possessed self-awareness enough to understand that in a century's time, readers would not find his odes to nature as compelling as anything written by Emerson or Thoreau. As a result, some of his "Letter" merely offered commonplace guidance on how to become a published author. Most of it, however, was devoted to why prospective writers should not allow themselves to be crippled by self-doubt. After reminding his readers that "every editor is always hungering and thirsting after novelties," he turned to the sort of inspirational advice he had surely given himself over the years: "Have faith enough in your own individuality. A man has not much intellectual capital who cannot allow himself a brief interval of modesty." Higginson scorned writers who imitated popular English novelists—such as Walter Scott, Dickens, or Thackeray—and he found much to praise in his own country: "Do not shrink from Americanisms." American literature, he believed, was now out of its infancy. Most of all, as a man who knew his own mind and judged his value to society to be high, Higginson warned his theoretical young contributor not to waste any time in trying to impress others with "the merit of your own performance." If writers did not believe their own prose, there was nothing they could do to "vindicate it." Should they never see their work in print, that did not mean they should cease their labors or think them unworthy. "Many fine geniuses have been long neglected," he concluded, before adding, presciently, "but what would become of us, if all the neglected were to turn out to be geniuses?"[20]

A reply was not long in coming. Walking home from the gymnasium on April 17, Higginson stopped at the post office to collect his mail. Waiting for him was an envelope postmarked from the town of Amherst. He tore it open and out tumbled four poems and a short note. "Are you too deeply occupied to say if my Verse is alive?" the brief letter began. "Should you think it breathed, and had you the leisure to tell me, I should feel quick gratitude." Years later, Higginson still marveled that "the most curious thing about the letter was the total absence of a signature." Inside the envelope, however, was a smaller one that contained a blank card on which she had penciled her name. "I enclose my name, asking you, if you please, sir, to tell me what is true?" The signature on the card, "in a handwriting so peculiar," was that of Emily Dickinson.[21]

"The impression of a wholly new and original poetic genius was as distinct on my mind at the first reading of these four poems," Higginson later reflected. Her work was so unlike his own conventional poems that he was bewildered by them, simultaneously "so remarkable" and yet "elusive of criticism." He did think it necessary, however, to provide Dickinson with some editorial suggestions of line editing and punctuation, followed by a series of queries as to what she was reading, how old she was, what sort of education she had obtained, and whether she had already published any of her poems. Dickinson responded immediately, and despite Higginson's admonition that writers should follow their own muse, she adopted his suggestions, saying "the surgery [was] not so painful" as she had supposed it might be. Dickinson's responses made it clear why she valued the older and much published author. Her mother, she admitted, "does not care for thought," while her father bought her "many books, but begs me not to read them, because he fears they joggle the mind." Her family was "religious, except me," she added. She admired the English romantic poet John Keats but had not read Walt Whitman's 1855 *Leaves of Grass*, as her father denounced it as "disgraceful."[22]

Each of Higginson's letters brought an instant reply, all in "the same birdlike script." Every missive contained new poems, and Higginson quickly recognized that his advice to follow more traditional forms paled against her brilliance. "Here was already manifest that defiance of form, never through carelessness, and never precisely from whim, which so marked her." Changing her word order would allow for her lines to rhyme, "but no; she was intent upon her thought, and it would not have satisfied her to make the change." Even so, Dickinson clearly desired his advice, but not, she claimed, because of his ability to get his essays and poems published. She did not wish to be a bother. "Because you have much business, besides the growth of me, you will appoint, yourself, how often I shall come, without your inconvenience. And if at any time you regret you received me, or I prove a different fabric to that you supposed, you must banish me." She hoped he would continue to read her poems, concluding one letter with the simple but touching request: "Will you be my preceptor, Mr. Higginson?"[23]

Dickinson evidently tried to take Higginson's editorial advice to heart, but only to a point. "I had no Monarch in my life, and cannot rule myself," she admitted to him. She promised to "observe your precept," although she did not "understand it, always." As but a workaday poet himself, Higginson was flattered by her requests that he offer improvements even as he doubted that she could tame what he regarded as her "wayward" forms. He noted that Dickinson kept him at arm's length in other ways as well. When he asked her for a *carte de visite*—a posed photographic portrait done in a studio—she replied, evasively, that she "had no portrait, now," offering instead that she was "small, like the Wren," with hair "like the Chestnut Bur" and eyes "like the Sherry in the Glass, that the Guest leaves. Would this do just as well?"[24]

In between reading Dickinson's poems, which arrived three or four in each post, Higginson found time to research one more slave conspiracy. While digging into Vesey and Turner, he had discovered evidence of a third, which, while even more "obscure in the darkness of half a century," was "perhaps more wide in its outlines than that of either." In Harvard's library, he pored over yellowing Virginia and New York newspapers from the fall of 1800, although he lamented that he was unable to locate several key documents, including any official statements from Virginia's governor. The historian in him observed that had he had those at his disposal, they "would no doubt have enlarged, and very probably corrected," his narrative. But he forged ahead, and Northern papers reported that the *Atlantic Monthly* for September 1862 would carry "Gabriel's Defeat, by Thomas Wentworth Higginson."[25]

The essay, about a failed conspiracy organized near Richmond by an enslaved blacksmith named Gabriel, made it clearer yet that while trying to craft an accurate picture of the past, Higginson continued to be inspired by John Brown and to believe that to absolve the nation's sins, the Civil War had to become a revolutionary abolition war. One newspaper reported at the time of Gabriel's attempt, incorrectly (although Higginson could not know that), that if his plan to capture Richmond and take Governor James Monroe hostage failed, he intended to retreat into the hills. "John Brown was therefore anticipated by Gabriel sixty years before," Higginson wrote, "in believing the Virginia mountains" might serve as "a place of refuge for fugitive slaves." Higginson was correct in regarding Gabriel's execution as a turning point in the history of the South. "Liberty was the creed or cant of the day," he observed. "Slavery was habitually recognized as a misfortune and an error," as even Thomas Jefferson had conceded in his *Notes on the State of Virginia*, "itself an anti-slavery tract." Had slavery ended decades before in the state that was home to more slaves than any other, Higginson mused, Americans would not now be slaughtering one another in northern Virginia. Two weeks after the essay appeared, the war witnessed its single bloodiest day at Antietam Creek, Maryland, a battle that prompted President Lincoln to retrieve a document he had drafted two months earlier and locked in his desk drawer.[26]

* * *

Events to the south soon drew Higginson away from his desk. In late February 1862, Congress discontinued the Department of New England, and its commander, General Butler, was dispatched to direct the land forces assisting the navy in the capture of New Orleans. With Governor Andrew again in charge of the state regiments, Higginson began to think anew about military service. In March, he contacted Worcester's mayor, saying that he did not "wish to be exempted on the score of profession, not being properly a clergyman" for some years. He was reluctant to broach the topic with Mary, but he decided that he would be a "broken man for the remainder of [his] days" if he continued to "sacrifice the public duty to this domestic one." Four Massachusetts regiments had taken part in the previous fall's humiliating defeat at the hands of Confederate forces at Ball's Bluff, Virginia. Norwood "Pen" Hallowell and Oliver Wendell Holmes Jr., Higginson's young allies in protecting abolitionist speakers (and in the case of Holmes, a future Supreme Court justice), were among those who were badly wounded but survived the debacle.[27]

Finally, in August Higginson signed three-year enlistment papers with the rank of captain. He had originally considered a shorter period of service, but as the young men of his acquaintance scorned short enlistments, he determined that he would let his actions match his words. Mary, he assured his mother, "will make the best of it, as she always does," and would either settle in a rooming house in Boston or remain in Worcester in the care of Caroline Andrews, an old friend from Newburyport. Given the "uncertainties of human life" in a time in which death visited both young and old, he reminded his mother, the dangers "seem hardly greater in war than in peace." Not surprisingly, the pacifist Garrison's response was mixed, writing that Higginson was not really "a Garrisonian abolitionist" because he had been supporting the Republican Party.[28]

The regiment, formally christened the 51st Massachusetts, filled quickly. "The city of Worcester is the big Abolition centre of Massachusetts," one friendly editor gushed, attributing this to Higginson. Colonel Augustus Sprague, the sheriff of Worcester County, took command of the regiment, with Dwight Foster, the state attorney general and "one of our best men," in Higginson's estimation, as lieutenant colonel. Higginson drilled his recruits for two hours each day. "They learn fast and their marching is much praised," he boasted. "I don't think I ever did anything better than I have done all this, so far." His lieutenants he well knew from hours spent in the gymnasium. In late August, his two companies relocated to barracks just outside of Boston at Camp John Wool, and as they marched toward the train station, the soldiers passed the Lincoln House, the boarding house that was to be Mary's home for the coming months. The spectacle met with Mary's approval and "edification," or at least that was Higginson's hope. His efforts made the news from Brattleboro, Vermont, where his brother Dr. Francis Higginson resided, to

New Bern, North Carolina, as it was expected that the 51st would soon sail south to join General John Foster's Department of North Carolina in the liberated coastal town.[29]

Higginson took pride in the sergeants of the ten companies, all of them from New England, that comprised the 51st. Although none was "highly cultivated" by Harvard standards, all were "intelligent & manly & the majority are fine looking." Correctly guessing that many of his Irish-born Catholic privates regarded their brahmin officer with suspicion, Higginson transferred several to other regiments, although he thought it somewhat humorous that "an inebriated Irish private" was heard singing "Old Higgie is so strict, so strict." Strict or not, Higginson did allow for weekly musicals. "Candles are stuck about the rafters," he told his mother, and "two fiddlers hoisted on a top bunk." The men engaged in "country dances," crashing about the barracks in "thorough heel-and-toe work" and creating such a din that Higginson could hear it even as he wrote. Away from his home and with his hours consumed by army paperwork, he had little time to review Dickinson's latest poems. His responses "might take time," Higginson warned her, which promoted wistful queries like hers of October 6: "Did I displease you, Mr. Higginson? But won't you tell me how?"[30]

Dickinson's isolation from the war tested Higginson's patience. Her letters, often "plaintive [and] always terse," fell to the bottom of a seemingly endless stack of official reports. "I have not had a trace of ennui, because I have no leisure," Higginson reported to his mother, together with an apology for not having written regularly. Nonetheless he cheerfully accepted his lack of free time. In addition to hectic days of drilling and correspondence, "four evenings in the week" were consumed with meetings. He was content to be a captain rather than a colonel, as he believed it folly for his "raw" regiment of Massachusetts clerks and farm boys to be led by someone of his limited experience. The regiment had yet to be issued rifles, but even so he warned his mother that they might be ordered to North Carolina at any moment. As for Higginson's claim, made on November 2, that he was happy not to have been promoted above the rank of "senior captain," he little guessed what the coming week's mail held in store for him.[31]

Returning to his room after yet another day of drilling, Higginson found a letter on his camp table, dated November 5 and sent from Beaufort, South Carolina. "I am organizing the 1st Regiment of South Carolina Volunteers" recruited from the Black runaways and refugees crowding into Beaufort, wrote General Rufus Saxton, the antislavery West Pointer Higginson had once hoped would lead his abortive regiment. "I take pleasure in offering you the position of Colonel in it, and hope that you may be induced to accept." Accompanying the offer was a lengthy explanation penned by Reverend James Fowler, a chaplain of Higginson's acquaintance. Several Massachusetts men had advanced Higginson's name to Saxton, he wrote, given his "deep interest in the cause" of antislavery. As did Higginson, Fowler hoped to transform the conflict into an abolition war, believing that the Black regiment could be the "solution to the whole Negro question." Saxton promised not to appoint any other man colonel until he heard from Higginson, and he begged him not to decline the position until he could tour the Carolina Sea Islands to judge the situation for himself.[32]

Higginson first hastened to Worcester to gauge Mary's response, and while he declined to pass news of her reaction along to his mother, he took solace in Greta's pleasure. "Will not Uncle Wentworth be in bliss!" she exclaimed. "A thousand men, every one as black as a coal." He then telegraphed Governor Andrew, who was in Washington, to obtain leave to travel to South Carolina and meet with Saxton. Andrew quickly confirmed the request, but when Higginson reached Manhattan, the quartermaster of the USS *Cosmopolitan* told him the ship was completely full and doubted that Saxton's pass would guarantee passage. Higginson next sought out the steamer's captain, who offered "a mattress on the cabin floor" if he was interested. Higginson accepted, and over the next three days met most of his fellow passengers. Many were army officers; others were teachers who had been employed by a school for Black children in Boston and now planned to teach in Beaufort as part of what was already known as the "Port Royal Experiment." "There is no love lost between these elements," Higginson observed, with the more conservative officers pronouncing the teachers guilty of "sectarianism" and the teachers denouncing the officers as "proslavery." Higginson spoke also with common soldiers, who warned him of the consensus among the ranks "that the negroes will not fight." Higginson thought otherwise.[33]

Sunday, November 23, found the *Cosmopolitan* just off the coast of Cape Fear, and the Massachusetts native who had not journeyed south since 1841 watched with fascination as the "mysterious land" passed by. Louisa had counseled against the appointment, arguing that her son should not "exchange the certain for the uncertain." But Higginson had already grown bored with the 51st, his labors having become "too smooth." Any of his junior officers there could fulfill his duties. By comparison, the colonelcy of the 1st South Carolina was "a position of great importance." He had long believed that anyone who commanded a Black regiment would perform "the most important service in the history of the War," although he never imagined that he would be the man to do it. At length, the steamer reached Beaufort and docked alongside other boats, among them the schooner *Planter*, a Confederate vessel liberated by Robert Smalls, formerly an enslaved mariner. Higginson disembarked and asked for directions to Saxton's headquarters. Off in the woods, Higginson spied a "broad encampment of white tents." A young officer pointed to "your regiment of Maroons," a term Higginson judged to be particularly fitting.[34]

Saxton welcomed his prospective colonel warmly, and Higginson took an immediate liking to the general, who was just one year his junior. "A shortish compact man, with a mild absorbed face," Higginson noted. Saxton "is quite absorbed in this regiment," and he "gave up all else for me." Saxton ordered several companies of the 1st Infantry to be mustered in for Higginson's inspection, and he marveled that they were "all black as coals as Margaret predicted, not a mulatto among them." He noted also that they wore the red pantaloons of the Zouaves, trousers donned by French regiments then serving in North Africa. Higginson thought that Black soldiers should dress just as did white ones, but Saxton was a man of "simple New England good sense and earnestness," and his "zeal for these poor people [was] inexhaustible." Although already inclined to accept Saxton's offer, Higginson was "embarrassed" at Saxton's confidence in him, given his lack of military experience. He hoped that Saxton did not "overlook means in his zeal for ends."[35]

In hopes of convincing Higginson to accept the task, Saxton ordered several companies to fall in for inspection. After Saxton said a few words of introduction, Higginson strolled among them. Their faces were "impenetrable," a habit, he guessed, having learned never to show emotion around white men. Higginson paused to speak with one soldier, who had been slightly wounded in an upriver raid in search of lumber. "Did you think that was more than you bargained for?" Higginson inquired. The Black private's answer came without hesitation: "I been a-ticking, Mas'r, *da's jess what I went for.*" Later that evening, Higginson carefully transcribed the freedman's accent and made a mental note to remind any soldiers under his command not to refer to white officers as "masters." He was pleased with his first exchange with the recruits.[36]

Much of what he discovered about this handful of raw soldiers concerned Higginson, however. The history of the regiment was a troubled one. Originally organized in April 1862 by General David Hunter, a New York–born career soldier who had been given command of the Department of the South (comprising Georgia, South Carolina, and Florida), the unit was to be filled with runaways fleeing toward the Carolina coast. The optimistic Hunter begged the War Department to ship him fifty thousand rifles and an equal number of "scarlet pantaloons" with which to arm and clothe men as loyal as he "could find in the country." Hunter never directly stated that he planned to arm runaway slaves, largely because he was acting well in advance of any statements from Washington regarding Black liberation. Some refugees enthusiastically signed on, but others had good cause to distrust all white men, and so Hunter finally resorted to conscripting men from the Sea Islands into his unit. When Hunter then tried to encourage enlistments by declaring free all slaves in the three states of his department, an exasperated Lincoln overruled his decree and finally, in late September, removed him as commander. Watching the fiasco from nearby Port Royal Sound was Charles Francis Adams Jr., a captain in the 1st Massachusetts Cavalry. Hunter, Adams thought, should have waited for both Black Southerners and white Northerners to get accustomed to the idea of Black military service. "The slaves would have moved when the day came," he predicted. Higginson could not have agreed more.[37]

Worse yet, on December 8, 1862, a small number of recruits arrived from the Georgetown region, up the coast. "Such forlorn looking recruits, lame halt & blind & not clearly understanding why they were brought here," Higginson lamented. "I felt like a slave driver as I partitioned them to eager captains, each anxious to make up his number." But just as he was preparing to decline Saxton's offer, he began to notice other things. "Their love of the spelling book is perfectly inexhaustible," he observed, "& they stumbled on by themselves, or aiding each other, with the most pathetic patience." On the evening of December 14, he quietly stood at the edge of that night's "shout," where the men prayed with a "mixture of piety & polka & its castanet-like clapping of hands." An older freedman, whom Higginson guessed to be a "stump orator," stood atop a barrel, "pouring out his mingling of liberty & Methodism in quaint eloquence." One private stepped forward, and Higginson, fascinated by Lowcountry dialects and songs, carefully recorded his prayer: "Let me lib wid de musket in one hand and de Bible in de oder, dat if I die at de muzzle of de musket, die in de water, die on land, I may know I hab de blessed Jesus in my hand, and hab no fear." Another took his place: "I hab leff my wife in de land ob bondage. But when I die, when de blessed morning rises, when I shall stand in de glory, den, O Lord, I shall see my wife

& my little chil'en once more." Higginson promptly sought out Saxton and accepted the colonelcy.[38]

By late 1862, with the U.S. Army growing almost daily as the war dragged on, the selection of colonels for new regiments almost never made national news. Higginson's appointment did, and with President Lincoln's final Emancipation Proclamation set to be issued in but a few days on January 1, Republican editors uniformly praised the choice of a militant abolitionist to lead the nation's first federally approved African American regiment. In an essay titled "A Fighting Parson," the editor of a Cleveland newspaper reminded readers of Higginson's many articles in the *Atlantic Monthly* and hoped that as a good antislavery man Higginson would accept the challenge. One Columbus newspaper was unenthusiastic, although it grudgingly praised Higginson for agreeing to the appointment "as a satisfactory index to his politics." Higginson, the editor observed, was "a lecturer of the radical stripe" and a "white man with African proclivities." The regiment was an "experiment which the Abolitionists have been insisting should be tried." The Columbus editor doubted the test case would prove successful, but promised his readers updates on "the Rev. Colonel Higginson."[39]

Democratic and Southern journals were even less charitable. Several Midwestern and one Kentucky newspaper scoffed at the pretensions of Republican "Abolitionists" to be the "only loyal party in the nation" on the grounds that Higginson, "a reverend," had been appointed to lead the country's first Black regiment. This was the same man, the editors reminded readers, who had organized an 1857 convention that had declared the nation a moral failure and "proposed disunion because of slavery." The appointment "would excite our indignation did it not first stir up our ridicule."[40]

Somewhat more serious were the charges leveled by Kentucky senator Garrett Davis. In a fiery speech that was reprinted in pamphlet form, Davis demanded a resolution calling for a congressional inquiry into the appointment. Higginson "was both a murderer and a traitor," he alleged, for taking part in the attempt to liberate Anthony Burns. While guard James Batchelder's wife and children were sleeping at home, Davis charged, Higginson had caused Batchelder to be "assassinated on the spot." Who fired the shot was unknown, Davis admitted, but as Higginson and his colleague Theodore Parker were supporters of Senator Sumner, he thought it crucial to raise the subject. Higginson "should have been twice hung"—once for the Burns affair and the second time for being a member of the "secret six." "But the present Executive has appointed him colonel of the Massachusetts

Fifty-fourth colored regiment." Lincoln, of course, had played no role in Higginson's selection, and Davis was confusing Higginson with Robert Gould Shaw, the young new commander of the Massachusetts unit. The Black editor of Beaufort's *Free South* rode to Higginson's defense, laughing that his real "unpardonable sin" was his opposition to the Fugitive Slave Law. But Davis continued to renew his demands well into the spring of 1864, when Illinois Republican Lyman Trumbull and Sumner finally called a vote on the resolution to be tabled. The final vote was 29 to 10, with Tennessee Democrat Andrew Johnson joining Davis in the nays.[41]

A few of Higginson's friends worried about the post, not merely because of the chaos of war but fearing the hatred white Southerners held toward the man they saw as John Brown's chief supporter. Poet and abolitionist John Greenleaf Whittier, for one, "tremble[d] in view of its peril. He will be a marked man." Despite his concerns, Whittier maintained that he understood Higginson's motives. "So beautiful in his glorious manhood, with his refinement, culture, and grade," he wrote of Higginson, "leading that wild African regiment to avenge the wrongs of two centuries of slavery! How this one act of his is making his name historic." The editor of Port Royal's *New South*, a newspaper launched by freedmen after the region's liberation, was equally effusive. "Mr. Higginson has laid down the pen to take up the sword," the editor noted. "May he be able to wield the latter as well as he does the former."[42]

For himself, Higginson never worried, at least not in any letter he wrote to Mary or his mother, about the dangers of his new post, assuring his family, as he had ever since the Burns riot, that military duties were no more perilous than everyday life. He did not believe that he was the only man for the job, nor that his few short months as a desk captain had adequately prepared him to lead a regiment of men just weeks out of bondage. But he believed that his life had inexorably led to this moment, and that when presented with the opportunity he could not refuse. "I have been an abolitionist too long, and had known and loved John Brown too well," Higginson later reflected, "not to feel a thrill of joy at last on finding myself in the position where he only wished to be."[43]

8

"Path of duty is the way to glory"

1862–1865

Higginson's return to Worcester was by necessity brief. Mary was settled into the Lincoln boarding house, with Greta Channing and the proprietor to watch over her. He made a quick trip to Vermont to visit his mother, now seventy-six. His unmarried sister Ann and brother Stephen resided in Boston and Cambridge, respectively, while his brother Francis, a doctor, lived in Vermont. All of them could be counted on to assist with their mother. The sibling he felt closest to and regularly corresponded with, Waldo, lived in Boston and was doing his part for the Union by acting as secretary of New England's War Claims Association. Higginson intended to supplement his monthly pay—colonels received a princely $212 by comparison to white privates, who drew but $13 each month—with occasional submissions to the *Atlantic Monthly*.[1]

Although the next two years of his life were to be among the most consequential, Higginson regarded his coming service in South Carolina as a new chapter but one in an ongoing story. For many white officers, a military posting far from home and the sudden transition from civilian tranquility to wartime violence was jarring. But for Higginson, who over the past decade had several times risked his life in the cause of freedom, leading Black troops into combat was little different from following Lewis Hayden through the Boston courthouse door. If Higginson supposed Senator Garrett Davis to be correct in any of his allegations, it was that his dedication to liberty, from attempting to free Anthony Burns to supplying rifles to Kansas free-staters, formed a seamless narrative. As Higginson later phrased it in a poem he titled "Duty," "For all truly noble men or nations the verdict of history is that 'path of duty is the way to glory.'"[2]

By mid-December 1862 Higginson was back in Beaufort. He had no sense of how long he would be there, or for how many more months or years the conflict would drag on. Initially, he had expected that General Ambrose Burnside's plan to cross Virginia's Rappahannock River and race toward

Richmond might bring the war to an early end, and initial rumors in his Beaufort encampment signaled a Union victory. Within days, however, more accurate accounts of the fighting in Fredericksburg revealed that Burnside had suffered over twelve thousand casualties, more than twice that of the entrenched Confederates. "Tonight the officers are rather depressed" by the news, Higginson recorded in his diary on December 21, and he hoped the word would not reach his recruits. It was well, he thought, "that the men know too little of the events of the war to feel excitement or fear." But he was pleased to discover that Seth Rogers, the resident doctor at the Worcester Hydropathic Institution, had accepted his offer to serve as the regiment's surgeon. Rogers, an antislavery Quaker, had been close to Higginson for years, and within the week he reported home that Higginson was a "splendid" leader, "beyond even [Rogers's] anticipation." Like Saxton, Rogers believed that his old friend was precisely the man who could "magically" bring these raw privates "under the military discipline" required to make them a cohesive unit. "Should we possibly ever increase to a brigade," Rogers believed, he could "already foresee that our good Colonel is destined to be the Brigadier General."[3]

Higginson and the men of the First settled into their quarters, which Higginson rechristened "Camp Saxton." The regiment was housed roughly two miles south of Beaufort on an abandoned plantation previously owned by James Joyner Smith. The mansion yet stood, but Higginson instead chose as his headquarters two wall-tents placed end to end, one for his sleeping quarters and the second for his office. Both had floorboards, and his desk, he laughed, was "a bequest of the slaveholders" taken from the big house. On it rested his paperwork, a copy of Victor Hugo's *Les Misérables*, and Shakespeare's *Sonnets*. For a chair, Higginson sat upon an old cane seat lashed to broken bedsteads, and his bed was "made of gun-boxes covered with condemned blankets." But the tent's flaps kept out dampness and drafts "and everything but sand." His days were devoted to drilling his recruits "into fighting trim," and at night he rode about the camp's perimeter, listening to the distant prayer "shouts" and attempting to write down the words of this or that song. Before blowing out his candle, he wrote to Mary or his mother, promising them that he was safe but threatening to eventually return home "jet black" from the Carolina sun. "Do not regret that I am here," he wrote Louisa. "I should have missed the best fortune of my life had I not come."[4]

The regiment had to date raised roughly eight hundred men. Higginson and Saxton planned for the day when they would have a full contingent of

Figure 8.1 As this 1863 image and other photographs taken during Higginson's time in South Carolina reveal, his service as colonel was the only time in his life when he exchanged his iconic cavalry whiskers—which revealed the scar on his chin earned in the failed Burns rescue—for a full beard. Taken just before returning to Beaufort, the photograph shows a robust Higginson whose health was not yet shattered by his near-death experience. From the collection of Graham Russell Gao Hodges.

ten companies of one hundred men each. A single well provided the entire camp with fresh water, but each company had its own latrine and cookhouse, where meals were grilled over an open fire. Behind them stood the soldiers' tents, lined up with precise regularity. Higginson ordered the camp swept clear of debris each day, a process assisted by wild pigs that rooted about. In the heart of the camp stood a huge circular tent constructed of sailcloth, thirty feet in diameter, that the men dubbed "the Pagoda." Ordered built by Chaplain James Fowler, the pavilion could shield two hundred men and was used as both a church and a school. Higginson thought it resembled a dilapidated circus tent but noticed that it never sat empty, given the men's determination to learn how to read.[5]

Christmas arrived, and in honor of the day Higginson dropped the curfew, signaled by the playing of "Taps," and allowed the soldiers "to have their little prayer-meetings as late as they desired." In preparation for January 1, when President Lincoln was expected to issue his final Emancipation Proclamation, Higginson read Saxton's order "of freedom to the regiment, the first slave regiment in the Civil War." Higginson judged the order to be the "finest Christmas present" he had ever received. After writing to Mary, he tried to sleep, but all night he was awakened by the soldiers' "praying and 'shouting' and clattering with hands and heels" about the Pagoda. The former minister thought their "innocent Christmas" joy compared favorably "with some of the convivialities of the 'superior race' hereabouts."[6]

To commemorate the day of jubilee, Saxton issued an order titled "A Happy New Year's Greeting to the Colored People in the Department of the South," together with an invitation to a January 1 celebration at the First's camp. The steamers *Flora* and *Boston* ferried freedpeople from the liberated Sea Islands to Beaufort's docks, and from there the band from the Eighth Maine led the procession to the regiment's drilling grounds in an oak grove behind the Smith mansion. A low stage had been hastily erected. Saxton and Fowler sat toward the rear with Dr. William Henry Brisbane, a federal tax commissioner, and Reverend Mansfield French, who had arrived on the coast as a teacher. Higginson stood on the edge of the stage, flanked by his two favorite Black officers, Sergeant Prince Rivers and Corporal Robert Sutton. Laura Towne, a Philadelphia teacher and abolitionist, found a seat amid the "dense crowd." Higginson, she thought, though a "tall and large man," appeared "small" when standing between his two color-bearers. The ceremony began promptly at 11:30 with a prayer from Chaplain Fowler. Brisbane next stepped forward to read the president's proclamation. Higginson considered that especially appropriate, as the South Carolina–born Brisbane had converted to abolitionism and carried his slaves to freedom in the North. French then presented Higginson with a new regimental flag he had obtained in Manhattan, a fact he had "very conspicuously engraved on the standard."

Thinking the day should be for Black Carolinians, that act and French's praise of white New Yorkers left "a bad taste" in Higginson's mouth.[7]

But then "followed an incident so simple, so touching, so utterly unexpected & startling," he wrote in his journal, that he could scarcely believe it. Just as Higginson received the flag and began to speak, an "elderly male voice" from the front row began to sing, "into which two women's voices immediately blended." The first words floated almost hymnlike above the crowd: "My county 'tis of thee, Sweet land of Liberty." One teacher in the audience noticed that those on the platform began to join in. Higginson turned, shushing, "Leave it to them." The freedpeople in the audience finished the song, with Higginson gazing down at them. Dr. Rogers remembered that Higginson was "so much inspired" that he "made one of his most effective speeches." Higginson thought otherwise. The day marked the first moment "they had ever had a country, the first flag they had ever seen which promised anything to their people," he marveled, and "here while others stood in silence, waiting for my stupid words, these simple souls burst out." The "choked voice of a race" had been, he wrote, "at last unloosed," and nothing he might say could match that eloquence.[8]

As the 1st Infantry neared its full contingent of one thousand men, the War Department prepared to raise a sister regiment of contraband soldiers, the Second South Carolina. To lead the unit, Saxton recommended James Montgomery, currently a captain in the 3rd Kansas and Higginson's old ally in the abortive plot to liberate John Brown. In late January, several days after Montgomery arrived in Beaufort, General David Hunter unexpectedly returned to the coast and paid Higginson a surprise inspection. Although no longer commander of the Department of the South—having been relieved of his command by Lincoln for overstepping his authority—Hunter still enjoyed the support of Northern abolitionists, and Higginson was anxious to earn good publicity for his regiment among the antislavery community. Marching his companies to the parade ground, Higginson displayed his men's skills at close order drills. "Their changes in front, formation in square, and preparation to charge in double column," one Ohio journalist reported, "were executed with a harmonious rapidity and precision scarcely to be surpassed by any regiment." Hunter then addressed the soldiers, saying he saw "no reason why you should not make as good soldiers as any in the world." His brief speech was heavily covered in the Northern press, although one Hartford, Connecticut, editor thought it unfair to "white regiments to have the negroes," who had yet to see combat, "complimented by the first

Figure 8.2 Some Northern abolitionists feared that at the last minute, President Lincoln would decline to issue his promised final Emancipation Proclamation on January 1, 1863, but understanding the importance of Black troops, Higginson never did. The celebration of freedom held at Camp Saxton was attended by teachers Charlotte Forten and Laura Towne, federal and military officials, and a journalist for the *New York Times*, who reported that it "was an important day to the negroes here, and one of which they will long retain the remembrance as the first dawn of freedom." Courtesy of the Library of Congress.

review and inspection." But if Hunter's traditional pleas to patriotism pleased most Republican editors, Higginson wished to appeal to his men in more personal terms. Remembering one of the prayers that had prompted him to accept Saxton's offer, Higginson urged them "to hold up their hands and pledge themselves to be faithful to those in bondage." To "enthusiastic cheers," the soldiers "entered heartily into this." That vow, Higginson supposed, would be "a good thing" to later remind them of, "at any time of discouragement or demoralization."[9]

Among Higginson's chief concerns during those early weeks in January was the rate of desertion, which had been considerable under Hunter. Unlike other commanders of the earliest Black regiments, such as Colonel Robert Gould Shaw, who was soon to take charge of the first unit of Northern freemen, the 54th Massachusetts Volunteer Infantry, Higginson instinctively understood that he had to oversee his men, most of them just weeks out of bondage, with the lightest possible touch. As word filtered inland of a new commander, bondsmen put aside their concerns about military life and fled toward Beaufort. Deserters also began to return, one of them, "his clothes in rags," heading directly for Higginson's tent in hopes of mercy. Higginson simply returned them to their sergeants. "Severe penalties would be wasted on these people," he later reflected, "accustomed as they have been to the most violent passions on the part of white men." While aboard the *Cosmopolitan*, Higginson had inquired of the teachers who had already worked with refugees if the freedmen could "appreciate *justice*." If they did, Higginson believed, "all the rest would be easy." Provided his officers were consistently understanding and kind, there would "be no sort of difficulty." The desertions slowed to a trickle and then stopped.[10]

Higginson also devoted a good portion of each afternoon to walking among the tents, listening to the soldiers' concerns and talking with them about their past lives. One private admitted that he had "been restless, nights," trying to decide whether to stay in slave country or run for Beaufort. When rumors reached the upcountry of the regiment being formed, he told Higginson that "his time to act had come." Unlike white soldiers, the recruit was not fighting for his country and certainly not for "rations and pay, but for wife, children, and people." Talking to another soldier, Higginson, who had recently composed some essays on enslaved rebels, wondered why there "had been so few slave insurrections." The young soldier replied that while he had heard rumors of revolts for years, especially during the presidential election of 1856, rural bondsmen lacked both the knowledge and the weapons to fight back. Each failed conspiracy "left a tradition of [white] terror for many years." Now, both the private and his colonel understood, Carolina Blacks had everything they needed to take part in what constituted the largest African American uprising in the nation's history.[11]

One of the features that made the First South Carolina unlike later Black regiments, and similar to white units, was their geographical cohesion. After Lincoln called up seventy-five thousand militiamen in the days after Sumter, white men flocked to county courthouses with their brothers, cousins, and friends and enlisted in regiments that bore state designations. By comparison, because conservative Northern governors were reluctant to follow Andrew's lead in raising Black regiments, the freemen who caught trains to Boston to volunteer for the Massachusetts 54th hailed from all over. They arrived from Northern states, loyal Upper South states, Confederate states, Canada, the Caribbean, and the western territories. Higginson's volunteers, to a man, had escaped from estates along the Carolina and Georgia coast and northern Florida. In most cases, they had fled in groups, sometimes with their families. On occasion, all the enslaved from a single plantation left for Beaufort in the dead of night. Although the colonel who had shared a Boston stage with Frederick Douglass never had any doubts that Black men could be effective combatants, what he witnessed in his camp reminded him of the "courage" it required to risk bodily harm by trying to reach Union lines. "There were more than a hundred men in the ranks," he understood, "who had voluntarily met more dangers in their escape from slavery" than he or any of his "young captains had incurred in all their lives."[12]

Higginson quickly grasped that as old friends and family members enrolled in the First, previous plantation hierarchies promptly reemerged. Leaders within the slave community—skilled artisans, literate domestics, and drivers—instinctively resumed their places within the military's ranks. Burdened by paperwork and reports, Higginson was content to turn the day-to-day management and training of his regiment over to his white captains and Black officers. The two he relied upon the most were Sergeant Rivers and Corporal Sutton. The literate former coachman to Henry Middleton Stuart, whose Oak Point estate was close enough to Beaufort to allow for escape, Rivers provided Higginson with daily accounts on the one hundred men in his company. He had been promoted to sergeant by Hunter, and while accompanying the general to Manhattan, had discovered that racism was not a strictly Southern phenomenon. While walking down Broadway, Rivers was attacked by toughs who objected to the chevrons on his arm. A "splendid figure of a man"—in Higginson's estimation—Rivers fought them off. "There is not a white officer in this regiment who has more administrative ability," Higginson marveled, "or more absolute authority of the men." "They do not love him, but his mere presence has controlling power over them."[13]

Higginson's other favorite, Corporal Sutton, had formerly been enslaved on the Alberti estate along the St. Mary's River, which divided Georgia from Florida. Laboring as a ship's pilot and lumberman at Woodstock Mills, a steam-powered sawmill run by slaves, Sutton knew the region's waterways well enough to escape in a canoe of his own creation. Having discovered the route to freedom, he returned to liberate his wife and child. Although illiterate, the "large, powerful" Sutton easily dominated his men, and his desire to learn impressed his colonel. "He had a massive brain and a far more meditative and systematic outlook" than those of greater education, Higginson later recalled. The corporal "yearned and pined for intellectual companionship," sitting up late with Higginson and discussing national affairs. Higginson was particularly impressed that Sutton understood the connection between abolitionism and military success. In that, Higginson wrote in his journal, "I could teach him nothing, and he taught me much."[14]

When it came to his white officers, Higginson was less concerned about their lack of previous military experience than he was with finding young men with solid antislavery credentials. Well aware that his soldiers had been trained from childhood never to trust white men, Higginson believed that the regiment's senior officers had to learn the "value of the habitual courtesies of the regular army." More than once, he had to caution his captains not to call the men by their first names but to use their surname or rank. In the same way, Higginson reminded the privates that they should not obey their officers simply because they were white but because they were superior officers. He also observed that when he spoke to his soldiers, they tended to doff their caps. Only slaves did that, he lectured them; soldiers saluted. His senior staff was required to return any salute. For recruits just out of bondage, especially for those who carried scars on their backs, that lesson was not easily learned. But as the regiment had capable men like Sutton and Rivers, the Black officers quickly caught on.[15]

The one deviation from the officer's manual that Higginson did permit was allowing the enlisted men to bypass both their Black sergeants and white captains and appeal directly to him with their concerns. The freedmen had "a particular dislike of all *intermediate* controls," he noted, as invariably they wished to go straight to him. He guessed this was partly due to the "old habit of appealing to the master against the overseer." But he suspected it was also because his soldiers had such distrust of white people that asking them to "trust more than one at a time was too much." He was gratified that his men had faith in him, and with patience and time, they would learn to trust his captains as well. "We, their officers, did not go there to teach lessons, but to receive them." Unhappily, that was never to be true of all white officers in the region. Captain Charles Steedman, a Charleston-born loyalist, commanded the steamer *Paul Jones* and on occasion ferried the soldiers of the First around the coast. Higginson admired his loyalty and thought him "manly," but Steedman had no use for antislavery colonels. The First was "composed entirely of Niggers & the fanatical sort of Nigger worshippers," he complained to his wife. "You have no idea how annoying it has been to me to be obligated to act with these people."[16]

Higginson knew that forcing Confederate officers to respect his men was highly unlikely. He was, nonetheless, determined to try. With Confederate forces just up the Broad and Coosaw rivers from Beaufort, the two sides often communicated with one another. In an episode that made national news, Confederate General William Walker and several junior officers sent a flag of truce into Port Royal in hopes of negotiation. Aware that there were Black soldiers in the region, Walker instructed his subordinates to refuse to communicate with their officers. When Captain James Lowndes arrived at the agreed-upon location, the young Carolinian was stunned to be met by Colonel Higginson, who had been rowed to the rendezvous by Prince Rivers, "in the full uniform in the sergeant of infantry." Lowndes was in the process of demanding to speak to another officer when Higginson remembered the name of Lowndes's commanding general. Previously a U.S. Army captain, General Walker had worked with Kansas governor John Geary in keeping free soil pioneers out of the territory, and it was Walker who had demanded that Higginson meet with the governor. Calling Walker "an old friend," recalled Seth Rogers, Higginson "took special pains to send word [to Walker] that his old acquaintance would have been happy to send his compliments had he been treated with due respect." Lowndes replied that had to follow his orders, and Higginson refused to send a substitute. The negotiations collapsed.[17]

By late January 1863, following six weeks of training and drills, Saxton believed Higginson and the 1st were ready for a major upriver raid. With more Northern regiments expected shortly, and with the naval siege of Charleston underway, the army required enormous amounts of lumber, brick, and steel. Packages of food routinely arrived from the North, to provide for both the army and the voluntary organizations—teachers and other participants in the Port Royal Experiment—but the soldiers needed a constant supply of food, particularly welcoming grilled meat. As freedmen native to the region, the men of the 1st were well suited for large-scale foraging operations. Rumors of abandoned railroad iron on St. Simons Island, Georgia, attracted the military's interest, and Corporal Sutton assured Higginson that if they could sail up the St. Mary's, there was "more lumber than [they] had transportation to carry." Saxton approved of the idea, and a plan was quickly formed. Higginson would take five companies and three small steamers down the coast before turning up the St. Mary's River. Saxton and Higginson both hoped they could liberate those still held in bondage in northern Florida. "We were, in short, to win our spurs," Higginson later wrote.[18]

The St. Mary's was wide enough at its mouth, where it joined the Cumberland River and flowed into the Atlantic. However, Higginson grew worried about the expedition as he pored over rough army maps of the river, which was rightly regarded by naval officers "as the most dangerous in the region." Its sudden turns hid hazardous shallows, and its bluffs offered entrenched Confederates ample places to attack. Escaped bondmen warned that a company of cavalrymen was encamped at Township Landing, some fifteen miles upriver from Beaufort. Sutton, however, was eager to engage the Confederate troopers, many of whom he had known while enslaved, and Higginson agreed that this was better for the men than foraging. Although Higginson assumed that at best they would face a skirmish, he judged it desirable to get his men exposed to live fire as soon as possible so that they might apply their training. His flagship was the *Ben De Ford*, supported by the confiscated Confederate steamer the *Planter* and the *John Adams*, an old Boston ferryboat unfit for sea service and captained by a man named Jack Clifton. Each steamer was armed with several thirty-pound Parrott guns—a muzzle-loaded artillery weapon—and two howitzers. After several delays, the officers and men, 462 in all, pushed away from Beaufort's docks on January 23, each vessel departing separately to hide the larger expedition from prying eyes, with plans to rendezvous at St. Simons, a barrier island on the Georgia coast roughly one hundred miles below Beaufort.[19]

Sunday, January 24, was unusually hot, the sun "very oppressive." Captain Charles Trowbridge sent word to Higginson that the boilers had blown on the *Planter* and that he would have to put in on St. James Island for repairs. Higginson put the interval to good use. The soldiers once enslaved on St. Simons discovered the cache of hastily buried railroad iron and spent the day loading it aboard the *Ben De Ford* and a confiscated flatboat. The metal "would have much value at Port Royal," Higginson knew, but in the meantime the soldiers piled some of the iron bars around the statehouses and engine rooms of both the *Ben De Ford* and *John Adams* as protection from Confederate snipers. By the day's end, the soldiers had loaded one hundred bars and a large number of five-inch planks, which they used to barricade the ships' pilot houses.[20]

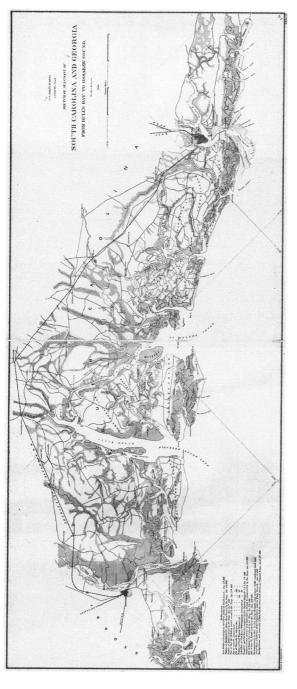

Figure 8.3 In one of the earliest amphibious operations of the war, combined Union army and navy forces captured Port Royal Sound on November 7, 1861. On this 1863 U.S. survey, Beaufort sits atop the bend in the river of the same name, with Camp Saxton roughly two miles to the town's southwest. Afterward Port Royal served as a base for the army's assaults on Charleston to the east, and for Higginson's upriver raids along the coast to the west. The camp is still managed by the U.S. Navy and may be found at 601 Old Fort Road. Courtesy of the Library of Congress.

As they slowly steamed upriver, the waters became too shallow for the *Ben De Ford*, so Higginson and two hundred of his men crowded below decks on the *John Adams*. Finally, long after darkness had set in on January 26, the ship reached Township Landing, some fifteen miles upriver. A runaway enslaved man emerged from the trees with word that the Confederate cavalry was camped five miles inland. Two roads stretched toward the encampment, one of them a lumber path Sutton had once helped to build. He and Higginson took a company of a hundred Florida men and trudged up the road. Sutton marched beside Higginson, pointing the way and assisted by the Black refugee. Governor Andrew had sent Higginson a large supply of printed Emancipation Proclamations, and Higginson handed one to their new "guide." While few could read it, Higginson observed, "they all seem to feel more secure when they hold it in their hands." A full moon illuminated their path, and for miles they heard nothing but the occasional barking of a dog. "This yelping always made Corporal Sutton uneasy," Higginson noticed, dogs being "the detective officers of Slavery's police."[21]

Just as Higginson was beginning to think the rest of their venture was "proceeding smoothly," a Confederate officer on a white horse reined up before them, taking a shot with his pistol and shouting, "Charge in among them! Surround them!" The 1st's advance guard returned fire, but without precision. Higginson shouted for his men to fix bayonets and close ranks, and for those in front to kneel and fire. Someone next to him—as it turns out a private named William Parsons—was hit almost immediately, Higginson later reported, but he barely noticed as he watched his men kneel in the underbrush on both sides of the road, "settling down in the grass as coolly and warily as if wild turkeys were the only game." As the Confederates began to pull back, some of the soldiers began to charge after them into the woods. Higginson and his captains labored to keep the men in formation, while Confederates in the woods on either side of the path fired toward them, mostly hitting the trees above their heads. As the Confederate fire began to diminish, Higginson called for a temporary ceasefire. "Why de Cunnel order *Cease firing*," he heard one private complain, "when de Secesh blazin' away." Surprised at how calm he had remained, Higginson reflected that "the taste of gunpowder was too intoxicating."[22]

Only later did Higginson realize that he had lost all sense of time: "I could hardly tell whether the fight had lasted ten minutes or an hour." Sutton argued they should continue up the road toward the cavalry's base, and Higginson admitted that he felt the impulse to do just that. But General Saxton had ordered him to risk little, understanding how the Northern public would regard a Confederate victory over the nation's first Black regiment. "We now have an honorable victory," Higginson wrote in his official report, and both the officers and men "were in good spirits." It was not yet daylight, and Higginson still had no clear idea of how many Confederates were in the region. "I judged it better to rest satisfied with the victory already gained." The skirmish would rank low in the annals of Civil War battles, Higginson knew, but to him personally, their small victory "was of the greatest value." Much ink had been spilled in the Northern press over the question of how well Black men would fight, but when faced with Confederate fire coming from two directions, his men "did not flinch."[23]

Higginson guessed that they had bloodied the troopers sufficiently that they would not return. He knew that Confederates would never allow their infantrymen to march two miles through wooden fields in the dark to renew the fight given what they had suffered. From a Florida newspaper he later learned that the lieutenant on the white horse had died, as had twelve others. The company's captain stated that "finding the enemy in strong force," they had abandoned their camp, taking with them "twelve negroes on their way to the enemy." The 1st lost only the young private who fell by Higginson's side, and suffered seven wounded, among them Corporal Sutton, who had a ball crease his skull. Another of the wounded had taken a ball through his lung, but as he was carried back to the *John Adams* he asked only whether Higginson had survived, as a rumor was circulating among the soldiers in the rear that he had fallen with Private Parsons. "Braver men never lived," Higginson marveled.[24]

With Seth Rogers tending to the wounded, the *John Adams* resumed its mission. Just before dawn on the 30th, the steamer reached the small Florida hamlet of Woodstock, roughly forty miles upriver. Higginson ordered the town secured and all white men of military age arrested as prisoners. Seven "forlorn specimens" were detained as potential hostages in case of further action as the boats descended the St. Mary's. The men rounded up a flock of sheep and a cannon, but there was far more lumber stored on the docks than could be loaded onto the small steamer. Most of the houses were empty, though the furniture was still in place; Higginson longingly gazed at the pianos, though he knew that he had no space for one aboard his cramped ship. Sutton, somewhat recovered from his wounds, wondered if his colonel wished to see where he had been enslaved. The two strolled to the plantation owned by Edwin Alberti, finding Alberti's widow at home. Aware that the town had been occupied by Union troops, she appeared on her front steps. "To what am I indebted for the honor of this visit, Sir?" she asked Higginson. He stepped aside to reveal his companion and suggested that she "had been previously acquainted with Corporal Robert Sutton." A look of "unutterable indignation" swept across her features. "Ah," she replied after a few moments. "We called him *Bob*." In that one instance, Higginson recalled, he had witnessed "the whole drama of the war to reverse itself," as his "tall, well-dressed, imposing" Black officer faced down the elderly white woman who had once owned his body. Sutton merely nodded and led Higginson off to see the estate's slave jail. Higginson confiscated the shackles and key as trophies of war.[25]

As the *John Adams* steamed back downriver, Higginson hoped that the 1st had seen action enough for the time being. They passed several high bluffs as the St. Mary's twisted but saw no sign of the enemy. Having had little sleep over the past twenty-four hours, he lay down on a settee in the ship's stateroom. The river widened in a turn and then narrowed again below a cliff called Scrubby Bluff. Suddenly from the Georgia side of the river "a roar and rattle as of a tornado let loose," Higginson later wrote. "A storm of bullets" rained into the side of the ship. Higginson raced for the gun deck as the Parrott guns fired shells up over the cliff's edge. The men had been quartered below, but a good number swarmed up onto the main deck, loading and firing. "Nebber big it up!" Higginson heard one private shout. Others remained below, firing from the portholes in the lower deck. One Confederate leaped aboard the ship but was shot by one of the Black sergeants. Amid the smoke, one of his majors found Higginson, shouting that Captain Clifton had been killed while on the upper deck. Furious, some of the men wanted to land and attack the Confederates, who Higginson presumed were the same cavalrymen they had faced days before. Higginson wisely thought the idea "madness," given the cliff's steep wall. Nonetheless the soldiers continued to load and fire "with inconceivable rapidity," taking turns at the portholes until the steamer floated far enough downriver to be out of range. "Nobody knows anything about these men who has not seen them in battle," Higginson wrote in his official report of the affair.[26]

The *John Adams*, its port side badly scarred but otherwise serviceable, and the *Ben De Ford* docked in Beaufort just before sunrise on February 2. Higginson handed over the iron bars, cannon, and lumber, together with forty bushels of rice, resin, cordage, the flock of sheep, the seven Confederate prisoners, and several families of Black refugees. To Saxton, Higginson gifted the shackles and key from the slave jail. Dr. Rogers counted one soldier killed and seven wounded, including Sutton. One of the wounded men was so badly injured that Rogers expected him to not survive the day. To his mother, an exultant Higginson wrote that he enjoyed the mission "inexpressibly." The soldiers "behaved splendidly," and when the "whole is known, it will establish past question the reputation of the regiment." Still thinking of John Brown's original plan of creating a series of maroon colonies in the Virginia hills, he hoped that this small success might prod the War Department into permitting them to establish camps in the interior. The 1st could forage for their provisions and recruit runaways. "A chain of such posts would completely alter the whole aspect of the war in the seaboard Slaves States," he informed Saxton, doing what no Northern white regiment could.[27]

Over the next weeks, Higginson was gratified to discover that news of their raid appeared in Northern newspapers. Higginson himself contributed to the word count, firing off an essay on the two skirmishes for the *Atlantic Monthly*'s April issue. Greeley's *New-York Tribune* endorsed Higginson's appraisal of Black combatants, and the Philadelphia *Christian Recorder*, an AME journal, reported that the Confederates were "shot down like dogs by the negro volunteers, who fought like tigers." Newspapers as far west as Iowa and Minnesota praised the 1st for fighting with "the most fiery energy." Even the conservative *New York Times* applauded the regiment's courage under fire. Most Democratic journals, however, fell silent, only a handful maintaining their earlier opposition to Black recruits. The *Hartford Daily Times*, which churned out a steady stream of hostile editorials, insisted that Higginson's official account would "not bear analysis" and that their correspondent in Hilton Head maintained that Higginson's recruits "still persist in deserting at every opportunity" and had "scattered with wondrous rapidity, upon a charge of twenty rebel horsemen."[28]

Perhaps as important was the fact that white soldiers were impressed by the 1st, and their letters had a significant impact on the home front. One officer's wife who had just visited soldiers of the 6th Connecticut told Dr. Rogers that those New Englanders "were full of praise of the bravery of our regiment." A private from the 8th Maine wrote that his previous doubts of how well Black soldiers would fight vanished after the upriver raid, adding that "they have won the praises of all." A third soldier initially cursed the Black soldiers as they marched back into Beaufort until he noticed the Confederate prisoners they prodded before them. With that, the entire band cheered, "Bully for the negroes." John Greenleaf Whittier assured

Philadelphia abolitionist Charlotte Forten, who was assisting refugees in Port Royal and the Sea Islands, that while he remained "a peace man," he believed that "twenty such regiments, under twenty such men as Higginson and Dr. Rogers, would soon give a new aspect to the struggle."[29]

News of the St. Mary's raid came at a most opportune time in Washington. In May 1863, the War Department created the Bureau of Colored Troops to facilitate the recruiting of Black soldiers and white officers. Pennsylvania congressman Thaddeus Stevens introduced legislation to enlist fifty thousand Black soldiers, and in speech after speech Republicans and antislavery activists cited the heroism of the 1st. Newspapers widely reprinted Higginson's report to Saxton that "no officer in this regiment now doubts that the key to the successful prosecution of this war lies in the unlimited employment of black troops." Saxton described the raid as "a complete success" to Secretary of War Edwin Stanton: "It foreshadows clearly the very important advantages which might result in our cause by the extensive arming of the blacks." That statement was reprinted across the North, and one Ohio editor reminded his readers that the West Point–educated Saxton was "a thorough military man" and not "a fanatic." Abolitionists joined in. Speaking at New York's Cooper Union, Wendell Phillips rephrased the old question, saying that while "slaves" would not fight, a free man would: "Will he fight? Ask Higginson!"[30]

Democrats continued to resist and in the House voted against Stevens's bill in an unsuccessful effort to stop the enlistments. Newspapers in Richmond and Memphis reprinted Higginson's statement without comment, evidently believing his words incendiary enough to require no formal condemnation, while the *Nashville Daily Union* denounced Higginson for "stealing" four of Mrs. Alberti's slaves. The reliably critical *Hartford Daily Times* regarded it as insulting for Republicans to believe that the Union could not be restored "without the help of negroes," and one Connecticut journal described a white soldier complaining that Higginson "has had nigger on the brain from the time of his conception." Many more newspapers regarded the creation of the U.S. Colored Troops as simple pragmatism. "We must have the negroes for us or against us," editorialized one Maine newspaper. "The Black Brigade has done noble service in Florida, under the lead of that 'muscular Christian,' Col. Higginson, who is as good with the sword as with the pen." An Iowa journalist observed that using Black soldiers "may save the lives of thousands of our [white] troops" and quoted Higginson as saying that Southern freedmen "know the country, while white soldiers do not." An editor in St. Paul remembered that

Confederate general Robert Toombs had once bragged that after a few more Southern victories, he would "call the roll of his slaves on Bunker Hill." Before Toombs could do so, the editor laughed, "Higginson got ahead of him, and called the roll of Toombs' slaves on the soil of South Carolina."[31]

* * *

Their successful raid behind them, Higginson awaited the regiment's next assignment. It was not long in coming. In Washington, both President Lincoln and Secretary of War Stanton were eager to launch an invasion into Florida and retake the town of Jacksonville, captured once before being evacuated in October 1862. In the Department of the South, Generals Saxton and Hunter were equally enthusiastic. Not only did Saxton believe that there were "large numbers of able-bodied negroes" who would enlist if liberated, but as the least populous of all Confederate states, Florida would provide an asylum for runaways from Georgia and Alabama who would then homestead on what had once been Seminole lands. Saxton reminded Stanton that the raid up the St. Mary's had "caused a perfect panic" among whites in the region. As several companies of the 1st were composed solely of Florida freedmen, Saxton understood that these soldiers knew northern Florida's waterways and swamps. Should Higginson's and Montgomery's two regiments take Florida at the same time that Admiral Samuel DuPont's ironclad ships assaulted Charleston harbor, Saxton argued, the tenor of war would change dramatically along the southeastern coast. Hunter concurred and informed the admiral that he intended to order Higginson into Florida and urged DuPont's officers to "render any assistance in their power" to support the invasion.[32]

Although gratified that the Northern press had taken notice of the St. Mary's raid, Higginson did not grasp the full extent to which the foray had captured the nation's attention, or how Saxton used it to persuade official Washington to build upon it with an incursion into Florida. Isolated from the larger world at Camp Saxton, Higginson was not privy to discussions within the War Department and suspected only that the army intended to recruit another Black regiment from the upper banks of the St. John's River before returning to the Carolina coast. Instructions to take with them twice as many uniforms, rations, and muskets as they required reinforced that theory. Not until orders arrived from Saxton that he and Montgomery were to take three steamers, including the hastily overhauled *John Adams*, occupy Jacksonville, and "intrench yourselves there" did Higginson grasp that Florida was to be the new home of the 1st and 2nd South Carolina Regiments for the coming months.[33]

Knowing how his Florida companies desperately wished to return home in search of their still-enslaved loved ones, Higginson tried to keep his orders as secret as he could. But as the men began to break camp, taking all of their belongings with them, it became clear that this would not be just another week-long raid. The navy established Fernandina Island, where the St. Mary's joined the Cumberland and flowed into the Atlantic, as the rendezvous points for the support ships being sent by DuPont. Montgomery and the soldiers of the 2nd transferred to the steamer *Burnside*. One teacher in Beaufort guessed that the soldiers would "probably never return," and as evidence that the occupation might be a lengthy and dangerous one a number of nurses accompanied the regiments, among them Susie King Taylor, once a Georgia bondswoman who had risen to become the first Black nurse in the war. As the *John Adams* pulled away from Beaufort's docks, Saxton honored the invasion force with a salute of thirty-two guns.[34]

Joined by the *Norwich* and the *Uncas*, the flotilla steamed up the winding St. John's. At 8:00 on the morning of March 11, the ships rounded the final bend and spied Jacksonville. The gunners had taken their posts, and the soldiers lined up, preparing to leap ashore. Rather to Higginson's surprise, all that awaited them was a handful of children playing on the docks. He spied a few women gazing at the ships out of windows and doors, but no soldiers could be seen. He and several companies disembarked on piers on the western side of the town, and Montgomery unloaded his men on the lower docks. Gunners rolled small howitzers onto the wharves, aiming down Jacksonville's main streets. "The pretty town was ours without a shot," Higginson later recalled. "The surprise had been complete, and not a soul in Jacksonville had dreamed of our coming." The *Uncas* dropped anchor in the middle of the channel and rounded to so that its guns could face any Confederate river traffic. As one journalist attached to the regiments stated, the two colonels ordered the railroad depot occupied and stationed men on the outskirts of town, blocking all major approaches. "This movement was executed with such promptness," the reporter observed, "that the first knowledge of the invasion only came to the townspeople when they saw the black soldiers marching past their dwellings."[35]

If Higginson was stunned at how easily Jacksonville had been taken, he was stunned again to discover just how many had wished the expedition to fail. In Democratic newspapers across the Midwest, editors reported that "the

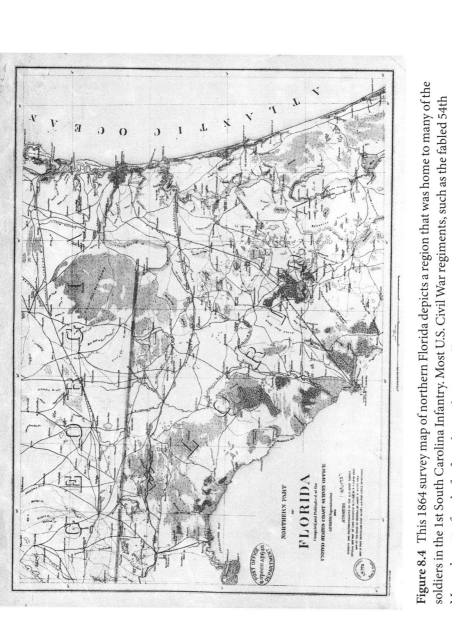

Figure 8.4 This 1864 survey map of northern Florida depicts a region that was home to many of the soldiers in the 1st South Carolina Infantry. Most U.S. Civil War regiments, such as the fabled 54th Massachusetts, fought far from home, but virtually all of Higginson's men had been enslaved in northern Florida and along the Carolina coast. At the top of the map is St. Mary's River and below is Jacksonville on the St. John's, which the 1st briefly occupied. Courtesy of the Library of Congress.

negro expedition" led by Higginson and Montgomery had been "captured by the rebels." One Washington journal gave the story a particularly grim twist that must have terrified Mary and Louisa. On the previous Christmas Eve, Confederate president Jefferson Davis had issued an executive order, threatening to sell captured runaway soldiers back into slavery and summarily execute their white officers, and Higginson, the editor predicted, "will probably be dealt with in accordance with Davis's retaliatory proclamation." A St. Paul newspaper went further still in celebrating the alleged failure of the regiments, gleefully suggesting that Higginson's capture "will not occasion much regret among those who are acquainted with the character of the officer." Higginson was "an out-and-out disunionist" who had enlisted to put down slavery rather than save the Union.[36]

Before anything could be done to slow the growing movement to recruit Black soldiers, Saxton hastened a formal statement on the affair to Stanton on March 14, an account that the politically astute secretary of war released to Washington-based journalists. "It gives me pleasure to report that so far the objects of the expedition have been fully accomplished," reported Saxton. "The town is completely in our possession and [with] many prisoners." Nearby Confederates had sent skirmishers into the outskirts of Jacksonville to probe for weaknesses in the Union Army's defenses and to scout for accurate numbers, but "in every action the negro troops have behaved with utmost bravery." Saxton speculated that no other action yet taken during the war had caused more panic on the Southern coast than the appearance of Black troops. Within days, Republican newspapers across the North either reprinted Saxton's statement in full or confirmed the successful Florida invasion. For his part, Higginson assured his mother that he was safe and warned her never to believe Democratic papers that were writing his obituary. The greatest praise arrived on April 1 from the executive mansion. "I am glad to see the accounts of your colored force at Jacksonville," President Lincoln wrote to General Hunter. "The enemy will make extra efforts to destroy them, and we should do the same to preserve and increase them."[37]

Although Saxton had no precise knowledge of just how much the invasion terrified white Southerners, his guess was accurate. Three days after the capture of Jacksonville, Confederate general Joseph Finegan, the commander of the District of East Florida, notified his superiors that their "unscrupulous enemy" had landed Black soldiers at Jacksonville under the command of white officers. Finegan urged the citizens of Jacksonville to flee the town, if they could, and to form companies immediately and then report to him.

The following day, Finegan fired off a second account, confirming the arrival of a large number of "Abolition troops, said to be negroes." As had Southern authorities during antebellum slave conspiracy scares, Finegan inflated the numbers facing him, estimating them at four thousand, roughly doubling the actual number under Higginson and Montgomery. His skirmishers, he insisted, had forced Higginson's pickets—soldiers placed in an advance position to warn against an enemy's advance—to retreat and flee "in confusion" back into the heart of the town, but he lacked adequate numbers to follow up. Finegan then contradicted that tale by admitting that unless Jacksonville was retaken "the entire negro population of East Florida" would be lost. As ever, Confederates found supporters in Northern Democrats. Speaking to a Democratic convention in Philadelphia, former state attorney general William Reed described "negro ruffians with their bloody pikes standing over the cradles of Southern babes." Unable to fathom the idea that former bondsmen in blue could occupy Jacksonville without atrocities, Reed alluded to the recent rebellion of soldiers in India—the so-called Sepoy Rebellion—and warned that "the next news we may hear will be the wail of violated women and affrighted children shrieking in terror, as Higginson and his Sepoys, pursue their career of outrage."[38]

Well aware of such sentiments, Higginson was especially careful not to offend any white Floridians. "All definite display of our force was avoided," he scribbled into his journal, and "dress parades were omitted." The soldiers consistently "behaved perfectly well, though many were owned here & do not love the people." He suspected that few whites were actually in fear of their lives, but rather were feeling humiliated at being occupied by Black troops. One Confederate captain's wife, however, assured Higginson that as she had known many of his soldiers in the years before the war, it was "pleasanter" than to be occupied by white Yankees. Republican editors also did their best to trumpet that "the negroes behave with propriety." Higginson's only concern was that he and Montgomery lacked the numbers required to hold the city should Confederates launch a concerted assault. He estimated that about five hundred white Southerners remained in the town, and many were so destitute that he was forced to distribute rations to them. Initially opposed to having white troops under his command, Higginson finally concluded that they would be needed, especially if they planned any forays further up the river or into the interior. He requested New England men be sent to join them. In the meantime, he quartered his regiment in riverfront warehouses on Bay Street but pitched empty tents where Confederates could see them and urged the navy's gunboats to steam "impressively up and down the river from time to time."[39]

Higginson also feared that Confederate gunners could set their cannon on rolling flatbeds on the rail tracks in the thick woods west of the town, a fear that was confirmed when on March 17 he received a formal warning from Confederate colonel Abner McCormick. Writing from his "camp near Jacksonville," McCormick gave Higginson twenty-four hours to evacuate the women and children from the town before shelling began. Any civilian who remained in Jacksonville did so under Higginson's responsibility. In response, Higginson simply observed that he had never placed any restrictions "on the passage of women and children across his lines" and would not start now. He promised to alert civilians to McCormick's implied threat and offered to use army wagons to carry any woman who wished to leave under a flag of truce. About the white men in town, however, Higginson said nothing, leaving it to McCormick to surmise that they were being held as hostages should the shelling start.[40]

Evidently the only person in the nation unaware of Higginson's whereabouts was Emily Dickinson. Having asked the previous fall whether his silence reflected his "displeasure" with her, in early 1863 she mailed off another poem asking for his advice. "You were so generous to me, that if possible I offended you, I could not too deeply apologize." By February somebody evidently brought the numerous stories printed in her local *Springfield Republican* to her attention. "I found you were gone, by accident," Dickinson admitted. Although she had earlier rebuffed his requests for an image of her, she insisted that she "should have liked" to have seen him before he sailed for the Carolina coast. "War feels to me an oblique place," she admitted to her "dear friend" the colonel. "Should there be other Summers," she thought, "would you perhaps come?" As if her suspicions that Higginson might not live to see future summers was not awkward enough, she concluded with the question of "who will inform me of the Exchange" should he trade life for death and "experience immortality." So far as his daybook indicated, Higginson declined to respond.[41]

Several days after Higginson's plea for reinforcements, Hunter ordered the 8th Maine and eight companies of the 6th Connecticut to sail for Jacksonville. The task of ferrying the soldiers south and then guarding the city from the river fell to Captain Charles Steedman, who complained that the "duty has been by no means to [his] taste" given his views of Black soldiers. Much to Higginson's dismay, the instructions from Hunter ordered him to cede command of the city to John Rust, colonel of the Maine regiment. "It is just what I begged *not* to have done," Higginson confided to his journal, as he doubted that Rust possessed the necessary tact for commanding contraband troops. Hunter regarded Rust as Higginson's senior, as he had been in the army for eighteen months, but Higginson judged him "mediocre, a heavy Maine livery stable keeper [who] has smelt no powder & sleeps on board the steamer." Perhaps, Higginson hoped, the white soldiers might garrison Jacksonville while his and Montgomery's forces could go further up the river and establish an outpost there.[42]

Despite the arrival of reinforcements, General Finegan gave the order to start the shelling on the night of March 21. Colonel McCormick had sent a subordinate into Jacksonville under a flag of truce to usher women and children out of the town, and shells began to land dangerously close to the abandoned mansion of John Sanderson, where Higginson had set up his headquarters. Susie King Taylor guessed the "bearer was evidently a spy," as the "shells were sent too accurately to be random." Higginson was forced to abandon his headquarters and urged Taylor to evacuate to a hotel that was being used as a hospital. The cannonading continued all night, and Higginson readied his men for an assault on the town, thinking the shelling was merely a prelude to an attack. But at dawn the shelling ceased, and in the silence Higginson believed the Confederates had drawn back and that there would be renewal of the bombardment unless they marched out to meet them, as he had suddenly determined to do. To his mother, Higginson wrote only that the troops seemed to have withdrawn. Just hours before, Taylor expected to be killed at any moment. Higginson evidently thought it unwise to mention the shelling to either Mary or Louisa.[43]

Three days later, on March 25, Higginson led a small reconnaissance force to the west of Jacksonville, following the rail tracks toward Four Mile Station. The soldiers carried two days' worth of rations and water, and their mission was to tear up the tracks that allowed the sixty-four-pound Confederate gun mounted on a flatbed to shell the city from as far away as two miles. Behind him marched four companies from Maine and Connecticut and five from the 1st, making this the first racially integrated army unit to see action in the war. The soldiers pushed and pulled a small flatcar holding a ten-pound Parrott cannon. In the distance, Higginson spied Confederate pickets on horseback riding away from them through the woods, carefully staying beyond their range. Higginson's men advanced in three columns, with the 1st taking the middle. "A long line—white, black, white—were deployed transversely,"

Higginson later reported. "For the first time I saw the two columns fairly alternate on the military chessboard; it had been the object of much labor and many dreams, and I liked the pattern at last."[44]

Finegan ordered his men, both cavalry and infantry, to advance and support their retreating pickets and to engage Higginson's force. The Confederates had used a rifled thirty-two-pound cannon to bombard the city, and as they pulled back up the tracks the gun began to throw shells toward Higginson's ranks. The Union gunners returned fire, blowing up a low bridge that had permitted the Confederates to get close enough to bombard Jacksonville. Higginson could see "a great black projectile hurled into the air," but it landed well clear of most of his unit. Both sides began to retreat back up the tracks, Higginson's men ripping up the rails as they went. Northern papers reported one soldier killed and another wounded, both of them from Maine. Finegan told his superiors that he had lost no men but that Higginson's soldiers had made off with a number of mules and wagons, and he ordered the court-martial of the officer who had lost them. The brief skirmish was "the hardest fight they had [yet] had," Taylor noted in her journal. "After this we were not troubled with General Finegan."[45]

Finegan concluded his report by explaining why his Confederates had not yet launched an infantry assault on the town: "The fortifications erected by the enemy around Jacksonville were formidable." Unhappily for Higginson's men, General Hunter had begun to take the advice of General Truman Seymour, his chief of staff and, according to Edward Pierce, a correspondent for the *New-York Tribune*, "a strong proslavery man, against arming negroes." For reasons Hunter felt no need to explain, on March 28 he ordered Higginson and Montgomery to evacuate Jacksonville and return to Beaufort. Higginson had expected orders to transfer several of his companies upriver, and he fumed that his soldiers had "so daunted the rebels" that they could venture outside the city for several miles in any direction without facing opposition. Jacksonville was the key to Florida, Higginson believed, but now he would have to abandon the Union population there to the "persecutions" of vengeful Confederates. Seymour was "strongly opposed to us," he confided to his diary; only the general's racism "defeated us in this case, just in the hour of success." Ever the optimist, however, Higginson prayed his "natural buoyancy" would get him past the disappointment.[46]

Higginson's men were far less easily consoled, and with good cause. One of his sergeants, "a Florida man" with most of his family still enslaved up the St. John's River, burst into tears upon hearing the news. "It was very natural that the men from that region should feel thus bitterly," Higginson admitted. The evacuation itself was a debacle. Departing white soldiers determined to burn down the town, and much of Jacksonville was left in ashes. Soldiers from Maine blamed those from Connecticut, who hurled the accusation back at the white soldiers of the 8th. Colonel Rust finally threatened to have any soldier found "applying the torch" shot. It fell to Higginson to take charge of loading his men and their arms and "government property" aboard the steamers. Terrified white Unionists begged to accompany his regiment to Beaufort, and Higginson allowed them to board. However, due to challenges of space he refused to allow them to bring their personal property, prompting an Ohio newspaper to run the story under the headline "Cruelty of Colonel Higginson." In a final insult, the 1st returned to their old camp to find it stripped by soldiers and civilians who had never expected them to return. "Every board gone from the floors, the screens torn down from the poles," Higginson observed. "Every man seemed crushed, officers and soldiers alike."[47]

Abandoning the ransacked Camp Saxton, Higginson and the 1st sailed down the Beaufort River roughly nine miles below their old site and pitched their tents on the northern edge of Port Royal Island, on what had been the Milnes estate. As yet, Saxton and Hunter had provided no clue as to their next assignment. Charleston remained under a naval blockade, and Higginson supposed that either they might take part in an assault on the harbor's outer defenses, or their task would be to guard their portion of the coast should the Confederates attack Port Royal Island to take the pressure off Charleston. In the meantime, he considered writing up his Florida adventures for the *Atlantic Monthly*, but temporarily abandoned the idea, as a mere essay seemed "a sort of profaning" of their sacrifices there. He instead put his new leisure to good use in writing to Mary and his mother. Mary was considering relocating to a health resort in Germantown, Pennsylvania; evidently Higginson had been led to believe that her health had continued to improve, and when she testily insisted otherwise, he placidly apologized. "I didn't mean to insult you dear by thinking you better—but you seemed so."[48]

Frustrated by inactivity, Higginson took some solace in an editorial drafted by editor Robert Hamilton, which appeared in his New York *Weekly Anglo-African*, to which Higginson had long subscribed. Hamilton admitted that the time had not yet arrived for Black men to serve as commissioned officers, not having "had the opportunity to study the art of war." But under the tutelage of the "gallant" Higginson and Montgomery, "our young men will soon be made sufficiently proficient for all work." One Ohio Republican editor agreed, adding that the "courage" the 1st demonstrated in Florida proved that the "experiment" in raising Black troops should continue. Higginson continued to believe that "the fate of the whole movement for colored soldiers rested on the behavior of this one regiment." Any Bull Run–like "panic" would have "blasted" everything and with it any prospects transforming the war into an abolition conflict and advancing the hopes of the formerly enslaved. As they abandoned Jacksonville, journalist Pierce had remarked to Higginson that his was the one regiment that had become "familiar" to the general public. Higginson hoped that might soon change.[49]

* * *

Higginson did not have long to wait. On the afternoon of June 3, the *DeMolay* docked at Beaufort, and the men of the 54th Massachusetts disembarked and marched through town on their way toward their camp on an abandoned cotton plantation already home to the 55th Pennsylvania. As the first Black regiment to be raised in the Northern states, the 54th contained few Southern men or runaways, and the small number who fit either description had lived in the North for some years. Many, however, such as Sergeant Major Lewis Douglass, the son of the great abolitionist, had been born to once-enslaved parents and had kin still enslaved in the Confederate states. One of the regiment's lieutenants was Higginson's nephew, twenty-two-year-old Francis Lee Higginson. Higginson had not yet met the unit's young colonel, Robert Gould Shaw, but was familiar with the colonel's abolitionist parents and recognized him as a fellow Harvard man, if separated by some fourteen years.[50]

As the second white colonel to lead Black soldiers, Shaw was even more eager to meet the first. On his initial night in camp, Shaw sent a bottle of champagne over to Higginson's camp, not knowing of his temperance views or his rules regarding a dry camp. Higginson tossed the bottle but rode over to see his nephew and meet Shaw on June 4. At the camp, he also met Shaw's second-in-command, Edward "Ned" Hallowell, with whose abolitionist parents he was also familiar. The four hit it off immediately; Higginson assured his mother that he was "delighted with the officers—the best style of Boston." Shaw returned the favor, writing home that he had never met anyone who put his "whole soul into his work" as did Higginson, and that he was "very much impressed with his open-heartedness & purity of character." However, at one point during their meeting, after Shaw agreed that Higginson's men had proven "effective in bush-fighting," he yet wondered "how they would fight in line of battle." A stunned Higginson assured the young colonel that he had absolutely no doubts on that score, and he hoped Shaw felt the same way. Not providing a direct answer, Shaw instead mused that it might be prudent to place white soldiers to their rear. Later Higginson wrote that he was "amazed" by Shaw's doubts.[51]

On July 2, Francis Higginson returned the visit, riding the ten miles to his uncle's camp. Higginson told his mother that he judged Frank "manly & quiet" when it came to bragging about his two brothers, who were serving in the 1st Massachusetts Cavalry. Sixteen days later, Shaw was killed and Hallowell badly wounded in the assault on Battery Wagner, a Confederate stronghold guarding Fort Sumter and the entrance to Charleston harbor. Francis Higginson was one of the few officers to survive the failed incursion, although a bout of fever soon forced him into the Beaufort mansion the army had commandeered as a hospital. Higginson visited his nephew and mourned Shaw's loss but took solace in the fact that the nation was electrified by the courage of the 54th. Within the month, the War Department announced that two new regiments, the 3rd and 4th South Carolina, would soon join Higginson's and Montgomery's Black troops.[52]

Regrettably, neither the heroism of the 54th nor the addition of two new Black regiments in the Department of the South altered the racism of some white officers. To Higginson's dismay, Hunter ordered several companies from the 1st to accompany Captain Francis Jackson Meriam and the 3rd South Carolina on a raid off the coast of Florida. According to Meriam and William Randolph, the eldest of Higginson's captains, a number of the men refused to go on shore, and, when ordered to disarm, one man, "the ringleader" of what Meriam regarded as a "mutiny," refused to do so. Meriam then shot one of the privates and wounded two more before the mutiny was "quelled." Although not directly involved in the revolt, Robert Sutton, now a sergeant, was thought by Meriam not to have used "his utmost endeavors to suppress the same." Sutton, although not the two wounded soldiers, was brought up on charges of mutiny. A court presided over by John Chatfield, a lieutenant in the 6th Connecticut, found Sutton guilty and sentenced him "to be hung by the neck until he is dead."[53]

Higginson believed not a word of it, and despite the fact that Meriam had been a minor ally of John Brown, he judged him "an insane young man." Higginson first appealed to Hunter, begging him to spare the men a punishment that properly should be meted out to the "incompetent officers." When that failed, Higginson appealed directly to his commander-in-chief,

Abraham Lincoln. Sutton was a sergeant of "good character, fidelity, and bravery," he averred. Higginson also disputed Meriam's account, noting that far from being ordered to disarm the mutineer, the captain had commanded him to "make him take an oar," and how Sutton was supposed to have done that, Higginson pointed out, was quite unclear. Lincoln chose to accept the word of the regiment's famous colonel over a junior officer and granted Sutton a full pardon. On August 23, Sutton returned with honor to his company. At the same time, Higginson cosigned a letter from Governor Andrew to the president, urging him to publicly promise reprisals should Jefferson Davis and the Confederate Congress follow through on their threats to summarily execute captured officers of Black troops and turn "captured negroes in arms to the Rebel States authorities."[54]

Sutton's return to Beaufort in mid-August meant that he was spared the 1st's latest inland raid, a July 9 incursion up the South Edisto River. Located between Charleston and Beaufort, the Edisto snaked more than two hundred miles into Carolina's upcountry. With the capture of Port Royal in the fall of 1861, planters had herded their laborers inland, and runaways informed the army that large numbers of slaves still worked rice plantations thirty miles upriver. Ironically, Higginson's earlier raids, and Montgomery's June expedition up the Combahee River with Harriet Tubman and the men of the 2nd, had increased the problem of Black refugees in the region. Liberated men were encouraged to join the army if they were the right age and healthy. Their dependents set up camps outside of Beaufort they dubbed Higginsonville and Montgomery's Hill, and the army was hard-pressed to provide adequate food and medical supplies to the growing and increasingly unsanitary settlements. General Quincy Adams Gillmore, the latest commander of the Department of the South, hoped that an upriver raid could at once seize rice stores, clean away the impediments the Confederates had thrown into the twisting Edisto, destroy any railroad bridges leading into Charleston, and liberate more Black Carolinians.[55]

Higginson's expedition steamed out of Beaufort on the afternoon of July 9. He brought with him three companies of his men, and two more from the 1st Connecticut Battery, guessing they would have to shell upriver bluffs to keep Confederates away from the cliffs. As ever, the *John Adams* provided the main transport, but, guessing that the larger steamer could not get far upriver, they also brought two smaller steamers, the *Enoch Dean* and the *Governor Milton*. The next morning, the force encountered "a solid structure of pilings" that took an entire day to remove. Once cleared, the Edisto proved too shallow to allow the *John Adams* to continue toward the bridge, which Higginson supposed to be another ten miles upriver. The soldiers squeezed into the smaller vessels, most of the men remaining on deck.[56]

Just before dawn on July 11, the steamers docked at Wiltown, located twenty-one miles upriver. Higginson could see "a three gun field battery there stationed." The Connecticut artillerymen opened fire, as did the two Parrott guns aboard the *Enoch Dean*. Higginson and one of his lieutenants took thirty men and raced up the bluff, finding it deserted save for clothing, equipment, and still-smoldering breakfast fires. Skirmishers on both sides fired at one another, but no soldier from the 1st was injured. Upon returning to the *Enoch Dean*, however, the ship's pilot informed Higginson that they had run aground and could go no farther. At that moment, the *Governor Milton*'s engineer took a bullet from above and died within minutes. Only when lifted by the tide did the steamer float free, and although Higginson estimated they were within two miles of the bridge Gillmore wanted destroyed, the captain of the *Governor Milton* spied another battery of four guns ahead. Reluctantly, and to the frustration of the soldiers who had been trained in the use of "combustibles," Higginson ordered a retreat.[57]

As the current tugged the steamers downriver, the ships sailed into a long, straight stretch of river. On the bluffs dead ahead, Confederates had hastily erected a battery, and as the ships drifted within range the guns opened fire. Higginson's Parrotts were placed to shoot from the sides and unable to return fire. Confederate balls crashed through the thin walls of the *Enoch Dean*, where Higginson stood on the deck. He later counted fifteen holes where the "projectiles passed through the vessel or cut the rigging." One killed Higginson's orderly, shearing his head off above the shoulders; others killed a second private and a Black refugee, while still another took a second refugee's leg. Higginson felt "a sudden blow in the side, as if from some prize-fighter." The impact knocked him to the ground, and he found it painful to breathe. The ship's captain dragged him onto a bench. Feeling his side, Higginson found no blood, and his uniform had not even been torn. He supposed the shock had been produced by "the wind of a ball," but surgeons later assured him that he had been grazed by an exploded shell. The Edisto at last turned, and the steamers rounded the bend toward the Wiltown bluff and the protection of the *John Adams*. Higginson realized that he had come "only half an inch from death," yet, he mused, quoting Shakespeare's Mercutio, "it was enough."[58]

Higginson was able to report that they had liberated "about 200 contrabands," which was his "immediate object." His men had seized six bales of cotton, several large bags of rice, and two Confederate prisoners with their horses and equipment. His report named the two privates killed, together with the engineer of the *Governor Milton*, which was so badly damaged that it could no longer be of use. Dr. Seth Rogers examined Higginson and discovered that most of his ribs on the injured side were cracked. A large bruise at least ten inches in diameter had already formed. Rogers assured his fellow temperance advocate that he had been spared "from the perils of peritonitis"—an inflammation of the membrane that lines the inner abdominal wall—"by the fact that [he] had never used whiskey." Higginson expressed surprise that the death toll was not higher, given the holes blasted through the steamers. Even so, he judged the expedition "should never have been sent without more accurate reconnaissance."[59]

Because the Northern press covered the failed raid, Higginson hastened to assure Mary that reports of his "so-called wound" were nothing but "a great humbug." He admitted that Rogers had ordered him to walk as little as possible and remain in his tent, but Higginson dismissed that as a waste of time. Although the bruise remained and was as large as "two hands," he insisted it was little different from "some mishap at the Gymnasium." He did concede that the area around the bruise felt a bit paralyzed and that his hip was "somewhat lame, like rheumatism," but Dr. Rogers promised that danger had now "entirely passed." Unless the 1st was ordered to Folly Island, just south of Charleston harbor, to take part in the ongoing siege of Charleston, he might even be granted a brief furlough to return home. Higginson signed off by claiming that his enforced leisure was most "pleasant." Aware that Mary's health was ever precarious and that she worried about his welfare, he added a final line: "Goodbye, dearest, don't despise me."[60]

Higginson prayed that his "strong constitution and good habits" would enable him to heal quickly, but at length he was forced to apply for a twenty days' leave. He sailed north on Thursday, July 23, and reached Manhattan just in time to catch the night train for Worcester. Neither Mary nor Louisa knew that he was coming. Higginson's sister Ann, who normally resided in Boston, had come for a visit and was washing Mary's hair when the door opened. "Why Mrs. Higginson only look here," she cried. The bruise had finally vanished, but he had not fully recovered his strength. Higginson's unexpected arrival in Massachusetts caught Garrison's attention, who reported on it. Evidently, Higginson was not able to visit his mother, who was about to turn seventy-seven, as by August 16 he was writing Louisa from Manhattan's Astor House. He boarded the *Arago* for Beaufort and was delighted to discover that his colleague Charles Steedman was also a passenger, the captain evidently being quite talented in disguising his disdain for the antislavery colonel. "I do not see that I am not perfectly well," he assured Mary, "& feel no anxiety about myself."[61]

On August 22, the *Arago* docked at Beaufort, and Higginson prepared to ride the few miles to their camp, which had been rechristened Camp Shaw after the late colonel. A handful of soldiers had been detailed for duty on the wharf, and when they saw Higginson standing on the deck they began to point and shout. Higginson disembarked and rode to the camp, where the welcomes continued. "Bless de Lord sa, for see my Cunnel once more," Higginson recorded in his journal, attempting as always to transcribe the Lowcountry accents. "Hab waited for you comin' sa, with eyes ob expectation." The commissioned officers were also relieved to have Higginson back, as a good number had been sick or promoted to other regiments. Higginson soon discovered that everything was essentially fine at the camp, and that his return and clear orders for their future would quickly "brighten up" the regiment.[62]

Seth Rogers was unsure that Higginson had recovered sufficiently to return. Higginson believed he had no choice. He was only one of a dozen officers who were "*not* on the sick list," he told the surgeon. John Strong, his lieutenant colonel, was so sick that he was shipping north on furlough, as was Charles Trowbridge, now a major, and his adjutant was "yellow as gold" with fever. Higginson quickly thought better of returning. Some officers were so dedicated, he admitted, that they injured their health by not taking a longer leave, and "such at least was [his] case" too, he later wrote. Mid-October found Higginson and Rogers's nephew James in the army's commandeered Beaufort hospital, being cared for by Dr. Esther Hill Hawks, a recent graduate of the New England Medical College. "They are both convalescent," Rogers reported home, "and I am not anxious about them."[63]

* * *

Higginson hoped the 1st would be deployed to Morris Island, the site of the recently captured Battery Wagner. The siege of Charleston continued, and with the arrival of the 55th Massachusetts, the 54th's sister unit, there were now six Black regiments on the coast, and as "the Senior Colonel of colored regiments," as one Ohio editor put it, Higginson would be in charge of a brigade, which was composed of four or five regiments. Like most abolitionists,

Higginson was thrilled at the prospect of leading Black troops into the city many regarded as the dark soul of the Confederacy. But instead, his men were drawn into another skirmish with Confederate pickets just across the Broad River. Two of his soldiers drowned in the fight, and six more were wounded. But his soldiers, as he noted in his journal, liberated twenty-seven slaves, "beat off a cavalry company," and captured "two rebel pickets." The most "edifying result," Higginson thought, was that when Major John C. Calhoun Jr., the son of the infamous proslavery politician, asked to discuss a prisoner exchange, he met with Major Trowbridge. As one Republican editor chuckled, without formally changing their policy, Confederate officers implicitly recognized "the gallant soldiers" of the 1st as equals to "the whisky-drinking and tobacco-chivalry of South Carolina" and spoke with Trowbridge "without protest." The *Chicago Times* saw it differently. Only because Lincoln had demanded that Confederates "recognize our niggers in uniform (or rather, *their* niggers stolen from them)" did Southern officers agree to meet with the "notorious Higginson and Montgomery."[64]

For a Christmas celebration, General Gillmore planned a grand reception at his headquarters on Hilton Head, and Higginson and Saxton steamed down to join the party. Although it was intended to be a surprise, one of the celebrants could not resist informing the two that the freedpeople of Beaufort planned to present them both with swords on New Year's Day. Ten newly prosperous Black men, including war hero Robert Smalls and a few who had "made money by keeping saloons"—for once Higginson relaxed his temperance scruples—had contributed $60 for Higginson's ceremonial blade. Evidently on Gillmore's recommendation they had sent it to Francis Shaw, the father of the late colonel, asking him to purchase one for them. Higginson was deeply touched by the gesture. To Mary, who continued to fret about his health and urged him to return home for at least another month, he confided that so far as the war was concerned, he believed he had "done his duty entirely" and had no "compunctions" on that score. But as to his men and those families still enslaved in the interior, he expressed his reluctance to leave the work undone. Only if his health truly took an ill turn could he consider leaving.[65]

The first day of the new year was "piercingly cold," teacher Laura Towne noted in her diary. Saxton's wife was present, and she raised the flag while the 8th Maine fired a thirty-five-gun salute. As an army band played "sweet, patriotic music," Reverend Hall, a Northern Black minister, presented the sword to Higginson, who had "the entire confidence of this regiment"; they wished only "that God will spare and protect your life to see peace once more." The surprise of the gift lost, Higginson had written a reply. He accepted the saber on behalf of his men. "The career of that regiment belongs to the history of the nation," he insisted. As the nation's first regiment of Black soldiers, the 1st had faced "a fortress of prejudice to be stormed, stronger than Fort Wagner." But now, because of their courage on the St. John's raid and their seizure of Jacksonville, "there were fifty thousand black soldiers filing through the breach." Leading these men, Higginson told the crowd, was "the greatest honor of [his] life."[66]

It was to be Higginson's last celebration on the Carolina coast. By early April, as the air grew warmer, he awoke each morning feeling as if "a thousand soft arrows" were shooting through him, draining his strength. For a man who prized physical exercise every bit as much as intellectual exertion, the prospect of another summer in the Lowcountry was too grim to consider. He ate almost nothing but rice and hominy and shed pounds he could ill afford to lose. "I feel very weak in these days," he admitted to his worried mother. "Every warm & sunny day now teaches me that I cannot safely stay more than a month longer." Saxton did not want to lose his favorite colonel and recommended a six-months' furlough rather than a permanent resignation, but Higginson knew that his body was telling him something. The surgeons in Beaufort certified him as suffering from toxicohaemia, blood poisoning by toxins from a local bacterial infection, and while Higginson doubted that diagnosis, he thought it unfair to the 1st that they be led by a "disabled officer." He dreaded saying farewell to his men, so much so that he was reluctant to leave the hospital for Camp Shaw. He was also irate that his beloved regiment had been redesignated the 33rd USCT by the War Department. "All the pride of my men was centered in 'de Fus' Souf,'" he groused, as "the very words were a recognition of the loyal South as against the disloyal."[67]

* * *

Rather than return to Worcester, the Higginsons decided to relocate to Newport, Rhode Island. Mary had spent the previous months there for her health, renting rooms at Hannah Dame's boarding house on Broad Street. Higginson informed his old Free Soil ally John Greenleaf Whittier that the "winter climate [there was] so very mild" it would do them both good. Mary had been seeing a homeopathic doctor in Newport, and although family friend and fellow *Atlantic* contributor Dr. Oliver Wendell Holmes Sr. was far from convinced by homeopathic methods, he advised Mary that their practices were at least preferable to recent fads she had been dabbling in, ranging from animal magnetism to electrical treatments. In any case, Higginson mused, what had initially attracted him so to Worcester "was the radical popular party that prevailed there." But with slavery and the Confederacy collapsing across the South, that phase of his life was behind him. Although he professed to dislike moving, his time in the South had changed him. Moreover, many of his old friends had left Worcester, and, as one newspaper observed, new ones awaited in Rhode Island. "A happier man is seldom met with," the editor noted of Higginson. "He is himself an overflowing fountain of joviality, wit, welcome and happiness."[68]

Just as Higginson's enlistment in the 1st had made national news, so, too, did his potential resignation. Forever afterward to label him "Col. T. W. Higginson," editors reported that he had been honorably discharged because of disability. Old friends wrote with condolences or to thank him for his service. "We are all in deep debt to you, I more than most," Emerson wrote. "I have heard with alarm that your health was seriously impaired, and so has deprived the Army of a rare & incomparable soldier." Emily Dickinson, who had spent recent months in the Boston area, was for once aware of his whereabouts. "Are you in danger?" she inquired in June. "I did not know that you were hurt." When Higginson failed to immediately reply, she wrote again, almost as if he had died. "Deity—does he live now? My friend—does he breathe?" she asked before helpfully adding, "Mr. Hawthorne died."[69]

More comforting missives arrived from South Carolina. Susie King Taylor wrote to say how much he was missed. "I meet manny of the old Soldiers [and] I spoke of you," one soldier wrote, "all hailed your name with that Emotion of the Soul when hearing of one who when in darkness burst light on their path way." Some of the soldiers' dependents had erected a freedmen's village near Beaufort and wished Higginson to know that the settlement had been named for him.[70]

Finally, in November 1864, Higginson at last made his resignation final. With the Confederacy in its death throes and Lincoln's reelection secured, Higginson judged it time to close this chapter of his life. That same month, Louisa died at the age of seventy-eight. Her death certificate, signed by her doctor son Francis in Brattleboro, where she had been living, listed the cause of death as "Disease of [the] Liver." Her will named Higginson as one of the trustees of her modest estate, all of which went to the unmarried women in her extended family. She had played the role of both parents during his childhood, and the dutiful son had written to her at least twice a week since he first left Cambridge. Louisa had been his one constant for the past three decades, even more so than Mary. In the privacy of his daybook, a grieving Higginson wrote only, "News from Brattleboro."[71]

Higginson had assured Mary that he could earn a good living by returning to the "literary trade," and he was not wrong. Newspapers across the North, and even a few in the South, announced that he would pick back up writing for the *Atlantic Monthly*. While writing Emerson in thanks for his good wishes, Higginson announced that literary romanticism, as he termed it, was a "revelation" to him, and he hoped to follow in Emerson's footsteps in crafting essays that tested both his intellectual powers and what he referred to as "moral nature." Still, the war had changed him. His antebellum sentimental odes to quiet walks in the woods gave way to journalism, mainly involving stories of his experiences with the 1st. In both the *Atlantic* and a new journal for youthful readers, *Our Young Folks*, he published "Expedition Up the South Edisto," "Up the St. Mary's," "Up the St. John's," "Regular and Volunteer Officers," "Leaves from an Officer's Journal," and "A Night on the Water." Northern audiences, so many of them with their own sons, brothers, and husbands at the front, or in graves, proved ready listeners. Higginson joined Emerson and feminist and abolitionist Anna Dickinson on the New England lecture circuit. Northern Democrats were naturally less eager to hear of Higginson's wartime exploits. "The Rev. Col. Higginson begins a series of papers on his experiences with his nigger regiment," sneered one Pennsylvania editor. "They will doubtless be entertaining."[72]

The veteran also threw himself into two causes dear to the soldiers of the 1st: their access to land and equal pay with white soldiers. Higginson had long understood that what made his regiment different even from the Black soldiers of the 54th was their ties to the region. The freedmen from Massachusetts wished only to end the war, liberate those still enslaved, and return home. For men like Sutton and Rivers, Florida and South Carolina *was* home, and they believed they had a right to its soil. More than a year earlier, Higginson had promised a visiting delegation from the American Freedmen's Inquiry Commission that potential recruits would "delight in the idea" of a land bounty for enlistment. When confiscated estates were put up for sale in January 1864 by federal tax commissioners, Higginson found that his men were "intensely interested." Bidders were required to put up only one-quarter of the final amount, and his former orderly and three other men under his command purchased a house and a town lot. Both Higginson and Saxton had lobbied a sympathetic Senator Charles Sumner to break the great rural estates into twenty-acre lots that soldiers might buy for $1.25 per acre. The tax commissioners, all of them white Republicans, favored Northern land speculators, Higginson and Saxton fretted, but Sumner assured them that Lincoln had adopted their proposal "over the heads" of the commissioners. While some of the region's freedpeople, including Robert Smalls, did succeed in obtaining the title to property they had worked while enslaved, many large estates were sold intact to Northern investors. Furious, Higginson and Saxton initiated a petition to Treasury Secretary Salmon Chase, denouncing "the failure of the U.S. Direct Tax Commissioners to carry out, in good faith, the wise and humane orders" of President Lincoln. Chase declined to act.[73]

More successful were the efforts of Higginson and Congressman Thaddeus Stevens to address the issue of pay inequality. According to the terms of the Militia Act of 1862, white privates received $13 each month, while Black recruits earned only $10, and then had $3 deducted from that to cover the cost of their uniforms. Just before being mustered out, Higginson spoke to his men about the problem, noting that two-thirds of the regiment refused to accept any pay at all. One soldier told Higginson that if they accepted the money, "it's because our chilen need it, but it *takes de sojer all out of we*, to be treated so unjustly." Higginson noted that in the case where three entire companies refused to accept the pay, the sergeants were "the best men in the regiment," while the soldiers who took it were "a poor set," the "regular invalids & shirks." Writing to Sumner and Maine senator William Pitt Fessenden, Higginson complained that he could not get a straight answer as to who was responsible. The War Department insisted that it was up to Congress to amend the 1862 law. "If the Secretary of War is an 'irresponsible recruiting officer,'" he fumed, then "who is responsible?" His regiment had bled for their country, he lectured Fessenden, but the "injury that has been done to them already, by impoverishing them at the time of the land sales, can never be undone."[74]

Sumner shared Higginson's frustration, promising him that if "the blunder" was not corrected by the War Department, "Congress must do it." Higginson also sent angry editorials to the *New York Times* and the *Chicago Tribune* and mailed a copy of his petition to Massachusetts senator Henry Wilson, who introduced the adjustment into Congress on January 8, 1864. "The memorial of Thomas Wentworth Higginson, late colonel of the 1st South Carolina volunteers," the Senate's scribe recorded in official minutes, not only demanded that the army immediately cease its racially based pay scale but also provide back pay from the moment of their enlistment. Finally, in June 1864, Congress granted equal pay to Black troops and made the action retroactive.[75]

Unhappily, Higginson's men were not eligible for the retroactive pay received by more recent Black regiments. An amendment to the 1864 law provided that only African Americans who were free before April 19, 1861—just days after Lincoln called for volunteers following the attack on Fort Sumter—would be eligible for back pay. As Higginson complained to Congressman James Garfield, "it was impossible to record the previous status of these men in the muster rolls except on their own statement." Those recruits who "were willing to *lie* were put down as freemen." But conscientious men who told the truth and admitted to being contraband soldiers "lost by [their] being put down as slaves." Higginson assured Garfield that he had instructed men to tell the truth and that "afterward they had reason to regret it." Congress never addressed the error.[76]

Months before, in a letter written during his last days in South Carolina, Higginson quoted Emerson that "no man can do anything well who did not feel that what he was doing was for the time the centre of the universe." He devoutly believed that no regiment had done more to create a "trust" than the 1st, one that would serve "at least until the problem of negro soldiers was conclusively solved before all men's eyes." And although he ever disparaged his courage compared to that of the Black soldiers who risked everything to serve, Higginson did think himself forever united with his men, as he put it in "A Song from Camp":

> And the hands were black that held the gun,
> And white that held the sword,
> But the difference was none and the color but one,
> When the red, red blood was poured.[77]

9

"The women's hour"

1865–1877

Like the nation, Higginson craved peace. The bruise on his side had vanished, although his ribs continued to ache, and he often had difficulty catching his breath. Unlike so many veterans who returned home with missing limbs and phantom pains, he required no crutch or cane, and decades of exercise had prepared him for a shorter period of recuperation than he might otherwise have faced, although his desire for complete fitness was frustrated by his lingering troubles. "Poor sleep two nights for my old breathing trouble," Higginson confided to his journal in February 1866. His friends and neighbors in Newport welcomed "the colonel" home. But due to what was then dubbed "battle fatigue," memories of the skirmishes along the Edisto and the death of men like Captain Jack Clifton faded but slowly. The Thirteenth Amendment, then working its way through the states, had been ratified in December 1865, ending one crusade to which Higginson had dedicated himself. Others beckoned, but for the time, he simply needed quiet.[1]

Higginson's diary, which had been filled with lengthy daily commentary while in South Carolina, grew quiet too. Days passed without a single word committed to the page, and often his entries contained but brief notations detailing a game of croquet, or swimming or sailing about the bay. "Rowed to Bishop Rock" was all Higginson noted for one sunny June day. "Went fishing for bass" was a typical August entry. For a reformer who had virtually lived in train cars that carried him from convention to convention in the years just before the war, Higginson had no desire to leave Newport. When Elizabeth Cady Stanton wrote in May 1866, begging him to speak at a women's rights conference, Higginson declined. "I never go to Conventions, now," he replied, "& dislike public speaking." At most, he added, "a letter I will *try* to write."[2]

Mary's delicate health also tied him to home, more so than in the antebellum years, due to the fact that she suffered more bad days than good ones, but also surely from a sense of guilt at having left her in the hands of others for so long. For a brief time in the first months of 1866, Higginson assured himself that Mary was "gaining decidedly—her hands spread as far as mine in proportion & fingers move more freely." In April she was able, with his help, to walk about their garden, "only the 4th time since October, & felt better since that time." Other journal entries were less promising. It was a trial, he admitted, to live in a house that was actually a "hospital" and to witness "the only object of his care in tears of suffering daily." Determined to get Mary into fresh air, Higginson had one side of his carriage removed so that her wheelchair could be lifted directly into the cab, allowing the two to ride around the town.[3]

Declining all invitations to speak, Higginson settled into a simple routine. Each morning he rose early for breakfast and then exercised for thirty minutes by sawing and chopping wood. Mary rose later, and Higginson sat beside her while she ate, and then, from ten to two, as he wrote, Mary sat nearby with a book propped open on a simple stand. Holding a pointer in her gnarled fingers, she was able to turn the pages on her own. Her friends dropped by to check on her, and, as Higginson cheerfully observed, his "writing was often done in the midst of lively conversation." Most visitors were struck by Mary's condition but impressed by Higginson's determined cheer. "On the whole I think him an astonishing success under difficulties!" Helen Hunt Jackson, a poet, told a mutual friend. "What would become of *you*, for instance, or me, to sleep where he sleeps—embrace what he embraces!"[4]

So isolated was Higginson from the larger world that he barely took notice of the events in Appomattox Court House or Ford's Theater. "News of Lee's surrender, occurring yest'dy," he wrote in his diary for April 10, devoting more words for that day and the next to the "rainy" weather. Despite the fact that Lee's submission effectively marked the end of the conflict to which Higginson had nearly lost his life, the retired colonel spent the next days reporting on his "First French lesson" and a long stroll on a "Delightful day" amid large "quantities of sheep & lamb." Higginson's wartime diary had filled pages each evening, but his April 15 entry said only, "News of President's assassination. Shops closed & sheets in mourning." Two days later he roused himself to travel to Boston to attend a meeting at Faneuil Hall, but never having warmed to the martyred president, he declined to speak and instead dined with Waldo and his sister Susan Louisa. "Streets draped with black & portraits of Mr. Lincoln everywhere," was all he noted.[5]

Only slowly was Higginson recalled to life. In the spring of 1866, he accompanied Charlotte Forten, whom he had met on the Carolina coast, to

Figure 9.1 This 1865 portrait shows Higginson as a veteran whose health was broken by the war. His pensive, almost sad gaze hints at a man whose normally optimistic nature had seen more than his share of death and suffering during his South Carolina and Florida campaigns. Courtesy of the Library of Congress.

Boston to hear Emerson speak on "the dignity of thought." On another occasion, he dined at Boston's Union Club, established in 1863 on Beacon Hill to serve officers, writers, and supporters of the Union cause. After a hiatus of eighteen months, Emily Dickinson resumed her correspondence, timidly asking, "Would you instruct me now?" and sending one poem, "Further in Summer than the Birds," for his thoughts. Higginson even took an interest in amateur theatricals, accepting a small part in a local production of John Morton's two-act comedy, *A Soldier's Courtship*. Reform conventions remained an activity of the past.[6]

Higginson's writings revealed a new fascination with the simple life of Newport. Although always a close observer of nature, whose poems and essays gloried in silent walks in the woods, he sent the *Atlantic* works increasingly focused on the minutiae of New England existence. Gone were the previous year's stories of soldiers and enslaved rebels and campaigns up Carolina's rivers. Instead, "Oldport Wharves" described several ancient docks in affectionate detail. "The Haunted Window" was no ghost story but a reminiscence of an old house from his youth. "A Drift-Wood Fire" depicted the calm of a crackling blaze, and "Oldport in Winter" was an ode to a silent, snowy night. While walking along Newport's cliffs, Higginson was suddenly struck by the idea of writing a "romance," that is, a full-length novel. He would not complete his only novel for several more years, but the idea for it was inspired by the tranquility of the coast.[7]

Newspapers promoting the *Atlantic* promised readers that Higginson "and all the old writers will continue their contributions," but Higginson's longtime editor, James Fields, was less sure that was the case. As Higginson tallied up his income and expenses on the last day of 1866, the totals disclosed the cost of writing versus speaking. Two local lectures had netted him $272, while essays in the *Atlantic* provided him only $300 collectively. He had agreed to edit two volumes of *Harvard Memorial Biographies* and write thirteen of the entries, and that gained him another $500. Essays for the local newspaper brought in $265. Together with undefined "sundries," Higginson's total income for the year was $2,427, but the rent for their home was almost half that. "Medical attendance" for Mary cost $160, and clothes for them both totaled $158. Because of Mary's health, two Irish "domestic servants," Mary and Joanna, resided with them and together earned wages of $77. Food, dental bills, and athletic equipment added to the count. "Remainder," Higginson carefully added, was a meager $540.61.[8]

A number of factors, including potential insolvency, prodded Higginson back into the world. On December 22, 1866, his forty-third birthday, he announced to his journal that he was "now physically well again." Mary's health also continued to improve. On one warm August day, she walked about the garden "further than before," and even as the cooler fall days of 1867 closed in, Higginson took solace in the fact that she walked "about the parlor almost every day at noon & has been for several times in the garden."[9]

The other issue that served to end Higginson's rustic retirement was an invitation to speak about the soldiers he had led and the cause they had served. The New England branch of the Freedmen's Union Commission was set to hold their first anniversary meeting in Boston in June 1866, and when Governor Andrew, who had agreed to preside, contacted Higginson about speaking, he felt he could not decline. "I hate public speaking more than ever, since the war," he assured his sisters Ann and Susan Louisa, but in the end, he admitted that "it was a fine meeting" and that he had "a very good time." Afterward he dined at the Union Club with Theodore Parker and George Luther Stearns, an old ally from the Harpers Ferry days. Rather surprised at Higginson's appearance, the *New York Herald* welcomed the "Colonel's" return to public life.[10]

As did many abolitionists, Higginson initially believed that the Thirteenth Amendment had put an end to the nation's greatest struggle. "The world has been transformed, since I used to write to you about Anti-Slavery matters," he reflected to Gerrit Smith in the spring of 1867. But the willingness of the accidental president Andrew Johnson—who became president after Lincoln's assassination in April 1865—to placate white Southerners had produced a series of state laws collectively known as the Black Codes, designed to virtually reenslave freedpeople, and had inspired a series of white-orchestrated massacres in Memphis and New Orleans. Near Beaufort, Higginson's wartime home, a former Confederate soldier shot a Black youth fifty-seven times. "What most men mean to-day by the 'president's plan of reconstruction' is the pardon of every rebel for the crime of rebellion," Higginson fumed to Smith, "and the utter refusal to pardon a single black loyalist for the 'crime of being black.'" Although a good number of white Republicans feared that endorsing Black suffrage would endanger their party in upcoming Midwestern elections, radicals like Higginson, Smith, and Stearns prodded Senator Sumner to accept no compromise on the issue. In a public statement sent to Greeley's *Tribune,* Higginson insisted that Black Southerners had earned the right to vote by donning Union blue. "As commander of a regiment of colored South Carolinians," he wrote, "I claim for those brave men a share in the government of the country, at least equal to that conceded to the Rebels who endeavored to destroy it."[11]

Inspired anew by his conversations with old allies, and aware that *Atlantic* readers preferred essays of glory over his recent submissions, Higginson began to accept requests to speak around New England about his wartime experiences. Rather than tell again of his leading invasions up Carolina's rivers, he crafted new topics, with an eye toward not only their publication as individual essays but combining all of his pieces into a larger book about his years with the 1st. In short order, "Out on Picket," "Up the Edisto," and "Negro Spirituals" appeared in 1867 issues of the *Atlantic*. The last piece in particular, described by one editor as "a lengthy essay on negro hymnology," grew out of Higginson's wartime transcriptions of religious songs conveyed in coastal dialect. Staid Northern audiences were fascinated by what they regarded as a nearly foreign culture; one Ohio newspaper described the essay as "interesting and amusing," as it "present[ed] a very curious collection of real negro melodies." Sales of the June issue reinforced Higginson's determination to compile his writings on the 1st into a single volume. One Charleston editor sneered that Higginson was "writing up glorification articles of himself and his colored troops," in which he "claims the credit for putting down the rebellion."[12]

As soon as his old allies realized that he might be available to speak, invitations poured in. Lucy Stone prevailed on Higginson to address the Manhattan Equal Rights Convention, which he was content to do in part because just two days before that he was due to speak at the anniversary meeting of the American Anti-Slavery Society. At the former, Higginson shared the stage of Steinway Hall with William Wells Brown and his old associate Wendell Phillips, the Society's president. After a series of speakers promoted Black suffrage but failed to address land reform, Higginson and Phillips rose to submit a resolution insisting that "a large measure of confiscation and the division of the confiscated land among the negroes is imperatively demanded to secure the rights of the negroes." The chamber approved the resolution with no opposition. The women's rights conference went equally well. "Home at night after happy visit," Higginson reflected in his diary, little knowing the harmony within the feminist movement was to be short-lived.[13]

In the decades before the war, the lyceum speaking circuit had been haphazardly organized. When Higginson had spoken in the West, it was usually because he was responding to a particular invitation, and he then contacted fellow reformers in nearby towns in search of other speaking opportunities. But in 1869, the Boston Lyceum Bureau began a formal booking system across all New England, and within two years had opened branch offices in New York and Chicago. The Bureau was formally affiliated with Higginson's old Brown ally, the journalist James Redpath, and the agency was particularly interested in booking speakers willing to address Reconstruction issues. The Bureau promptly signed Higginson, Frederick Douglass, and Phillips, paying each speaker $100 per lecture and covering "expenses for rent, fuel, printing, [and] janitor." (Less interested in women's issues, the Bureau paid Elizabeth Cady Stanton $75 per speech.) Because speakers traveled a circuit and gave up to fourteen lectures before returning home, Higginson was able to earn almost as much in two weeks as he had pocketed in all of 1866. Typical was his venture of the late fall in 1867. A Wisconsin newspaper announced that he and Douglass were heading west. After boarding the New York and Erie Railroad, Higginson spoke in Buffalo, Toledo, Oshkosh, and Racine; made two stops in Iowa; and concluded in Chicago and Alton. "I had the satisfaction of it, which pays for itself," he wrote his sister Ann from Illinois. But in the privacy of his diary, Higginson noted that he "got $100 a night," or roughly $2,200 in today's currency.[14]

The Grand Army of the Republic (GAR), a fraternal organization of veterans and an advocacy group founded in Illinois in 1866, spread east, and Higginson became a fixture at their meetings. He was elected president of his regiment's Association of Ex-Officers and Enlisted Men when they met at Manhattan's Astor House. Seth Rogers, the unit's doctor, attended the organizational meeting, as did former sergeant Prince Rivers, who had recently been elected to the South Carolina Assembly. Higginson also served as chairman of Ex-Officers of U.S. Colored Troops, which met annually in New York's Union Club. The organizations allowed for the fireside camaraderie of the war to continue, and, as Higginson admitted to his diary, he gradually came to "quite enjoy" these public dinners. At one Philadelphia meeting, he dined with Congressman Stephen Hurlbut, the older brother of his "former friend." In addition to the comradeship, Higginson understood the need to keep Black military service and sacrifice in the public eye as President Johnson turned his back on their claims. "Resolved," Higginson announced at the second conclave, "It is expedient to perpetuate the ties and continue the work of the colored troops who served during the late war." Speaking at yet a third meeting, this one at Boston's John A. Andrew GAR

Post, with what an admiring journalist described as "well known eloquence and pure diction," Higginson argued that Black soldiers had "brought the nation equality." Although many white soldiers initially resisted serving beside Black regiments, he remarked, they quickly changed their minds, as their combined numbers meant a quicker victory and a faster return to "prosperity."[15]

Higginson also became a popular speaker at Decoration Day ceremonies, observations held shortly after Appomattox to honor whose who had died in the nation's service. Usually marked with speeches and the decorating of graves with flowers, the service initially had no fixed date, which permitted Higginson to speak at several each year. At Mount Auburn cemetery in Cambridge, he reminded his audience that "no matter what [the war] has cost us individually," it provided "Union, Freedom, and Equal Rights." Several months later found Higginson in St. Alban's, Vermont, speaking on what was rapidly becoming the established Decoration Day in late May. Shortly afterward, he delivered a speech in Bangor, Maine, when a "beautiful monument" to the city's sailors and soldiers was unveiled. So accustomed did audience and newspaper readers become to reading Higginson's words at such moments that a Philadelphia editor complained about one unnamed orator's "tame and uninteresting" speech delivered at the dedication of Harvard's Memorial Hall. "If Col. Higginson had been called to the platform on this occasion," the *Commonwealth* complained, "we should have had ringing words, such as warm the blood and stir the soul." Higginson was so pleased by the piece that he cut it out and pasted it into his diary.[16]

For many veterans, GAR events were occasions to escape the boredom of peacetime and relive old glories. For Higginson they were opportunities to connect with like-minded reformers and advance the cause of civil rights, and not merely in the defeated South. He alerted Greeley and the *Tribune* to the struggles of former army chaplain Henry McNeal Turner, who was forced to resign as postmaster of Macon, Georgia, due to false allegations of counterfeiting. When speaking in Boston at an Annual Anti-Slavery Festival, Higginson reminded the convention that even in New England, "a colored man would not go to a hotel and be properly treated." Why focus only on South Carolina, he questioned, when basic social equality had yet to "be fully secured" in the North? Black men could at least vote in Massachusetts, but the Empire State retained its 1821 property qualifications, and Black veterans returning home to the Midwest could nowhere cast a ballot. In response to the rising ride of Southern violence, Congress had passed a Civil Rights Act in 1866. However, that law, like most Republican politicians, was silent on the franchise. "Organizations which aim to enfranchise the freedmen are as legitimately the successors of the Antislavery movement as are the organizations which aim to educate them," Higginson wrote Charles Allen, the Massachusetts attorney general.[17]

Rather to his surprise, Higginson discovered that "since attending these meetings," he felt "more restored to the world than last year without loss of literary power." Far from inhibiting his ability to produce essays, public speaking inspired him. "It may be that I can yet combine both, though this at one time seemed impossible." Over the space of just a few weeks in January 1868, Higginson attended a GAR meeting in Philadelphia, met with Connecticut senator William Barnum regarding temperance, and "spoke with uncommon freedom" at a Boston civil rights convention. His renewed activity attracted the attention of his critics. When Jamaicans protesting poverty and a poll tax designed to deny them voting rights led to the burning of a courthouse in Morant Bay, one Northern Democratic editor used the affair to praise President Johnson's public attacks on "negro equality and negro suffrage" while attempting to cast blame on "northern agitators and radicals, such as Phillips, Fred Douglass, Garrison, and Higginson" and their "insane doctrines of negro equality."[18]

Higginson's activism remained largely local, and he did not much focus on affairs in Washington, if only because he knew few Republicans would now embrace his radical agenda. He was furious at those Republican moderates who voted to acquit Johnson at his Senate impeachment trial, especially Lyman Trumbull of Illinois and William Pitt Fessenden of Maine, who changed their earlier position. "If two and two were four last February, in the mind of a Senator," he groused, "we ask that they shall make four now." Higginson wished the Republican presidential nomination would go to Sumner, and if not to him then to Chief Justice Salmon Chase. He was nonetheless hardly surprised when the convention instead tapped Ulysses Grant. In a speech at a meeting of the Anti-Slavery Society, Higginson reluctantly endorsed the general and even chided his old friend Phillips for "not loving Grant enough." Yet in the end he delivered only one speech at a Grant rally that fall. Although Higginson—like Douglass and Garrison, for that matter—remained a Republican, he had no illusions that the party would adopt a truly progressive program in the near future.[19]

Higginson's efforts to make a clear connection between Black military service and postwar demands for civil rights grew more explicit, however, when he took his latest speech, "The Nation's Debt to the Soldiers," to the nation's capital in early 1869. Higginson could be his own toughest critic, and, as he told his sister Ann, he was "prone to humility about speaking." But this lecture, he wrote Mary, "was a real success": "I think I seldom have spoken so well." President-elect Grant, he noticed, did not attend, though Massachusetts senator Henry Wilson, who did, assured him that Grant had purchased "extra tickets & urged his friends to do so." The press appeared to support Higginson's assessment. "Higginson is a tall, raw-boned man," one reporter noted. "He has a long beard but looks unlike a literary character; he is a clear case of 'Yankee Colonel.'" Only Charles Sumner "surpassed him in stature." Another reported that "Col. Higginson is naturally the most popular of this class of speakers, combining as he does a literary reputation with a military record." Few of Higginson's critics bothered to attend, but nobody in the audience could have missed his point on Black voting rights. Men like those in his regiment, Higginson continued to insist, risked their lives more than those who had led them, and to those Black soldiers "the nation owes a debt that must be paid during the whole of their lives."[20]

***

Newport offered some opportunities for reform. Shortly after relocating to Rhode Island and just before he resigned his commission, Higginson accepted a local judge's invitation to serve on the city's school board. A majority of the committee approved his nomination, the judge arguing that the Harvard-educated writer and advocate of gender equality in schools would prove to "be a very useful man." Only one member dissented, evidently not grasping the distinction between commissioned and junior officers in Black regiments. "Don't know anything about" Higginson's qualifications, he snapped. "But I'm not going to sit on the same Committee with a *black* man." Higginson loved the anecdote.[21]

As he had when serving on the Worcester school board years earlier, however, Higginson immediately gained more than one critic. In the case of Worcester, he had championed the right of Catholic parents to substitute their preferred translation of the Bible over the King James Version in mandatory religion classes. That had gotten him "honorably dismissed," as he put it. The same thing happened in 1866 in Newport. Congress had just passed the Civil Rights Act, prompting Higginson to push for integrated public schools. Hoping to appeal to residents' pocketbooks, he argued that apart from the injustice of segregation, it was uneconomic for the city to maintain separate schools for Black children. Racism proved stronger than pragmatic appeals, however, and Higginson lost his bid for reelection. Ironically, just as he was again being forcibly retired, Rhode Island's legislature passed legislation requiring integrated schools. Higginson's efforts earned him the support of Newport's progressives, and a few years later, in 1870, a number of Republicans advanced his name for an open seat in the state assembly. Not notified before the fact, Higginson was unable to campaign and probably would not have done so in any case. Even so, voters in his district cast 74 ballots in his name, placing him third behind former congressman William Sheffield, who won with 496 votes.[22]

A few years later, in 1874, Higginson achieved vindication when he was again elected to the board. "I am pleased at this reversal of one of the most marked slights I have received," he exulted, "when I was dropped for having promoted the abolition of the colored schools." He was especially pleased that joining him on the committee was Mahlon Van Horne, a New Jersey–born Black minister who had previously served as principal of the African Methodist Episcopal Zion School in Charleston, South Carolina. At Higginson's prodding, and for the first time in their history, Newport schools required calisthenics of all pupils, and he raised money to build and equip a gymnasium in the city's center.[23]

Higginson also renewed his old interest in spiritualism, both as a way to avoid what he regarded as damaging sectarianism and as a purer path to what he called divine perfectionism. His brush with death during the war may also have had something to do with it. Initially, in the months after he resigned his commission and required solitude, Higginson was content to write editorials in New York's *Friends of Progress*, the leading spiritualist journal. Quakerism, he believed, had lost adherents "through its formality, Universalism through its narrowness, and Unitarianism through its indecision." Only when "rational Spiritualists and radical Unitarians" could unite and merge the wisest teachings from other faiths, he argued, might religion find the "right middle path." As Higginson once explained it to Wendell Phillips, his mother had taught him not to rely on churches, which allowed him a "happy escape" from the pulpit. Louisa might not have agreed with that statement, but the fact that Higginson now desired a more "rational" spiritualism suggested he no longer had any interest in the physical and aural manifestations—the knocking and disembodied voices—that had once fascinated him. The fact that Southern editors, who normally had little use for Higginson, reprinted his words revealed that many across the nation shared his grief and loss in the years after 1865.[24]

By May 1867, however, just as Higginson slowly began to return to public life, he was persuaded to attend a "Free Religion" conference in Boston. Together with Unitarian minister Octavius Frothingham, Lucretia Mott, Ralph Waldo Emerson, and Robert Dale Owen, the Scots-born politician and founder of the socialist community New Harmony in Indiana, Higginson helped craft a series of resolutions that encouraged "the scientific study of theology" and promoted what they all called "the interests of pure religion." The leading delegates all delivered speeches, which were then published in pamphlet form. The group promised to meet every May, and elected Frothingham the organization's permanent president. When the society met for the third time in 1869, they were joined by feminist and poet Julia Ward Howe and a correspondent for Manhattan's *Jewish Times*. The members all agreed to a free and open exchange of ideas, and Higginson praised the participants as numbering among them the leading reformers in "the most successful reforms of the day." Because of the presence of Higginson and Mott, one Vermont reporter observed that several of the "chief actors" had previously taken part in women's suffrage meetings. Some ministers and editors, those who had no interest in women's rights and evidenced no desire to abandon some of their dogma in hopes of achieving a broader faith, took a dim view of the proceedings. A Charleston journalist derided the conferences as a "*thoroughly out of kilter*" group of "atheists, deists, spiritualists and free lovers." If mainstream churches were declining in membership, an Ohio editor huffed, it was "because the church has been prostituted into partisan fellowship with such men as Higginson." Higginson, of course, sought just the opposite, though agreed with their determination to "make reason the supreme guide."[25]

Higginson dutifully attended the conference each May. He also began to lecture from New York to New England on "The Sympathy of Religions," sometimes by himself and at other times sharing a stage with Phillips and Howe. When challenged by Unitarians in the audience, Higginson responded that those adherents were "wasting effort in the attempt to bring that organization to the platform of Free Religion." What was needed instead was a "religion of the heart." Higginson reminded his audiences that he had once lost his place on the school board "for denying [the] right of the Committee to compel a little Irish girl to read the Protestant Bible," and he noted that even when reading the same Bible, there were "scarcely two intelligent beings who will receive exactly the same impression from any inspiration." What he called "free thought" had been the "origination of the anti-slavery and the temperance reforms, and the woman's rights movement." Nearly as many editors, Higginson was pleased to note, were approving as censorious. "Those who know his bright and witty way of putting things can conceive of the capital manner" of his address, one Boston newspaper gushed. "The lecture was several times applauded and the audience were unanimously pleased with the discourse," Higginson himself recorded in his diary.[26]

In between lectures and conferences, Higginson found time to produce more essays for the *Atlantic*. Apart from his articles on his time with the 1st Infantry, the one that attracted the most attention was "A Plea for Culture" in the January 1867 issue. The path to a truly American culture, Higginson argued, was not to abandon "the fine arts" but to support them with a modern curriculum: "Our educational system requires a process of addition, not subtraction." Thinking back to his teenage years at Harvard, in which so many courses were taught by rote, or earlier still, at William Wells's academy and the whippings so common there, Higginson proposed that universities "undertake to deal with men, not children, and assume that they have come to learn, and not to be feruled," that is, punished with a stick or cane. Higginson valued his classical education and knowledge of Greek and Latin, but in the rapidly changing postwar nation, it was imperative to "give young men the opportunity to study anything" that they or their parents thought necessary to rise in society. Making them read something that neither they nor their parents desired resulted only in "ignorance and the torturing of freshmen." Newspapers from Maine to Missouri praised the essay for its practicality, and it prompted a response from Emily Dickinson, who had fallen silent during the previous twelve months after Higginson had invited her to join him in Boston. She sent her usual brief request: "Bringing still my 'plea for Culture,' Would it teach me now?"[27]

Several months later, Higginson completed the novel he had been working on sporadically. *Malbone: An Oldport Romance* was loosely based on his own life, family, and friends. Just after the war, he had purchased a set of Jane Austen's novels, and his hope was to craft a similar tale of courtship and dashed hopes. Antebellum Newport and the old Hunter mansion provided the setting, with his protagonist, Philip Malbone, by Higginson's admission, a mixture of William Henry Hurlbut's charm and beauty and his own sunny optimism. "He liked everybody and everybody liked him," Higginson wrote of his leading man, and then, remembering his youthful attraction to Hurlbut and his dismay at his friend's moral decline, added, "He had a personal beauty, which, strange to say, was recognized by both sexes." Aunt Jane, "the head of the house," was a composite of Aunt Nancy, Louisa, and Mary, as she had "spent more than fifty years in educating her brains and battling her ailments." Hope, the novel's heroine, was so clearly an amalgam of his unmarried sisters Ann and Susan Louisa that he felt the need to privately beg them not to be "dismayed" at finding themselves in his story. "I had to write it," he explained to them. "I enjoyed it so much."[28]

The slim novel worked best when Higginson paused to describe the town and its people, and his ear for dialogue proved natural, perhaps because so many of the conversations were drawn from life. But the plot was slight, and the surprise ending, in which Emilia, the treacherous counterpoint to Hope, vanished at sea, appeared implausible even for those who knew the fate of Higginson's brother Samuel Thatcher. As was often the case with Victorian fiction, the novel was serialized, and Higginson assured his sisters that his longtime editor, James Fields, "liked it very much though he made excellent criticisms," which Higginson "mostly followed." Over the course of the fall of 1868, Higginson intended to make final revisions, but after Fields promised to publish it in six installments starting in January 1869, its "acceptance of publication seems to have so far detached it for me that I cannot modify it continually." Fields, however, evidently was not as confident in the novel's success as Higginson. He offered only $1,000 for the book's publishing rights, an amount, Higginson complained, that "does not at all satisfy me & is a great disappointment." At this late date, Higginson decided not to sell it elsewhere, though he warned Fields that he could take no less than "$200 per number—$1200 for the whole." Even then, he cautioned, he would "be fractious for some time to come & not love the Atlantic as loyally as I have."[29]

Fields had a better sense of the market, or perhaps a more realistic appraisal of the novel's merits. The national press simply noted, as they invariably did, that beginning with the first *Atlantic* issue of 1869, *Malbone* was to appear as a serial story. Only a handful of newspapers characterized the story as "excellent," and that was possibly due more to Higginson's reputation as an essayist than an actual assessment of the book's qualities. When the serial ended in June, Fields reprinted the novel in hardcopy. One year later, Higginson observed in his journal, the book had sold just under two thousand copies, and the amount he received in royalties was less than he earned in a single *Atlantic* installment. Even so, he was convinced the novel had increased his literary reputation.[30]

Higginson had far greater success the following year when he pulled together and revised the eight essays the *Atlantic* had published on his service with the 1st Infantry as *Army Life in a Black Regiment*. This time Fields offered little editorial advice, suggesting only that the final title was preferable to Higginson's initial thought of "Leaves from an Officer's Journal." Unsurprisingly, Higginson's account of his alliance with contraband troops sparked new controversy across the South. In an indignant essay reprinted in newspapers from West Virginia to South Carolina, one editor reminded readers that Higginson had "acquired notoriety during the war as the colonel of a thieving and murderous gang of negroes." His soldiers, the piece alleged, "were guilty of inhumanities which Indians on the war-path would hesitate to commit." Although Higginson had returned home poor in purse and physically broken, the story claimed that he kept "a share of the plunder of his gang" and that "none but those afflicted with 'nigger on the brain' will suppose that Higginson tells the truth in his narrative." Higginson was rightly proud of his book, and Fields was pleased enough to promise him "$150 per article," prompting him to churn out six more pieces for the *Atlantic*'s 1870 issues, including an essay on the healthy benefits of swimming. By that December, several newspapers guessed that among American writers, "the genial Higginson rates 'way up in the thousands" of income for each year.[31]

Higginson's literary output caught the attention of the trustees of the University of Michigan. When the institution's presidency became vacant in July 1869, several trustees advanced Higginson's name for the position. No formal offer appeared, but in any case, Higginson was too involved in his latest cause, which fused his renewed interest in publishing with his ongoing belief in spiritual freedom. In the fall of 1867, while in Boston for a meeting of the Free Religious Association, Higginson and Mott had begun to discuss the possibility of formalizing their occasional discussions of literature, theology, and science into a club with regular meetings and traditional presentations of essays in progress. The plan that was adopted was for the group, henceforth to be known as the Radical Club, to meet on the first Monday of each month. Presenters would submit essays in advance, with one member appointed to then deliver a formal response before turning to a general discussion. Unitarian minister John Turner Sargent volunteered the use of his spacious Chestnut Street home. A number of reformers, theologians, aging Transcendentalists, and women's rights activists promptly signed on, including Emerson, Frothingham, Phillips, Bronson Alcott and his daughter Louisa May, Julia Ward Howe, and Higginson's old classmate Samuel Longfellow. Mary Sargent promised to open her door to any reform-minded Bostonian as a guest.[32]

The club shared a good number of members with a second group. Organized by Howe, the Women's Club also met monthly in Boston's Tremont Temple, usually on the 23rd to honor the birthday of the late feminist and writer Margaret Fuller. Both clubs promised that men and women would "meet on terms of equality," but the chief difference is that while the Radical Club engaged a wide variety of topics, the Women's Club was organized around members reading each other their poems. Although the Radical Club drew occasional fire from ministers and conservative editors who regarded any discussion of religious liberty as heresy, a society dedicated to feminism and the notion that women might craft brilliant poems attracted even greater ridicule. "Mrs. Howe will supply its bland atmosphere of scholarship," sneered one Philadelphia editor, "Garrison will agitate the same with carnal thunderbolts of gratuitous fanaticism, and Higginson will reason from the wrong premise to the wrong conclusion."[33]

The press covered each meeting of the Radicals, often in great detail. Newspapers as far west as Chicago also chronicled the debates, perhaps because educated readers delighted in seeing literary luminaries they had long enjoyed gently spar with one another and try to outdo other members in witticisms. "On one side of the room is Thomas Wentworth Higginson, lusty and healthy in body," wrote one Boston journalist, "a fighter who strikes with Cromwellian directness at the heart of his antagonist's thought." When Howe presented a paper on "Limitations," author David Wasson replied that "a man who tries to do everything naturally fails to do anything," before indicating that he was referring to "Col. Higginson." Higginson blandly noted that as their discussions often reached the pages of the *London Saturday Review*, they "were in small danger" of not having their ideas accomplish some good in modern societies. On another occasion, Bronson Alcott—"the white-haired sage of Concord"—spoke on "Inspiration." Higginson disagreed with what he called Alcott's "discouraging" tone, arguing that "there were two kinds of inspiration—the one which we receive from the man who knows and says everything, the other which comes from the very stillness of some[one] who says nothing, and so makes us say everything." Higginson added that "women of this type wrought the charm of the French salon," which prompted Alcott to concede the point "to his martial neighbor." With good reason, such guests as feminist Abby Kelley Foster and Charlotte Forten, whom Higginson had known from his Beaufort days, crowded into each monthly session.[34]

"I have been wandering about more than usual," Higginson reflected in his diary in early 1869, "lecturing & read[ing] before the Radical Club." Whether Mary objected to his return to the road was an issue upon which he did not comment in his journal. Nor is there any evidence that she complained about the occasional references to her husband in the press that paired him with Julia Ward Howe, whose unhappy marriage to a man eighteen years her senior was a subject of common gossip. Howe was present in December 1870 when Higginson delivered his lecture on "Sappho," which was published the following July in the *Atlantic*. "A man whose friends are legion, and all whose friends wanted to hear him," reported the *New-York Tribune*, and they packed Sargent's home to hear what the newspaper described as "the Lesbian Swan." Perhaps to his audience's dismay, Higginson avoided the prurient and instead painted Sappho in a fashion that any feminist in the audience could appreciate. "Now why is it that, in case of a woman thus famous some cloud of reproach has always mingled?" he wondered. "In part, perhaps, because she was a woman and thus subject to harsher criticism in course periods of the world's career." Higginson supposed that if today "a Lesbian woman collected around a class of young pupils for instruction," it was as much beyond the understanding of a Greek male as of a Frenchman "pondering the relationship between Margaret Fuller and George Sand," the pen name of French novelist and feminist Amantine Aurore Lucile Dupin. Taking on Victorian writers who believed Sappho to have been "a corrupt woman" and her school at Lesbos "a nursery of sin," Higginson, who could read Greek and advanced his own translations of her poems, concluded by marveling that "a woman's genius could play such a part in molding the great literature that has molded the world." Proud of the essay, Higginson included it as one of the twelve pieces published in his 1882 *Atlantic Essays*.[35]

Higginson's writings captured the attention of a recent visitor to Newport, when in the winter of 1874 Samuel Clemens and his wife, Olivia, briefly abandoned Hartford, Connecticut, for a nearby vacation resort. Clemens had just published *Mark Twain's Sketches, New and Old*, and after Julia Ward Howe served the Clemenses tea, she put him in contact with Higginson. An invitation to dine with the Clemens family in February began a friendship that stretched on for years. In the privacy of his journal, the former minister reflected that "it seemed odd to have [Clemens] say grace, yet it seemed a genuine thing." Increasingly sad about the state of his own marriage, Higginson was immediately drawn to Olivia's kindness. "He has a very sweet refined wife."[36]

In the years after the war, Higginson devoted his energies to his other great antebellum cause, women's rights. While some abolitionists, believing slavery to be the greatest sin in American life, had insisted that the "Negro's hour" should precede "the women's hour," Higginson had always refused to privilege one cause over the other. With the ratification of the Thirteenth Amendment, many of Higginson's old male allies put down their pens, regarding their task as completed. But, as Higginson had assured Elizabeth Cady Stanton in 1866, his "*convictions* as [to] the political rights of women [were] unchanged." As he had believed about the battle against slavery, he maintained that "men can never secure women's rights vicariously for them." He was ever the ally, though he understood that feminists had no need for a male leader or spokesman. He was "haunted," however, by how many Northern women appeared to be indifferent to the cause and accepting of their oppression, particularly after seeing formerly enslaved people embrace their rights. Younger Americans of both genders, he feared, thought that with the war over and slavery gone, the country was "nearly at the end of those great public wrongs which require a special moral earthquake to end them." Together with a few of his old allies, Higginson was determined to attach himself to yet another good if unpopular cause.[37]

As Congress was still debating voting rights for Black men, something guaranteed to Southern freedmen by the 1867 Military Reconstruction Act but still denied to Black men in most Northern states, many women's rights advocates believed the time had come to push for voting rights for women as well. When the American Equal Rights Association, founded in 1866 for the express purpose of securing "Equal Rights to all American citizens, especially the right of suffrage, irrespective of race, color, or sex," met in May 1867, male feminists were divided on the question. Wendell Phillips restated his "Negro's hour" proposition, insisting that universal Black male suffrage took precedence, given the rising tide of violence in the former Confederacy, a position endorsed by Garrison. When Henry Ward Beecher rose to argue that it should be "the favored hour for all," Phillips gaveled him out of order. He dared not do so when Higginson got to his feet. Higginson pointed out that the wives of the soldiers in his regiment suffered the same attacks from Southern whites as did Black men, and that the "extension of the suffrage to the women of the South" would serve to strengthen the Black community. He also joined with Beecher, Gerrit Smith, and Ohio senator Benjamin Wade in drafting a public "Pronunciamento to the Voters of the United States," stating that "suffrage is the right of every adult citizen, irrespective of sex or color."

Higginson then permitted his 1854 essay "Women and Her Wishes," an early call for voting rights, to be reprinted in the anthology *Women's Rights* alongside essays by Beecher, Parker Pillsbury, and Stanton.[38]

Stanton, for one, welcomed Higginson's assistance. "We shall be glad to have anything from your pen," she advised him in early 1868. "You know the 'white male' is the aristocracy of this country, [and] we belong to the peasantry." Especially as "such men as Garrison, Phillips, [and] Sumner" continued to "push us aside saying 'this is the negro's hour,'" Stanton promised that while feminists "do care what all good men like you *say*, just now the men that will *do* something to help us are more important."[39]

Stanton's alliance with Higginson did not last long. At the time she was writing Higginson, she and Susan B. Anthony began to publish *The Revolution*, a weekly newspaper. Financing for the paper came from George Francis Train, a businessman as devoted to women's rights as he was critical of Black suffrage. Garrison denounced Train as a "raging egotist and blackguard," and a number of abolitionists, including Higginson, fired off letters of complaint. Stanton, with admirable courage, published the letters together with her rebuttals, which often descended into vitriol. To Higginson, Stanton responded that "time will show that Ms. Anthony and myself are neither idiots or lunatics." The spat between what one New York editor dubbed the "Train" and "Anti-Train" factions became even more public when the American Equal Rights Association met at Manhattan's Cooper Institute in May 1868. Stanton presided over the conference, and speakers were to include Anthony, Lucy Stone, Higginson, and Douglass. Just before the meeting opened, Higginson and Stone approached Anthony, begging her "*not to bring up anything unpleasant*" in the name of keeping the focus on women's suffrage. Anthony, however, regarded the speech by Henry Blackwell, Stone's husband, as "opening [a] chapter of complaints against" her. Higginson regretted the incident and admitted to Harriet Beecher Stowe that while he subscribed to *The Revolution* and was "constantly annoyed" at what he read, he was also "constantly impressed of the positions of these women." Society, he mused, "has always had more respect for the unwisely zealous than for those who are fastidiously impartial."[40]

Higginson and Anthony set aside their differences long enough to collaborate on *Eminent Women of the Age*, a volume of forty-seven biographical sketches published as a fundraiser. For Greeley's *Tribune*, Higginson also penned the essay "Women's Wages," renewing a demand for equal pay for equal work in New England's textile mills that had been going on for years.

As a member of the Committee of Arrangements for the fall 1868 women's rights convention in Boston, Higginson had helped to compose a call for attendance that he hoped "was so large & comprehensive" that it could result in "a strong meeting which should merge all petty differences & personalities." When the convention opened in Boston's Horticultural Hall, Higginson was elected to serve as one of the sixteen vice presidents, only six of whom were women. The meeting went smoothly, and when Douglass spoke in favor of "the more vital importance" of Blacks gaining the right to vote and then turning to female suffrage afterward, "if possible," Higginson countered that it was "emphatically the woman's hour." In his main speech, Higginson urged the gathering to be "charitable to each other," and in a pun that drew chuckles, he added that "we must expect our friends to make mistakes," just as "we must expect them sometimes to train in strange company." In the end, Higginson confided to his diary, "A very fine Convention, harmonious & strong throughout."[41]

Higginson alone seemed to believe that the peace could long survive. With the American Equal Rights Association, which in May 1869 had been rechristened the National Woman Suffrage Association, focused on including women in proposed amendments to the Constitution, Stone believed it necessary to form a second organization dedicated to lobbying individual state legislatures to expand the right to vote to women. At an October 1869 women's rights meeting in Providence, Rhode Island, Higginson and Paulina Davis passed a resolution regarding the upcoming convention in Cleveland calling "a new National Woman's Rights Suffrage" organization to be named the American Woman Suffrage Association (called AWSA in the newspapers). Perhaps because the Providence group wished to explicitly address voting rights by including the word "suffrage" in the title, the conservative press enjoyed mocking these "strong-minded women" and their male allies, describing them as "aged spinsters" and noting that during the speeches, "Colonel Higginson stroked his flowing beard in ecstasy." But the real impediment, as Stone and Higginson both knew, was not Democratic journalists but Stanton and Anthony. In a public letter, Stone and Higginson tried to clarify that they were not "depreciating the value of Associations already existing," but they thought it time for "an organization at once more comprehensive and more widely representative" of American women. Stanton promptly wrote to Higginson, tartly promising that if she was to be "a stumbling block in the way of the saints or the young converts," she would absent herself from Cleveland. "I can honorably retire," she added, hinting that Stone should as well. "Mrs. Stone is at that period of a woman's life when they are often morbid," she observed of her rival—who was actually three years Stanton's junior—and "hers has taken a jealous turn in a few years." Explaining in an article in *The Revolution* why she would absent herself from the upcoming convention, Stanton accused Higginson and the other "Boston malcontents" of "ostracizing" her and again promised to resign from the Equal Rights Association.[42]

The Cleveland convention convened on November 24 in Case Hall. Stone, described as "Lucy Stone Blackwell" in conservative newspapers, called the meeting to order "and read the circular letter" she and Higginson had crafted that explained the need for a new organization before turning the gavel over to Higginson. A few longtime activists, such as Lucretia Mott and Isabella Beecher Hooker, the younger sister of Harriett Beecher Stowe, hoped to maintain membership with both groups, but most of those hostile to Train, and even to Stanton and Anthony, whom Garrison derided as "untruthful, unscrupulous, and selfishly ambitious," pledged themselves to the new society. Julia Ward Howe, Abby Kelley Foster and her husband Stephen Foster, and Henry Ward Beecher all followed. Just as the meeting was underway, James Bradwell, an Illinois delegate, rose to suggest that Anthony, who had just arrived, be honored with a seat on the stage. Stunned at discovering her present, Anthony observed, the normally loquacious Higginson "hesitated, stumbled in speech," but finally found his voice and invited her to the platform. Anthony made only a brief and conciliatory speech, in which she suggested that "these independent and separate movements show that we are alive." The conference ended without further incident. The group elected Higginson as president for the next year, with each of the fifteen states represented in Cleveland getting one vice president. Stone was to serve as chair of the Executive Committee, with Howe as foreign corresponding secretary and journalist Franklin Sanborn, Higginson's old ally from their Harpers Ferry days, as treasurer.[43]

As the voice for the new organization, and to counter *The Revolution*, the Executive Committee decided to relocate a regional women's rights journal, Chicago's *Agitator*, to Boston and rechristen it the *Woman's Journal*. Mary Livermore, the *Agitator*'s editor, would continue in that role, with Stone, Higginson, Garrison, and Julia Ward Howe as coeditors. Howe thought to house the journal in the same Tremont Temple building rented by the Women's Club. The first issue made its appearance on January 8, 1870, and at $3 for a year's subscription, the magazine was priced low enough for middle-class readers. Perhaps because editors regarded it as a more temperate response to *The Revolution*, most were surprisingly charitable and eschewed the usual mocking tone they took when discussing feminist demands. Collectively, one Vermont paper observed, the editors were "all good and honorable names, and if any can convince us of the merits of woman suffrage, they will." One Philadelphia newspaper went further still, conceding that when the names of "Julia Ward Howe, Lydia Maria Child, and T. W. Higginson are added to those of the old leaders in this cause, we must conclude that the reform is to be carefully and practically considered."[44]

In hopes of reconciling the breach between the two groups, poet and editor Theodore Tilton invited leading members of both organizations to meet with him at Manhattan's Fifth Avenue Hotel on April 6 for what he called "an arbitration." Stone, Higginson, and civil rights advocate George Williams Curtis represented the AWSA, and Josephine Griffing and Parker Pillsbury appeared on behalf of the National Woman Suffrage Association. Stanton and Anthony declined to attend, and the typically serene Mott, who did attend, was still annoyed with Higginson for his behavior in Cleveland, wondering why he had "to hesitate when S. B. Anthony was called for." The conclave met for several hours, and Tilton read a letter from Anthony calling for "union," which Mott endorsed, hoping for "such concessions as each should make to the other." Stone and Higginson disagreed and insisted that while they were quite in favor of union, they did not wish to be "absorbed." Higginson asserted that he wished for harmony but saw "no reason for any modification of the present position of the American Woman Suffrage Association." Stone concurred, adding that "the olive branch was extended at Cleveland." The conference ended in failure, the two sides farther apart than before. "I didn't like Higginson's spirit & his & Lucy's flushed face & Curtis's determined spirit & manner—so little idea of yield'g," Mott complained. In a belated concession to their critics, Stanton and Anthony repealed the National's earlier ban on male leadership and elected Tilton its president. Garrison, Douglass, Phillips, Greeley, and even Stanton's cousin Gerrit Smith sided with Stone and Higginson.[45]

The division within the feminist movement grew yet more bitter and more personal when the AWSA again met in Cleveland in November 1870. Douglass was in attendance and encouraged a second attempt at union, but when Anthony arrived and spoke, any hopes of unity were dashed. *The Revolution* had begun to advocate for more equitable divorce laws, a contentious topic the *Woman's Journal* shied away from. In her prepared remarks,

Anthony charged that the *Journal* was "the last paper in the world that ought to speak against greater freedom for women in marriage and divorce, for one of its editors—Lucy Stone—at her wedding, refused to submit to the legal form of marriage" and instead "issued a solemn protest about the traditional vow of obedience." The moment Anthony finished speaking, a furious Higginson rose, shouting, "I cannot allow one who is admitted to the floor of this Convention by courtesy to attack the character of a prominent officer of this society, and go unrebuked." Anthony retorted that she resented the charge that she had "attacked" anyone, but was gaveled into silence by Higginson, who was also chairing the meeting, and who pointed out that he had "made no interruption while you were speaking." He then stated that if any woman in Massachusetts was legally married, that woman was Lucy Stone, and he knew this because he had "tied the knot myself." The reprimand brought applause from the floor, and far from winning over converts, Anthony succeeded only in alienating old allies by essentially repeating allegations made by conservative editors at the time of Stone's 1855 protest. Anthony later apologized, asserting that she "had no such intentions, as she honored Lucy Stone very much." The damage, however, was done.[46]

The crippling "war in the woman suffrage camp," as the Washington *Evening Star* dubbed it in a banner headline, was covered in newspapers across the nation. Perhaps because most editors, being male, sided with "the decorous *Woman's Journal*" and condemned Stanton's support "of free divorce," Stanton's and Anthony's denunciations of their critics grew both more personal and more public, and they turned their fire almost exclusively on Higginson. Stanton drafted a series of letters to her supporters, insisting that "Cleveland was a fizzle—no audience, no enthusiasm, no speakers." In a public letter, she denounced the "person known as T. W. Higginson [as] merely a man of straw, a dapper authority in dress, manners, and culinary utensils." Stanton's attempt to paint the former colonel as foppish was merely strange, but Anthony aimed lower yet when she confided to Martha Coffin Wright that she had "*heard gossip* of undue familiarity with persons of *the opposite sex*—relative to Beecher and Higginson." The National was preparing to meet in Washington, and before she should "consent" to allow Victoria Woodhull "or any other *earnest woman worker*" to attend, Anthony insisted that there be a full investigation of the "*scandals* afloat about those men." By tying Higginson to Beecher, who had been linked to Elizabeth Tilton, Theodore's wife, just the previous year, or with Woodhull, a twice-married feminist who championed legalized prostitution, Anthony evidently hoped to damage the reputation of the AWSA. But no publication picked up the allegation, and as with Anthony's maladroit criticism of Stone's wedding vows, suggesting that Higginson had not been faithful to his ill wife surely won her no new allies within the movement.[47]

Higginson simply ignored the accusations and declined to respond, knowing that any private missive would quickly become public and cause Mary considerable pain. Instead, he continued to speak about suffrage rights, sometimes, as in Washington and Rhode Island, in tandem with Stone and Howe. In Manhattan, in what one journalist described as his "rich, thrilling, dignified Boston voice," Higginson demolished the standard postwar argument that women had not been able to perform "military" service. Apart from the role that many played as nurses, he asked, did that mean Congress now intended to deny the ballot to "that certain class of weak-lunged, liverless, dyspeptic draft-dodgers?" In February 1871, just as Anthony was spreading rumors about his private life, Higginson made a similar argument to the Massachusetts Assembly and stumped across Vermont, where the state legislature was preparing to approve a new constitution without submitting the document to the people. It was "undemocratic" enough to deny women the right to vote in that method, Higginson insisted in one speech, but even more so given that only male legislators, rather than all Vermont residents, would get to decide the question. No matter was too small to give way on. When the American Social Science Association held their annual meeting in Boston, Higginson unexpectedly appeared and demanded that two women be added to the all-male board, a motion that was carried "by a unanimous vote." And when invited to speak at Harvard, Higginson "made a manly protest against the exclusion, by this institution, of the girls of New England."[48]

*****

Oblivious to the whispers against Higginson was his correspondent in Amherst. The two finally met in August 1870. Higginson told his colleagues at the Radical Club that he thought it the responsibility of older writers to discover and promote new talent. He had recommended Celia Thaxter, a poet and writer of short stories, to Fields in 1861, and he was the first established author to send a note of praise to Elizabeth Stuart Phelps, who composed stories of New England life. Higginson had long encouraged Dickinson to come to Boston to meet with him and other writers. Each time, she demurred. "I should be glad to see you, but think it an apparitional pleasure not to be fulfilled," she replied in early 1866, asking him instead to visit her in Amherst. "You would find a minute Host but a spacious Welcome." Not knowing of her reputation as a recluse, sometimes even to the extent that she declined to leave her bedroom to receive guests, Higginson chided her gently for being "elusive." Dickinson simply mailed Higginson more poems for his approval, and when he again mentioned Boston, she blamed her father, insisting that he "object[ed]" when she left home and once more requested that he be her "Guest to the Amherst Inn." Annoyed, Higginson failed to reply, creating a silence between them that lasted throughout the next year.[49]

The pace of their correspondence rose and fell as they debated whether or where to meet, with a brief renewal in the summer of 1867, followed again by a lengthy pause. Dickinson wrote in June 1869, sending Higginson several poems and renewing her invitation to host him in Amherst. Should he visit, she would be "very glad," but she warned, "I do not cross my Father's ground to any House or town." Her previous letters to him often read like her poems, short and sometimes obscure, but this one was unusually lengthy and concluded with an admission that clearly stunned Higginson. "You were not aware that you saved my Life," Dickinson confessed. "To thank you in person has been since then one of my few requests. The child that asks my flower, 'Will you,' he says—'Will you'—and so to ask for what I want I know no other way." Her confession elicited an equally blunt response, and one that revealed Higginson's intellectual ties to her poems and perhaps also contained an admission of his unhappiness with his private life. "I have the greatest desire to see you," he admitted, "always feeling that if I could take you by the hand I might be something to you." But her refusal to meet in Boston—a subject Higginson broached yet again by mentioning both the Radical and Women's clubs—meant that "you only enshroud yourself in this fiery mist & I cannot reach you." He frequently thought of traveling to Amherst, but because he was so often traveling for lectures he was rarely able to travel "for pleasure." Higginson concluded with the hope to "hear from you very often" and expressed astonishment that anybody could wish to "live so alone."[50]

In mid-August 1870, eight years after she had first approached him through the mail, Higginson found himself lecturing near Amherst and sent Dickinson a brief note asking if he might visit. "I will be Home and glad," was her brief reply. "The incredible never surprises us because it is the incredible." Higginson arrived at 2:00 in the afternoon at what he characterized as "a large country lawyer's house, brown brick," and was admitted to the parlor, where he was pleased to spy a copy of *Malbone* on the shelf. "A step like a pattering child's in entry & in glided a little plain woman with two smooth bands of reddish hair," he reported that evening to Mary. "A very plain & exquisitely clean white pique & a blue net worsted shawl." Higginson noticed also that she carried two lilies, which she placed in his hands "in a sort of childlike way," saying, "These are my introduction" in "a soft frightened breathless childlike voice." Gazing up at Higginson, seven years her senior and more than a foot taller than she, Dickinson apologized for being "frightened," as she rarely saw "strangers & hardly" knew what to say. But the two dined together, and Higginson lingered until nine o'clock. "Gratitude is the only secret that cannot reveal itself," she remarked as they parted. The next morning, she sent Higginson a brief note of thanks, assuring him, as he told Mary, that she "dreamed all night of you (not me)" and urged Higginson to return soon with Mary. Higginson admitted that he had barely mentioned Mary, and confided to his diary that the meeting was "a remarkable experience, quite equaling expectations."[51]

The fact that the tall warrior was as much at home with the diminutive Dickinson as he was in a Boston melee says much about Higginson's many worlds. But while the two corresponded with one another and exchanged thoughts on poetry for the next sixteen years, with Dickinson mailing Higginson more than one hundred poems and he sending her a copy of his collected *Atlantic Essays*, they met only once more, when Higginson was invited to lecture in Amherst in December 1873. As in their previous meeting, Dickinson "glided in, in white, bearing a Daphne odora for me, & said under her breath, 'How long are you going to stay?'" This time, Higginson was so baffled by their meeting that he mentioned only his lecture and honorarium in his diary for December 3. To his sister Ann he reported that he saw his "eccentric poetess Miss Emily Dickinson who never goes outside her father's grounds & sees only me & a few others." After Dickinson mailed Higginson more poems in early 1874, he wrote to assure her that she had not been "forgotten" and that he "enjoyed being with you." Despite rarely meeting, Higginson promised, "we seem to come together as old & tried friends." Mary was less patient with Dickinson, and perhaps a bit jealous of their intellectual connection. "I don't dare die and leave the Colonel," she confided to one friend, as "there are so many women waiting for him." To her husband, Mary simply wondered, "Oh why do the insane so cling to you?"[52]

*　*　*

With his reputation as a former soldier and a writer growing on both sides of the Atlantic, and with a steady income thanks to the *Atlantic*, in the summer of 1872 Higginson decided to accompany his brother Waldo and sister-in-law Mary when they traveled to Britain. Unlike other New England reformers, who often sailed for Britain to attend antislavery or women's rights conventions, Higginson had never demonstrated much interest in developing transatlantic connections. But Newport, unlike Worcester, attracted a good number of English tourists, and over the past years he had become friendly with the English writer and attorney Thomas Hughes, who, like Higginson, occasionally wrote for young people, and with John Russell, a Liberal member of Parliament and a women's rights activist. Armed with letters of introduction to Prime Minister William Gladstone, Irish nationalist and editor William McCarthy, and Scottish essayist and historian Thomas Carlyle, Higginson arrived in London on May 18. As always, he believed he had left Mary in good hands, though his diary said less about her health than about Waldo's and his sister-in-law's, writing that both were "rather tired [and] will take things more slowly than I can." Like all tourists, Higginson promptly visited Westminster Abbey, Shakespeare's Stratford, and Cambridge University. "I am having the most amazing time," he reported to his sisters, "perfectly overwhelmed with attention & kindness."[53]

During his brief visit, Higginson managed to combine sightseeing with reform, meeting with feminists and activists involved in industrial and franchise reform. Mostly, however, conversations with other writers occupied his time. Thanks to Hughes, Higginson was invited to speak at a gathering of the Anglo-American Society at London's Century Club, where he dined with Hughes and poet Matthew Arnold. Elizabeth Chase, a member of the Century Club, reported that "Col. H., as a scholar, writer, and reformer [delivered] a neat speech of commendation." Arnold was the son of Thomas Arnold, the celebrated educator and himself an advocate of state-supported secondary schools, so the two reformers had much to discuss.[54]

Far and away Higginson's favorite moment came when he called on naturalist Charles Darwin. Higginson had recently read Lewis Carroll's *Through the Looking-Glass*, and after the two fell into a conversation about its author, Emma Darwin pulled the book from a shelf and urged her husband to read aloud. "It was altogether delightful to see the man who had revolutionized the science of the world giving himself wholly to the enjoyment of Alice and her pretty nonsense."[55]

Both friends and supporters followed Higginson's travels in the press. Emily Dickinson wrote, saying that she had often seen his "name in illustrious mention" in the *Springfield Republican* and "envied an occasion so abstinent." She was happy Higginson had enjoyed the travel that he had "so long desired" and, as she had during the war, she prayed that her "Master met neither accident nor Death." Higginson was never quite sure how to respond to Dickinson's curious observations about his mortality. He did take pleasure in the praise of one of Boston's women's rights newspapers. Reporting on Higginson's meeting with English journalist Charles Bradlaugh, who had recently been prosecuted by the British government for blasphemy and sedition, the editor hoped that Higginson was "a secret emissary sent to drill the Republicans there as he did the black Federals of the South." Higginson was back in Newport by December 22, his forty-ninth birthday, and he reflected on both his successes and his sorrows. "Looking back at my work, I can see that I have improved in public speaking very much—chiefly by a better method of preparation & self-management." As for his publications, he judged them "as good work as I shall ever perhaps produce." But then: "Of my home life, there is little to be said."[56]

As Higginson moved into his fifth decade, life, at least for a time, began to take away more than it gave him. His robust health and the fact that he was by far the youngest in his family made this unsurprising, yet still painful. Of his half-siblings, the children born to his father and Martha Salisbury, Higginson had already lost Elizabeth Keith, who had died in 1840 at the age of forty-two; two other half-siblings had died before Higginson's birth. Of his full siblings, most of them much older than he, Higginson had seen Samuel Thatcher vanish at sea, and Mary Lee and Edward Cabot died when he was only three years old and one year old, respectively. In September 1870, word arrived that his brother Stephen, fifteen years his elder, had died at the age of sixty-two of "heart disease." A Boston-based merchant with business ties to the Royal Insurance Company of Liverpool, Stephen had done well for himself and owned a country estate in Deerfield, Massachusetts, and a smaller home in Cambridge, where he died. His wife, Agnes, survived him, as did most of their ten children, including his son Francis Jackson Higginson, who had served as a lieutenant with the 54th Massachusetts before joining the navy. Obituaries invariably mentioned Stephen's famous sibling, noting that he was "the elder brother of Col. T. W. Higginson." Higginson and his sisters attended the Cambridge funeral, Ann taking "the news with her usual wonderful strength & Louisa quietly." There "was a particular sweetness & affectionateness about Stephen which we all feel," Higginson reflected. Despite the fact that he and Stephen had rarely corresponded, the loss prompted Higginson to think more deeply about mortality. In one speech, he observed that "everyone wishes to go to heaven, but most people are willing to take a great deal of very disagreeable medicines first" to avoid it.[57]

Two years later, in March 1872, Francis John Higginson, Louisa's eldest child, died at his home in Brookline at the age of sixty-six. Newspapers reported that he had practiced medicine in Brattleboro, Vermont. He was survived by his wife, Susan, and two daughters, and had "left two brothers, Waldo Higginson and Col. T. W. Higginson." Higginson caught the train for Vermont for the burial at Prospect Hill Cemetery. "I am sorry your Brother is dead," Dickinson wrote after reading the obituary in the *Springfield Republican*. "I should be glad to know you were painlessly grieved." As was often the case with such kind but curious thoughts from Amherst, Higginson simply did not reply.[58]

"News of L.'s death," was all Higginson said to his journal on August 27, 1875. Susan Louisa, who had never married and had turned fifty-nine the previous March, died in Portland and was buried in Brattleboro's Prospect Hill Cemetery near her mother. To honor her, when the Boston Women's Club met that fall, Higginson read the works of "two unknown Poetesses, Louisa & Emily Dickinson." He explained to the group who Louisa was and talked about her education both from tutors and from her own reading, but, respectful of Dickinson's wish for privacy, did not identify her by name. He read a dozen of Louisa's poems, a few of which had been published in the *Harbinger*, a religious journal. "As there has been nothing written about Louisa, as yet," Higginson explained to his sister Ann, "I thought I should like to recall attention in this way to her poems." Of the ten children Louisa Storrow had given birth to, only Wentworth, Waldo, and Ann remained alive.[59]

Even more than after Stephen's death, the loss of Louisa prompted him to ponder his remaining years. Evidently Higginson mentioned his sister's death and Mary's poor health to Dickinson, as she wrote to suggest that Susan Louisa "has no suffering now," and she asked Higginson to pass her "remembrance [to] Mrs. Higginson." After Dickinson, whom Higginson described to his sister Ann as "my partially cracked poetess," asked if she might write directly to Mary, she did so from the summer of 1876 into the following spring. The missives were well intentioned but perhaps not much welcomed by the recipient. "I wish you were strong like me," one began. "I am sorry you need Health, but rejoice you do not [need] Affection." In another, Dickinson wished Mary a "Good Night with fictitious lips, for to me you have no Face." In a third, she made an oblique reference to Mary's inability to walk, promising that she "half resent my rapid Feet, when they are not your's." To Higginson, she hoped only that she had "not fatigued her."

Higginson patiently replied that he prayed her brother, who had been ill, was feeling better.[60]

Perhaps because of family considerations, Higginson paid little attention to electoral matters in 1876; he had always been more a regional reformer than a national one. In 1872, he had given only one pro-Grant speech and thought it advisable for Republicans to nominate another candidate. Even then, he did so only because he was invited to lead a march of "nearly a hundred Boys in Blue" through the streets of Newport. Privately, as he informed John Greenleaf Whittier, he judged both candidates—Grant and Greeley—"miserable" and thought it "folly for Grant to run again or for [Democratic nominee] Greeley to run at all."[61]

Four years later, in 1876, Higginson's focus on Mary's health and inattention to the larger world led to several inconsistencies regarding national politics. He publicly denounced a riot in Hamburg, South Carolina, in which armed Democrats attacked Black militiamen and burned the home of Judge Prince Rivers, Higginson's former sergeant. However, he also publicly praised the actions of the new president, Rutherford B. Hayes, in withdrawing federal soldiers from South Carolina and Louisiana. If Higginson thought their removal would reduce tensions in the South, he was being naive, and the fact that Southern editors now lauded "the old guard of abolitionism" should have alerted him to that fact. Unhappily, he was not alone in his faith in Hayes, as poet James Russell Lowell wrote to praise his public statements "about the President & Southern policy [as both] timely & wise."[62]

"Please recall me to Mrs. Higginson," Dickinson wrote in June 1877. The letter barely arrived in time. On September 2, Mary died at the age of fifty-six. Her end was not unexpected, and for most of August, Higginson's diary contained no entries. Finally, on September 5, he pasted in his diary, without comment, the obituary he sent to the *Boston Evening Traveler*. Mary's funeral, Higginson wrote, attracted "a large number of friends, but there was not that terrible gloom that usually accompanies funeral services." The Reverend James Freeman Clarke, who had served as chaplain for the 1st Infantry, conducted the simple service, and "the lady friends of the deceased sang the hymn." For once, Dickinson's letters were both heartfelt and sensible. "We must be less than Death, to be lessened by it," she wrote later that month, "for nothing is irrevocable but ourselves." Her father had suffered a stroke and died in 1874, and she observed that the "Wilderness" of such loss was "new—to you. Master, let me lead you." When Higginson was slow to reply, she quickly sent another: "I think of you so wholly that I cannot resist to write again, to ask if you are safe." A third, never published elsewhere, contained only this thought:

> Perhaps she does not go far
> As you who stay—suppose—
> Perhaps comes closer, for the lapse
> Or her corporeal clothes.[63]

10
"The happiest day of my life"
1877–1888

Twelve years earlier, at the end of the Civil War, Higginson had been badly in need of quiet. Now, with Mary gone, his house was far too silent. He began to crave companionship. Ann remained in Newport with him for a time, and numerous friends called each day. "I find the presence of friends very gratifying," he confessed to his diary shortly after Mary's death. He noted that most of them did not mention her death to him, and while they tried to "cheer" him, he would have to grieve on his own. Ann left after several weeks, and Higginson found the house silent and cheerless, so he decided to rent it out. Wandering about the house, Higginson reflected that the rooms provided "touching memories of Mary," but he would be happy to get away. On September 15, two weeks after Mary's death, Higginson awoke feeling that the worst was over. He was finally able to sleep and was "rested & seem[ed] to have come back to life." As is often the case with those who have witnessed the long, lingering decline of loved ones, Higginson took solace in the fact that his own health would soon improve. Caring for Mary to the point of carrying her around the house had proven hard, even for a man of Higginson's size. "What danger may not M. & I have escaped," he mused, "some worse condition in her & perhaps [an] entire break-down for me." That afternoon, he boarded the train for Brattleboro.[1]

"I go somewhere impromptu to tea, & the days go fast," Higginson reflected, although that was hardly enough to diminish his sorrow. But in late October 1877, a letter arrived from Frederick Wines, a Congregational minister and prison reform advocate. Higginson had never written about prison conditions, but Wines, who had briefly served as president of St. Louis University, regarded him as an activist devoted to all good causes, and very likely Mary's death was known in reform circles. Wines hoped to entice Higginson to attend the upcoming August Prison Congress in Stockholm, which was set to deal with the problem of innocent but mentally disturbed people being sentenced to prison. As Higginson had been contemplating foreign travel, the invitation lent "a definite public air" to his trip. In preparation for his voyage, that January he attended the annual meeting of the American Social Science Congress in Boston, where he and Wines were formally elected to serve as delegates in Stockholm. Rather than return home prior to sailing, Higginson opted to journey southward for the first time in fourteen years. After a brief stop in Richmond, where he met with his cousins ("formerly secessionists to a man"), he returned to Beaufort, and then revisited Jacksonville, Florida. "It was strange," Higginson reflected, "to touch at Jacksonville as a quiet passenger, where I could once have burned the city to the ground with a word." He called on a few old comrades from the war and spent a week as the guest of Harriet Beecher Stowe, who had purchased an estate in nearby Mandarin.[2]

May 1878 found him back in London. Once again, he called on Charles Darwin, and this time the two discussed Samuel Clemens's short stories. Darwin had loved "The Celebrated Jumping Frog of Calaveras County" and was amazed that Higginson had not read it, despite his acquaintance with the author. On the morning of May 30, Higginson arrived in Paris, hoping to hear Victor Hugo speak at the celebration commemorating the centenary of Voltaire's death. The event was sold out, but Higginson found a sympathetic policeman, whom he told he had journeyed to France for just this reason. Accustomed to speaking before American audiences, Higginson was pleasantly surprised that Parisians clapped only when pleased and did not also stamp their feet as did Americans. Upon returning to London, he resumed his old contacts with reformers, addressing a conference of suffragettes and, after receiving a letter of introduction from Darwin, meeting with biologist Thomas Henry Huxley and sociologist Herbert Spencer. He remained in Britain until sailing to Stockholm for the conference, which opened on August 20 and lasted six days. He then sailed for home.[3]

Higginson arrived back in the States in October. A letter waited for him from Emily Dickinson, who urged him to pay her another visit, promising that she had "thought of [him] often since the Darkness" of Mary's death. He gently declined. Newport held too many sad memories, so he moved back to Cambridge, renting a small apartment on Kirkland Street, quite near the house where he had been born. Then he began preparations to build the only house that he was ever to own. Friendly journalists were pleased, commenting that his move back to Cambridge added "another to the interesting literary circle of that university town." Located on Buckingham Street, halfway between Harvard College and Mount Auburn Cemetery, the three-story, Queen Anne–style house was painted a fashionable dark brown (Figure 10.1). A brass knocker reading "S. Higginson," taken from Susan Louisa's home, was bolted to the front door, and just inside, in the front hallway, hung the officer's sword gifted to him by the men of the First Regiment. "It is such inexpressible happiness to have at last a permanent home," Higginson wrote to Ann.[4]

As he shifted his books and furniture from Newport to Cambridge, Higginson renewed an acquaintance with Mary Thatcher, the niece of Henry Wadsworth Longfellow's wife. Born in Rockland, Maine, in 1844, Mary was thirty-three and still living with her father, attorney Peter Thatcher, her mother, Margaret, and her five siblings in 1870. But shortly afterward her parents relocated to West Newton, Massachusetts, and she to Newport, where she began to write essays and poems, some of which attracted attention in the nation's women's magazines. As had Dickinson, Thatcher and her circle of friends sought out Higginson and asked him to read their drafts.

Figure 10.1 Constructed on Higginson's instructions in 1880, the 5,859-square-foot house was added to the National Register of Historic Places in 1982 and is now numbered 29 Buckingham Street. The house is roughly one mile from the Kirkland Street house in which Higginson was born in 1823. Privately owned, the home is today valued at $7,300,000. Courtesy of the Library of Congress.

Writing of Higginson in her essay "Water-Lilies in Newport," Thatcher observed that her mentor, "having no sons or daughters, made all childhood and youth his own, thus keeping his heart forever young, [and] usually kept a watchful eye upon us." Thatcher was unusually well traveled; one of her essays described a journey up the Mississippi, and another chronicled a trip to the Midwest. In 1877, she published a collection of nineteen essays in *Seashore and Prairie*, and as most of the pieces featured images of New England life, with its "fearless old preachers" and "seafaring men," the volume was just the sort to capture Higginson's attention. The author, who had never married, was "exquisitely refined and dainty," he told a friend one month after returning from Europe.[5]

Thatcher had "a sweet face & very loving nature," Higginson assured Ellen Conway, who, like her husband, Moncure Daniel Conway, was a former ally from abolitionist days. "I have known her some five years in a literary way." But apart from her growing scholarly fame, Thatcher was quite unlike many of the public women he had encountered at feminist conventions. "She is shy & modest," although "bright & winning," and was "in some ways rather an 'old fashioned girl,'" who has "never worn a low necked dress or had her ears bored." Higginson chuckled when writer and reformer Kate Gannett Wells informed him that his friends who saw them together guessed Thatcher to be "a brilliant society woman," given Higginson's postwar activities in Northern literary circles. But understanding the character of a man who longed to be a father, Wells wisely guessed that in reality, she was "a modest domestic girl."[6]

Just weeks later, in December 1879, the two announced their engagement. A bereavement of just fourteen months was a bit brief, even in Victorian America, but as his diary entrances revealed, Higginson believed that he had lost his first wife years before. "A man of any feeling must feed his imagination," he had written in *Malbone*, and "there must be a woman of whom he can dream." Thatcher had just turned thirty-four, and although Higginson was twenty-one years her elder, he was yet vital and robust, and the fact that he remained childless was the regret of his life. The news reached Dickinson, who wrote to say "there is no one so happy [that] her Master is happy as his grateful Pupil." Although Dickinson was far closer to Higginson's age than was Thatcher, there had never been anything more than an intellectual connection between the two poets, despite his late wife's suspicions. "The most noble congratulation it ever befell me to offer," Dickinson added, "is that you are yourself."[7]

The two were married on February 6, in Peter Thatcher's home in West Newton. Newspapers announced that the wedding of "Miss Mary Thatcher to Col. T. W. Higginson" was private. Her uncle and Higginson's theology classmate, Reverend Samuel Longfellow, the brother of the poet, performed the ceremony, and Henry Wadsworth himself attended. Old friends wrote congratulations. John Greenleaf Whittier sent "very best wishes for your happiness," and Dickinson, returning to her earlier curious form, thanked Higginson for a copy of *Seashore and Prairie* but added that should the three meet, "I think I could see her Face in that." For February 6, Higginson's diary read only, "The happiest day of my life." The next day's entry followed with "At my lovely home, now ours."[8]

For a honeymoon, Higginson squired Minnie—as he preferred to call her out of deference to his late wife—first to Philadelphia and then into West Virginia to visit Harpers Ferry and relive his John Brown days. He had never actually been to the site of the failed revolt, and although he was unsure of what they might find, he was shocked by the town's dilapidated state. He had cabled ahead to Dr. Nicholas Marmion, an elderly Irish-born physician who had once attended to Brown. "The train stopped in a dismantled sort of station," Higginson reported to his sister, "where stood an old man with soft white hair on his shoulders, holding a lantern & attended by two fair haired daughters." The two women "seized us with joy" but apologized that they owned neither horse nor cart. The group set off across "ruined pavements," marched up several flights of stone stairs, and finally reached a number of "high manor stone houses," also dilapidated. One of them was the "Marmion abode." The entire town turned out to welcome "the bridal party" with the "largest round of beef" Higginson had ever seen, "with only us two to eat it." The table, he noted, bore bullet holes from federal pickets who had fired from the Maryland heights across the river. The Marmions were disappointed that the Higginsons remained only one night, but the couple caught the train for Arlington, then visited both Mount Vernon and the White House. "Found Mrs. Hayes as pleasing as ever," Higginson reported to Ann of the First Lady. He noted also that Justice John Marshall Harlan, who would go on to write stinging dissents in the *Civil Rights Cases* and *Plessy v. Ferguson*, was present.[9]

Although Higginson had been devoted to Mary, their final years together had been a trial, and his frequent speaking engagements had provided him with excuses to escape the sorrow of home. Now he almost refused to leave Cambridge. "I have now had six weeks of such happiness as I never imagined," he reflected on March 20, "& my love for my darling has grown with every day." As a man who had long embraced gender equality, Higginson believed that marriage was "a mutual surrender," in which "the two partners are morally equivalent." That December he recorded that he had "a very happy birthday," and with good reason. Minnie was eight months pregnant. At fifty-six, Higginson was about to become a father. Having just turned thirty-five herself, Minnie was a dozen years above the average age for giving birth for the first time, and the pregnancy was evidently a rocky one. For several months, Higginson drove her about town every morning. "It is the one thing she needs & keeps her well," he noted, and although he judged the trips "a delight," the hours spent in their carriage were "destructive to [his] day's work" and writing schedule.[10]

"God!" Higginson scribbled into his diary on January 24, 1880. "May I be worthy of the wonderful moment when I first looked round and saw the face of my child." They named the girl Louisa Wentworth after Higginson's mother. "How trivial seem all personal aims and ambitions beside the fact that I am at last the father of a child." Henry Wadsworth Longfellow called and promised the happy parents that he spied "beauty and intelligence" in their daughter's face, and that her tiny fingers resembled the hands of a musician. Higginson thought Longfellow's pronouncements the equivalent of those of a fairy godmother. Having buried a spouse and several siblings in recent years, he was aware of how fleeting life might be, and the former theology student believed that "should she die to-morrow she will still be my child somewhere" in some spirit world. "But she will not die," he added.[11]

But the child did die. Although Louisa appeared "very robust" at birth, within weeks she developed meningitis and died on March 19, five days shy of her second month. "Cerebral affliction," the doctor wrote on her death certificate. The doctor assured the heartbroken couple that there was "no fault in our care of her," but Higginson was deeply anxious about Minnie. "Thus ends our pride and our earthly hope," the grieving father sighed. "O the hopes, the dreams, the fancies all now gone, or exchanged for profounder thought belonging in the world unseen." Dickinson sent a note, assuring the bereaved Higginson that "it grieves me that anything disturbs you—the dearer sorrow of which you spoke." At the funeral, one niece observed, "I shall never forget Uncle Wentworth's beautiful, transfigured look when he said in a broken yet strong voice, 'The Lord gave, the Lord hath taken away.'"[12]

In July 1881, a second daughter arrived and was named Margaret Waldo. Higginson was overjoyed, and when Margaret remained healthy after three months, he assured one friend that "a more blissful possession no one ever owned." That December, Higginson tore himself away long enough to lecture in Maine, and when he returned home, he told Ann, "the darling little baby's face gleamed & laughed all over & she seemed to wish to put out her arms to me." On the eve of Margaret's second birthday, he marveled at how active she was, "running or rather toddling all about the house & lawn." The proud father was sure that the child was unusually bright, and he bragged that "talking has come almost too fast; she puts together a long string of words, 'Papa come by see dear baby.'" Everything Margaret did delighted her parents. "She has just begun to be put in a tub instead of sponging & does not like it," Higginson told his sister. "The second time it was done she said, whimpering, 'No wash baby, wash at baby.'" Even before she turned four, Margaret was herself writing to Ann, whom she dubbed "Aunt Annie Hig."[13]

Somewhat disbelieving that he had become a father on the eve of his fifty-eighth birthday, Higginson behaved more like a doting grandparent than a typical Victorian father. Far from being the reserved, middle-class father who returned home from work each evening after his child had gone to bed, Higginson eagerly shared parenting duties with Minnie. Each morning, he told a friend, "I take baby out to see the 'lilly chilen,' as she calls some children from the street she plays together with" before walking her to school. A Memphis journalist thought Higginson had "always been a pattern of domesticity" and was "a most affectionate father." Every utterance from Margaret charmed him immensely, to the extent that he took to bragging about her sweet comments to friendly reporters. Enough of them, as well as their readers, found these sufficiently delightful to publish. In one story carried in a Montana newspaper, "Col. Higginson's little daughter" had so enjoyed her third birthday celebration that she assumed each day would be a party. "When she woke up the next morning" to discover that life had returned to normal, Margaret cried out, "Oh, mamma, where is my birthday?"[14]

* * *

In November 1879, just months after his marriage, Cambridge reformers advanced Higginson's name for election to the lower house of the state legislature. His friends did so without asking his permission, perhaps suspecting that Higginson might decline to stand for office. Rather to their surprise, though, he accepted. Republicans controlled both chambers, and after attending the state party convention in Worcester, he admitted he "enjoyed the sense of being again at work & recognized." Because the nomination had been unsought, Higginson decided that he take a stab at public service. "I

Figure 10.2 When the late-in-life father—here in 1885 at the age of sixty-two—constructed a special seat on his velocipede for Margaret, even his old enemies found the widely distributed image by Ernst Haechel charming. The *Richmond Dispatch* noted, "his little daughter enjoys many a delightful ride with her father for engineer and motive power." Courtesy of Todd-Bingham Pictures Collection, Yale University.

had never thought for an instant of 'going into politics,' as people say," he confessed, but as each session lasted less than four months, from January 7, 1880, to April 24, and each term but one year, the days spent away from Minnie and his writing table were few enough. The state paid a salary of $500, enough to cover a few missed submissions to the *Atlantic*. For several years, Massachusetts women had submitted petitions demanding the right to vote in school board elections, and the previous winter Higginson had delivered several lectures on just that topic and spoken in the statehouse on the issue, insisting that "it was the inevitable next step to be taken in the improvement of our educational system." Although Higginson would be just one of 240 members, the press took notice. "It is a good omen of reform in the right direction," one editor observed, "when such a man as Col. Thomas Wentworth Higginson accepts service in a State Legislature."[15]

"I had, in the legislature, my fair share of successes and failures," Higginson later reflected. His activities mirrored his long-held reform agenda, together with whatever new worthy cause was brought to his attention. When informed that impoverished sailors and veteran soldiers were in danger of losing the right to vote due to a lack of property or income, Higginson introduced an amendment to the state constitution stating that nobody who had been "honorably discharged" from the military could "be disqualified on account of being a pauper." The House approved Higginson's motion on January 16, 1880, just nine days after the session began. As he had as a school board member, Higginson also introduced legislation guaranteeing children the right not to read a particular Bible "against the wish of their parents," while a third bill funded the building of a new Normal Arts School.[16]

Just as his term was coming to an end, Higginson found himself drawn back into national politics, when former president Grant let it be known that he was interested in a third term. As early as 1872, alarmed by the growing number of scandals in the Grant administration, Higginson had hoped the party would select a different candidate. Now he joined a chorus of reformers who actively opposed an unprecedented third term. Banding together with a good number of prominent Republicans, including Charles Francis Adams Jr., former Massachusetts governor William Washburne, Maine general and governor Joshua Chamberlain, Massachusetts congressman George Hoar, and the Reverend James Freeman Clark, the former chaplain of the First South Carolina, Higginson agreed to serve as a delegate to the April Anti–Third Term Convention in St. Louis. "We all honor Gen. Grant for what he did in the war," he told one journalist, "but we cannot be proud of his administration."[17]

Higginson also rekindled his growing friendship with Samuel Clemens, in part because they shared the same politics. Both men endorsed Ohio Republican James Garfield for the presidency, largely because the former general had been an early advocate of Black voting rights and a critic of Andrew Johnson. Clemens thought his friend William Dean Howells might make a splendid minister to Holland—a position that ultimately went to attorney William Dayton—and drafted a letter of support he planned to circulate to his friends. "Won't you, or Higginson (somebody who is on good terms with all the New England literary folks) get up a letter to Garfield which shall be an improvement on the rough draft herewith enclosed?" Clemens asked Boston publisher James Osgood. "We can get an array of bully signatures which would not only convince the said Garfield, but come derned near to amounting to a command." When Howells appeared reluctant, Clemens joked that perhaps they should organize "the Modest Club—& the first & main qualification for membership is modesty." Clemens thought the term might not apply to himself, but he volunteered to nominate "Higginson & a few more—together with Mrs. Howells, Mrs. Clemens, & certain others of her sex."[18]

In his second term, which began on January 5, 1881, Higginson continued his service on the Education Committee, but he also asked to be appointed to the Committee on Woman Suffrage. From that perch, he sought to translate his cherished beliefs into legislation. He introduced legislation to permit women to vote for members of the School Committee, urged the House to consider a bill to legalize "military instruction" in the public schools, formally inquired into the legality of requiring calisthenics in the public schools, and submitted petitions in support of women's suffrage. He crafted a bill to provide state assistance to homeless veterans who could not apply for city or county aid, and as a lifelong temperance advocate, he proposed that local liquor licensing laws be suspended until Massachusetts might put a statewide ban on the sale of alcohol on the ballot. One new issue was his bill to establish a reformatory for youthful offenders who otherwise would be sentenced to prison with hardened criminals. Less successful was his bill to allow avowed atheists to provide testimony in court; never one to give up easily, even after returning to private life Higginson lobbied the Assembly to pass his bill, which prompted one critical journalist to doubt his credentials as a "Rev" and suggest that if passed, the law would somehow make "the death penalty for murder only a dead letter." Higginson had been involved in reform circles long enough to know that success was rarely the work of a moment, and he was far from done crusading.[19]

Early on, Higginson had discovered that his legislative duties required only a few hours a day, and so even before the assembly adjourned for the year on May 13, 1881, he had already published a number of essays in *Scribner's* and the *Atlantic Monthly*. For the *International Review*, he published "Two Anti-Slavery Leaders," reflections on Levi Coffin and William Lloyd Garrison, who had died in 1877 and 1879, respectively. (Higginson had spoken at Garrison's funeral the year before; the eulogy grew into a longer essay he later published in the *Atlantic*.) In the *North American Review*, Higginson joined Lucy Stone, Wendell Phillips, and Julia Ward Howe in castigating historian Francis Parkman for his essay in the previous issue denouncing calls for women's suffrage. "Colonel Higginson and Mr. Phillips make their points with a force that must be acknowledged by all readers," a Memphis editor conceded. Certainly, Higginson hardly held his fire, attacking Parkman's "very absurd argument" that only those who fought for the nation during the Civil War should be permitted to vote. "Of [the] one thousand clergymen" who might have served, "nine hundred and fifty-four were disqualified for military duty; of the same number of journalists, seven hundred and forty" were excused from active duty, Higginson observed. Parkman apparently did not dispute their right to the ballot. "We will never know peace until the words 'male' and 'female' are eliminated from our statutes, and all are equal before the law," Higginson concluded.[20]

Just as his legislative work was wrapping up in the spring of 1881, Higginson was contacted by Massachusetts governor John Davis Long about representing the New England states at the May dedication of the monument marking the American victory at the Battle of Cowpens, South Carolina, one of the turning points of the Revolutionary War. Long had first asked Higginson in December 1880, but he had declined, insisting he could not leave his pregnant wife for a week. But when the ceremony was delayed for a year, Higginson decided to accept, as it would afford him another opportunity to visit old friends from the war, including former state senator Robert Smalls, who was then considering a run for a seat in Congress, and Prince Rivers, who had been in ill health since being attacked by a white mob during the 1876 election. A handful of Southern editors declared Higginson's selection inappropriate, given his activities during the Civil War. One Savannah newspaper nonetheless urged that his reception be a peaceful one. Despite his antislavery views and the fact that he had "commanded the first negro troops formed into a regiment in the late war," Higginson was "a gentleman of fine presence [and] polished manners." The editor hoped that "the new South will find in him as good a friend in peace as he proved to be an enemy in war."[21]

The affair was a strange one, and Higginson would have been wise to have declined to attend. He tried to recruit President Garfield to accompany him, demonstrating that the recently elected Republican was "the president of the nation, not of a party," but with no success. The presiding officer was South Carolina governor Johnson Hagood, who as a Confederate officer had given the order to have the body of Colonel Robert Gould Shaw stripped and buried in a sandy pit beside his Black soldiers as a calculated insult. Representing the South was Senator Wade Hampton III, whose paramilitary unit, known as the "Red Shirts," had murdered four of Rivers's men in an attack on an armory in the town of Hamburg. Thirteen hundred white troops marched in parade; besides Higginson, no veterans of the 1st Infantry attended in uniform or sat upon the platform. When he rose to speak before the crowd of twenty thousand spectators, Higginson ignored the Revolutionary era in favor of current events, going well beyond trying to heal old sectional wounds. He claimed that having spoken to more than one hundred of the men once under his command, "only one complained of poverty," but he guessed that was due to his being "given to whisky." By comparison, Higginson observed, one of his former corporals owned a livery stable in Beaufort worth several thousand dollars, while one of his sergeants earned a good living as a master carpenter in Jacksonville. He had not been able to visit his former corporal Robert Sutton, but only because he was "a traveling minister up the river."[22]

Having praised what he perceived to be Southern progress in race relations, Higginson then focused on the sins of his own region. "I do not know a Northern city which enrolls colored citizens in its police," he remarked, adding that he had seen Black officers in Charleston, Beaufort, and Jacksonville. Rhode Island's legislature had recently declined to repeal its colonial ban on interracial marriage, "while the legislature of South Carolina has refused to pass such a bill." Although true, Higginson's determination to appeal to national unity ignored the rising tide of violence across the South, and the fact that within his own lifetime, he would witness South Carolina revise its state constitution to eliminate Black voting rights and impose a ban on interracial marriage.[23]

The event was covered by dozens of newspapers, and Higginson's speech was widely praised by Southern journalists and Northern Democrats. His habitual optimism fueled his reform impulses, but his confidence in a brighter future for civil rights betrayed him in this instance. While in camp upriver with the 1st Infantry in early 1863, Higginson had reflected "that revolutions may go backward." At that time, facing Confederates, he suspected that "the habit of injustice seems so deeply impressed upon the whites that it is hard to believe in the possibility of anything better." In 1881 he devoutly wished to believe that the blood shed by his soldiers had made a difference in Southern life, though the evidence, then as now, made clear that this was a false hope.[24]

Higginson's other activities, from his books to his ongoing support for women's rights, did not sit as well with white Southerners. In the mid-1870s, following the commercial failure of *Malbone*, he considered writing an American history primer for younger readers. James Fields, his editor, was as unenthusiastic about the prospect as he had been excited about Higginson's novel. However, once the idea took hold, the educational reformer in Higginson refused to abandon it. Most histories written for high school students, he fretted, were crafted on the lowest possible level and favored white male politicians. Published in 1875 as *Young Folks' History of the United States*, the book was, as a gratified Higginson later crowed, "incomparably the most successful venture" of his career, selling more than 200,000 copies. The volume was revised and expanded over the next two decades to cover William McKinley's assassination in 1901, was twice translated into French and once into German and Italian.[25]

The thick tome of nearly five hundred pages was written in clear, fluent prose, and contained illustrations, primary documents, a timeline, and a detailed bibliography, as well as suggestions for further readings and study questions in an appendix. Higginson virtually ignored the famous statesmen of the late antebellum era, except to denounce South Carolina senator John C. Calhoun for wishing to "uphold the interests of slavery, extend its influence, and secure its permanent duration." Republicans and reformers, such as Charles Sumner, Horace Mann, Wendell Phillips, Benjamin Lundy, William Lloyd Garrison, and Theodore Parker, earned as many mentions as did Henry Clay, one of the most dominant politicians of antebellum America. Unlike later textbooks, which would depict John Brown as mentally unwell, Higginson praised his old friend: "He frankly announced his object to be the freedom of the slaves; and he promised safety to all property except slave-property." Higginson declined to mention his own service during the war, though Rufus Saxton and Robert Gould Shaw received mention, as did the men of the First South Carolina, the battle at Battery Wagner, and the Confederate massacre of Black and loyalist soldiers at Fort Pillow. Still believing that Lincoln had not done enough to equalize the pay for his Black soldiers, Higginson remained as lukewarm toward the martyred president as he had been during Lincoln's lifetime, but Reconstruction reforms drew acclaim, while Andrew Johnson's vetoes drew condemnation.[26]

The Republican press was as passionate about the book as they had been disapproving of Higginson's Cowpens talk. The Massachusetts *Springfield Republican* insisted that the colonel "was well qualified to write such a history," and Maine's *Portland Daily Press* judged it a "new departure in child literature [and] an improvement on the diluted article which has hitherto been given." Black schools across the South turned the book into a classroom staple; Oberlin graduate Caroline Putman told one correspondent that her academy was "the only school in Virginia that teaches [Higginson's] history—praising John Brown!" Conservative Democrats thought otherwise. When an Idaho school board voted to find a substitute for *Young Folks*, Higginson wrote a polite rebuttal, wondering "how any patriotic citizen can object to teaching the history of the Rebellion." The "history of the Mexican War," he noted, was "distasteful to some" but glorified by others. How could the nation's youth grow into "intelligent citizens" if textbooks expunged these events from the past? Higginson believed he had written an honest account of American history, one that even noted the existence of slavery in the colonial North. "If American history is to be taught at all, I should most strenuously insist upon its being taught as a whole and not in shreds to suit the whims of individuals."[27]

The surprise success of *Young Folks* prompted Higginson to believe that it was his fate to join the growing ranks of professional historians. He was familiar with the works of biographer James Parton and fellow Harvard graduate George Bancroft. But many scholars regarded Parton's multivolume studies of Andrew Jackson and Thomas Jefferson as partisan works of hagiography, and, at ten volumes, Bancroft's *History of the United States*, which he had completed just several years before, in 1878, was hardly designed for casual readers. Higginson envisioned a work of about the length of *Young Folks*, a single volume that might "reduce these accumulations into compact shape [and] make the results readable." He also planned to revise and expand his earlier essays on slave rebellions into a single volume, *Travelers and*

Outlaws. As ever, to get a sense of what his readers wished, and to maximize his profits, Higginson began by publishing potential chapters in *Harper's Weekly*, an increasingly popular Manhattan-based magazine largely known as the forum for political cartoonist Thomas Nast. "First Americans," "Visit of the Vikings," and "Spanish Discoverers" all appeared in back-to-back issues in the fall of 1882, with "French Voyagers" in the spring of 1883. Although Higginson continued to publish the occasional literary piece in the *Atlantic*, he had found a new home. "There is nothing equal to Harper's Magazine," averred the *New-York Tribune*.[28]

The *Harper's* essays, which continued into 1884 as his subject matter drew closer to the Revolutionary era, were so popular with readers that the magazine began to highlight the pieces in their newspaper advertisements. Higginson's editors assigned Howard Pyle, a young artist who had recently gained fame painting scenes from the Revolutionary War, to produce illustrations for Higginson's chapters. Five more articles quickly appeared, all of them exclusive to *Harper's*, and as the essays approached the founding generation, the illustrations grew ever more prominent. "The Dawning of Independence," for example, published in October, contained a full-length portrait of Alexander Hamilton.[29]

When finally published in book form in the fall of 1885 as *A Larger History of the United States to the Close of President Jackson's Administration*, Harper and Brothers, the magazine's parent company, spared no expense. The 498-page volume contained dozens of maps and illustrations, which Higginson judged to be "the finest series of portraits of American statesmen yet seen in any American book." Although more traditional in approach than *Young Folks*, the book was unusual in that the lengthy first chapter chronicled life in North America before the arrival of the first Europeans. The words "slave" and "slavery" received thirty-eight mentions, and Native peoples more than twice that. The son of merchant Stephen Higginson could not resist mentioning that the 1807 Embargo Act "brought ruin to so many households that it might well be at least doubted whether it brought good to any," but otherwise Higginson sought to achieve a truly bipartisan approach to his final chapters, a balance Parton, for example, had never even attempted. By ending his narrative in the mid-1830s, Higginson avoided wading into the sectional controversies of the late antebellum years, though he was critical of the 1830 Indian Removal Act, noting also that the capture of Seminole leader Osceola was achieved in "violation of a flag of truce." That view was safe enough in New England, if less so in the South. Even so, newspaper reviews of the book were effusive.

Higginson "takes issue with [Nathaniel] Hawthorne that our history is commonplace and unpoetic," noted a Sacramento journalist. "He believes, on the contrary, that no historic subject more varied or picturesque is offered by the world." A Maine reviewer predicted that, as with his *Young Folks*, "Col. Higginson is destined to find a very large circle of appreciative readers." Even Virginia's *Richmond Dispatch*, while acknowledging that the author "was one of the Greeley stripe of northern abolitionists," thought the book "written in a kindly and most sensible manner." The editor warned his readers that there were some things in the book that they "might not admire" but nonetheless urged Virginians to give it a read: "You will get your money's worth."[30]

* * *

Although many of the reforms he had long championed were national in scope, Higginson was a New Englander and a sectionalist at heart. In part because he championed a variety of causes, his name appeared almost daily in some newspaper, and his essays and books enhanced his fame. Many veterans had used their military service as a stepping stone to political office, yet apart from his brief service in the Massachusetts statehouse, Higginson had never much thought about higher office or national politics. That changed in early 1883. The former Free Soiler had endorsed Lincoln in 1860—only because of his opposition to slavery and not due to the party's Whiggish economic policies—and remained a Republican. But with Reconstruction receding and the party increasingly deaf to the plight of Black Southerners, the Republicans had become ever more the party of financiers and businessmen, just the sort of wealthy elites Higginson had denounced in his 1848 Thanksgiving sermon. As did most progressive reformers, Higginson regarded protective tariffs as a tax on working Americans and found himself increasingly drawn to the free trade policies long associated with the Democratic Party.

In early May 1883, Higginson was invited to speak in Boston at the Tariff Reform League meeting. The conference elected Charles Francis Adams Jr. as its president. Like Higginson, Adams was a former colonel who had led Black troops during the war, in Adams's case the Fifth Massachusetts Cavalry. He had done so with far less enthusiasm than Higginson. Still, Higginson admired his fellow Harvard man and son of New England. Later that month, Higginson journeyed to Pennsylvania to speak to the Society of Progressive Friends, another group that hoped to have an impact on national politics.[31]

Higginson's estrangement from the Republicans he had supported for more than two decades became more obvious in the following month, when the party met in Chicago in early June and selected Maine senator James G. Blaine as their presidential nominee. For nearly a decade, Blaine had been burdened by rumors that he had taken a bribe from the Union Pacific Railroad, when the company paid him $64,000 for worthless stock. Two years earlier, in January 1881, Higginson had written to President-elect Garfield, insisting that "the more independent class of Republicans in Massachusetts" hoped to have New England represented in the cabinet, but not Senator Blaine. The mere "rumor" that Blaine might find a place in Garfield's cabinet, Higginson warned, "has greatly chilled the feeling of prospective confidence in your administration." Garfield ignored the advice, and Blaine received the top spot of secretary of state.[32]

The day after the Republican convention adjourned, the Massachusetts Reform Club met. "The attendance was unusually large," one journalist reported. The Reverend James Freeman Clarke, Higginson's former chaplain during the war, opened the meeting. Harvard president Charles Eliot, former colonel Norwood Penrose Hallowell, and civil service reformer Charles Dana were also present. Adams was unable to attend, but he sent a letter to be read that rebuked the delegates who had nominated Blaine and promised to "at once organize to defeat them." Higginson then rose to submit a resolution. Claiming that Blaine was "named in absolute disregard for the reform sentiment of the nation," Higginson urged all independent-minded Republicans to consider voting Democratic should that party—whose convention was to open on July 8—select a clean candidate. The Democrats, Higginson observed, had "several proper men," among them New York governor Grover Cleveland. Cleveland had gained bipartisan support for taking on Manhattan's influential Tammany Hall organization, and when Higginson mentioned his name, the Club's members burst into "loud applause." As a final act, the group created a committee to organize a second meeting after the Democratic convention to "carry out the sense of this meeting with practical effect."[33]

The response to the meeting, despite Higginson's hopes of bipartisanship, broke along party lines. In a day when party affiliation was strong and Republicans continued to paint the Democrats as the party of treason and Jefferson Davis, for officers who had led Black regiments during the war, as had Higginson and Adams and Hallowell, to consider voting against their longtime party was unsettling. "T. W. Higginson is one of those Boston gentlemen who find themselves too great and good to support the Republican nominees," one Indianapolis editor chided. Another noted that "Col. Tom Higginson" had been defeated as a candidate for the Massachusetts legislature, failing to note that Higginson had in fact declined to run for a third term. The solidly Republican *New-York Tribune* wrote that Higginson "tried to persuade himself that he did not think the Democratic party after all was so dreadful as he knew it was." Democratic newspapers, understanding their party represented a minority of voters, welcomed the breach in Republican ranks. "It is plain that the moral sense of the people has been deeply affronted" by Blaine's nomination, a Kentucky paper editorialized, while the *Delaware Gazette* observed that the "sneering" names applied to the reformers by the Republican press, "such epithets as kickers and soreheads," would hardly dissuade such high-minded men as "Charles Francis Adams Jr., James Freeman Clarke, and Thomas Wentworth Higginson." Enough voters, the editor hoped, were no longer willing to support "even the devil if he is the regular nominee."[34]

Undeterred, Higginson persevered, joining with his publisher, Joseph W. Harper, Henry Ward Beecher, and Carl Schurz, former secretary of the interior and a founding member of the Republican Party, at a Manhattan meeting of "Independent Republicans" in late June. One week later, he and President Eliot spoke to a group of independents in Cambridge. A second meeting in Cambridge in late July drew an even larger crowd, prompting Higginson to say it reminded him of the days of antislavery agitation. That agitation had been successful, and so would this be. He then immediately boarded a train for a national conference at New York City's University Club Theater, where 459 delegates from sixteen states met to endorse Democratic nominee Cleveland. In a lengthy speech, Higginson announced that he had severed his allegiance to the Republican Party for the first time, a statement that obscured the fact that Higginson had voted Free Soil or Liberty until 1860. Republican editors again jeered, one Philadelphian dubbing Higginson "the royal grand of the Boston mugwumps," the favorite Republican epithet for reformer, predicting (incorrectly as it turned out) that he would attempt "to cross back again" from the Democrats "after the skirmish was over."[35]

Although, as one editor conceded, the independents' position was "not that they hate Cleveland least, but Blaine more," the Democrats' selection of Indiana governor Thomas Hendricks for the vice presidency placed Higginson in the strange position of defending a conservative Democrat who as a senator in 1864 had supported a resolution to investigate whether

Higginson had been involved in the attempt to rescue Anthony Burns. Republican newspapers enjoyed pointing out that Hendricks had opposed putting Black troops on the same footing as white. Hendricks's speeches, one editor jested, "will interest not only Col. Higginson but colored voters everywhere."[36]

More troubling still was the revelation that years before, as a young lawyer, Cleveland had fathered a child out of wedlock with Maria Halpin. Cleveland immediately admitted to being the father, but pages in the *Woman's Journal* promptly filled with outraged letters. As one of the journal's editors, Higginson understood that he needed to take a stand, and he did. "Deeply as I deplore that transaction," he stated in the magazine, "I must distinctly decline to abandon for that reason only, a candidate whose public record is so admirable." Higginson also noted that Cleveland—to whom he was distantly related on his father's side—was much younger at the time, adding that he had received a personal letter from a Buffalo clergyman who testified that since that time the candidate's "professional and private life has been and is correct."[37]

Long accustomed to criticism from Northern Democrats and white Southerners, Higginson was nonetheless surprised by the rebukes from his old allies. One normally friendly Maine newspaper observed that far from being a young man at the time of the pregnancy, Cleveland had been thirty-three. A Republican editor in the Midwest scoffed that Higginson evidently believed that "the moral law involved in the seventh commandment may be barred by the statute of limitations." The angriest rebuttals appeared in the *Woman's Journal*, and painful though they must have been, Higginson made no effort to deny the subscribers their opinions. One writer gave Higginson credit for his "lofty moral purpose" but added, "I feel sorry for his judgment." Another observed that Higginson was "a household god in our family," and that both young and old devoured his books. "It is with real sorrow that I manage to keep the young folks from reading his articles on this very new and singular code of ethics." Lita Barney Sayles, a fellow Massachusetts resident, wrote to say how sorry she was to differ with Higginson, "for his words always find an echo in my soul." Sayles had thought of him as "half-feminine in his nature" in his ability to "understand the needs of women." His endorsement of and continued support for Cleveland, she concluded, revealed "the old masculine habit" of ignoring private sins in favor of public policy. "Let us pray that his usual good sense will make him see his path clearer, before voting time comes."[38]

To the surprise of nobody who knew him well, Higginson refused to change course. He took to the road to present the case for Cleveland and "the Independent Republicans." His speech in Boston at the Tremont Temple—where he had delivered so many antislavery lectures—brought out a large audience in which, rather to Higginson's surprise, "women formed a conspicuous element." Whether they came in support or to censure remained unclear. Higginson lectured a second time in Boston, at Young's Hotel, before catching the train for late October lectures in Manhattan and Jersey City. While in New York, he discovered that he and candidate Cleveland were both staying at the Hoffman House. "I hope to have a look at him," Higginson wrote Minnie. He "sent up [his] card and was at once admitted & cordially received." Cleveland "has not an air of polish," Higginson reported to his father-in-law, "but is prepossessing through frankness and strength." Higginson was impressed that Cleveland pressed him for details on the campaign in New England. Another visitor arrived, and so Higginson excused himself. But he left with the impression that nobody who met Cleveland could "regard him as a weak man, but the contrary; he makes an impression of essential manliness and even goodness," if not "of refined manners."[39]

While speaking around the Northeast, Higginson generally avoided discussing Cleveland's private life, preferring to focus on Blaine's vices and the Democrat's public record. When speaking in Jersey City before a "tremendous" crowd, seventy-year-old Henry Ward Beecher, who himself had publicly confessed to adultery, waded into the debate and, as an uncomfortable Higginson noted, "said something about Cleveland's sins that might well have given Lucy Stone a test." Higginson confessed to Minnie that he "felt ashamed" of sharing the stage with Beecher, "who spoke so coarsely," but the campaign season was nearly at an end. He bought gifts for Margaret, who at three was still his "baby," and caught the train for Cambridge.[40]

One week later, Cleveland lost Massachusetts but carried his home state of New York, and with it the electoral college. Furious Republican newspapers denounced Higginson and the Reverend Clarke as "malignants" and judged their politics "indefensible." The Republicans will never accept them back, one journalist insisted, while the "Democracy will spurn them" as insufficiently supportive of the party's platform. Higginson, however, neither desired nor expected political favors from the president-elect, assuring Cleveland that he had not endorsed any New Englander for any office and steadily refused any such requests from other independents. Instead, he returned home to Minnie and Margaret and resumed his writings, mailing off a very critical review of George Palmer's translation of *The Odyssey* to the

Atlantic, which editor Thomas Aldrich judged "cruelly good." Two years later, Higginson received the gift of two silver salt spoons that had once belonged to Cleveland's family; they were sent by Frances Folsom Cleveland, who had been the president's ward and, at the age of twenty-one, became his wife.[41]

From Higginson's perspective, the only casualty of the affair was that by mutual decision, he ceased any formal connection with the *Woman's Journal*, which he had coedited since its inception fourteen years earlier. Lucy Stone could not accept the idea of a man who had fathered a child out of wedlock sitting in the White House, and one of her editorials denounced his election as "an indignity." As one critical Republican journalist put it, Higginson had "slurred over [Cleveland's] disgraceful private record," and his views were "not in harmony" with the magazine's readership. When the first issue of 1885 appeared in January, Higginson's name had vanished from its masthead, and Alice Stone Blackwell joined her parents Lucy and Henry as the journal's third editor. Higginson understood the necessity of the literary divorce, and he remained friendly with Lucy Stone until her death in 1893, just as he remained loyal to the cause. At the same time, local unhappiness with his views prompted him to resign from his latest stint with the Cambridge school board. But he took comfort in the fact that that June he was reelected president of Boston's Round Table Club for the next twelve months.[42]

* * *

Losses of a more personal kind plagued Higginson in mid-decade. In August 1884, the *New York Times* announced the marriage of Higginson's onetime friend William Henry Hurlbut (now calling himself Hurlbert) to New York socialite Katharine Parker Tracy. The two men had not been in contact for decades, but the fact that so much of the fictional character of Philip Malbone was based on Hurlbut revealed how often Higginson thought of his long-ago companion. Higginson had not been much surprised when the announcement of an 1863 marriage came to nothing. Since the scandal of 1856, in which Hurlbert had a very public affair with the wife of prominent Manhattan attorney, he had largely resided in Britain, briefly returning to Manhattan to edit the New York *World*. That venture did not last long, and Hurlbut and Tracy were married in London. That too did not last, and after he denied writing salacious letters to his latest mistress, he was indicted for perjury by a British court and avoided jail only by fleeing to Italy.[43]

Higginson's old abolitionist ally Wendell Phillips died in Boston on February 2, 1884, at the age of seventy-two. His memorial service at the

Tremont Temple, according to the press, "attracted a more notable audience than any similar occasion." Higginson spoke, as did Louisa May Alcott, Julia Ward Howe, and Beecher. "Wendell Phillips belonged to the heroic type," Higginson told the crowd. "Whether we regard him mainly as an orator or a participant in important events, it is certain that no history of the United States will ever be likely to omit him." The fact that Phillips, who was but twelve years older than Higginson, was gone surely reminded the new husband and father not to squander any of his remaining years with his family.[44]

Two years later, on May 15, 1886, Emily Dickinson died at the age of fifty-five. The two had corresponded until the end, with her second-to-last letter written to Higginson. Knowing that her end was close, her brief note to the former minister carried a reference to the Bible's beginning, the story of Jacob wrestling with the angel in Genesis. "Audacity of bliss, said Jacob to the angel, 'I will not let thee go except I bless thee'—Pugilist and Poet, Jacob was correct." Higginson had known she was ill and had contributed to a fund "to promote the recovery of her health." She had planned every aspect of her funeral, from what gown she was to be buried in to who would carry her casket. She requested that her family telegraph Higginson and urge him to attend her memorial in Amherst, and she never doubted that he would. "To Amherst to the funeral of that rare and strange creature," he scribbled into his journal. Upon arriving, Higginson was taken into the library where Dickinson lay in a small, open casket. "E.D.'s face [was] a wondrous restoration of youth," he marveled, "and looked 30, not a gray hair or wrinkle, and perfect peace on the beautiful brow." At the graveside, he read Emily Brontë's "Last Lines," telling the small group it was "a favorite with our friend." "How large a portion of the people who have most interested me have passed away," Higginson reflected.[45]

Haunted by death, Higginson returned to a story he had begun in 1877, just after Mary's death, but had been unable to finish. Shortly after returning from Dickinson's funeral, he completed work on a novella he entitled *The Monarch of Dreams*. Part fantasy, part autobiography, and partly a meditation on the tension between his desire to lead a solitary life as a literary man and the call of reform movements that so often had pulled him away from the pen. If Philip Malbone was largely Hurlbut, Francis Ayrault was unmistakably Higginson himself. "Coming from a race of day-dreamers," Higginson's protagonist abandoned his home in a Rhode Island seaside town to return to the place where he was born. Although he had a much younger stepsister, "Little Hart," the child of his father's second marriage, life had "ravaged him," and he felt as if "there was no one left on earth whom he profoundly loved." The story was set in 1861 and the war beckoned, yet Ayrault, who was in mourning, needed "utter rest." One night, after seeing an image of France's Mont Saint-Michel, a dream transported him to a lovely hillside. Determined to experience the dream each night, Ayrault willed it to happen, and much to his surprise, his "control of his visions became more complete with practice." But while the hillside he visited each night was filled with people, Ayrault noticed that no ties connected him to them. When their demands on his time and attention grew too great, he "drew with conscious volition a gleaming light over them," creating a "certain hardness in his state of mind toward them."[46]

When awake, the realities of life intruded. "The storm of the Civil War began to roll among the hills," and Ayrault realized that he would serve as an officer. As "Old Susan" often reminded him, five-year-old Hart was unwell. Ayrault sent for doctors, and sitting up with her each night, "he did not dream." Miraculously, Hart suddenly improved, and Ayrault returned to his visions. But Hart had been changed and remained "pale and thin." Ayrault realized he could not avoid his responsibilities, that he could not be both imaginative dreamer and public citizen. "Life, action, duty, honor, a redeemed nation, lay before him," and in the wake of the "great defeat" at Bull Run he was placed in charge of a "half-organized regiment, undrilled, unarmed, and not even uniformed." At the last moment, however, a weary Ayrault fell asleep in his quarters. When he awakened, he grew conscious of "the rolling of railway wheels"; the "train with young soldiers was in motion." He had missed the war, and "the lost opportunity of his life [rolled] away—away—away."[47]

The parallels to Higginson's own life were too obvious for his family and friends to ignore. From the fact that Hart shared Margaret's age to the deaths of his child Louisa and his wife Mary, those closest to Higginson found the tale alarming, and his sister Ann worried that he was struggling mentally in the face of so much death. Ann was also offended by the fact that some of the dialogue given to Hart were things she had actually said to her brother decades earlier. "I feel dreadfully sorry at your feeling about my little story," Higginson assured Ann. "Pray do not imagine that I wrote it when I was ill or depressed but on the contrary was getting more well." In fact, Higginson was "in high spirits at being able to write something that" had been on his "mind for years."[48]

Publishers thought otherwise. The *Atlantic* declined to serialize the novella, either because editor Aldrich found it too curious or because Higginson had begun to flatly demand certain prices for his essays. Higginson, however, regarded the book as his "favorite child," in part because it was the only thing he had ever had rejected by the *Atlantic*, which to his mind was proof of its uniqueness. *Monarch* finally found a home with the Boston publishers Lee and Shepard, which had published his profitable *Young Folks' History*. Although it did not sell as well as the *History*, it was soon translated into German and French. For those who did not know Higginson intimately, the novella was, as one critic gushed, "a marvelous conception, so rich in its fancy and so charmingly written." Another argued that it gave "in a nutshell a world of philosophy; and no one who reads it will fail to admit its power and originality." A New Haven newspaper not only compared it to the best of Nathaniel Hawthorne but claimed it had far "deeper insight." Only one Chicago reviewer caught the author's real-life tension between his desire for literary solitude and the demands on a public reformer. "It is difficult to exactly define the true literary character of this little book," the critic confessed.[49]

* * *

Higginson had just returned home from lecturing on the history of abolitionism in Colorado Springs and revisiting former adventures in Kansas when word unexpectedly arrived from the Massachusetts Democratic Committee that they wished to nominate him for Congress in his Fifth District. The seat was a Republican stronghold, only twice since the election of 1856 captured by non-Republicans—one a Constitutional Unionist and the other a Democrat. But longtime congressman Edward Hayden had declined to seek reelection, and Democrats saw a chance with Higginson's name recognition and, they hoped, bipartisan popularity. Whether to run or not, Higginson reflected, "was a good deal like going to the war," as there "seemed plenty of cogent reasons against it, yet it seemed unmanly to let these reasons prevail." Congress did not yet meet year around, and if elected, Higginson would serve only from December 3 to March 3, although his term would delay their planned trip to Europe. Minnie "behaved as an angel about it," Higginson told his sister, "as she always does about everything." His only concern was that he was about to turn sixty-five and sometimes felt as if he "were 100 years old." But a new chapter in life, he reflected, "may do some good physically," and the decision to run gave him "a renewal of life." Given his resignation from the *Woman's Journal*, Higginson knew that he would "be abused, but probably not too much as four years ago," and in any case, he had "a way of ignoring such things."[50]

Higginson was formally nominated by the state party convention in late September. His Republican opponent was seventy-three-year-old Nathaniel Banks, who had served six nonconsecutive terms in Congress. "Both were famous before this generation was born," observed one reporter. But the "especial facility of Col. Higginson has been to unite the activities of a political and social reformer with the grace and dignity of a man of letters." A Washington editor added that while the nomination of abolitionist Higginson by the Democrats revealed "the strange mutations of American politics," the same newspaper praised him as a man with "the courage of his convictions in the highest degree," which, he added, would be necessary in running in a district that so heavily favored Republicans. The old sectional issues had "been definitely and permanently settled," and it was a sign of hope that both parties "today stand on the same level so far as devotion and loyalty to the Constitution are concerned."[51]

Four years before, Higginson had said little about Cleveland's platform, preferring to focus on evidence of Blaine's corruption when defending his endorsement. As a congressional candidate, however, Higginson could not avoid taking a stand on a variety of issues, and for the first time in his career he was forced to read widely on economic policy. In his district, Higginson filled his speeches with data, arguing that in 1884, one of every eighty-two businesses failed, whereas by 1886, thanks to Cleveland's low tariff and free trade policies, the number had declined to one in ninety-six. This was a sign that business was booming, he insisted again and again, and that the nation's spending power had increased. One Republican editor conceded the point but defended a high protective tariff as necessary "for preserving the industrial system under which this prosperity proceeds," a theory not likely to win over many working-class residents in Higginson's district.[52]

As numerous observers noted, Higginson's was just one of many strange campaigns in 1886. Although Banks had a lengthy and impressive résumé, including a term as Massachusetts governor and serving as a major general during the war, as a young Democrat he had endorsed the 1850 Fugitive Slave Act, while, at the same time, one editor observed, "Higginson was in the hottest of the abolition fight." Charles Francis Adams Jr. endorsed Cleveland's reelection, as did Republican Party founder Carl Schurz, William Lloyd Garrison Jr., and John F. Andrew, the son of the late governor. In Illinois, Owen Lovejoy Jr., the son of "the first martyr of the anti-slavery cause," was also a candidate for Congress as a Democrat. "Truly we have fallen upon strange times," Frederick Douglass remarked to one journalist, "when William Lloyd Garrison [Jr.] and Thomas Wentworth Higginson boldly proclaim their purpose to support the nominee of the Democratic party." Douglass remained a loyal Republican, but when it came to race relations and civil rights, neither party was what it had been twenty years before. "These men or their fathers all fought for anti-slavery principles," one Missouri editor boasted. "They stood for freedom" then, he added, and they campaigned for free trade now.[53]

Higginson promised Minnie that he would spend none of their money on his campaign, so his key supporters formed the Higginson Club of Cambridge. Higginson "represents independence of thought and vote," they declared in a November 3 circular. "His past career assures his influence for the purity of elections and freedom of the ballot." Guessing his neighbors already knew where he stood on the issues of the day, he initially agreed to make only six public addresses. When sizable crowds turned out to hear him speak, however, he consented to more, speaking fifteen times over eleven days. In one speech in Lexington, he was asked whether he could be truly independent in Washington in the face of party pressure. "I don't say it's an easy thing for a man to stand up against his own party," he replied, but, if elected, "what I *ought* to do is plain, and what I *desire* to do is known to the searcher of all hearts." Despite his age, Higginson was never short on vigor. "It is a great thing to have so tested my strength & found myself in good condition," he assured his sister.[54]

Election night, November 6, found Higginson at home, quietly reading a novel. A reporter from the *Boston Globe* stopped by and was surprised to find the house so quiet. Most candidates, he remarked, spent that night at newspapers, or at least in home offices, surrounded by "newspapers & telegrams & tables of figures." John Woods, a leading Boston lumber merchant, had confidently predicted that Higginson was certain to beat Banks. Turnout was heavier than usual, and in the early vote, one journalist reported, "the independent vote went to the Democrats." As the evening wore on, that began to change. "I got hold of an 8 PM Herald," Higginson wrote Ann, "which looked unfortunate." The next morning, newspapers reported that Banks had won by 1,381 votes. Higginson had earned 13,456 votes, an impressive increase over the previous election cycle, when Hayden had won with 3,457. Higginson also ran ahead of Cleveland in his district, who captured the national popular vote but lost his home state of New York and with it the electoral majority. Presidential years brought out more voters, Higginson understood, and so party affiliation meant more "than any personal considerations." The lingering reporter from the *Globe* thought Higginson took the bad news "very quietly, as we certainly did," he promised Ann.[55]

Higginson admitted that he was disappointed only in that he had grown so interested by tariff reform, although, with Benjamin Harrison in the White House, he knew the tariff was sure to rise. "I have never supposed that I should like the life in Congress," he mused, "though I might have liked the experience." Both Ann and Waldo sent messages to assure him that they bore "no personal disappointment" in his loss, and Minnie, who had promised to support her husband in whatever he desired, was quietly pleased with the news. Seven-year-old Margaret, Higginson reported, "danced about the floor with delight," shouting, "Oh, papa! I'm so glad you won't have to go to Washington." Higginson, of course, had never regarded himself as a single-issue reformer, and only one month away from his sixty-fifth birthday he felt both renewed and energetic. There were yet more campaigns to be waged, more books and essays to write, more causes to be taken up, and more countries to visit. "There is plenty else to do," Higginson wrote in his diary.[56]

11

"The crowning years"

1889–1911

Having reached an age when most men—or at least men of means—began to curtail their activities, Higginson exhibited no desire to slow his pace, whether it came to writing and lecturing or to spending time with his family. Twenty-one years his wife's senior, and fifty-seven years older than Margaret, Higginson was determined to remain as active as he had been decades before. William Lloyd Garrison had spent the fourteen years he had left to him after the war declaring victory over slavery and seeking to dissolve the American Anti-Slavery Society. Wendell Phillips disagreed, arguing that so long as Black men were denied equal rights, the old organization remained necessary. But apart from supporting political rights for Native Americans, Phillips had remained largely focused on Reconstruction-era reforms in the South until his death in 1884.

By comparison, Higginson hoped to remain vigorous so that he might enjoy fatherhood, but also to support the lengthy list of reforms he had devoted his entire life to, from women's rights to freedom of religion, with new advocacies of socialism and anti-imperialism. The last two decades of Higginson's life remained as full and consequential as any period in his career, his health finally giving way only weeks before his death.

As a man in his late sixties, Higginson simply decided that his occasional health troubles meant he needed to find new ways to extend his life. In the first months of 1890, he suddenly fell ill with a stomach ailment and had to cancel a scheduled lecture in Providence titled "People I Have Met." More frightening yet was that Minnie was diagnosed with "nervous prostration" and was cautioned by her doctor to remain in bed for several months. Having buried one wife, Higginson was nearly frantic about Minnie's condition, although he assured his equally concerned sister Ann that both were on the mend. "I have had a little fall-back from doing too much," he promised her, "but nothing serious."[1]

Higginson's solution was simply to spend more time each day riding his velocipede. One journalist observed that Higginson was hardly "the first man of advanced years to find virtue in cycling" but wondered why he "wastes effort on three wheels when two would serve him better." Higginson patiently explained that it was harder to propel a velocipede than a traditional bicycle, and given that he was focused on his health, his daily "run on wheels" was quickly restoring his strength. He also told the reporter that on solitary rides, he was able to sketch out essays in his head and so was "combining literature and riding on a tricycle." On other days, young Margaret accompanied the "enthusiastic wheelman," now on her own bicycle, and was "her father's most congenial companion."[2]

Higginson also used his time away from the lecture circuit to brush up on his languages. He believed he had received but a "rather shallow" education in languages while at Harvard, but over the years he consistently worked at improving his Greek and Latin. More recently, he had broadened his studies to include German, Portuguese, Hebrew, and "a little Swedish," and he told one reporter that he hoped "to live long enough to learn at least the alphabet in Russian." On the eve of his sixty-eighth birthday, he reassured Ann that Minnie's health was improving and so was his. Margaret, as ever, was a happy and "perfectly jubilant" young girl.[3]

Higginson used his convalescence to start what would become a four-year-long collaboration with Amherst author Mabel Loomis Todd in editing and publishing Emily Dickinson's poems. Higginson initially approached Houghton Mifflin, who had an extensive list of poetry volumes, but they were not interested in investing in an unknown poet, despite Higginson's strong endorsement. The two then turned to the Boston-based Roberts Brothers, who had published one of Dickinson's poems in a collection edited by Helen Hunt Jackson, a poet and former classmate of Dickinson's. Senior editor Thomas Niles approved, but only if Higginson cut his proposal of 199 poems in half, and with an initial run of but five hundred copies. Niles also insisted that the editors make the poems conform to the conventions of literary verse by altering Dickinson's punctuation and capitalization, and by adding titles, which Dickinson had almost never used. Higginson agreed and set to work, dividing the poems into the categories "Life," "Nature," and "Time/Death/Eternity." Newspaper editors had given titles to a few of her anonymously published poems, and Higginson used those, but on other occasions he simply bestowed his own choices on the poems. "Although I admire Mr. Higginson very much," Todd complained in her journal, "I do not think many of his titles good." But Higginson enjoyed his labors, telling Todd that "there are so many new to me which take my breath away."[4]

The project was complicated by the animosity that Dickinson's unmarried sister, Lavinia Norcross Dickinson, bore Todd. Vinnie, as she was known to her family, had learned of Todd's affair with her married brother, Austin, and wrote to Higginson demanding that Todd's name not appear on the title page. Higginson was unable to decipher Vinnie's handwriting, so he showed the letter to Todd, who responded that she was "trying hard not to be furious." Higginson had no desire to be trapped in a fight between the two and promised Todd that not only should her name appear, but that "it is proper that yr name shld come first as you did the hardest part of the work." To prepare readers for Dickinson's unusual verse, Higginson published a brief portrait of the poet, "Emily Dickinson's Letters," in the *Atlantic Monthly*, telling his audience to be ready for "a suddenness of success almost without parallel in American literature." The volume, simply entitled *Poems, by Emily Dickinson*, with much of Higginson's essay reprinted as its preface, appeared in late 1890.[5]

As Houghton Mifflin's senior editors had predicted, reviewers were unsure what to make of the poems. The *Providence News* praised Higginson's "intelligent editorship" but thought the poems themselves "curious, sometimes startingly beautiful, more often mere jerky and powerless rhapsodies." But readers heeded Higginson's advice, and within the year the volume had been reprinted eleven times. Higginson found it suggestive that "no two critics quote the same poems," as "each finds something different" to emphasize. He was "distressed" to discover, however, as he read through Dickinson's papers "poems as good as any we printed." Another volume had to be published. Todd agreed, and this time Niles was enthusiastic. A second volume, bearing the same title, followed within twelve months.[6]

Higginson was far less enamored of another poet who defied conventions. After Walt Whitman published *Drum Taps*, his collection of Civil War poetry, Higginson went public with his long-standing disdain for Whitman's work. Whitman's brother George had enlisted in the 51st New York Infantry and been captured by Confederate troops, but Whitman himself remained in Washington, working in the army's paymaster office and volunteering in area hospitals. Higginson had never thought much of Whitman's verse, claiming it displayed "a certain quantity of hollowness," and he believed that was "nowhere more felt than in the strains called 'Drum-Taps.'" Evidently, the veteran colonel could admire women who served the nation in the nursing corps but maintained different standards for men. "Hospital attendance is a fine thing, no doubt," Higginson wrote to one journalist, "yet if all men, South and North, had taken the same view of their duty that Whitman held, there would have been no occasion for hospitals on either side." Whitman finally tired of Higginson's public criticisms. "Oh! damn Higginson!" he grumbled to a reporter in 1890. Whitman's rebuttals, however, revealed the same sorts of cultural biases as Higginson's original criticisms. Higginson's literary judgments, he charged, were those of a "lady's man," one "who had an awful belief in respectability—an awful hunger to be gentlemen." The feud escalated when William Sloane Kennedy, a mutual friend, attempted to secure a war pension for Whitman. Writing in *Harper's Bazar*, Higginson again questioned Whitman's manhood. "There were many men who, being rejected from enlistment for physical defects, sought honorably to serve their country as hospital nurses," Higginson observed, but "in the case of the proposed pension for Mr. Whitman, the poet," he "deliberately preferred service in the hospital rather than in the field." Kennedy sought to reconcile the two, with no success on either side.[7]

Undeterred by Whitman's critiques of his work, Higginson published another collection of poetry, *The Afternoon Landscape*, in 1889. Reviews were mixed, with the *New-York Tribune* praising "Colonel Higginson's verse [as] smooth and harmonious," before conceding, "Higginson's warmest friends will hardly claim that his mind is at its best in these musical, but rather thin and insubstantial exercises." Four years later, however, Higginson and Minnie brought out *Such as They Are: Poems*. The volume, published by Roberts Brothers, contained nineteen of Higginson's poems and twenty-one of Minnie's, separated into two parts by author. This time the *Tribune* was more charitable, and the slim volume of seventy-three pages sold well enough to inspire the two to persevere in their efforts.[8]

Higginson also maintained an active speaking schedule. Although he begged off one speaking invitation in Connecticut on the grounds that he was fighting "the temptation to undertake too much," he rarely declined a request to lecture at the Massachusetts Historical Society, the Boston Public Library, or Manhattan's Reform Club. When possible, he brought Margaret with him, placing her in the balcony so that she might evaluate the strength of his voice. Higginson was then in the process of writing a two-volume history, published as *Massachusetts in the Army and Navy during the War, 1861–1865*, and so he especially responded favorably to requests to relive his wartime experiences, even traveling as far as Washington on one occasion to address veterans of the South Atlantic Blockading Squadron.[9]

Higginson's speeches on the war filled auditoriums, and the proud lecturer habitually wrote down the number of people in the audience in his diary. His speeches, such as one to the Loyal Legion of Massachusetts in 1895, were effusive in praise for Northern officers and soldiers, but less so for Northern political leaders, who he continued to believe had been too slow to raise Black troops and too tardy in correcting racially based pay inequities. Nor did he have any kind words for Confederate politicians or generals. Speaking in May 1904 at Harvard's Decoration Day ceremony—a legal holiday in every Northern state increasingly known as Memorial Day—he reflected that Union veterans might consider honoring common soldiers "who had fought bravely on the other side." That brief nod toward sectional reconciliation was not enough for one unforgiving Virginia editor. Higginson "believes in social equality, mixed schools, mixed marriages, and in the abolition of the color line," he wrote. "He is to us one of the most offensive of all New England negro lovers." In fact, Higginson had never written a word about interracial marriage, and what the editor wrote in condemnation Higginson would have surely seen as high, if unintended, praise.[10]

Northern audiences thought otherwise. Speaking alongside his old friend Julia Ward Howe at Boston's College Club, Higginson was introduced as the "great American eagle," and an approving journalist thought it a "great privilege to hear them read together." In 1894, in honor of his seventieth birthday, Boston's Round Table Club presented him with a silver loving cup inscribed with quotations from Tennyson on friendship. The year before, Higginson made one of his rare appearances in the Midwest, to read from his *Army Life in a Black Regiment* and to reminisce about his days in Kansas. Reporter Rufus Wilson heard the lecture and spoke to Higginson afterward. "At sixty-nine he is still a splendid specimen of vigorous manhood," Wilson gushed, "sturdy, erect, clear-eyed, and deep voiced." When asked about his next project, Higginson confessed that he was finally considering writing his memoirs and discussing "the men and women he has known and the events in which he has taken part during the last fifty years."[11]

Higginson chipped away at his memoirs, writing and cutting for most of 1896, even as he continued to publish short essays in *Ladies' Home Journal*, *Harper's Bazar*, and *Century* magazine. He waded through old newspaper clippings and his early diaries "with great delight," but, typical of his era, he preferred to describe the fascinating men and women he had encountered over the years rather than dwell on personal issues. His first wife earned only three mentions, and never by the name of Mary, only as "my wife." But neither did he emphasize his own exploits, instead praising John Brown and the men of the 1st Infantry for their valor in Kansas and South Carolina. (Higginson did, however, devote several pages to his ongoing feud with Whitman, characterizing him as a "dandy roustabout.") Houghton Mifflin promptly agreed to publish the volume, but, as always interested in maximizing profit, Higginson decided to first publish seven of the eleven chapters in the *Atlantic* for $150 each, a proposition the magazine "accepted at once." Like most authors, Higginson considered a number of possible titles, including "The Recollections of a Radical" and "From the Table of My Memory," before finally settling on *Cheerful Yesterdays*.[12]

Publishing the chapters in serial form first turned out to be a wise marketing strategy. Newspapers across the country praised the first installments, one remarking that "Colonel Higginson's career as a writer, soldier, public servant, and man of letters covers the last half century, and there is hardly a man or movement of that time that he has not come into intimate relations with." Most reviewers observed that the autobiography actually said more about other people than about the author: "There is not an important movement or event, and hardly an important personage, that does not come into these cheerful recollections." Newspapers uniformly commended it as "among the most readable reminiscent papers ever printed." Only Samuel Clemens and Henry James discovered a sadness in many of its pages. "Higginson's Cheerful Yesterdays is one long record of disagreeable services which he had to perform to content his spirit," Clemens observed. "He was always doing the fine and beautiful and brave disagreeable things that others shrank from and were afraid of—and his was a happy life." As for James, although he thought "action and art have been unusually mingled, with the final result of much serenity and charity," he noted also that "in spite of its cheer," it was "a book of ghosts, a roll of names, some still vivid, but many faded." Among the youngest of his antebellum reform generation, Higginson was one of its few survivors in the 1890s.[13]

James was more right than he knew. Several years before finishing his memoirs, Higginson had accompanied Lucy Stone and William Lloyd Garrison Jr. to the 1889 funeral of Lewis Hayden, the Black activist Higginson had followed through the Boston courthouse door thirty-five years before in their unsuccessful attempt to liberate Anthony Burns. The funeral was held in Boston's Charles Street African American Episcopal Church, where so many turned out to honor Hayden that dozens had to be turned away. The old abolitionist followed a procession led by the Wendell Phillips Club and the Robert G. Shaw Veteran Association and was afforded a seat on the front "platform near the pulpit for prominent participants."[14]

Ann, Higginson's last surviving sister, died in November 1892 of pneumonia at the age of eighty-three. Six years earlier, upon the death of Waldo's wife, Ann had abandoned the Brattleboro, Vermont, home she had shared with her mother and Aunt Nancy, to help care for Waldo's grandchildren. "It was a touching thing thus to close the half century of our family's residence in Brattleboro," Higginson mused, "where they went in 1842." Waldo himself died in May 1894 at the age of eighty. A lengthy obituary in the *Vermont Phoenix* chronicled his extensive career and service as president of the New England Railroad Insurance Company. But as did Ann's obituary in the same newspaper, the editor could not resist adding that the deceased "was a brother of Colonel Thomas Wentworth Higginson." That fall, Minnie's father, Judge Peter Thatcher, died at his home in Newtonville, Massachusetts, at the age of eighty-four. The obituary noted that "one of his daughters married Col. Thomas Wentworth Higginson."[15]

The passing of Higginson's oldest friend, albeit long an estranged one, and the only man Higginson ever confessed that he "loved," received far less press attention. William Henry Hurlbut (or Hurlbert) died in exile in Italy in September 1895. The man who had helped make the *New York World* into a leading Democratic voice was ignored in death by the Manhattan press. Only a handful of provincial newspapers in Maine and Sacramento devoted even a single line to Hurlbut's life, stating that he "died after a long illness." Higginson said nothing for three years, until finally confiding to a St. Paul reporter that "the utter indifference with which the announcement of his death was received was a tragic comment upon a wasted life."[16]

Far more painful was the death his old ally Lucy Stone. Despite their disagreement over Grover Cleveland's campaign and his being asked to resign from the *Woman's Journal*, the two remained friendly. After her death in November 1893, Higginson contributed testimonials to *Harper's Bazar* and the *Woman's Journal*. At her funeral, he spoke of her "beautiful and helpful life" and paid tribute to her marriage "protest" without mentioning the role he had played in the wedding. Funerals not being the appropriate venue for dredging up past misdeeds, and since Henry Blackwell was still alive, Higginson talked only of the "great love" Stone and Blackwell had for one another. "Her voice was herself, tender, sympathetic, true, musical, but with a peculiar ring that came from her sense of justice," Higginson assured those in attendance.[17]

"The gradual disappearance of early friends never visibly depressed him," Minnie later commented. "He lived in the present." There were always other old companions to visit, such as Clemens, who often summered near the Higginsons' vacation cottage in Dublin, New Hampshire. An early riser, Higginson often caught Clemens "in bed, where he prefers to write," still in "night clothes, with curly white hair standing up over his head." There were also new acquaintances. In 1896, Higginson enjoyed a bicycle ride with sixteen-year-old Helen Keller and her tutor Anne Sullivan; the two women shared a "tricycle" similar to Higginson's, and he pronounced the adventure "amazing." The next year, he was asked to preside over a dinner hosted by the Massachusetts Suffrage Association for reformer Jane Addams. "Colonel Higginson never presided with more grace," one reporter thought. There was also his July 1900 dinner with young Winston Churchill, who was touring New England and Canada in promotion of *Ian Hamilton's March*, a memoir of his South African experiences. Higginson judged the twenty-six-year-old, who had just won a seat in Parliament, "a pleasing manly young fellow" and was impressed by his "great publishing success."[18]

*　*　*

For the most part, Higginson avoided politics. To the dismay of his feminist friends, he endorsed Cleveland's campaign to recapture the White House in 1892. But he spoke on behalf of Cleveland on only one occasion. Appearing on the Boston stage, Higginson once again joined Charles Francis Adams Jr., Garrison Jr., and Harvard president Charles Eliot in denouncing Benjamin Harrison's domestic and foreign policies. As an advocate of free trade, Higginson was as infuriated by Harrison's support for the high McKinley Tariff as he was by the president's annexation of Hawaii. This time, Higginson said nothing about Cleveland's personal life, reserving his ire for what he regarded as Harrison's "departure from the old and safe policy of the founders" and his "courting rather than avoiding foreign entanglements." Curiously, Higginson was silent on Harrison's unsuccessful advocacy of Congressman Henry Cabot Lodge's Federal Elections Bill, which was designed to protect Black voting rights and battle the rising tide of Jim Crow legislation in the South. Higginson was even more ambivalent four years later, in 1896, responding to an inquiry about his position on Republican William McKinley and Democrat William Jennings Bryan by stating, "I hardly expect to support either nomination."[19]

Instead, Higginson preferred to devote his hours to his long-standing crusades, especially religious freedom and women's rights. In 1894, he attended the founding meeting of the American Congress of Liberal Religious Societies in Chicago. The Reverend Hiram Thomas, the head minister at Chicago's People's Church, a Unitarian congregation, was elected to serve as the organization's president. The fact that Thomas had once been fired from his Methodist church for progressive views only endeared him to Higginson, who was elected one of the group's vice presidents. Among those in attendance who were also given the title of vice president was Higginson's former ally Susan B. Anthony, but if that concerned Higginson, he failed to mention it in his diary. The aims of the Congress, noted the official statement, was to "unite in a larger fellowship and co-operation such existing societies and liberal elements as are in sympathy with the movement toward undogmatic religion." Speaking at a regional convention in Plymouth later that year—with Anthony again sharing the stage—Higginson said he felt particularly "welcomed" there as "it was the greeting conveyed to the Pilgrim Fathers by the native race," a reference to the so-called first Thanksgiving in 1621. His account of the first encounters in his *Young Folk's History* was a bit more nuanced. However, not wanting to spoil the moment, he simplified the story in his following remarks on Plymouth's history. He took pleasure in being followed by speakers Swani Vive Kanada of India and Professor J. Estlin Carpenter of Oxford.[20]

Neither Anthony nor Higginson commented on their troubled relationship when they again met in Boston's Tremont Temple to commemorate the anniversary of the pioneering 1850 women's rights convention in Worcester. Higginson had been only twenty-six and a silent observer when he had attended the conference, but together with Julia Ward Howe, Garrison Jr., Anthony, and Dr. Emily Blackwell, he was advertised as being among "the eminent [to] be present at this historic celebration." (Not long afterward, a Maine journalist reported that Higginson and Elizabeth Smith-Miller were the last two survivors of the eighty-nine people who had signed the 1850 Worcester convention's statement so many years earlier.) Higginson shared his thoughts on why men should support women's rights in "Concerning All of Us," an essay first published in *Harper's Weekly* and then expanded into a slim volume. Hoping to frame his line of reasoning in ways that Gilded Age readers might understand, Higginson argued that "the greater imitativeness of girls is, on the whole, an aid to civilization." Especially when it came to appearance and deportment, "the presence of a few girls better dressed and better mannered than the rest is a great stimulus" to working-class males, who would require such polish when entering into business.[21]

Advocating education for girls or property rights for women was safer than promoting suffrage for women, though Higginson never shied away from that fight. He served as the keynote speaker at the annual fundraising banquet of the Rhode Island Woman Suffrage Association, and one week later joined Howe in Boston for the twenty-fifth anniversary of the New England Woman Suffrage League. Together with William Warren, the president of the newly founded Boston University, Higginson publicized a petition to at least allow women to vote in municipal elections and published a list of one hundred books by American authors suitable for "A Young Girl's Library" in the *Ladies' Home Journal*. To better support that venture, Higginson donated his collection of books on "the history of women in all lands and ages" to the Boston Public Library. That collection, he told several reporters, began fifty years before, in 1846, when he purchased a copy of Scottish feminist Marion Reid's *A Plea for Women*.[22]

Perhaps foolishly, Higginson maintained the schedule he had followed as a younger man, and in October 1895, two months before he turned seventy-two, he fell ill with gastric "trouble." Higginson's doctor, John Hildreth, confined him to bed and prescribed a milk diet. "He has been compelled to cancel all his lecture engagements," a Portland newspaper reported. "His recovery will not be so speedy as in the case of a younger man." Minnie turned away all visitors but family and physicians. Determined not to abandon his writing, though, Higginson worked propped up on pillows, churning out essays for the *Boston Evening Transcript*, *Harper's Bazar*, the *Nation*, *Century* magazine, and *Youth's Companion*. "Voice weak but not excessively weak on legs," he confided to his journal on January 6, 1896, and "for first time today went halfway downstairs." His doctors believed he suffered from at least two ulcers. Higginson had hoped to take his family to Europe that summer, but Minnie vetoed that idea. He complained that he was too weak to lift the heavy history books he required for his next project. Nonetheless his habitual optimism never diminished. "I enjoy life & have adapted myself wonderfully to my recumbent condition," he noted in March. Later that month he was able to make it down the stairs and lie on the parlor sofa. One of his doctors seemed pleased with his progress and guaranteed him "he need have no fear for the future." Europe was out, the physician said, but their summer cottage in New Hampshire remained a possibility.[23]

The return of spring, with its "perfection of beauty," made Higginson only keener to get to the cottage as he "grew better & the time shorter." But the summer came and went, and, depressed, he noted on October 30 that "1 year ago today [he] was sent upstairs to bed." He celebrated his seventy-third birthday two months later, and was "most happy by restored health." Just to be cautious, he maintained a milk-heavy diet and resolved to stay close to home. More painful was the need to decline the presidency of the New England Historical Society "from considerations of health."[24]

The one invitation Higginson was pleased to accept was the May 1897 unveiling of Boston's Robert Gould Shaw Memorial, a large bas-relief commemorating the men of the 54th Massachusetts Infantry. Higginson was invited to speak. The role of keynote went to Thomas Livermore, on the curious grounds that, as the organizing committee put it, he "did not belong to the colored regiment service [and so] could speak of it impartially." Higginson was invited to contribute "Colored Troops under Fire" to a special issue of the *Century*, and he joined Adams, colonel of the Black Massachusetts 5th Cavalry, former Sergeant Lewis Douglass, and Shaw's mother and sisters in the ceremony. Higginson was pleased by the monument and its depiction of marching soldiers, and five years later he braved a cold January night to see it again. Sitting in the dark at 2:30 in the morning and remembering his own brush with death, he was inspired to write:

> Even before mine eyes the beautiful pageant is passing
> Colonel & dusky braves, who are marching around forever
> But for some inches of space, one trivial course of Fates.[25]

Their trip to Europe delayed for a year by Higginson's ill health, the moment the dedication ceremony was over, the Higginsons boarded a steamer for Liverpool, a private family event that nonetheless made national news. "Col. Higginson, with his wife and daughter, is summering in Europe," one Kentucky editor noted. Margaret was about to turn sixteen, and her parents wanted her to make the grand tour before she began college. Minnie and Margaret had their list of places to visit, but they also had to endure Higginson's reform tendencies. In London, as he put it in his diary, he met with "two heretical clergymen & another two semi-socialist." An American who joined them as they toured Britain judged Higginson "too soft-hearted" to travel in the old country. "He has discovered great holes in the roofs of some of the cottages near us," and the thought that the incessant English rain might flow in "makes him unhappy." Higginson himself was saddened to find London "so confoundedly empty to me." Although they visited during Queen Victoria's Diamond Jubilee, joining huge crowds in the city, he deeply missed "the circle of great men" with whom he had conversed during his 1878 visit.[26]

Higginson squired Minnie and Margaret to the usual sights. At Oxford, they toured Christ Church and the Bodleian Library, and Higginson was pleased to discover that the senior librarian recognized him from a talk he had given there in 1878. Back in London, they visited the British Museum, which Higginson pronounced a "fascinating place," and nearby Windsor Castle. Fame, as ever, opened doors for the Higginsons. Novelist and socialist H. G. Wells invited the group to attend his reception for John Hamilton-Gordon, then home on leave from his post as governor general of Canada. Higginson called on Emma Darwin, the naturalist's widow, and dined with Peter Kropotkin, a Russian geographer and anarchist living in exile, before the family crossed the channel for Paris. "The best thing I have done is to go to the top of the Eiffel Tower," the seventy-three-year-old Higginson bragged to a friend. "There was a high wind when we got up and the building did not tremble." After passing through Dublin, the group boarded a steamer for home, arriving in Boston in time for Higginson to check on conditions at the Old Colored Women's Home. "74th Birthday [and] in good condition," he reported that December 22, dutifully recording that he received "12 callers, 3 reporters, [and] 14 presents."[27]

* * *

A quiet retirement was never a consideration. In the spring of 1898, Higginson addressed the Massachusetts legislature on what he regarded as an "outrageous bill" that sought to ban Sunday concerts. Larger, national issues intruded when on April 25, Congress declared war on Spain. Harvard students called on Dean LeBaron Briggs, demanding that they be allowed to enlist, but Briggs begged off speaking with them, claiming he was suffering from a severe cold. Someone suggested they instead seek the advice of the most famous veteran in Cambridge, and they marched to Higginson's Buckingham Street home. Higginson, too, insisted he was "not fit to speak," but after reconsidering the matter, walked over to address the students from the steps of Thayer Hall. He warned them that given European interest in Cuba and the Philippines, the nation might well face "a combination of European powers, and then our patriotism will be tested to the utmost." Having led men younger than some of the students up Carolina rivers during the Civil War, Higginson added that nobody should persuade them that they were too young to fight, as a "young and educated man makes the best kind of soldier." He distrusted President McKinley enough to doubt that liberating the Cuban people from the Spanish yoke was the sole reason for the conflict, yet he concluded his remarks by conceding that, whether right or wrong, the war had begun, and "we must finish it come what may." The students cheered, and three days later Higginson thought even better of the war when he read of Admiral George Dewey's "victory" in the battle of Manila Bay.[28]

Higginson's reluctant support for the conflict hardly translated into supporting the American occupation of the Philippines. Together with Adams, labor leader Samuel Gompers, and industrialist Andrew Carnegie, Higginson co-authored and signed "An Address to the People of the United States." The lengthy statement, which was widely reprinted, demanded the McKinley administration "take immediate steps toward a suspension of hostilities in the Philippines," recognize the legitimate claims to leadership of Philippine nationalist Emilio Aguinaldo, and assure the residents of the island chain that Washington would respect "such a government as the people shall prefer." Any right to retain the islands, the group argued, ultimately rested on "conquest," a policy they felt incompatible with the principles of the republic. That argument gained little support in the South, where politicians employed Jim Crow opinions in defending their view that dark-skinned Filipinos were unprepared for self-government. Abraham Lincoln had used military force in "establishing sovereignty over some millions of vehemently dissenting white Americans," one editor grumbled. "Col. Higginson personally assisted in that work of coercion." The editor, at least, referenced the race of Southerners fighting the federal government and made no attempt to suggest that the men of the First South Carolina believed they were being coerced by Lincoln or Higginson.[29]

As always, once Higginson had committed to a crusade, he was all in. In February 1900 he spoke "on Freedom" at Boston's Century Club, and although he believed he had defended his anti-imperialist arguments adequately, he was also aware of time passing. His performance itself, he feared, was "not very satisfactory," and he was "not feeling in good form." Typically, Higginson spoke from memory or from an outline, but on this occasion he had to resort to reading parts of the address, something he had not done in some time. The lecture attracted national attention, particularly in the emerging progressive press. In it, Higginson had been especially critical of Captain Alfred Mahan, an imperialist whose writings on naval power and recent essays supporting McKinley's course in the Philippines earned considerable praise among Republicans. "It is unfortunate that we have a man, honored in literature and naval service, who will state an absolute falsehood," Higginson charged. "Captain Mahan lays down the general principle that neither a state nor a people possess any right to govern itself or to independence," a racist view Higginson regarded as in violation of American principles. Activist Ella Ormsby praised Higginson's speech in *Labor World*, remarking that it was "particularly appropriate" that those living in Boston object to the government's rejection of the Filipino Declaration of Independence.[30]

Higginson's opposition to the Republican Party grew after the party's convention, when they tapped New York governor Theodore Roosevelt, a war hero and avowed advocate of empire, to replace Garret Hobart, the late vice president. In a political leaflet, the aged abolitionist warned Black voters that "the imperialist Republican Party of today is not the liberty loving party of that name which set the American Negro free forty years ago." In another speech, Higginson conceded Roosevelt's bravery under fire and shared the candidate's belief in vigorous physical activity. Yet Higginson argued that to oppose imperialism "might often require more courage than the winning of battles." Well aware of the unpopularity of his position—and knowing that McKinley was assured of reelection—Higginson doggedly insisted that the nation was in danger of going from a republic, founded on the Declaration of Independence, into a "vulgar, commonplace empire, founded on physical force."[31]

Democrats hoped that meant Higginson might publicly endorse Bryan, once again the party's nominee. The *Chicago Journal* thought Higginson's approval would be a "valuable acquisition" to their ranks. The *New York World* agreed that Bryan was sure to capture the support of "anti-imperialists" like Higginson "and many other representatives of the intellect and conscience of the Republican party in its better days." But not only was Higginson dismayed to read that Bryan had moderated his anti-imperialist stance; he discovered that Bryan had published an essay that appeared to support Mahan's view that Filipinos were not yet prepared for "social equality." In a scathing personal letter to Bryan, who had asked Higginson to serve as the state chairman of his campaign, Higginson denounced Bryan's position as "utterly retrograde and mediaeval." Bryan had stated that no one had ever advocated "equality between the white man and the black man." Higginson replied that nobody involved "in the great anti-slavery movement in its early days ever advocated anything else." Noting that he had "raised emigrant parties and accompanied them into your state and Kansas," he was appalled that any candidate calling himself Democratic should "assume such a position." Higginson acknowledged that he agreed with Democrats on free trade, but the stand on race was "so utterly in the wrong" that he could have no part in Bryan's campaign.[32]

* * *

Determined now to avoid politics, Higginson suggested the family return to Europe. Thanks to his publishing and regional lectures, which typically earned him from $125 to $250 per speech, the Higginsons were quite comfortable as the new century dawned. Census takers in 1900 found "author" Higginson, then seventy-six, living with his wife of twenty years, his daughter Margaret, age eighteen, and two Irish "servants," thirty-seven-year-old Hannah Fay and twenty-nine-year-old Kate Rafferty. With *Cheerful Yesterdays* selling well, and four new *Atlantic* essays over the previous two years providing additional income, Higginson decided on an extended visit to Britain and the continent, essentially giving Margaret, soon to be twenty, more of the classic grand tour than she had received in 1897. Heads of households could then obtain passports for the entire family, so Higginson applied for a new one on March 5, 1901. Gazing at the applicant, a State Department functionary noted Higginson's "sapphire" eyes, "iron grey" hair, "florid" complexion, and "high" forehead. Later that month, the three boarded a steamer for Italy.[33]

Aided by a Spanish guide named Ernest, the group visited Morocco before heading for Spain and the Alhambra. Higginson judged the palace "utterly beyond expectation," as he did with Pompeii after returning to Italy. "I could hardly believe my eyes, so long have I dreamed about it," he marveled. Rome, Florence, and Venice followed: "no matter how much one hears about Venice beforehand, it is really more unlike any other place one can imagine." Margaret wished to see Paris and Innsbruck, and Higginson was happy to oblige. He was dismayed by the various travelers he encountered in Britain's Lake District, and not merely because they apparently cared "absolutely nothing for the literary" connections to the region. Support for the Boer War in South Africa, he feared, had "intensified the love of royalty everywhere," and he found little of the republican sentiment he had found on his first visit to Britain years before. Perhaps Victoria's reign had accustomed the English to accept royalist "institutions bad in themselves." Despite that, the Higginsons accompanied Charles Francis Adams Jr. to the September unveiling of a statue of Alfred the Great, king of the Anglo-Saxons. "We are now with our faces turned homeward," the satisfied traveler wrote in early October.[34]

Margaret may have received some college education prior to their 1901 tour, but there is no evidence that she ever graduated from any New England women's college. Instead, in early 1905 she announced her engagement to a physician named James Barney. Margaret had just turned twenty-four, and the groom was twenty-seven. The wedding was set for September 2, with a simple ceremony to be held at the village church near the Higginsons' summer cottage in New Hampshire. Higginson fretted about falling ill the week of the wedding, but then rallied. The wedding day itself was a rainy one, and with Higginson's siblings gone, only a few of Minnie's family attended. During the honeymoon, the first letter received from Margaret "made us very happy," Higginson noted in his journal. Three months later, Higginson celebrated his eighty-second birthday: "82 years young, as several journals say, and not unjustly."[35]

One year later, Margaret, who had settled with her husband in Boston, gave birth to a healthy boy, Wentworth Higginson Barney. Higginson was overjoyed: "The beautiful and happy baby makes my health or illness a secondary trifle, if I can only pass quietly away without these melancholy intermediate days or weeks when I may be only a burden." Despite his fears, Higginson was quite alive two years later, when in June 1908 his daughter gave birth to Margaret Dellinger Barney. "One of the happiest days of my life," Higginson wrote. He rejoiced "in the birth of a beautiful baby girl with abundant black hair and fine health."[36]

* * *

Higginson had one final crusade left in him. Since his days as a young pastor, he had believed there was more to life than the acquisition of money. Even before delivering his 1848 "Thanksgiving Sermon," he thought it an unworthy path to suppose that "*temporal goods*" were the "one thing needful in life" and finding "happiness in securing those." That belief only grew stronger over the decades, especially as the Civil War had fueled the growth of factories and railroads across the North and into the Midwest. As early as 1892, Higginson began to lecture on "The Aristocracy of the Dollar," although his thinking on the economic inequality, intensified by immigration and the rise of the industrial age, did not coalesce until 1904, when he published the speech as an essay in the *Atlantic*. "The advance in the standard of wealth in the last century is recognized by all as something formidable," Higginson warned. In his own boyhood, shipping magnate John Perkins Cushing was the only

Figure 11.1 Although eighty-two years old in 1905, Higginson had no interest in slowing down his pace of writing. In that year alone, he published a second autobiography, *Part of a Man's Life*, an enlarged version of his *History of the United States*, and eleven essays in the *Atlantic Monthly*, *Harper's Weekly*, *Outlook*, and the *Independent Nation*. Courtesy of the Library of Congress.

man in Boston thought to be a millionaire. Yet by the dawn of the new century, $1 million appeared to many to be "almost poverty; at any rate, a step toward the almshouse." It was sad enough, Higginson thought, that so few men of wealth also pursued intellectual activities, but the real danger of such fortunes was political. "Great monopolies [and] giant trusts begin to have power to control government, and tax people indiscriminately without their consent." The current "gulf between rich and poor," he cautioned, "was a danger to republic institutions." At present, "two thousand capitalists own more than the rest of our 65,000,000 population," and those atop society, he feared, cared little about those on the bottom.[37]

The answer, Higginson believed, was the introduction of socialist ideas into the American political system, if not the state control of the means of production advocated by Karl Marx, at least a recognition of the just claims of laboring people, an argument made years before by his friend Theodore Parker. Higginson could well remember the cooperative experiments of his youth, such as Brook Farm, which had taken shape just outside of Boston in West Roxbury. To that end, Higginson believed socialism needed to be taught in universities beside courses on business and capitalism. In 1905, at a large meeting held in New York, he joined journalist Upton Sinclair, attorney Clarence Darrow, novelist Jack London, and feminist Charlotte Perkins Gilman in forming the Inter-Collegiate Socialist Society. The organization's avowed purpose was "to promote an intellectual interest in socialism among college men and women, graduate and undergraduate, principally by the formation of student chapters in the universities and colleges of the country." One journalist reported that Higginson "astonished his friends by signing a socialist manifesto," but his astonishment only meant that he had never read Higginson's sermons or essays on entrenched wealth, intellectual freedom, and the desire for a moral life. Higginson continued to attend socialist meetings and lecture on the topic into February 1909.[38]

* * *

Two months later, Higginson was lecturing in Boston when he realized he was perhaps speaking for the last time. His throat had been sore, so he had refrained from speaking at all before the lecture. Even so, he felt "somewhat hoarse" during the talk. The large audience received him "more warmly than anyone save the president," though he judged his own performance mediocre, and for Higginson presentation had always been as crucial as content. When he was done, he left the platform, in very awkward fashion, embarrassed and thinking it was "the worst" aspect of his performance. Margaret had been in the audience, and she gently suggested that he best withdraw from speaking while he still enjoyed his reputation as orator. Higginson continued to write, however, submitting short pieces to *Harper's Bazar*, *Outlook*, and the *North American Review*.[39]

At about the same time, Higginson donated his personal papers, dating back to his college journals, together with a large number of books, to

Harvard. With novelist William Dean Howells, he established a $2,000 scholarship in the name of the late poet Paul Laurence Dunbar, whose father had served with the Black 55th Massachusetts Infantry. Even as he donated books to his alma mater, however, Higginson continued to acquire more, ordering books by Frances "Fanny" Kemble and Harriet Beecher Stowe.[40]

For the time being, he and Minnie lived a quiet, private life in their Buckingham Street home, with two housekeepers to care for them. Newspapers remarked on his eighty-sixth and eighty-seventh birthdays. "The last survivor of the group of famous New England scholars and writers," one Texas editor noted, Higginson "received an almost countless number of congratulatory messages from friends and admirers in all parts of the country."[41]

"During the winter of 1911, strength gradually failed," Minnie wrote later, but in fact the end came swiftly. On February 8, Higginson called in his usual doctor, John Hildreth, who again diagnosed him as suffering from ulcers. "He thinks me not seriously ill," an optimistic Higginson noted, "& that I can be cured by certain food." But his mind also wandered, and on several occasions in March, sentences in his diary either trailed off unfinished or were completed by Minnie. Later that month, Higginson found himself unable to walk or even stand without assistance. "A day of illness in bed & not knowing just why," he observed on March 29, and one month later he complained that he was "still lame and helpless." On April 21, he rallied enough to walk "a little in afternoon but was now lame." Hildreth and a nurse visited daily, as did Margaret. Days passed with no diary entry, until Minnie finished the story on Tuesday, May 9, writing only, "Passed from earth 11:30 p.m."[42]

Higginson's memorial service was held two days later in Cambridge's First Parish Unitarian Church. Six Black soldiers currently serving in the National Guard escorted the coffin, covered by the regimental flag from the 1st South Carolina Infantry, from Higginson's home. The choir sang a song of Higginson's own composition, "Waiting for the Bugle." Former Harvard president Charles Eliot, Charles Francis Adams Jr., industrialist Andrew Carnegie, Edward Waldo Emerson, the son of the poet, Norwood Penrose Hallowell, who had served in both the 54th and 55th Regiments, and Franklin Sanborn, the last of the Brown conspirators, were pallbearers. Minnie had also invited educator Booker T. Washington to serve, but Washington cabled from Charlottesville that he could not arrive in time. In keeping with Higginson's wishes, the service was brief and simple, and while the Reverend S. M. Crothers officiated, there was no eulogy. The burial at Cambridge Cemetery was private, attended only by Minnie, Margaret, and Margaret's husband, James.[43]

Dozens of lengthy newspaper obituaries, most of them featuring a drawing of the elderly Higginson, ran nationwide, from New England to Alaska, one appearing in a Czech-language Minnesota journal. "Noted Abolitionist Dead" was the most common headline. Still unwilling to forgive Higginson's wartime exploits, not a single editor in what had been a Confederate state carried the news. Most noted Higginson's dedication to antislavery. "A link with the distant and most stirring period of United States history is broken by the death of Col. Thomas Wentworth Higginson," the *Washington Times* lamented. "When war broke out, he took up the sword with the same zeal with which he had wielded the pen." Others, such as Iowa's *Evening Times-Republican*, observed that with William Lloyd Garrison, Wendell Phillips, and Frederick Douglass (in 1895) gone, Higginson "was the last of that group of men who made the middle of the nineteenth century famous for all time to come." Their lives "were devoted to a noble cause and the freedom of this country from the curse of slavery," the editor added. "We do not believe that any age or nation ever produced a group of men their equal." The Washington *Evening Star* concurred: "Americans of the older generation do not forget that in the early days of the Civil War this polished gentleman and fine scholar forsook his studies and willingly underwent the hardships of the camp and the march."[44]

Higginson would have been pleased to discover that other papers emphasized his support for women's rights and his many crusades. Still others discussed his literary career and support for public education or reprinted his poem "To Duty." "In his passing it seems as if the last living link between the early coterie of famous poets, essayists, and historians and the men of to-day were broken," the *Journal of Education* remarked. A South Dakota newspaper carried a lengthy obituary that was reprinted widely in the Midwest. "Historian, author, clergyman, soldier and abolitionist," the writer noted, ticking off the diverse aspects of Higginson's life, "he was active in many lines and leaves enduring works to perpetuate his name." One newspaper in Oregon called him "the last of that New England coterie which included Longfellow, Whittier, Holmes, Emerson, and Lowell."[45]

Minnie did her best to keep her late husband's memory alive. Just months after his death, she announced that she was planning to write his biography and urged journalists to publicize her need for "the loan of letters written by him to friends and acquaintances." It took Minnie three years to complete, but *Thomas Wentworth Higginson: The Story of His Life* was published by Higginson's old press, Houghton Mifflin, in 1914. Although the volume was crafted in the style of the period, with lengthy quotations from letters and Higginson's diary, Minnie's own words revealed a clear and lively prose style. The 435-page biography was heavily weighted toward his early decades, with two-thirds of the pages devoted to the years before 1865. Mary Channing Higginson was granted extensive and sensitive coverage, while Minnie herself never appeared even once. Hoping her readers would continue to consume Higginson's writings, her book ended with a detailed bibliography. Willing to overlook her husband's occasional dalliance with the Democrats, the Republican press widely advertised the biography.[46]

Minnie quietly lived on in their Cambridge home; a cousin, Francis Thatcher, resided nearby. She published the occasional poem, including "The Call" in April 1917, inspired by the nation's entrance into the Great War. Four years later, she edited a second volume dedicated to her husband, *Letters and Journals of Thomas Wentworth Higginson, 1846–1906*, also published by Houghton Mifflin. In 1926, on the eve of her eighty-second birthday, she boarded the exclusive RMS *Aquitania* for a return visit to Britain. Census takers in 1940 found the ninety-five-year-old widow still living at home with a servant, Catherine Sullivan. Minnie died on January 21, 1941, having just turned ninety-six. Her daughter buried her in the Cambridge Cemetery. Margaret herself survived her first husband before marrying William Hallowell, with whom she had two children. She died on April 13, 1985, in Meriden, Connecticut, at the age of seventy-six. Less successful in life, Higginson's first grandchild, Wentworth Higginson Barney, never attended school and became a permanent patient at Boston's McLean Hospital. Listed in the 1950 census as a "private mental" patient, he died unmarried in 1952.[47]

Despite Minnie's best efforts, both Higginson's name and the causes he championed fell into either disuse or disfavor, at least among white journalists and scholars. When references to Higginson did appear in the national press, they were invariably about his friendship with Emily Dickinson or his views on literature or education, but rarely about antislavery or feminism. The few stories that praised his radicalism appeared in union newspapers, such as *The Labor Journal*, which reprinted his poem "Heirs to Time," with its stanzas:

> I hear the tread of marching men,
> The patient armies of the poor,
> But waking early, toiling late.
> The heirs of all the earth remain.[48]

That historical erasure was not limited to Higginson. As the nation wrestled with problems of rapid urbanization and a rising tide of Eastern European immigration, Progressive Era historians focused on disparities in wealth and the battles between organized labor and big business. When scholars did take note of earlier struggles, they suggested that the abolitionists' "obsession" with slavery ignored the larger sectional issue of industrialization versus attachments to rural life. Historian W. E. Woodward's 1936 *New American History*, a best-selling volume lauded by many New Dealers, suggested that slavery "benefitted the negro, in that it served as a vast training school for African savages." Popular works on the Civil War emphasized the courage of combatants and generals on both sides, and when they did mention causation, those historians derided abolitionists as "fanatics" and insisted they bore as much blame for a bloody, unnecessary conflict as did reactionary Southern fire-eaters. Margaret Mitchell's Lost Cause novel, *Gone with the Wind*, won the Pulitzer Prize for fiction and sold more than a million copies during its first year in print, while historian W. E. B. Du Bois's *Black Reconstruction in America* sold but 376 copies during its first year and was never reviewed by the prestigious *American Historical Review*. Frederick Douglass's first autobiography, *Narrative of the Life*, went out of print, its last print run in the early 1850s. In 1891, Archibald Grimké, a former slave turned diplomat and attorney, published what would be the last biography of William Lloyd Garrison until 1963.[49]

With the onset of the civil rights movement in the 1950s, the country's attitudes toward race, and so also abolitionism and the Civil War years, at long last begin to shift. Young scholars watched on television as Black ministers and student activists were brutalized by Southern authorities and began to reconsider the view that both sides bore blame for the war or that abolitionists were oddly fanatical about a "benevolent" institution. After more than a century, Douglass's *Narrative* came back into print in 1960, and three years later appeared the first scholarly biography of Garrison in seventy-two years. That same year, the Washington *Evening Star*, a newspaper founded in 1852, was scouring their long-ago back issues and discovered a series of stories from March 1863 about Higginson and the 1st

South Carolina Infantry. The *Star* reprinted the stories verbatim, added documents from the *Official Report* drafted by General Rufus Saxton, included photographs, and supplied modern "background" on Higginson. That fall, Collier Books rushed an inexpensive paperback reprint of *Army Life in a Black Regiment* onto the market aimed at lay readers and emerging college courses on slavery and the Civil War.[50]

For a man who worried that he might never attract a biographer, Higginson would have been pleased by the attention heaped on *Army Life*, just as he would have been delighted to find that today no study can be published on nineteenth-century American poetry and literature, religious toleration, abolitionism, women's rights, temperance, or the turbulent 1850s and 1860s without a reference to his contributions.

Yet Higginson might also be saddened to discover that when it came to the issues he cared about most passionately, much remains to be completed two centuries after his birth. "Personally, I should like to live to see international arbitration secured," he remarked late in life, rather than to see borders contested by force of arms. He hoped one day to see "the legal and educational rights of the two sexes equalized," to read that "natural monopolies [are] owned by the public, [and] not in private hands," and to live in a nation where there was "absolute as well as nominal religious freedoms." As realistic as he was optimistic, Higginson—a man on fire—was nonetheless content to leave his readers with one final thought: "Let my memory perish, if only humanity may be free."[51]

Acknowledgments

In the spring of 2020, I received a lovely summer stipend from the National Endowment for the Humanities for research on Thomas Wentworth Higginson's life—for which I am most grateful—just in time for COVID to upend the world and shutter libraries and archives across the country. Conducting research during a pandemic posed obvious challenges, but also unexpected opportunities. In many cases, closed libraries continued to employ staff who had no physical patrons to assist and so kindly offered to copy and send me materials relevant to Higginson. Archivists at the New York Public Library, the University of Rochester, and the Columbia University Library were more than generous with their time and assistance. At the Redwood Library and Athenaeum, Michelle Farias was of immense help, as were James Cusick and historian Matt Gallman at the University of Florida, and Elizabeth Burgess at the Harriet Beacher Stowe Center.

The staff at Harvard's Houghton Library, which houses the main collection of Higginson's papers, were immensely helpful. Houghton has digitized many of Higginson's diaries and letters, but they were always prepared to help me navigate the vast Higginson collection, which contains not just Thomas Wentworth's materials but also that of his immediate family. Anne Boyd took time away from her own graduate studies to make several final visits to Houghton in search of documents I had somehow missed along the way, and I am most grateful for her help. At the closed Kansas State Historical Society, Sara Keckelsen sent me vital information about Higginson's time in "Bleeding Kansas."

As I have noted before, perhaps the best part of spending nearly forty years in this profession is the wonderful and wise friends one meets along the way. A large number of dear pals put their own work aside long enough to read one or more of my chapters, while others, knowing what I was working on, sent me documents they had discovered while conducting their own research. For their advice and archival finds and the occasional catching of embarrassing mistakes, I am deeply grateful to Brian Kelly, Peter C. Hoffer, Lesley

Gordon, Nicole Etcheson, and Gordon Barker. As our modern plague began to recede, I was able to try out some of these chapters at the annual meetings of BrANCH (British American Nineteenth Century Historians) and at the Society of Civil War Historians, where I shared a panel with Tom Brown, who also read one of my chapters and enlightened me on Zouave trousers, of which Higginson took a dim view. Fun dinners with Carol Faulkner and Andrew Cohen often turned into discussions of Higginson's complicated relationships with Lucretia Mott and William Henry Hurlbut. Thomas Balcerski provided me with numerous book and article suggestions when it came to wrestling with young Higginson's intense college friendships.

I first met John Belohlavek decades ago at a conference in Worcester, where Higginson spent much of his life, and as always, John readily agrees to read any pages I send his way. One of the worst aspects of the pandemic, for me, anyway, was not being able to share our annual martinis and good cheer. I met Gary Kornblith not long after, when I lucked into sharing an airport cab with him, and our adventures, invariably with Carol Lasser and sometimes in period garb, are the stuff of memories. Both read portions of this book and improved it immeasurably. Other valued friends, Craig Friend and John Quist, leading authorities on abolitionism and antebellum politics, sent me their thoughts, and at least as the world has begun to reopen, I have had the opportunity to quaff a few ales with John in various British locales.

Special thanks go to my pal of thirty-three years, Don Wright, who pretty much reads as many chapters as I send him. The only downside to his now reading my pages online is that I cannot see the doodles and cartoons he used to draw in the margins. As ever, Jeanann Wieners, a talented and wonderfully artistic photographer, helped me in cleaning up some of the images in this volume, without laughing too much at my low-tech skills.

My amazing agent, Dan Green, agreed with me that after fifty-six years, it was time for a new Higginson biography, and he continued to believe in the project when others did not. At Oxford University Press, Tim Bent was a superb editor, both in raising larger questions about the manuscript but also in routinely reining in my tendency to let a sentence drag on a bit too long or let Higginson's prose overwhelm my own. The final book is far smarter and tighter for Tim's careful and skillful work.

My brilliant daughters, Hannah and Kearney, didn't contribute to this book, besides patiently listening to a Higginson story or two. But together with Marc, Evie, and Margot, they make my life a joy. As ever, my biggest debt is to Leigh Fought, who good-naturedly endured endless Higginson anecdotes, helped me decipher poor nineteenth-century handwriting, and recommended books on antebellum feminism. Leigh just generally puts up with me and makes waking up each day a pleasure. To borrow a thought from my longtime companion Paul, "Only love can stand the test, Only you outshine the rest, Only fools take second best."

Notes

ABBREVIATIONS USED IN THE NOTES

ASH	Anna Storrow Higginson
BPL	Boston Public Library
ECS	Elizabeth Cady Stanton
ED	Emily Dickinson
HLH	Houghton Library, Harvard
KSHS	Kansas State Historical Society
LC	Library of Congress
LSH	Louisa Storrow Higginson
MCH	Mary Chandler Higginson
MSH	Massachusetts Historical Society
MTH	Mary Thatcher Higginson
NA	National Archives
NYHS	New-York Historical Society
OR	Official Report of the War of the Rebellion
SLH	Susan Louisa Higginson
TWH	Thomas Wentworth Higginson

Introduction

1. University *Missourian*, May 16, 1911; TWH Diary, November 24, 1881, Higginson Papers, HLH. Mine is not the first full-length biography of Higginson. The first, *Thomas Wentworth Higginson: The Story of His Life* (New York, 1914), was written by Mary Thatcher Higginson only three years after her husband's death (hereafter MTH, *Story of His Life*). In 1963, mystery writer Anna Mary Wells published *Dear Preceptor: The Life and Times of Thomas Wentworth Higginson* (Boston, 1963), a work that emphasized his relationship with Emily Dickinson and other poets. Three years later, attorney Howard Meyer published *Colonel of the Black Regiment* (New York, 1967), which focused on Higginson's military service. Neither included notes or scholarly apparatus of any sort. The following year, Tilden Edelstein published his revised doctoral dissertation, *Strange Enthusiasms: A Life of Thomas Wentworth Higginson* (New Haven, 1968), and although scholarly and thoroughly documented, it was, as its title suggests, written at a time when the historiography of antislavery suggested a variety of psychological issues that motivated abolitionists. More recently, Brenda Wineapple's dual biography, *White Heat: The Friendship of Emily Dickinson and Thomas Wentworth Higginson* (New York, 2008), provided unique insights into the relationship of these two poets.
2. Ronald Walters, *American Reformers*, 1815–1860 (New York, 1978), ix; MTH, *Story of His Life*, 47.
3. Belinda Robnett, "African American Women in the Civil Rights Movement, 1954–1963," *American Journal of Sociology* 6 (May 1996): 1661–1693. On Garrison's attacks on Douglass, see Leigh Fought, *Women in the World of Frederick Douglass* (New York, 2017), 96–99; Stephen

Ash, *Firebrand of Liberty: The Story of Two Black Regiments That Changed the Course of the Civil War* (New York, 2008), 7.
4. *New-York Tribune*, December 23, 1871; MTH, *Story of His Life*, 47; Unidentified letter, 1862, in *Letters from Port Royal, Written at the Time of the Civil War*, ed. Elizabeth Pearson (Boston, 1906), 168.
5. Joseph Felt, *Memoir of the Rev. Francis Higginson* (Boston, 1852), 3–6; Leslie Butler, *Critical Americans: Victorian Intellectuals and Transatlantic Liberal Reform* (Chapel Hill, 2007), 20–25; TWH to MCH, January 26, 1855, Higginson Papers, HLH.
6. Norman Dann, *Gerrit Smith and the Crusade for Social Reform* (New York, 2009), 447; Peter Wirzbicki, *Fighting for the Higher Law: Black and White Transcendentalists against Slavery* (Philadelphia, 2021), 168; TWH, *Merchants* (Newburyport, 1851), 28.
7. Butler, *Critical Americans*, 26; Wirzbicki, *Fighting for the Higher Law*, 19; TWH, "Saints and Their Bodies," *Atlantic Monthly* (1858): 580–582; TWH to David Wasson, November 17, 1851, TWH Diary, May 1859, Higginson Papers, HLH.
8. George Frederickson, *The Inner Civil War: Northern Intellectuals and the Crisis of the Union* (New York, 1965), 37; TWH, *Cheerful Yesterdays* (New York, 1898), 202, 211–212.
9. TWH, *Contemporaries* (New York, 1899), 246–247; Oswald Villard, *John Brown: A Biography Fifty Years After* (Boston, 1910), 511; Wineapple, *White Heat*, 4, 86–87.
10. Richard Henry Dana, *Journal*, ed. Robert Lucid (Cambridge, 1968), 2: 629; Wineapple, *White Heat*, 86.
11. Carol Faulkner, *Lucretia Mott's Heresy: Abolition and Women's Rights in Nineteenth-Century America* (Philadelphia, 2011), 170–171; Manisha Sinha, *The Slaves' Cause: A History of Abolition* (New Haven, 2016), 548; David Reynolds, *John Brown, Abolitionist: The Man Who Killed Slavery, Sparked the Civil War, and Seeded Civil Rights* (New York, 2005), 450; TWH, *Army Life in a Black Regiment* (Cambridge, 1900), 5.
12. Benjamin Quarles, *Black Abolitionists* (New York, 1969), 15; *Washington Union*, May 22, 1857.
13. Richard Boyer, *The Legend of John Brown: A Biography and a History* (New York, 1973), 433; Robert Churchill, *The Underground Railroad and the Geography of Violence in Antebellum America* (Cambridge, 2020), 17.
14. Stacey Robertson, *Parker Pillsbury: Radical Abolitionist, Male Feminist* (Ithaca, 2000), 157; Michael Kimmel, "From 'Conscience to Common Sense' to 'Feminism for Men': Pro-Feminist Men's Rhetoric of Support for Women's Equality," in *Feminism with Men: Bridging the Gender Gap*, ed. Steven Schacht and Doris Ewing (Lanham, 2004), 27–29; Katharine Rodier, *Separate Spheres No More: Gender Convergence in American Literature* (Tuscaloosa, 2000), 52.
15. Joan Hedrick, *Harriet Beecher Stowe: A Life* (New York, 1994), 288; Henry James, *The American Essays*, ed. Leon Edel (Princeton, 1990), 239. In 1882, Higginson reprinted his twelve favorite *Atlantic* pieces in *Atlantic Essays* (New York, 1882); six years later, he revised and republished some of his historical essays, mostly from the *Atlantic* but also from *Harper's Magazine* and the *Century* as *Travelers and Outlaws: Episodes in American History* (Boston, 1889). More recently, Howard Meyer collected fifty-five of Higginson's essays in *The Magnificent Activist: The Writings of Thomas Wentworth Higginson* (New York, 2000).
16. TWH Diary, March 13, 1879, Higginson Papers, HLH; *Memphis Daily Appeal*, December 27, 1885; *Richmond Dispatch*, December 2, 1885.
17. Johari Jabir, *Conjuring Freedom: Music and Masculinity in the Civil War's "Gospel Army"* (Columbus, 2017), 31. Higginson had cameos in Madeleine Olnek's 2018 film, *Wild Nights with Emily*, and in Elizabeth Cobbs's novel *The Tubman Command* (New York, 2019), 17, although she incorrectly suggests that Higginson "had thickened around the waist" by 1863.
18. TWH, *Army Life in a Black Regiment* (Cambridge, 1900); *Washington Evening Star*, September 9, 1962, March 31, 1963.

Chapter 1

1. TWH, *Cheerful Yesterdays*, 3–4; LSH to TWH, February 20, 1841, Higginson Papers, HLH.
2. Felt, *Memoir of the Rev. Francis Higginson*, 3–6.
3. TWH, *Life of Francis Higginson* (New York, 1891), 34–40; *Wilmington Journal*, November 11, 1853.
4. TWH, *Life of Higginson*, 128; TWH, *Descendants of the Reverend Francis Higginson* (New York, 1910), ix; *Chronicles of the First Planters of Massachusetts*, ed. Alexander Young (Williamstown, 1978), 14, 143; Washington *Daily National Era*, July 11, 1854.

5. TWH, *Descendants of Higginson*, x, 6; Mary Beth Norton, *In the Devil's Snare: The Salem Witchcraft Crisis of 1692* (New York, 2002), 164, 234; Marilynne Roach, *The Salem Witch Trials: A Day-by-Day Chronicle of a Community under Siege* (New York, 2002), 164.
6. TWH, *Life and Times of Stephen Higginson* (Boston, 1907), 43, 111–117, 252.
7. TWH, *Life of Stephen Higginson*, 241–244; Stephen Higginson, Federal Census, 1790, Boston, Massachusetts, p. 56, National Archives (hereafter NA). On these court cases, see my *Death or Liberty: African Americans and Revolutionary America* (New York, 2009), ch. 7.
8. TWH, *Cheerful Yesterdays*, 10; *Richmond Enquirer*, February 27, March 16, December 11, 1810.
9. *Boston Commercial Gazette*, September 23, 1813; *Boston Daily Advertiser*, March 4, 1814, October 24, 1817; Federal Census, 1820, Brookline, Massachusetts, p. 106, NA; Keene *New Hampshire Sentinel*, November 28, 1828.
10. TWH, *Life of Stephen Higginson*, 271–277.
11. TWH, *Life of Stephen Higginson*, 277; TWH, *Cheerful Yesterdays*, 4–6.
12. TWH, *Descendants of Higginson*, 28–29.
13. TWH, *Cheerful Yesterdays*, 7–9; Massachusetts Town and Vital Records, 1620–1988, MHS.
14. TWH, *Cheerful Yesterdays*, 9; MTH, *Story of His Life*, 5; Massachusetts, U.S. Compiled Marriages, 1633–1850, MHS.
15. TWH, *Descendants of Higginson*, 28.
16. TWH, *Cheerful Yesterdays*, 370; MTH, *Story of His Life*, 14; Alexandria *Phenix Gazette*, August 26, 1831; Francis John Higginson, Federal Census, 1860, Brattleboro, Vermont, p. 206, NA. Stephen's house, later numbered 7 Kirkland Street, no longer stands; the house now at that address was built around 1880.
17. TWH, *Cheerful Yesterdays*, 10–11; TWH, "The Woman Who Most Influenced Me," *Ladies' Home Journal*, October 1895, 8; LSH to Harriet Jackson, 1818, Higginson Papers, HLH.
18. Andrew Peabody, *Harvard Reminiscences* (Boston, 1888), 17–19; *Salem Gazette*, February 28, 1834.
19. LSH Journal, December 25, 1827, January 16, 1828, Higginson Papers, HLH.
20. LSH to Harriet Jackson, 1824, LSH Journal, November 21, December 4, 1827, Higginson Papers, HLH.
21. LSH Journal, December 12, 13, 1827, January 21, February 19, 26, 28, March 6, 1828, Higginson Papers, HLH.
22. LSH Journal, November 22, 1827, February 6, March 20, 1828, Higginson Papers, HLH.
23. Samuel Eliot Morrison, *Three Centuries of Harvard* (Cambridge, 1936), 220; *Salem Gazette*, April 9, 1829; *Literary Cadet and Rhode-Island Statesman*. December 1, 1827; Stephen Higginson to John Davis, October 30, 1822, LSH Journal, October 29, November 16, 1827, Higginson Papers, HLH.
24. LSH Journal, November 10, 1827, March 2, 1828, Higginson Papers, HLH.
25. TWH, *Cheerful Yesterdays*, 7; MTH, *Story of His Life*, 11; Boston *Christian Examiner*, May 1, 1834; *New-York Mirror*, April 12, 1834; Keene *New Hampshire Sentinel*, February 27, 1834; Stephen Higginson, Will, 1834, Massachusetts Wills and Probate Records, 1635–1991, MHS.
26. TWH, *Cheerful Yesterdays*, 122–123. TWH misremembered the location of the conversation, writing that it took place when the parents of a Southern student brought an enslaved driver north. As slavery was then illegal in Massachusetts, that would have been foolhardy. Francis John placed the story "in the vicinity of Harper's Ferry."
27. MTH, *Story of His Life*, 14–15.
28. TWH Diary, August 28, 1837, Higginson Papers, HLH.
29. TWH Diary, August 29–30, 1837, Higginson Papers, HLH.
30. Morrison, *Three Centuries of Harvard*, 260–262; *Cape Girardeau* (MO) *Democrat*, January 23, 1897.
31. TWH Diary, March 29, May 9, May 23, 1839, Higginson Papers, HLH. Higginson reminisced about Longfellow's teachings in the *Princeton Union*, February 21, 1907.
32. TWH Diary, May 9, 1839, Higginson Papers, HLH. On such friendships, see Thomas Balcerski, *Bosom Friends: The Intimate World of James Buchanan and William Rufus King* (New York, 2019), 12–13.
33. TWH Diary, May 29–June 1, July 1–2, October 5, 1839, Higginson Papers, HLH.
34. TWH, *Cheerful Yesterdays*, 47; TWH Diary, October 5, 1839, July 2, 1839, January 31–February 1, 1840, Higginson Papers, HLH.
35. TWH Diary, February 28, 1840, Higginson Papers, HLH.
36. TWH, *Cheerful Yesterdays*, 47; TWH Diary, February 8, 1840, Higginson Papers, HLH.

37. TWH Diary, July 21, 1840, Higginson Papers, HLH.
38. TWH to LSH, August 1840, LSH to TWH, January 28, 1841, Higginson Papers, HLH.
39. LSH to TWH, January 28, 1841, TWH Diary, March 1–2, 1841, Higginson Papers, HLH. For Elizabeth's death date, see TWH, *Descendants of Higginson*, 28.
40. TWH to Francis Parker, February 17, 1841, TWH to LSH, April 1844, Higginson Papers, HLH.
41. LSH to TWH, February 17, February 20, 1841, Higginson Papers, HLH.
42. LSH to TWH, February 20, 1841, Higginson Papers, HLH.
43. TWH, *Cheerful Yesterdays*, 67–68; MTH, *Story of His Life*, 41; TWH Diary, September 20, 1841, Higginson Papers, HLH.
44. MTH, *Story of His Life*, 42; TWH Diary, September 20, 1841, January 7, 1842, Higginson Papers, HLH.
45. MTH, *Story of His Life*, 41; TWH Diary, September 19, November 11, 1841, Higginson Papers, HLH. Higginson's eye color was noted on a later passport. See TWH, Passport, March 5, 1901, Higginson Papers, HLH.

Chapter 2

1. TWH chose that for the title of chapter 4 of his *Cheerful Yesterdays*.
2. MTH, *Story of His Life*, 54; TWH, *Cheerful Yesterdays*, 78–81.
3. Ethan Kytle, *Romantic Reformers and the Antislavery Struggle in the Civil War Era* (Cambridge, 2014), 211; TWH to Ralph Waldo Emerson, July 6, 1864, Higginson Papers, Huntington Library; TWH, *Cheerful Yesterdays*, 87–88.
4. LSH to TWH, January 28, 1841, Higginson Papers, HLH; TWH, *Descendants of Francis Higginson*, 29; Samuel Thatcher Higginson, Will, March 15, 1842, Massachusetts Wills and Probate Records, Vols. 225–227, MHS. The Brattleboro *Vermont Phoenix*, April 11, 1861, identified Francis Higginson as a "physician and surgeon" located on Green Street.
5. TWH Diary, May 9, 1842, TWH to Anne Storrow, July 24, 1824, Higginson Papers, HLH.
6. TWH to Anne Storrow, July 24, 1842, TWH to LSH, January 31, 1843, Higginson Papers, HLH.
7. TWH, *Cheerful Yesterdays*, 90–91.
8. Theodore Parker, *The Transient and Permanent in Christianity* (Boston, 1841), 45, 147–150; TWH to MCH, October 6, 1844, July 6, 1844. On Waldo's December 29, 1845, marriage to Mary Schier, see Massachusetts Town Records, Boston, 1845, MHS.
9. *New York Herald*, December 29, 1844; John Chadwick, *Theodore Parker: Preacher and Reformer* (Boston, 1900), 200; Sydney Ahlstrom, "The Middle Period," in *The Harvard Divinity School: Its Place in Harvard University and American Culture*, ed. George Williams (Boston, 1954), 78–79.
10. Ahlstrom, "Middle Period," 88–89; Morrison, *Three Centuries of Harvard*, 243, identified Higginson as "among the more distinguished graduates [from] before 1850."
11. Ahlstrom, "Middle Period," 156–157; Samuel Johnson and Samuel Longfellow, eds., *A Book of Hymns for Private Devotion* (Boston, 1846), 187.
12. TWH, *Cheerful Yesterdays*, 97–98.
13. TWH, *Cheerful Yesterdays*, 122–126; Samuel Perkins, *Reminiscences of the Insurrection in St. Domingo* (Boston, 1886).
14. TWH, *Cheerful Yesterdays*, 126; *Liberator*, July 14, 1846; TWH, "Sonnet to W. L. Garrison," in *The Liberty Bell*, ed. Maria Weston Chapman (Boston, 1846), 19–20.
15. TWH, *Contemporaries* (Boston, 1899), 246–248; Sinha, *The Slaves' Cause*, 469.
16. TWH, *Contemporaries*, 247–248, 255–256, 296; Henry Mayer, *All on Fire: William Lloyd Garrison and the Abolition of Slavery* (New York, 1998), 49; Leslie Butler, *Critical Americans: Victorian Intellectuals and Transatlantic Liberal Reform* (Chapel Hill, 2007), 23–26; TWH, *Wendell Phillips* (Boston, 1884), viii–ix.
17. TWH, "Anti-Slavery Days," *Outlook* 52 (1895): 55; MTH, *Story of His Life*, 76.
18. TWH to LSH, March 11, 1845, Higginson Papers, HLH.
19. LSH to TWH, March 22, 1845, Higginson Papers, HLH.
20. TWH to LSH, September 20, 1845, Higginson Papers, HLH.
21. TWH, *Cheerful Yesterdays*, 107–108; TWH to LSH, September 20, 1845, November 16, 1847, Higginson Papers, HLH.
22. William Henry Hurlbut to TWH, September 3, 1847, TWH to LSH, 1848, Higginson Papers, HLH; MTH, *Story of His Life*, 126; TWH, *Malbone: An Oldport Romance* (Boston, 1869), 7.
23. MTH, *Story of His Life*, 72, 125; William Henry Hurlbut to TWH, September 3, 1847, Higginson Papers, HLH. Anya Jabour, "Male Friendship and Masculinity in the Early National South: William Wirt and His Friends," *Journal of the Early Republic* 20 (2000): 91–92, is

especially useful on what she calls "homosocial" friendships, as are E. Anthony Rotundo, *American Manhood: Transformations in Masculinity from the Revolution to the Modern Era* (New York, 1993), and Karen Hansen, "'Our Eyes Behold Each Other': Masculinity and Intimate Friendships in Antebellum New England," in *Men's Friendships*, ed. Peter Nardi (Newbury Park, 1992), 35–51, although Jabour dissents from Rotundo's view that such New England friendships were limited to the young. Balcerski, *Bosom Friends*, 41, discusses how such friendships were often critical to academic success.

24. Jabour, "Male Friendship and Masculinity," 96–99; Gail Bederman, *Manliness and Civilization: A Cultural History of Gender and Race in the United States* (Chicago, 1995), 17.
25. TWH to Anne Storrow, September 6, 1847, TWH to Samuel Johnson, January 13, 1847, Higginson Papers, HLH. On these free churches, see Nancy Isenberg, *Sex and Citizenship in Antebellum America* (Chapel Hill, 1998), 94–95.
26. Butler, *Critical Americans*, 23; TWH to Samuel Johnson, January 13, 1847, Higginson Papers, HLH; MTH, *Story of His Life*, 81–82. TWH, "The Woman Who Most Influenced Me," 8, noted that Louisa "never quite accepted Woman Suffrage." On TWH's collection of books on feminism, see *Marble Hill* (MO) *Press*, March 12, 1896.
27. TWH to LSH, August 2, 1847, July 2, 1847, Higginson Papers, HLH.
28. William Hurlbut to TWH, September 3, 1847, Higginson Papers, HLH.
29. TWH, Marriage Record, September 11, 1847, Massachusetts Marriage Record, MHS; TWH to Waldo Higginson, November 30, 1847, Higginson Papers, HLH; MTH, *Story of His Life*, 121.
30. TWH, *Contemporaries*, 344; Octavius Frothingham, *Memoir of William Henry Channing* (Boston, 1886); 239; MTH, *Story of His Life*, 85; Boston *Christian World*, November 13, 1847; Newburyport *Herald*, September 16, 1847. The church still stands and was added to the National Register of Historic Places in 1976. Channing was the grandson of Stephen Higginson and Higginson's first cousin; he was distantly related to Mary as well.
31. TWH to Samuel Johnson, October 7, 1847, Higginson Papers, MTH; MTH, *Story of His Life*, 84. On Newburyport's "proslavery sentiment," see Stanley Campbell, *Slave Catchers: Enforcement of the Fugitive Slave Law, 1850–1860* (Chapel Hill, 1970), 69.
32. TWH to LSH, November 16, 1847, TWH to Waldo Higginson, November 30, 1847, Higginson Papers, HLH. On the impact marriage had on such intense male friendships, see Jabour, "Male Friendships and Masculinity," 101.
33. MTH, *Story of His Life*, 98–99; TWH to Waldo Higginson, November 30, 1847, Higginson Papers, HLH.
34. TWH to Samuel Johnson, June 1847, Higginson Papers, HLH; MTH, *Story of His Life*, 95–96, 107.
35. MTH, *Story of His Life*, 96; Butler, *Critical Americans*, 25–26.
36. Robert Remini, *Daniel Webster: The Man and His Time* (New York, 1997), 686; Maurice Baxter, *One and Inseparable: Daniel Webster and the Union* (Cambridge, 1984), 405.
37. TWH to Samuel Johnson, January and March, 1848, *Letters and Journals*, ed. MTH, 14–15.
38. Charles Francis Adams Diary, October 31, 1847, June 4, 1848, Adams Papers, MHS; Frederick Blue, *The Free Soilers: Third Party Politics, 1848–1854* (Champaign, 1973), 100; *Report of the Proceedings of the National Free Soil Convention* (Buffalo, 1848), 19–20.
39. Newburyport *Herald*, October 31, 1848; TWH, *Cheerful Yesterdays*, 128; D. O. Quimby to TWH, October 20, 1848, Individual Manuscripts, UR; TWH to WH, October 11, 1848, MH to LSH, October 1848, in MTH, *Story of His Life*, 89, 97; TWH to LSH, September 19, October 19, 1848, Higginson Papers, HLH.
40. Newburyport *Herald*, January 24, 1849; Montpelier *Green-Mountain Freeman*, January 11, 1849.
41. Charles Francis Adams Jr. to TWH, June 14, 1848, Higginson Papers, Harriet Beecher Stowe Center, Hartford.
42. Reinhard Johnson, *The Liberty Party, 1840–1848: Antislavery Third-Party Politics in the United States* (Baton Rouge, 2009), 90; *Burlington Free Press*, November 17, 1848; Washington *Daily Union*, November 21, 1848; TWH to WH, October 11, 1848, in MTH, *Story of His Life*, 89; TWH, *Cheerful Yesterdays*, 128; TWH to John Greenleaf Whittier, August 3, 1848, in *Whittier Correspondence*, ed. John Albee (Salem, 1911), 105–107; TWH to LSH, November 14, 1848, Higginson Papers, HLH.
43. Lee Chambers-Schiller, "The Political Culture of the Boston Antislavery Fair," in *The Abolitionist Sisterhood: Women's Political Culture in Antebellum America*, ed. Jean Fagan Yellin and John Van

Horne (Ithaca, 1994), 258–259; TWH, "The Fugitives' Hymn," in *The Liberty Bell*, ed. Maria Weston Chapman (Boston, 1848), 94–97.
44. TWH to LSH, November 2, 1848, Higginson Papers, HLH; TWH, *A Thanksgiving Sermon: Preached in Newburyport, November 30, 1848* (Boston, 1848), 4–5. Before 1863, Thanksgiving did not have a fixed calendar date and was usually celebrated around the middle of the month.
45. TWH, *Thanksgiving Sermon*, 5–12.
46. TWH to LSH, December 3, 1848, Higginson Papers, HLH; *Liberator*, December 8, December 22, 1848; Richard Webb to Maria Weston Chapman, February 7, 1849, Weston Papers, BPL.
47. Peter Wirzbicki, *Fighting for the Higher Law: Black and White Transcendentalists against Slavery* (Philadelphia, 2021), 172; Emerson Journal, December 10, 1848, in *The Heart of Emerson's Journals*, ed. Bliss Perry (Boston, 1926), 241; TWH to Theodore Parker, September 11, 1848, HLH; Ralph Waldo Emerson to TWH, May 16, 1849, HL; Anne Warren Weston to Caroline Weston, May 22, 1849, BPL.
48. TWH to LSH, September 6, 1849, September 18, 1849, in *Letters and Journals,* ed. MTH, 19–22; Newburyport *Daily Evening Union*, September 17, 1849.
49. MTH, *Story of His Life*, 105–107.

Chapter 3

1. TWH Diary, May 1849, Higginson Papers, HLH; TWH to LSH, September 1849, in *Letters and Journals*, ed. MTH, 20–21; Federal Census, August 26, 1850, Essex County, Massachusetts, p. 663, NA.
2. Sinha, *Slave's Cause*, 496; MTH, *Story of His Life*, 112.
3. TWH to LSH, October 1849, *Letters and Journals*, ed. MTH, 22–23; TWH to LSH, June 5, 1850, in MTH, *Story of His Life*, 98.
4. *Portland* (ME) *Transcript*, January 27, 1849. On the antebellum lyceum movement, see Angela Ray, *The Lyceum and Public Culture in the Nineteenth Century United States* (East Lansing, 2005).
5. Holman Hamilton, *Prologue to Conflict: The Crisis and Compromise of 1850* (Lexington, 1964), 204; Fergus Bordewich, *America's Great Debate: Henry Clay, Stephen A. Douglas, and the Compromise That Preserved the Union* (New York, 2012), 214–215; New Lisbon *Anti-Slavery Bugle*, September 28, October 5, 1850.
6. Mayer, *All on Fire*, 406; unidentified newspaper clipping, Higginson Papers, HLH; James Stewart, *Wendell Phillips: Liberty's Hero* (Baton Rouge, 1986), 152; MTH, *Story of His Life*, 111–112; New-Lisbon *Anti-Slavery Bugle*, February 1, 1851.
7. Newburyport *Daily Evening Union*, October 11, 1850; TWH, *Cheerful Yesterdays*, 128, 145; TWH to WH, October 13, 1850, in MTH, *Story of His Life*, 89.
8. LSH to TWH, September 17, 1850, TWH to Waldo Higginson, 1850, Higginson Papers, HLH; *New York Herald*, October 12, 1850; *New-York Tribune*, November 4, 1850; *Washington Republic*, January 22, 1851; *Liberator,* November 1, 1850.
9. TWH to Waldo Higginson, 1850, Higginson Papers, HLH.
10. TWH to Waldo Higginson, 1850, Higginson Papers. Although both this letter and the one cited above are undated, the topic marks them as 1850. On the early, insolvent days of the *North Star*, see Leigh Fought, *Women in the World of Frederick Douglass* (New York, 2017), ch. 4.
11. Charles Francis Adams Sr. to TWH, May 25, 1850, Higginson Papers, Harriet Beecher Stowe Center. On Adams's short-lived ownership of the *Boston Daily Whig*, see my *Heirs of an Honored Name: The Decline of the Adams Family and the Rise of Modern America* (New York, 2019), 60.
12. TWH to WH, 1850, Higginson Papers, HLH; TWH, *Mr. Higginson's Address to the Voters of the Third Congressional District of Massachusetts* (Lowell, 1850), 4.
13. TWH, *Higginson's Address*, 5–6.
14. Washington *National Era*, November 21, 1850; Washington *Southern Press*, November 19, 1850; *New York Herald*, November 13, 1850; Washington *Daily Union*, November 14, 1850; *Lancaster Gazette*, November 15, 1850; *New-York Tribune*, January 22, 1851; *Middlebury Register*, January 22, 1851; *Washington Republic*, January 22, 1851; TWH to LSH, January 18, January 29, 1851, Higginson Papers, HLH.
15. TWH, *Merchants* (Newburyport, 1851), 1–2; Washington *Southern Press*, November 21, 1851; *American Slavery: Report of a Meeting of Members of the Unitarian Body, Held June 13, 1851,*

in Reference to Slavery in the United States (London, 1851), 2. For the obituary of Stephen Higginson, see *Salem Gazette*, February 28, 1834.
16. David Donald, *Charles Sumner and the Coming of the Civil War* (New York, 1961), 186–187; Charles Francis Adams Diary, August 24, 1851, Adams Papers, MHS; Charles Sumner to John Greenleaf Whittier, October 7, 1851, Charles Sumner to TWH, September 5, 1851, in Beverly Palmer, ed., *Selected Letters of Charles Sumner* (Boston, 1990), 1: 337–339; TWH to LSH, October 5, October 30, November 154, 1851, Higginson Paper, HLH.
17. *Liberator*, October 10, 1851.
18. TWH, *Cheerful Yesterdays*, 139; Sinha, *Slaves' Cause*, 508; John Buehrens, *Conflagration: How the Transcendentalists Sparked the American Struggle for Racial, Gender, and Social Justice* (Boston, 2020), 177; Washington *Daily Union*, April 6, April 16, 1851.
19. Richard Archer, *Jim Crow North: The Struggle for Equal Rights in Antebellum New England* (New York, 2017), 202; Stephen Kendrick and Paul Kendrick, *Sarah's Long Walk: The Free Blacks of Boston and How Their Struggle for Equality Changed America* (Boston, 2004), 174; TWH, *Cheerful Yesterdays*, 139–140.
20. TWH, *Cheerful Yesterdays*, 145; Stephen Kantrowitz, *More Than Freedom: Fighting for Black Citizenship in a White Republic* (New York, 2012), 194; Gordon Barker, *Fugitive Slaves and the Unfinished American Revolution* (Jefferson, 2013), 18; Kytle, *Romantic Reformers*, 208–209.
21. Stewart, *Phillips*, 154; Mayer, *All on Fire*, 410–411; TWH, *Cheerful Yesterdays*, 143–144; *New York Herald*, April 9, April 12, April 13, 1851; Leonard Levy, "Sims' Case: The Fugitive Slave Law in Boston in 1851," *Journal of Negro History* 35 (1950): 68.
22. TWH to Samuel Longfellow, June 29, 1851, Adin Thayer to TWH, March 18, 1852, Higginson Papers, HLH.
23. TWH to "sister," April 16, 1852, TWH to "Dear Sir," May 17, 1852, LSH to TWH, April 16, 1852, and A. P. War to TWH, May 3, 1852, Higginson Papers, HLH. On TWH's attendance at the 1850 Worcester convention, see Little Rock *Women's Chronicle*, January 31, 1891.
24. TWH to "sister," November 9, 1852, Higginson Papers, HLH; TWH to Theodore Parker, January 10, 1853, June 24, 1852, Higginson Papers, Huntington Library; Henry Howland, *The Worcester Almanac, Directory, and Business Advertiser for 1860* (Worcester, 1860), 73.
25. *Liberator*, November 25, December 23, 1853; TWH to LSH, January 30, 1853, Higginson Papers, HLH.
26. Undated *Worcester Spy* in New-Lisbon *Anti-Slavery Bugle*, December 4, 1852; Jesse Olsavsky, "Runaway Slaves, Vigilance Committees, and the Pedagogy of Revolutionary Abolitionism, 1853–1863," in *A Global History of Runaways*, ed. Marcus Rediker (Berkeley, 2019), 221–222.
27. WLG to Samuel May, July 19, July 22, 1852, in *Letters of Garrison*, ed. Ruchames, 4: 206–207; TWH to "Dear Sir," April 1, 1852, Higginson Papers, Huntington Library; Raleigh *North-Carolina Standard*, April 24, 1852.
28. Stanley Harrold, *American Abolitionism: Its Direct Political Impact from Colonial Times into Reconstruction* (Charlottesville, 2019), 136; *Liberator*, February 12, 1853.
29. WLG to TWH, February 1, 1853, in *Letters of Garrison*, ed. Ruchames, 4: 228; *Liberator*, October 20, 1854; Washington *National Era*, July 29, 1852; St. Clairsville *Belmont Chronicle*, June 10, 1853.
30. Francis Underwood to TWH, November 21, 1853, TWH to Francis Underwood, November 21, 1853, "Lecture on the Romance of Slavery," October 9, 1853, Higginson Papers, HLH. For Fitzhugh's statement on "the weak," see his *Cannibals All! or Slaves without Masters* (Richmond, 1857), 278. The best discussions of Northern free-wage capitalist thought and Southern proslavery theory remains Eric Foner, *Free Soil, Free Labor, Free Men: The Ideology of the Republican Party before the Civil War* (New York, 1970), and Eugene Genovese, *The World the Slaveholders Made* (New York, 1969).
31. Washington *National Era*, November 10, 1853; *Liberator*, December 9, 1853; New-Lisbon *Anti-Slavery Bugle*, November 12, December 17, 1853; *Thibodaux* (LA) *Minerva*, November 19, 1853.
32. TWH, *Cheerful Yesterdays*, 120; Worcester *Massachusetts Cataract*, October 2, 1851; New York *Torch Light*, January 1, 1852; TWH to LSH, November 14, 1848, December 8, 1851, undated 1852, Higginson Papers, HLH.
33. *New York Times*, May 13, 1853; New York *Independent*, April 7, 1853; Brattleboro *Windham County Democrat*, April 20, 1853; *Liberator*, February 18, 1853.
34. *New York Herald*, May 13, 16, 1853; Westerly (RI) *Literary Echo*, May 26, 1853; TWH to LSH, May 16, 1853, TWH to Molly, May 1853, Higginson Papers, HLH.

35. *New York Herald*, May 13, 16, 1853; Cincinnati *Ohio Organ*, June 3, 1853; TWH, *Part of a Man's Life*, 81.
36. Sally McMillen, *Lucy Stone: An Unapologetic Life* (New York, 2016), 105; Lucretia Mott to TWH, April 6, 1854, in *Selected Letters of Lucretia Mott*, ed. Beverly Palmer (Urbana, 2002), 230–231; TWH to LSH, January 30, 1853, Higginson Papers, HLH; Washington *National Era*, April 20, 1854; New York *Independent*, February 16, 1854. Although one of the creators of the 1848 Seneca Falls Convention, Mott disagreed with Elizabeth Cady Stanton on demanding the immediate right to vote. See Faulkner, *Lucretia Mott's Heresy*, 139.
37. TWH, *Women and Her Wishes: An Essay, Inscribed to the Massachusetts Constitutional Convention* (Boston, 1853), 6–17; Wendell Phillips, ed., *Women's Right Tracts* (Boston, 1854); Susan B. Anthony, "Enclosure: Women's Rights, Circulate the Petition," in *Selected Papers of Elizabeth Cady Stanton and Susan B. Anthony*, ed. Ann Gordon (New Brunswick, 1997), 1: 276–277; James Russell Lowell to TWH, August 31, 1853, Higginson Papers, HLH.
38. *Buchanan's Journal of Man*, May 1, 1853; *New York Herald*, June 6, June 23, 1853; Newburyport *Herald*, June 21, 1853; *Liberator*, June 10, 1853.
39. TWH to Mary Higginson, September 4, 1853, Higginson Papers, HLH; Montpelier *Green-Mountain Freeman*, September 15, 1853; Washington *National Era*, September 1, September 22, 1853; *Memoir of William Henry Channing*, ed. Octavius Frothingham (Boston, 1886), 271; Raleigh *Weekly North Carolina Standard*, September 7, 1853.
40. Washington *Daily Evening Star*, October 10, 1853; *Alexandria Gazette*, October 11, 1853; Baton Rouge *Weekly Comet*, October 18, October 23, 1853; Washington *Daily Union*, October 11, 1853.
41. TWH to Mary Higginson, October 18, 1854, Higginson Papers, HLH; Boston *Una*, July 1, 1854; Washington *Evening Star*, October 20, 1854; Georgetown (CA) *Weekly News*, December 7, 1854; *Liberator*, December 23, 1853; Lucretia Mott to Elizabeth Gay, October 9, 1854, in *Letters of Mott*, ed. Palmer, 232; WLG to Helen Garrison, October 19, 1854, in *Letters of Garrison*, ed. Ruchames, 4: 322.
42. Washington *Sentinel*, April 27, 1854; *Liberator*, February 17, 1854.
43. *Liberator*, February 17, 1854; Stewart, *Phillips*, 168; Charles Emery Stevens, *Anthony Burns: A History* (Boston, 1856), 16–17; Barker, *Fugitive Slaves*, 139–140; TWH, *Cheerful Yesterdays*, 147–148; Ann Warren Weston to "Dear Folks," May 30, 1854, Weston Papers, BPL.
44. TWH, *Contemporaries* (Boston, 1899), 296–298; Dean Grodzins, "Constitution or No Constitution, Law or No Law: The Boston Vigilance Committees," in *Massachusetts and the Civil War: The Commonwealth and National Disunion*, ed. Matthew Mason (Amherst, 2015), 68; Vincent Bowditch, *Life and Correspondence of Henry Bowditch* (Boston, 1902), 1: 265; John Stauffer, *The Black Hearts of Men: Radical Abolitionists and the Transformation of Race* (Cambridge, 2002), 23–24.
45. Evan Carton, *Patriotic Treason: John Brown and the Soul of America* (New York, 2006), 224; TWH, *Cheerful Yesterdays*, 149–150; TWH, *Wendell Phillips*, ix; receipt for axes, May 26, 1854, Higginson Papers, HLH.
46. James Oliver, *Boston Slave Riot and the Trial of Anthony Burns* (Boston, 1854), 7–8; TWH, *Cheerful Yesterdays*, 152–154; Sterling Brown, "Saving the Cargo: Sidelights on the Underground Railroad," *Negro History Bulletin* 4 (1941): 152–153. This was evidently not James W. C. Pennington, as he did not mention the Burns affair in his memoirs.
47. Albert Von Frank, *The Trials of Anthony Burns: Freedom and Slavery in Emerson's Boston* (Cambridge, 1998), 71; Charles Francis Adams Jr., *Richard Henry Dana: A Biography* (Boston, 1890), 300–301; Barker, *Fugitive Slaves*, 147; Earl Maltz, *Fugitive Slaves on Trial: The Anthony Burns Case and Abolitionist Outrage* (Lawrence, 2010), 64; TWH, *Cheerful Yesterdays*, 154; unidentified newspaper clipping, Higginson Papers, HLH. In the chaos, Hayden evidently believed that he had fired the shot that killed Batchelder, but Higginson thought it was Stowell. See John Stauffer, "The Union of Abolitionists and Emancipationists," in *Massachusetts and the Civil War*, ed. Mason, 19.
48. Irving Bartlett, *Wendell Phillips: Brahmin Radical* (Boston, 1961), 180; Von Frank, *Burns*, 74, 122–123; TWH, *Cheerful Yesterdays*, 160; E. J. Mannix to TWH, October 21, December 24, 1908, Higginson Papers, HLH.
49. TWH, *Cheerful Yesterdays*, 160; Harrold, *American Abolitionism*, 142; TWH, *Massachusetts in Mourning: A Sermon* (Boston, 1854), 11–15; *Frederick Douglass' Paper*, July 21, 1854; *Liberator*, June 16, 1854; Washington *National Era*, July 11, 1854.

50. Undated reminiscences of William Channing, Higginson Papers, HLH; Boston *Massachusetts Life Boat*, June 13, 1854; unidentified newspaper clipping and undated *Boston Transcript*, both in Higginson Papers, HLH; Nashville *Union and American*, June 18, 1854; Baton Rouge *Weekly Comet*, June 25, 1854; Evansville *Daily Journal*, June 17, 1854; Washington *Daily Union*, June 13, 1854; *Barre Patriot*, June 16, 1854; Richmond *Daily Dispatch*, June 13, 1854; *Worcester Spy*, June 12, 1854; *New-York Tribune*, June 12, 1854.
51. Von Frank, *Burns*, 170; TWH, *Cheerful Yesterdays*, 160–161; Francis Higginson to TWH, June 20, 1854, Higginson Papers, HLH.
52. Little Rock *True Democrat*, August 9, 1854; *Pittsfield Sun*, July 27, 1854; New Orleans *Daily Crescent*, July 24, 1854; Washington *Daily Union*, July 18, 1854; *Washington Sentinel*, July 16, 1854; New Lisbon *Anti-Slavery Bugle*, September 1, 1855; Bartlett, *Phillips*, 184; Steven Lubet, *Fugitive Justice: Runaways, Rescuers, and Slavery on Trial* (Cambridge, 2010), 150; *Liberator*, August 24, 1855.
53. TWH, *Cheerful Yesterdays*, 162; *New York Herald*, October 31, 1854.
54. TWH, *Cheerful Yesterdays*, 164; MTH, *Story of His Life*, 149; *New York Herald*, October 31, 1854; New-Lisbon *Anti-Slavery Bugle*, November 4, 1854; *Worcester Spy*, October 31, 1854; *Bradford* (PA) *Reporter*, November 4, 1854; *New-York Tribune*, October 31, 1854; Washington *National Era*, November 9, 1854; *Nashville Union and American*, November 10, 1854. The local newspapers identified Butman's assailant only as "a negro named Dutton," but according to *Worcester Almanac*, ed. Howland (Worcester, 1854), 80, William Dutton was the only person with that surname in the city.
55. *Alexandria Gazette*, November 1, 1854; Raleigh *North Carolina Standard*, November 8, 1854; Newburyport *Herald*, November 3. 1854; *Worcester Spy*, October 31, 1854; *New Orleans Daily Crescent*, November 9, 1854.
56. Washington *Evening Star*, December 6, 1854; Washington *Daily Union*, December 19, 1854; *New-York Tribune*, December 12, 1854; Washington *National Era*, December 14, 1854; TWH to LSH, November 20, December 6, December 28, 1854, and undated *Worcester Spy*, Higginson Papers, HLH.
57. Sinha, *Slaves' Cause*, 518; *New York Times*, April 4, 1855; Nashville *Union and American*, April 6, 1855; Biddeford *Union and Eastern Journal*, April 20, 1855; *Bradford* (PA) *Reporter*, April 7, 1855; Lucy Stone to TWH, July 15, 1854, TWH to Maria Weston Chapman, November 1854, TWH to LSH, December 3, 1854, March 5, 1855, April 5, 1855, TWH to Aunt Nancy, April 5, 1855, Higginson Papers, HLH.
58. TWH, *Cheerful Yesterdays*, 154.

Chapter 4

1. TWH, *Cheerful Yesterdays*, 2; Nicole Etcheson, *Bleeding Kansas: Contested Liberty in the Civil War Era* (Lawrence, 2004), 57–62.
2. TWH to MCH, January 26, 1855, TWH Diary, January 1855, TWH to LSH, January 21, January 26, 1855, Higginson Papers, HLH; *Liberator*, May 28, 1858. On Samuel Porter and the gossip about Julie Griffiths, see Fought, *Women and the World of Frederick Douglass*, 135–136.
3. TWH, *Cheerful Yesterdays*, 172, 180; TWH to LSH, December 28, 1854, Higginson Papers, HLH; *Plymouth* (OH) *Advertiser*, May 6, 1854.
4. *Liberator*, June 26, 1857; *Washington Evening Star*, March 8, 1855; TWH, *Part of a Man's Life* (Boston, 1905), 122; MTH, *Story of His Life*, 153.
5. Larry Gara, *The Liberty Line: The Legend of the Underground Railroad* (Lexington, 1961), 76–77; Robert Churchill, *The Underground Railroad and the Geography of Violence in Antebellum America* (Cambridge, 2020), 187–188; Eric Foner, *Gateway to Freedom: The Hidden History of the Underground Railroad* (New York, 2019), 187; *Liberator*, June 8, 1855; *New-Lisbon Anti-Slavery Bugle*, June 23, 1855; *Richmond* (IN) *Palladium*, June 21, 1855.
6. *New-Lisbon Anti-Slavery Bugle*, November 10, 1855; *Boston Mob of "Gentlemen of Property and Standing": Proceedings of the Anti-Slavery Meeting held in Boston, On the Twentieth Anniversary of the Mob* (Boston, 1855), 53–54.
7. *Liberator*, August 8, 1856; *New-Lisbon Anti-Slavery Bugle*, August 30, 1856; Charles Sumner to Ann Bramhall, August 8, 1856, in *Letters of Garrison*, ed. Ruchames, 4: 401; TWH to Gerrit Smith, November 22, 1856, Smith Papers, Syracuse University.
8. TWH to MCH, January 21, 1855, TWH to LSH, April 27, 1855, no date 1855, Higginson Papers, HLH; McMillen, *Stone*, 126. On Blackwell's probable infidelity, see Carol Faulkner,

Unfaithful: Love, Adultery, and Marriage Reform in Nineteenth-Century America (Philadelphia, 2019), 125.
9. Jean Baker, *Sisters: The Lives of America's Suffragists* (New York, 2005), 23; *Washington National Era*, May 17, 1855; TWH to LSH, April 27, May 1, 1855, Higginson Papers, HLH.
10. *Washington Evening Star*, May 5, 1855; *Ottawa Free Trader*, May 19, 1855; *Carroll* (OH) *Free Press*, May 17, 1855; *Richmond* (IN) *Palladium*, May 11, 1855; *Wilmington Journal*, May 11, 1855; *Evansville Daily Journal*, May 11, 1855.
11. *Burlington Tri-Weekly Hawk-Eye*, May 11, 1855; *Baton Rouge Weekly Comet*, May 13, 1855; *Bath Eastern Times*, May 17, 1855.
12. *Richmond Daily Dispatch*, September 22, 1855; *Washington Daily Union*, August 8, August 17, 1855; *New Orleans Daily Crescent*, August 223, 1855; *New York Herald*, September 20, 1855; Sallie Holley to unknown, in *A Life for Liberty: Anti-Slavery and Other Letters of Sallie Holley*, ed. John Chadwick (New York, 1899), 149; TWH to LSH, undated 1855, Higginson Papers, HLH.
13. *Richmond Daily Dispatch*, November 29, 1856; *New-York Tribune*, November 18, 1856; Sylvia Hoffert, *When Hens Crow: The Woman's Rights Movement in Antebellum America* (Bloomington, 1995), 82–84, 112; Sally McMillen, *Seneca Falls and the Origins of the Women's Rights Movement* (New York, 2008), 116; TWH to ASH, November 30, 1856, Higginson Papers, HLH.
14. TWH to LSH, September 13, 25, December 19, 1851, Higginson Papers; HLH; Frederick McGill, *Channing of Concord: A Life of William Ellery Channing II* (New Brunswick, 1967), 130–133.
15. McGill, *Channing*, 140–147; Margaret F. Channing, Massachusetts State Census, 1855, Federal Census, 1860, National Archives. In *Girl in Black and White: The Story of Mary Mildred Williams and the Abolition Movement* (New York, 2019), 227, Jessie Morgan-Owens writes that because of Mary's degenerative illness, she "did not allow him to lie with her though [Higginson] was her husband." While possibly true, Morgan-Owens lists no citation for that assertation.
16. LSH to MCH, January 20, 1852, TWH to LSH, January 4, 30, August 23, 1853, Higginson Papers, HLH; William Channing Gannett Diary, August 8, 1860, Gannett Papers, University of Rochester.
17. TWH Diary, September 3, 1855, TWH to LSH, September 5, 1855, TWH to MCH, September 1855, Higginson Papers, HLH. Hunt's still exists as Hunt's Resort and R.V. Park.
18. TWH Diary, October 30, November 8, 9, 1855, TWH to "Dear Bab," November 5, 1855, Higginson Papers, HLH.
19. TWH to LSH, December 26, 1855, TWH to "Dear Friends," February 21, March 17, 1856, Higginson Papers, HLH. For "Scripture Idolatry," see *Liberator*, October 6, 1854, and for "The Sympathy of Religions," see *Radical*, February 1871.
20. THW to "Dear Friends," March 17, 1855, Oramel Martin to LSH, April 23, 1856, Higginson Papers, HLH.
21. TWH to LSH, June 8, 1856, Higginson Papers, HLH; TWH, *Cheerful Yesterdays*, 196–197; TWH, *Contemporaries*, 283. Higginson's memory played him false here; he returned from Fayal in September rather than in June.
22. William Freehling, *The Road to Disunion: Secessionists Triumphant, 1854–1861* (New York, 2007), 72; Etcheson, *Bleeding Kansas*, 77; Eli Thayer and Amos Lawrence, *Organization of Objects and Plan of Operations of the Emigrant Aid Company* (Boston, 1854), 6; Eli Thayer, *A History of the Kansas Crusade: Its Friends and Its Foes* (New York, 1889), 27.
23. Thayer, *Kansas Crusade*, 25, 103.
24. TWH to MCH, June 29, July 1, 1856, TWH to LSH, June 26, 1856, Higginson Papers, HLH.
25. *Liberator*, July 18, 1856; Brattleboro *Vermont Phoenix*, August 16, 1856: *Marshall County* (IN) *Democrat*, August 14, 1856; *Grand River* (MI) *Times*, July 23, 1856; *Ashland* (OH) *Union*, July 23, 1856; Lucy Stone to Susan B. Anthony, July 22, 1856, in *Selected Papers*, ed. Gordon, 1: 328.
26. *London Anti-Slavery Advocate*, September 1, 1865. In *Cheerful Yesterdays*, TWH remembered that the conversation with the enslaved girl took place at "John Lynch's slave-dealing establishment," but according to his letter in the *Advocate*, while he did visit Bernard Lynch's pen, the exchange was at Thompson's office. According to the Federal Census, 1860, St. Louis, both Bernard Lynch and Thompson were "negro traders."
27. TWH to LSH, August 24, 29, 1856, both in Higginson Papers, HLH; TWH to Theodore Parker, September 1, 1856, Higginson Papers, Huntington Library.

28. TWH to LSH, August 31, 1856, Higginson Papers, HLH; Bill of Sale, August 17, 20, 1856, B. B. Newton to TWH, August 26, 1856, Martin Stowell to TWH, August 15, 1856, Higginson Papers, KSHS.
29. TWH letter to *New-York Tribune*, October 23, 1856; TWH to LSH, September 3, 12, 24, 1856, Higginson Papers, HLH; Franklin Sanborn to TWH, September 7, 1856, Higginson Papers, KSHS; MTH, *Story of His Life*, 175–176; John McKivigan, *Forgotten Firebrand: James Redpath and the Making of Nineteenth-Century America* (Ithaca, 2008), 30.
30. David Grimsted, *American Mobbing, 1828–1861: Toward Civil War* (New York, 1998), 256; Vermont *Phoenix*, August 16, 1865; TWH, *Cheerful Yesterdays*, 209; TWH to LSH, September 24, 1856, Higginson Papers, HLH; James Bassett to TWH, September 21, 1856, J. A. Davies to TWH, September 27, 1856, both in Higginson Papers, KSHS; TWH to "Dabney family," October 9, 1856, in *Letters and Journals*, ed. MTH, 142–143.
31. TWH, *Cheerful Yesterdays*, 202, 211–212; *McArthur* (OH) *Democrat*, November 20, 1856.
32. TWH, *Cheerful Yesterdays*, 210–211; Lydia Maria Child to Lucy Osgood, in *Letters of Lydia Maria Child*, ed. John Whittier (Boston, 1882), 84.
33. TWH, *Out-Door Papers*, 41; TWH, *Cheerful Yesterdays*, 216–217. In the latter volume, Higginson reproduced a February 1858 letter from Brown in which he said he "should be most happy to meet you again."
34. *Holmes County* (OH) *Republican*, October 23, 1856; *New-Lisbon Anti-Slavery Bugle*, October 25, 1856. Higginson reminisced about his appointment in the *Topeka State Journal*, May 5, 1897.
35. TWH to Thaddeus Hyatt, October 14, 1856, Higginson Papers, KSHS; THW, *Cheerful Yesterdays*, 212–214; *New-York Tribune*, October 23, 1856.
36. Lucretia Mott to Lucy Stone, October 31, 1856, in *Letters of Mott*, ed. Palmer, 254; Susan B. Anthony to Lucy Stone, August 2, 1857, in *Selected Papers*, ed. Gordon, 1: 348; J. Fuller to TWH, October 25, 1856, Franklin Sanborn to TWH, October 16, 1856, Thaddeus Hyatt to TWH, October 20, 1856, TWH to Thaddeus Hyatt, October 26, 1856, Higginson Papers, KSHS.
37. Samuel Tappan to TWH, October 16, 1856, Higginson Papers, KSHS; *New-York Tribune*, October 23, 1856. Higginson's dispatches from Kansas filled an entire page of Greeley's newspaper.
38. *New-York Tribune*, October 23, 1856; Samuel Tappan to TWH, April 7, 1858, Higginson Papers, KSHS; TWH Journal, undated, 1856, Higginson Papers, HLH. On the racism of many free-state settlers, see David Potter, *The Impending Crisis, 1848–1861* (New York, 1976), 203.
39. James Birney to TWH, October 27, 1856, C. Robinson to TWH, August 27, 1856, Richard Hinton to TWH, November 6, 1856, Samuel Tappan to TWH, November 6, 1856, Franklin Sanborn to TWH, November 6, 1856, Edward Anderson to TWH, November 10, 1856, Higginson Papers, KSHS.
40. *Wakarusa* (KS) *Herald of Freedom*, December 6, 1856; C. J. Higginson to John Brown, January 10, 1857, in *Life and Letters of John Brown*, ed. Franklin Sanborn (Boston, 1885), 384; TWH to MCH, undated, 1856, Higginson Papers, HLH; John Sergent to TWH, November 8, 1856, James Kimball to TWH, November 25, 1856, Franklin Sanborn to TWH, September 19, 1856, State Kansas Committee, July 29, 1856 to January 8, 1857, W. F. Channing to TWH, October 17, 1856, Gerrit Smith to TWH, November 27, 1856, TWH to James Blood, October 27, 1856, Higginson Papers, KSHS.
41. Stanley Harrold, *Border War: Fighting over Slavery before the Civil War* (Chapel Hill, 2010), 166; Mayer, *All on Fire*, 447–448; Etcheson, *Bleeding Kansas*, 77; Dorothy Sterling, *Ahead of Her Time: Abby Kelley and the Politics of Antislavery* (New York, 1991), 302; Samuel Smith to TWH, November 26, 1856, Albert Fuller to TWH, January 23, 1857, John Wells to TWH, October 22, 1856, Franklin Sanborn to TWH, November 22, 1856, Caleb Pratt to TWH, December 1, 1856, Higginson Papers, KSHS.
42. TWH to Gerrit Smith, November 1, 22, 1856, both in Smith Papers, Syracuse University; Robert McGlone, *John Brown's War against Slavery* (Cambridge, 2009), 205.
43. Thayer, *History of the Kansas Crusade*, 116–117.
44. Jonathan Daniel Wells, *Blind No More: African American Resistance, Free-Soil Politics, and the Coming of the Civil War* (Athens, 2019), 116–117; *New York Herald*, December 28, 1856; *Richmond Daily Dispatch*, December 19, 1856.
45. Peter Wirzbicki, "Today Abolitionist Is Merged in Citizen," in *Massachusetts and the Civil War*, ed. Mason, 76; Samuel May to TWH, December 14, 1856, Hugh Forbes to TWH, undated January 1857, Daniel Mann to TWH, January 4, 1857, all in Higginson Papers, HLH; TWH to Gerrit Smith, November 22, 1856, Smith Papers, Syracuse University.

46. TWH to William Seward, December 29, 1856, Seward Papers, University of Rochester.
47. William Seward to TWH, January 3, 1857, Seward Papers, University of Rochester; TWH to LSH, December 19, 1856, Higginson Papers, HLH.
48. Harrold, *American Abolitionism*, 149; *Nashville Union and American*, January 27, 1857; *Washington Evening Star*, January 27, 1857; *Washington Daily Union*, January 20, 1857; *New-York Tribune*, January 17, 1857.
49. TWH to LSH, undated January 1857, in *Letters and Journals*, ed. MTH, 77.
50. Harrold, *American Abolitionism*, 149; Francis Bird to TWH, January 8, 1857 (misdated 1856), Samuel May to TWH, January 9, 1857, Arnold Walker to TWH, January 30, 1857, TWH to LSH, undated January 1857, Higginson Papers, HLH; *Newburyport Daily Herald*, January 5, 1857.
51. Mayer, *All on Fire*, 470; McKivigan, *Redpath*, 34; *Washington Daily Union*, January 16, 1857; *New-York Tribune*, January 17, 1857; *St. Paul Minnesota Weekly Times*, January 31, 1857; *Boston Evening Ledger*, January 23, 1857; *New-Lisbon Anti-Slavery Bugle*, January 24, 1857.
52. *New-Lisbon Anti-Slavery Bugle*, January 31, 1857; TWH to unknown, January 27, 1857, Higginson Papers, HLH; *Liberator*, February 6, 1857.
53. *New York Herald*, January 19, 1857; *Frederick Douglass's Paper*, January 24, 1857; *Boston Courier*, January 24, 1857; *Pittsfield Sun*, January 22, 1857.
54. TWH, *Cheerful Yesterdays*, 238; Robert Durden, *James Shepherd Pike, Republicanism and the American Negro, 1850–1882* (Durham, 1957), 27; R. B. Merritt to TWH, February 12, 1857, Samuel May to TWH, February 7, 1857, Samuel Joseph May to TWH, March 16, 1857, A. Brooke to TWH, February 11, 1857, Higginson Papers, HLH.
55. *Washington Union*, May 22, 1857; *Cadiz* (OH) *Democratic Sentinel*, May 28, 1857; *Burlington* (IA) *Hawk-Eye and Telegraph*, May 20, 1857; *New-Lisbon Anti-Slavery Bugle*, May 23, 1857; TWH, *The New Revolution: A Speech before the American Anti-Slavery Society* (Boston, 1857), 4–5, 13.
56. *Pittsfield Sun*, August 21, July 2, 1857, *New-York Tribune*, June 25, 1857; *New York Herald*, June 25, 1857; *Nashville Union and American*, July 10, 1857.
57. *Liberator*, October 16, 1857; *Bloomsburg Star of the North*, July 29, 1857; *Placer* (CA) *Herald*, August 1, 1857; WLG to *Boston Evening Herald*, June 17, 1857, and TWH, WLG, Wendell Phillips, and Francis Bird, "To the Antislavery Men and Women," July 8, 1857, in *Letters of Garrison*, ed. Ruchames, 4: 395, 454–456; *McGregor North Iowa Times*, August 14, 1857.
58. *New-Lisbon Anti-Slavery Bugle*, October 17, 1857; *Emporia Kansas News*, August 22, 1857; Lucretia Mott to Martha Coffin Wright, September 3, 1857, in *Letters of Mott*, ed. Palmer, 261; WLG to Wendell Phillips, October 18, 1857, WLG to Samuel Joseph May, October 18, 1857, both in *Letters of Garrison*, ed. Ruchames, 4: 489–490; TWH to Theodore Parker, October 3, 1857, Higginson Papers, Huntington Library.
59. *Liberator*, June 12, 1857; Kytle, *Romantic Reformers*, 220.
60. Stewart, *Phillips*, 177; Franklin Sanborn to TWH, February 19, September 11, 1857, Higginson Papers, KSHS.
61. MTH, *Story of His Life*, 201.

Chapter 5

1. Franklin Sanborn to TWH, January 5, 1856, Brown Papers, BPL.
2. Reynolds, *Brown*, 208; Wendell Phillips Garrison, "The Prelude of Harpers Ferry," *Andover Review* 13 (1890–1891): 18.
3. Sandra Petrulionis, *To Set This World Right: The Antislavery Movement in Thoreau's Concord* (Ithaca, 2007), 119; Kytle, *Romantic Reformers*, 227; Stephen Oates, *To Purge This Land with Blood: A Biography of John Brown* (New York, 1970), 216.
4. Tony Horwitz, *Midnight Rising: John Brown and the Raid That Sparked the Civil War* (New York, 2011), 75; Evan Carton, *Patriotic Treason: John Brown and Soul of America* (New York, 2006), 229; John Brown to TWH, April 1, 1857, Brown Papers, BPL.
5. Reynolds, *Brown*, 216–217; James Oakes, *The Radical and the Republican: Frederick Douglass, Abraham Lincoln, and the Triumph of Antislavery Politics* (New York, 2007), 96; Jesse Olsavsky, "Runaway Slaves, Vigilance Committees, and the Pedagogy of Revolutionary Abolitionism, 1853–1863," in *A Global History of Runaways*, ed. Marcus Rediker (Berkeley, 2019), 226; Louis Decaro, *"Fire from the Midst of You": A Religious Life of John Brown* (New York, 2002), 253.
6. James Redpath, *The Roving Editor: Or, Talks with Slaves in the Southern States* (New York, 1959), McKivigan, *Forgotten Firebrand*, 44; Reynolds, *Brown*, 216; Horwitz, *Midnight Rising*, 76–78; McGlone, *John Brown's War*, 167.

7. TWH to James Redpath, February 2, 1857, George Stearns to TWH, February 28, 1857, Reuben Randall to TWH, March 1. 1857, A. J. Stone to TWH, March 12, 1857, Daniel Foster to TWH, April 2, 1857, TWH Papers, KSHS.
8. Elvira Pratt to TWH, April 3, June 30, August 27, 1857, Franklin Sanborn to TWH, August 28, 1857, TWH Papers, KSHS.
9. TWH, *Cheerful Yesterdays*, 220–221; Bonnie Laughlin-Schultz, *The Tie That Bound Us: The Women of John Brown's Family and the Legacy of Radical Abolitionism* (Ithaca, 2013), 48; Olsavsky, "Runaway Slaves, Vigilance Committees," 225; Decaro, "*Fire from the Midst of You*," 36; Patrick Rael, *Eighty-Eight Years: The Long Death of Slavery in the United States, 1777–1865* (Athens, 2015), 229.
10. Samuel Tappan to TWH, January 24, 1858, TWH Papers, KSHS. Tappan began spelling Brown's latest pseudonym "Br" but crossed that out and replaced it with "Blood."
11. David Blight, *Frederick Douglass: Prophet of Freedom* (New York, 2018), 296; Eric Walther, *The Shattering of the Union: America in the 1850s* (Lanham, 2003), 145; Carton, *Patriotic Treason*, 241; John Brown to TWH, February 2, 12, 1858, TWH to John Brown, February 8, 1858, Brown Papers, BPL.
12. Franklin Sanborn to TWH, February 11, 19, 1858. John Brown to TWH, February 12, 1858, John Brown to Franklin Sanborn, February 17, 1858, Brown Papers, BPL.
13. Newburyport *Daily Herald*, February 26, 1858; TWH, *Cheerful Yesterdays*, 219.
14. John Brown to Theodore Parker, March 4, 1858, John Brown to (son) John Brown, March 6, 1858, in *Life and Letters of Brown*, ed. Sanborn, 440, 447; *Topeka State Journal*, May 13, 1897.
15. Mayer, *All on Fire*, 477; John Brown to TWH, March 4, 1858, Brown Papers, BPL.
16. George Stearns to TWH, April 1, 1858, Brown Papers, BPL.
17. Franklin Sanborn to TWH, March 8, March 21, April 20, May 1, 1858, Brown Papers, BPL.
18. Reynolds, *Brown*, 239–241; Franklin Sanborn to TWH, May 5, May 7, May 11, 1858, Brown Papers, BPL.
19. Carton, *Patriotic Treason*, 265; TWH to John Brown, May 7, May 18, 1858, TWH to Theodore Parker, May 9, 1858, John Brown to TWH, May 14, 1858, Brown Papers, BPL.
20. Reynolds, *Brown*, 266; Franklin Sanborn to TWH, May 18, 1859, TWH to Theodore Parker, May 18, 1858, Theodore Parker to TWH, May 20, 1858, Brown Papers, BPL.
21. George Stearns to TWH, May 21, June 2, 1858, Franklin Sanborn to TWH, May 31, 1858, TWH, Memorandum, June 1, June 6, 1858, Brown Papers, BPL.
22. *Life and Letters of Brown,* ed. Sanborn, 464; Franklin Sanborn to TWH, June 4, July 6, 1858, Brown Papers, BPL.
23. Hugh Forbes to TWH, June 6, 1858, Brown Papers, BPL; TWH to LSH, June 17, 1859, in *Letters and Journals*, ed. MTH, 81.
24. TWH to LSH, June 16, 1848, TWH to Francis Underwood, November 21, 1853, TWH to William Hurlbert, October 31, 1852, Higginson Papers, HLH; Mary Blanchard, *Oscar Wilde's America: Counterculture in the Gilded Age* (New Haven, 1998), 29.
25. Daniel Crofts, *A Secession Crisis Enigma: William Henry Hurlburt and "The Diary of a Public Man"* (Charlottesville, 2010), 46–47; George Templeton Strong, Diary, December 6, 1856, March 8, 1857, in *The Diary of George Templeton Strong*, ed. Allan Nevins (New York, 1952), 312–313, 356, 402–403; TWH to LSH, June 26, 1856, Higginson Papers, HLH.
26. The elder Nathaniel Willis owned a number of newspapers, including *The Youth's Companion*, before his retirement in 1857. See *New Orleans Daily Crescent*, April 20, 1857.
27. Baton Rouge *Sugar Planter*, May 16, 1857.
28. R. Laurence Moore, "Spiritualism and Science: Reflections on the First Decade of the Spirit Rappings," *American Quarterly* 24 (1972): 474; Bret Carroll, *Spiritualism in Antebellum America* (Bloomington, 1997), 45, 98–199; Nancy Hewitt, *Radical Friend: Amy Kirby Post and Her Activist Worlds* (Chapel Hill, 2018), 140–141.
29. *Opelousas* (LA) *Courier*, July 4, 1857; Boston *Banner of Light*, June 12, June 25, 1857; New York *Spiritual Age*, January 23, 1857.
30. Boston *Banner of Light*, January 23, December 18, 1858; New York *Spiritual Age*, January 23, 1858; Grand Rapids *Wood County Reporter*, October 26, 1858.
31. Boston *Banner of Light*, March 12, June 25, July 9, July 16, 1859; New York *Spiritual Age*, July 2, 1859; TWH, *The Results of Spiritualism, A Discourse, delivered at Dodsworth's Hall* (New York, 1859).

314 NOTES

32. *Liberator*, August 12, 1859.
33. New-Lisbon *Anti-Slavery Bugle*, February 27, 1858.
34. *Washington Union*, May 16, 1858; New-Lisbon *Anti-Slavery Bugle*, May 1, May 22, 1858; Susan B. Anthony to Antoinette Brown Blackwell, April 22, 1858, in *Selected Papers*, ed. Gordon, 1: 360. On the article, see TWH, "Saints and Their Bodies," *Atlantic Monthly* 1 (1858): 582–595.
35. Green Mountain *Sybil*, April 1, 1859; TWH, "Murder of the Innocents," *Atlantic Monthly* (1859): 71; Burlington (IA) *Weekly Hawk-eye*, September 3, 1859; Woodstock *Spirit of the Age*, September 8, 1859; Baltimore *Daily Exchange*, August 19, 1859; *Vermont Phoenix*, October 1, 1859; *Nashville Union and American*, September 29, 1959.
36. *Liberator*, February 18, 1859; *New-York Tribune*, January 22, 1859; *Cass County* (MI) *Republican*, January 27, 1859; Sandusky *Fremont Journal*, January 29, 1859; TWH, *Atlantic Essays* (Boston, 1882), 99, 103, 109, 118, 121.
37. Faulkner, *Mott*, 170–171.
38. Stirling, *Abby Kelley*, 315; *Liberator*, February 5, 1858.
39. Benjamin Quarles, *Black Abolitionists* (New York, 1969), 233; *Liberator*, May 28, 1858; Richmond *Daily Dispatch*, June 28, 1858.
40. *Liberator*, October 15, 1858; *Wheeling Daily Intelligencer*, December 14, 1858.
41. Stewart, *Phillips*, 200; Reynolds, *Brown*, 242.
42. Franklin Sanborn to TWH, September 14, October 6, 1858, both in Brown Papers, BPL.
43. Jill Lepore, *These Truths: A History of the United States* (New York, 2018), 282; TWH to John Brown, October 29, 1858, Brown Papers, BPL.
44. Robertson, *Parker Pillsbury*, 120; New-Lisbon *Anti-Slavery Bugle*, January 15, February 19, 1859.
45. William Lloyd Garrison to Parker Pillsbury, June 3, 1859, Garrison Papers, BPL.
46. Franklin Sanborn to TWH, January 19, March 4, March 14, 1859, Brown Papers, BPL.
47. Carton, *Patriotic Treason*, 277; TWH, *Cheerful Yesterdays*, 222; TWH to John Brown, May 1, 1859, Franklin Sanborn to TWH, April 19, May 9, May 30, 1859, Brown Papers, BPL.
48. New-Lisbon *Anti-Slavery Bugle*, June 11, 1859; Washington *National Era*, June 23, 1859; McGlone, *John Brown's War*, 255; Franklin Sanborn to TWH, August 24, 1869, Brown Papers, BPL; TWH, *Cheerful Yesterdays*, 222–223.
49. TWH, *Cheerful Yesterdays*, 223; *Cleveland Morning Leader*, October 18, 1859; *Richmond Enquirer*, October 18, 1859; *Wheeling Daily Intelligencer*, October 18, 1859; Richmond *Daily Dispatch*, October 18, 1859; Cincinnati *Penny Press*, October 18, 1859; Baltimore *Daily Exchange*, October 18, 1859; *New-York Tribune*, October 18, 1859; *New York Herald*, October 18, 1859.
50. *Alexandria Gazette*, October 18, 1859; TWH, *Cheerful Yesterdays*, 223; McGlone, *John Brown's War*, 223–224; Laughlin-Schultz, *The Tie That Bound Us*, 64.
51. TWH to Oswald Villard, November 12, 1909, Villard Papers, Columbia University Library.

Chapter 6

1. David Reynolds, *Abe: Lincoln and His Times* (New York, 2020), 469; McKivigan, *Redpath*, 48.
2. Samuel May to TWH, November 10, 1859, Samuel Blackwell to TWH, October 27, 1859, Daniel Stickley to TWH, November 29, 1859, William Fall to TWH, October 27, 1859, Brown Papers, BPL.
3. Printed circular, November 2, 1859, Wendell Phillips to TWH, October 26, 1859, William Ingersal Bowditch to TWH, October 26, 1859, George Sennott to TWH, November 28, 1859, Brown Papers, BPL; *Wilmington Journal*, October 28, 1859.
4. Wendell Phillips to TWH, October 26, 1859, Brown Papers, BPL; McKivigan, *Redpath*, 50; TWH to LSH, October 27, 1859, in *Letters and Journals*, ed. MTH, 85; TWH, *Cheerful Yesterdays*, 224–225.
5. Octavius Frothingham, *Gerrit Smith: A Biography* (New York, 1878), 242; Bartlett, *Phillips*, 211; Blight, *Douglass*, 306; Norman Dann, *Practical Dreamer: Gerrit Smith and the Crusade for Social Reform* (New York, 2009), 510; Franklin Sanborn to TWH, November 19, 1859, Brown Papers, BPL.
6. Horwitz, *Midnight Rising*, 208–209; *New York Herald*, November 17, 1859; *Lowell Daily Citizen*, June 6, 1860; Franklin Sanborn to TWH, October 21, 1859, Charles Miller to TWH, November 11, 1859, Brown Papers, BPL.
7. Walther, *Shattering of the Union*, 180; TWH, *Cheerful Yesterdays*, 224; TWH to Franklin Sanborn, November 17, 1859, Brown Papers, BPL.

8. TWH to Samuel Gridley Howe, November 15, 1859, Brown Papers, BPL.
9. Samuel Gridley Howe to TWH, February 16, 1860, Franklin Sanborn to TWH, November 10, November 17, 1859, Brown Papers, BPL; *Life and Letters of John Brown*, ed. Sanborn, 514.
10. *Liberator*, November 4, 1859; *New Oregon* (IA) *Plaindealer*, November 25, 1859; Stephen Vincent Benét, *John Brown's Body* (Garden City, 1928), 59.
11. Villard, *Brown*, 574; TWH, *Cheerful Yesterdays*, 226; TWH to LSH, November 5, 1859, in *Letters and Journals*, ed. MTH, 86–87.
12. Carton, *Patriotic Treason*, 325; TWH, *Contemporaries*, 222–229.
13. Laughlin-Schultz, *The Tie That Bound Us*, 20–21; TWH, *Contemporaries*, 231.
14. Edward Renehan, *The Secret Six: The True Story of the Men Who Conspired with John Brown* (New York, 1995), 215; TWH, *Contemporaries*, 230, 242; TWH, *Cheerful Yesterdays*, 228; *Emporia* (KS) *News*, December 3, 1859; *Fremont* (OH) *Journal*, November 11, 1859; *Alexandria Gazette*, November 9, 1859; *New York Herald*, November 7, 1859; Richmond *Daily Dispatch*, November 8, 1859.
15. Villard, *Brown*, 512–513; George Sennott telegram to TWH, November 5, 1859, George Hoyt to TWH, November 7, 1859, John LeBarnes to TWH, November 7, 1859, Samuel Gridley Howe to TWH, November 9, 1859, Brown Papers, BPL; *New-York Tribune*, November 7, 1859.
16. John Brown to TWH, November 9, 1859, Mary Ann Brown to TWH, November 15, 1859, Brown Papers, BPL.
17. Ruth Brown Thompson to TWH, November 14, 17, 1859, Brown Papers, BPL.
18. Annie Brown to TWH, December 9, 1859, Brown Papers, BPL.
19. John Brown to TWH, November 22, 1859, Brown Papers, BPL.
20. Potter, *Impending Crisis*, 379; *Opelousas* (LA) *Courier*, December 17, 1859.
21. St. Paul *Weekly Pioneer and Democrat*, December 2, 1859; *New York Herald*, November 21, 1859; "A Southerner" to TWH, November 1, 1859, Brown Papers, BPL.
22. Henry Clarke to TWH, November 18, December 14, 1859, H. W. Wayland to TWH, November 18, 1859, E. F. Roberts to TWH, December 1, 1859, Brown Papers, BPL.
23. Francis Jackson to TWH, December 6, 1859, Richard Webb to TWH, March 11, 1860, Brown Papers, BPL.
24. Mary Mann to TWH, January 16, 1860, James Fitch to TWH, February 13, 1860, Samuel May Jr. to TWH, February 16, 1860, Annie Brown to TWH, January 11, 1860, Brown Papers, BPL; Richmond *Daily Dispatch*, March 22, 1860.
25. J. D. Fowler to TWH, March 6, March 9, 1860, Edward Spring to TWH, March 11, 1860, Brown Papers, BPL; James Redpath to TWH, June 26, TWH Papers, KSHS.
26. Freehling, *Road to Disunion*, 220; Oates, *To Purge This Land with Blood*, 351–352.
27. James McKim to TWH, October 28, 1859, Nathan Cheney to TWH, November 8, 1859, Franklin Sanborn to TWH, November 24, 1859, Salmon Brown to TWH, November 30, 1859, Brown Papers, BPL.
28. Craig Simpson, *A Good Southerner: The Life of Henry Wise of Virginia* (Chapel Hill, 1985), 212; Franklin Sanborn to TWH, November 28, 1859, John LeBarnes to TWH, November 27, telegram November 28, 1859, Brown Papers, BPL; Horowitz, *Midnight Rising*, 228.
29. Baltimore *Daily Exchange*, October 31, 1859; *Staunton Spectator*, November 1, 1859; Rebecca Buffom Spring to TWH, January 23, February 10, 1860, Richard Hinton to TWH, December 31, 1859, Brown Papers, BPL.
30. Charles Tidd to TWH, December 8, December 18, 1859, Richard Hinton to TWH, December 13, December 27, 1859, Brown Papers, BPL.
31. Lucy Pomeroy to TWH, January 23, 1859, John LeBarnes to TWH, January 11, 1860, Brown Papers, BPL.
32. Charles Tidd to TWH, December 8, 1860, Richard Hinton to TWH, December 27, 1859, James Redpath to TWH, January 19, 1860, G. F. Warren to TWH, January 18, 1860, Brown Papers, BPL.
33. James Montgomery to TWH, February 1, telegram February 10, 1860; John LeBarnes to TWH, January 19, 1860, telegram February 15, 1860, TWH to Richard Hinton, February 16, 1860, TWH to MCH, February 17, 1860, Brown Papers, BPL.
34. Villard, *Brown*, 574; John LeBarnes to TWH, February 18, 1860, Rebecca Buffam Spring to TWH, January 19, February 13, 1860, TWH, memorandum, February 1860, Brown Papers, BPL.
35. TWH to MCH, February 18, 19, 21, 1860, Brown Papers, BPL.
36. Edward Spring to TWH, March 10, 1860, Mary Ann Brown to TWH, July 25, 1860, TWH to Aaron Stevens, March 12, 1860, Brown Papers, BPL.

37. Robert Young, *Senator James Murray* (Knoxville, 1998), 90; *New York Times*, October 31, 1859; Chicago *Press and Tribune*, December 26, 1859.
38. John LeBarnes to TWH, November 14, 1859, Franklin Sanborn to TWH, November 14, December 25, 1859, Brown Papers, BPL. Andrew was also descended from Francis Higginson. See TWH, *Francis Higginson*, 132.
39. Franklin Sanborn to TWH, December 20, 1859, January 2, 1860, John Andrew to TWH, December 23, 1859, Henry Wilson to TWH, December 24, 1859, Brown Papers, BPL; Walter Stahr, *Seward: Lincoln's Indispensable Man* (New York, 2012), 180.
40. Renehan, *Secret Six*, 240–241; TWH, Federal Census, 1860, National Archives; TWH to Franklin Sanborn, February 30, 1860, Brown Papers, BPL.
41. James Redpath to TWH, April 20, 1860, William Handy to TWH, April 6, April 16, 1860, Higginson Papers, KSHS; TWH to MCH, February 16, 1860, Brown Papers, BPL; McKivigan, *Redpath*, 56.
42. *New York Herald*, April 7, 1860.
43. TWH to James Abbott, July 21, 1860, TWH Papers, KSHS; Charles Plummer Tidd to TWH, September 18, 1860, Elizabeth Tidd to TWH, October 20, 1860, Brown Papers, BPL.
44. Washington *Evening Star*, January 21, April 19, 1860; "The Maroons of Jamaica," *Atlantic Monthly* 31 (1860): 222–223; "The Maroons of Surinam," *Atlantic Monthly* 32 (1860): 557. Higginson later identified his sources when these articles were reprinted in his *Travelers and Outlaws*, 328–329.
45. Robertson, *Parker Pillsbury*, 120–121; Biddeford (ME) *Union and Journal*, June 8, 1860; Lansing *State Republican*, May 16, 1860; Wheeling *Daily Intelligencer*, May 11, 1860, *Emporia News*, May 12, 1860; Perrysburg (OH) *Journal*, May 17, 1860; Baton Rouge *Sugar Planter*, June 2, 1860; Sunbury (PA) *American*, June 2, 1860; Wisconsin *River Falls Journal*, June 6, 1860.
46. *Albany Evening Journal*, June 5, 1860; *New York Herald*, July 18, 1860.
47. Foner, *Free Soil*, 302–303; Richard Sewell, *Ballots for Freedom: Antislavery Politics in the United States* (New York, 1976), 340–341; *Liberator*, March 9, 1860.
48. TWH, *Contemporaries*, 255–256.
49. *Liberator*, September 28, 1860; Mayer, *All on Fire*, 512; Stirling, *Ahead of Her Time*, 327; TWH, "Anti-Slavery Days," *Outlook*, September 1898, 51.
50. Harold Holzer, *Lincoln President-Elect: Abraham Lincoln and the Great Secession Winter* (New York, 2008), 12; Elizabeth Griffith, *In Her Own Right: The Life of Elizabeth Cady Stanton* (New York, 1984), 105.

Chapter 7

1. *New York Herald*, April 13, 1861; *New-York Tribune*, April 15, 1861; TWH to LSH, April 17, 1861, Higginson Papers, HLH.
2. Norwood Hallowell, *Selected Letters and Papers of N. P. Hallowell* (Peterborough, 1986), 67; Stewart, *Phillips*, 214; TWH, *Cheerful Yesterdays*, 241–242.
3. TWH, *Cheerful Yesterdays*, 243–245; Lydia Maria Child to Sarah Shaw, January 1861, in *Letters of Lydia Maria Child*, ed. Child (Boston, 1882), 147–149; Washington *Evening Star*, January 26, 1861.
4. TWH to Harriet Prescott, January 1861, in MTH, *Story of His Life*, 181; Muscatine (IA) *Journal*, February 1, 1861; New Oregon (IA) *Plaindealer*, February 22, 1861.
5. TWH, *Cheerful Yesterdays*, 235, 245; Mayer, *All on Fire*, 518.
6. TWH to John Andrew, January 24, 1861, in *Letters and Journals*, ed. MTH, 154; Laughlin-Schultz, *Ties That Bind Us*, 92; Douglas Egerton, *Thunder at the Gates: The Black Civil War Regiments That Redeemed America* (New York, 2016), 35.
7. John Bailey to TWH, April 26, 1861, John Brown Jr. to TWH, April 25, 1861, C. C. Chickering to TWH, April 25, 1861, T. L. Davis to TWH, April 26, A. D. Jackson to TWH, April 23, 1861, J. W. Winkley to TWH, April 25, 1861, Higginson Papers, Stowe Center.
8. George Stearns to TWH, April 23, 1861, TWH, "Interview with Gov. Curtin," April 26, 1861, Higginson Papers, Stowe Center; TWH, *Cheerful Yesterdays*, 246.
9. TWH to LSH, April 17, 1861, Higginson Papers, HLH; Bridgetown *West-Jersey Pioneer*, May 18, 1861.
10. Hillsboro *Highland Weekly News*, September 18, 1862; *Cleveland Morning Leader*, February 27, August 26, 1861; Clearfield *Raftman's Journal*, April 3, April 17, May 8, 1861; Dowagiac (MI) *Cass County Republican*, November 28, 1861; St. Paul *Weekly Pioneer and Democrat*, January

20, April 5, 1861; Towanda *Bradford Reporter*, September 5, 1861; Stauffer, *Black Hearts of Men*, 205.
11. *Cincinnati Daily Press*, October 31, 1860; *Kenosha Telegraph*, May 23, 1861; St. Johnsbury (VT) *Caledonian*, November 2, 1860; Burlington *Free Press*, September 6, 1861; William C. Nell to TWH, February 6, 1860, Brown Papers, BPL; Lydia Maria Child to TWH, March 17, 1860, William Palmer Collection, Western Reserve Historical Society. Higginson published his "Appendix of Authorities" in *Travelers and Outlaws: Episodes in American History* (Boston, 1889), 332–333.
12. *Kenosha Telegraph*, May 23, 1861; TWH, "Denmark Vesey," *Atlantic Monthly* 7 (1861): 730–744.
13. Sinha, *Slaves' Cause*, 443; TWH, "Nat Turner's Insurrection," *Atlantic Monthly* 8 (1861): 175–181.
14. TWH, "Nat Turner's Insurrection," 185; Montpelier (VT) *Daily Green Mountain Freeman*, July 24, 1861; *New-York Tribune*, July 15, 1861; *New York Times*, December 5, 1861.
15. TWH to LSH, August 13, 1861, in *Letters and Journals*, ed. MTH, 156–157; *Emporia News*, July 13, 1861.
16. TWH to LSH, September 6, 1861, in *Letters and Journals*, ed. MTH, 158–159; TWH to LSH, November 1, 1861, in *The Complete Civil War Journal and Selected Letters of Thomas Wentworth Higginson*, ed. Christopher Looby (Chicago, 2000), 224–225; TWH, *Cheerful Yesterdays*, 248–249.
17. TWH to LSH, November 1, 1861, in *War Journal*, ed. Looby, ed., 224; TWH Journal, January 25, 1862, in *Letters and Journals*, ed. MTH, 62–163.
18. TWH to LSH, November 1, 1861, in *War Journal*, ed. Looby, 226; *Providence Journal*, November 18, 1861; *Cincinnati Daily Press*, November 19, 1861; Grand Rapids *Wood County Reporter*, November 30, 1861; Millersville (OH) *Holmes County Republican*, December 5, 1861.
19. Henry Pearson, *The Life of John A. Andrew* (Boston, 1904), 309; TWH, *Cheerful Yesterdays*, 248; TWH to James Field, January 1862, TWH to Harriet Spofford, January 1862, in *Letters and Journals*, ed. MTH, 105, 113; *Chicago Daily Tribune*, January 21, 1862; *Lewistown Gazette*, January 22, 1862.
20. TWH, "Letter to a Young Contributor," *Atlantic Monthly* 9 (1862): 79–85; ED to TWH, April 15, 1862, in *Letters of Emily Dickinson*, ed. Thomas Johnson (Boston, 1958), 2: 403.
21. TWH, "Emily Dickinson's Letters," *Atlantic Monthly* 68 (1891): 444–447; ED to TWH, April 25, 1862, in *Letters of Dickinson*, ed. Johnson, 2: 404.
22. TWH, "Emily Dickinson's Letters," 448. Before Dickinson died in 1886, she instructed her sister Lavinia to burn her papers, and so while Higginson kept her incoming correspondence, his responses to her are lost. See Wineapple, *White Heat*, 13.
23. TWH, "Emily Dickinson's Letters," 450; ED to TWH, June 7, July 1862, in *Letters of Dickinson*, ed. Johnson, 2: 408–409, 411–412.
24. ED to TWH, July, August 1862, in *Letters of Dickinson*, ed. Johnson, 2: 411–412, 414–415.
25. TWH, "Gabriel's Defeat," *Atlantic Monthly* 10 (1862): 337; TWH, *Travelers and Outlaws*, 331; *Cleveland Morning Leader*, August 19, 1862.
26. TWH, "Gabriel's Defeat," 337–339, 344.
27. MTH, *Story of His Life*, 211.
28. TWH to LSH, August 15, 1862, in *War Journal*, ed. Looby, 229; *Liberator*, September 5, 1862.
29. TWH to LSH, August 15, 22, 29, September 7, 14, 1862, in *War Journal*, ed. Looby, 229–234; Woodsfield (OH) *Spirit of Democracy*, September 30, 1863; Brattleboro *Vermont Phoenix*, September 4, 1862; *New Burn Weekly Progress*, October 11, 1862.
30. TWH to LSH, October 4, 13, 1862, in *War Journal*, ed. Looby, 237–238; ED to TWH, October 6, 1862, in *Letters of Dickinson*, ed. Johnson, 2: 417–418.
31. TWH to LSH, October 26, November 2, 9, 1862, in *War Journal*, ed. Looby, 239–244.
32. TWH, *Cheerful Yesterdays*, 251; Rufus Saxton to TWH, November 5, 1862, and James Fowler to TWH, November 10, 1862, in *War Journal*, ed. Looby, 243–245.
33. TWH to LSH, November 16, 1862, TWH Journal, November 22, 1862, in *War Journal*, ed. Looby, 246, 39–41.
34. TWH Journal, November 23, 24, 1862, in *War Journal*, ed. Looby, 42–44.
35. *New-York Tribune*, December 4, 1862; TWH Journal, November 25, 27, 1862, in *War Journal*, ed. Looby, 45–52.
36. TWH, "Leaves from an Officer's Journal," *Atlantic Monthly* 13 (1864): 522.
37. Ash, *Firebrand of Liberty*, 22; Charles Francis Adams Jr. to Charles Francis Adams Sr., July 28, August 10, 1862, in *A Cycle of Adams Letters*, ed. Worthington Ford (Boston, 1920), 1: 169–170, 174–175.

38. TWH Journal, December 8, 11, 14, in *War Journal*, ed. Looby, 63–66.
39. *Chicago Daily Tribune*, December 8, 1862; Indianapolis *Indiana State Sentinel*, December 3, 8, 1862; *Alexandria Gazette*, December 4, 1862; St. Paul *Weekly Pioneer and Democrat*, December 12, 1862; Keokuk (IA) *Daily Gate City*, December 12, 1862; *Cleveland Morning Leader*, November 25, 1862; Columbus *Daily Ohio Statesman*, December 4, 1862.
40. *East Saginaw Courier*, July 14, 1863; Maysville *Dollar Weekly Bulletin*, April 16, 1863; *Indiana State Sentinel*, June 30, 1863.
41. Garrett Davis, *Speech of Hon. Garrett Davis, of Kentucky, on the State of the Union* (Washington, 1864), 21–22; Washington *Evening Star*, March 14, 1864; Placerville (CA) *Mountain Democrat*, March 28, 1863; Tunkhannock (PA) *North Branch Democrat*, March 18, 1863; Raleigh *Spirit of the Age*, June 22, 1863; Charlotte *Western Democrat*, June 16, 1863; Muscatine *Weekly Journal*, March 25, 1864; Georgetown (DE) *Union*, March 25, 1864; *Cleveland Morning Leader*, March 18, 1864; *Cass County* (MI) *Republican*, March 24, 1864; Beaufort *Free South*, April 9, 1864; *Congressional Globe*, 38th Cong., 1st. Sess, 1155.
42. John Greenleaf Whittier to Mary Curzon, December 24, 1862, in *Letters of John Greenleaf Whittier*, ed. John Pickard (Cambridge, 1975), 33–34; Port Royal *New South*, December 6, 1862.
43. TWH, *Army Life in a Black Regiment*, 5.

Chapter 8

1. Montpelier (VT) *Daily Green Mountain Freeman*, July 13, 1862; *Portland Daily Press*, December 15, 1862.
2. *Washington Herald*, November 21, 1920.
3. TWH, "Leaves from an Officer's Journal," 744; Seth Rogers to unknown, December 27, 1862, Florida History Online.
4. MTH, *Story of His Life*, 216; TWH, *Army Life*, 26–27, 270; TWH, Regimental Description Book, December 1862, 1st South Carolina Infantry, NA.
5. Ash, *Firebrand of Liberty*, 31–32.
6. TWH, "Leaves from an Officer's Journal," 745; TWH, Diary, December 1862, Higginson Papers, HLH.
7. Beaufort *Free South*, January 17, 1863; *Chicago Daily Tribune*, January 10, 1863; *Letters and Diary of Laura Towne, Written from the Sea Islands*, ed. Rupert Holland (Cambridge, 1912), 98; TWH Journal, January 1, 1863, in *War Journal*, ed. Looby, 76.
8. *Cleveland Morning Leader*, January 12, 1863; TWH Journal, January 1, 1863, in *War Journal*, ed. Looby, 76; TWH, *Army Life*, 54–55; Charlotte Forten, "Life on the Sea Islands," *Atlantic Monthly* 14 (1864): 668; *Letters from Port Royal, Written at the Time of the Civil War*, ed. Elizabeth Pearson (Boston, 1906), 130; Seth Rogers to unknown, January 1, 1863, Florida History Online.
9. Junction City (KS) *Smoky Hill and Republican Union*, February 28, 1863; *Edgefield Advertiser*, February 11, 1863; *Cleveland Morning Leader*, January 30, 1863; *Hartford Daily Times*, January 30, 1863; TWH, *Army Life*, 64–65.
10. TWH, *Army Life*, 58–59.
11. Edward Pierce, "The Freedmen at Port Royal," *Atlantic Monthly* (1863): 313; TWH, "The First Black Regiment," *Outlook*, July 2, 1898, 527–526.
12. TWH, *Army Life*, 330–331. On the composition of the 54th, see my *Thunder at the Gates*, 81–82.
13. TWH, *Army Life*, 77; TWH Journal, January 13, 1863, in *War Journal*, ed. Looby, 88.
14. TWH, *Army Life*, 84–85; TWH, "Up the St. Mary's," *Atlantic Monthly* 16 (1865): 422.
15. Joseph Glatthaar, *Forged in Battle: The Civil War Alliance of Black Soldiers and White Officers* (New York, 1989), 37; Frances White, "Thomas Wentworth Higginson's Idea of Democracy," *Negro History Bulletin* 6 (1942): 71; TWH, *Army Life*, 38–39; TWH Journal, January 7, February 20, 1863, in *War Journal*, ed. Looby, 79, 106.
16. TWH, *Army Life*, 71, 331; Charles Steedman to Sally Steedman, March 20, 1864, Steedman Papers, University of Florida.
17. TWH Journal, April 19, 1863, in *War Journal*, ed. Looby, 133; William Walker to Thomas Gordon, April 20, 1863, in *The War of the Rebellion: Official Records of the Civil War: A Compilation of the Official Records of the Union and Confederate Armies* (Washington, 1880; hereafter *OR*), series 1, vol. 14, 903; Seth Rogers to unknown, April 19, 1863, Florida History Online; *Alexandria Gazette*, April 29, 1863; Washington *Weekly National Intelligencer*, April 30, 1863; *New-York Daily Tribune*, April 28, 1863.
18. TWH, *Cheerful Yesterdays*, 259; TWH, *Army Life*, 95; TWH, "Up the St. Mary's," 423.

19. TWH, *Cheerful Yesterdays*, 260; TWH, *Army Life*, 95; Burlington (IA) *Weekly Hawk-eye*, February 21, 1863; *Liberator*, February 20, 1863.
20. TWH, *Army Life*, 93; *Chicago Daily Tribune*, February 13, 1863.
21. TWH, *Army Life*, 95–97; TWH, "Up the St. Mary's," 426.
22. *Liberator*, February 20, 1863; TWH, *Army Life*, 100; TWH, "Up the St. Mary's," 426.
23. TWH, "Up the St. Mary's," 427; Report of TWH, February 1, 1863, *OR*, series 1, vol. 14, 195.
24. Tama County *Iowa Transcript*, February 26, 1863; Port Royal *New South*, February 7, 1863; TWH, "Up the St. Mary's," 428.
25. TWH, *Army Life*, 116–119; TWH, "Up the St. Mary's," 423; TWH Journal, February 4, 1863, in *War Journal*, ed. Looby, 93–95. Looby, n133, identified the hamlet as being in Georgia, but Woodstock Mills was approximately three miles below Kings Ferry, Florida, and not close to either Woodstock, Georgia, or Woodstock, Florida.
26. TWH, *Army Life*, 122–123; TWH, "Up the St. Mary's," 434–435; *Hartford Daily Times*, February 10, 1863; *Chicago Daily Tribune*, February 13, 1863; *Daily Evansville Journal*, February 18, 1863; Report of TWH, February 1, 1863, in *OR*, series 1, vol. 14, 196. Scrubby Bluff sits where I-95 now crosses the St. Mary's River.
27. *Liberator*, February 20, 1863; Boston *Banner of Light*, February 21, 1863; TWH, *Army Life*, 104; TWH, "Up the St. Mary's," 433–436; Report of TWH, February 1, 1863, *OR*, series 1, vol. 14, 196; TWH to LSH, February 1, 1863, in *War Journal*, ed. Looby, 261.
28. Chardon (OH) *Jeffersonian Democrat*, March 31, 1865; TWH, "Up the St. Mary's," 436; Keith Wilson, "In the Shadow of John Brown: The Military Service of Colonel Thomas Higginson, James Montgomery, and Robert Shaw in the Department of the South," in *Black Soldiers in Blue: African American Troops in the Civil War Era*, ed. John David Smith (Chapel Hill, 2002), 314; Tama County *Iowa Transcript*, February 26, 1863; St. Paul *Weekly Pioneer and Democrat*, February 20, 1863; *Hartford Daily Times*, February 4, 17, 1863.
29. Ash, *Firebrand of Liberty*, 198; John Greenleaf Whittier to Charlotte Forten, 1863, in *Letters of Whittier*, ed. Pickard, 35.
30. Glatthaar, *Forged in Battle*, 38; *Weekly Perrysburg* (OH) *Journal*, February 18, 1863; Report of Rufus Saxton, February 2, 1863, *OR*, series 1, vol. 14, 194; *Belmont* (OH) *Chronicle*, April 2, 1863; *Liberator*, February 20, 1863; *Muscatine* (IA) *Weekly Journal*, May 22, 1863.
31. Wilmington *Delaware State Journal*, February 6, 1863; *Richmond Palladium*, February 20, 1863; *Nashville Daily Union*, April 16, 1863; *Memphis Daily Appeal*, February 23, 1863; *Hartford Daily Times*, February 16, 1863; Ash, *Firebrand of Liberty*, 43; Portland (ME) *Daily Press*, April 3, 1863; *Muscatine* (IA) *Weekly Journal*, March 6, 1863; *Chicago Daily Tribune*, March 25, 1863; St. Paul *Weekly Pioneer and Democrat*, May 22, 1863.
32. Rufus Saxton to Edwin Stanton, March 6, 1863, and David Hunter to Samuel DuPont, March 6, 1863, *OR*, series 1, vol. 14, 421–423.
33. TWH, "The Re-occupation of Florida in 1863," Higginson Papers, HLH; TWH, *Army Life*, 135; TWH, Regimental Description Book, January 1863, 1st South Carolina Infantry, NA.
34. TWH, *Army Life*, 134–135; *Letters from Port Royal*, ed. Pearson, 168; Portland (ME) *Daily Press*, March 26, 1863; *Cleveland Morning Leader*, March 18, 1863.
35. TWH, *Army Life*, 142–143; Noah Trudeau, *Like Men of War: Black Troops in the Civil War, 1862–1865* (Boston, 1998), 67; Washington *Evening Star*, March 25, 1863; *Vermont Watchman and State Journal*, April 3, 1863.
36. *Daily Evansville Journal*, March 20, 1863; Cadiz (OH) *Democratic Sentinel*, March 25, 1863; Burlington (IA) *Weekly Hawk-Eye*, March 21, 1863; Washington *National Intelligencer*, March 26, 1863; St. Paul *Weekly Pioneer and Democrat*, March 27, 1863.
37. Rufus Saxton to Edwin Stanton, March 14, 1863, and Abraham Lincoln to David Hunter, April 1, 1863, *OR*, series 1, vol. 14, 226, 435–436; Rutland (VT) *Weekly Herald*, April 2, 1863; Fremont (OH) *Journal*, April 3, 1863; *Chicago Daily Tribune*, March 30, 1863; *Cleveland Morning Leader*, March 30, 1863; Burlington (IA) *Weekly Hawk-Eye*, April 4, 1863; TWH to LSH, April 10, 1863, in *War Journal*, ed. Looby, 270.
38. Reports of Joseph Finegan, March 13, 14, 1863, *OR*, series 1, vol. 14, 226–229; William Reed, *A Northern Plea for Peace, Address of the Hon. William Reed, Delivered March 28, 1863* (London, 1863), 21–22.
39. TWH, *Army Life*, 146–149; TWH Journal, March 13, 1863, in *War Journal*, ed. Looby, 109; *Dayton Daily Empire*, April 17, 1863; *Chicago Daily Tribune*, March 26, 1863.
40. Abner McCormick to TWH, March 17, 1863, and TWH to Abner McCormick, March 18, 1863, *OR*, series 1, vol. 14, 839.

41. ED to TWH, undated 1863 and February 1863, in *Letters of Dickinson*, ed. Johnson, 2: 423–426.
42. *New-York Tribune*, April 8, 1863; Report of Joseph Finegan, March 31, 1863, *OR*, series 1, vol. 14, 236; Charles Steedman to Sally Steedman, March 20, 1864, Steedman Papers, University of Florida; TWH Journal, March 22–24, 1863, in *War Journal*, ed. Looby, 114–115.
43. Susie King Taylor, *Reminiscences of My Life in Camp* (Boston, 1902), 22–24; TWH Journal, March 22, 1863, and TWH to LSH, March 22, 1863, in *War Journal*, ed. Looby, 114, 267.
44. Justin Iverson, *Rebels in Arms: Black Resistance and the Fight for Freedom in the Anglo-Atlantic* (Athens, 2022), 187; Seth Rogers to unknown, March 25, 1863, Florida History Online; Trudeau, *Like Men of War*, 68–69; Ash, *Firebrand of Liberty*, 148.
45. *Emporia News*, March 28, 1863; *Burlington* (IA) *Weekly Hawk-eye*, March 21, 1863; *Portland* (ME) *Daily Press*, April 21, 1863; Report of Joseph Finegan, March 31, 1863, *OR*, series 1, vol. 14, 234–236; Taylor, *Reminiscences*, 24–25.
46. Report of Joseph Finegan, March 31, 1863, in *OR*, series 1, vol. 14, 236; Edward Pierce to John Andrew, July 3, 1863, in Andrew Papers, MHS; TWH Journal, March 28, 1863, and TWH to LSH, March 30, 1863, in *War Journal*, ed. Looby, 117–118, 268.
47. *New-York Tribune*, April 8, 1863; Washington *Weekly National Intelligencer*, April 23, 1863; *Dayton Daily Empire*, April 17, 1863; TWH, *Army Life*, 321.
48. TWH Journal, April 6, 1863, and TWH to MCH, May 9, 16, 1863, in *War Journal*, ed. Looby, 123, 278–279.
49. New York *Weekly Anglo-African*, June 20, 1863; Warren (OH) *Western Reserve Chronicle*, June 3, 1863; TWH Journal, May 10, 1863, in *War Journal*, ed. Looby, 145. I am grateful to historian Kelly Mezurek for pointing out to me that the standard microfilm copy of the *Anglo-African* was taken from Higginson's collection, with his name written across most copies.
50. On this, see my *Thunder at the Gates*, 98–99.
51. Robert Gould Shaw to Sarah Shaw, June 6, 1863, in *Blue-Eyed Child of Fortune: The Civil War Letters of Colonel Robert Gould Shaw*, ed. Russell Duncan (Athens, 1992), 339; TWH to LSH, June 5, 1863, in *War Journal*, ed. Looby, 283; TWH, *Cheerful Yesterdays*, 257.
52. TWH to LSH, July 2, July 27, 1863, in *War Journal*, ed. Looby, 292, 297; *Diary of Laura Towne*, ed. Holland, 118–119; Washington *Evening Star*, July 28, 1863; St. Paul *Weekly Pioneer and Democrat*, August 14, 1863.
53. Court-Martial Case File MM-484, RG 153, Records of the Office of the Judge Advocate General, NA.
54. TWH to Abraham Lincoln, June 28, 1863, in Court-Martial Case File MM-484, RG 153, Records of the Office of the Judge Advocate General, NA; TWH to LSH, June 5, 1863, August 28, 1863, in *War Journal*, ed. Looby, 282, 303; John Andrew to Abraham Lincoln, June 18, 1863, Lincoln Papers, LC.
55. Willie Lee Rose, *Rehearsal for Reconstruction: The Port Royal Experiment* (New York, 1976), 264–265; TWH, *Army Life*, 231.
56. TWH, *Cheerful Yesterdays*, 262; TWH, *Army Life*, 232.
57. TWH, *Army Life*, 244–245; *Letters from Port Royal*, ed. Pearson, 195–196.
58. TWH, *Cheerful Yesterdays*, 263; *Army Life*, 247.
59. TWH, *Cheerful Yesterdays*, 262–263; Beaufort *Free South*, July 18, 1863; Washington *Evening Star*, July 20, 1863; Taylor, *Reminiscences*, 26–27.
60. TWH to MCH, July 14, 1863, in *War Journal*, ed. Looby, 296.
61. TWH, Regimental Description Book, July 1863, 1st South Carolina Infantry, NA; TWH, *Army Life*, 301; *Liberator*, July 31, 1863; TWH to LSH, July 27, August 16, 1863, TWH to MCH, August 19, 1863, in *War Journal*, ed. Looby, 297, 300–301.
62. TWH Journal, August 22, 1863, in *War Journal*, ed. Looby, 159–160.
63. MTH, *Story of His Life*, 232; TWH, *Army Life*, 301; Seth Rogers to unknown, October 16, 1863, Florida History Online.
64. MTH, *Story of His Life*, 233–234; TWH Journal, November 6, 1863, in *War Journal*, ed. Looby, 173; Wheeling *Daily Intelligencer*, December 18, 1863; St. Clairsville (OH) *Belmont Chronicle*, December 17, 1863.
65. TWH to MCH, December 21, 1863, January 28, 1864, in *War Journal*, ed. Looby, 342–343, 351; Beaufort *Free South*, December 12, 1863.
66. *Diary of Laura Towne*, ed. Holland, 122; Beaufort *Free South*, January 30, 1864; Port Royal *New South*, January 9, 1864; TWH, *First Anniversary of the Proclamation of Freedom in South Carolina, held at Beaufort, S.C., January 1, 1864* (Beaufort, 1864), 16–17.

NOTES   321

67. TWH Journal, April 11, 25, 1864, in *War Journal*, ed. Looby, 216, 220; MTH, *Story of His Life*, 248–249; TWH, *Army Life*, 355; TWH, Regimental Description Book, April 1864, 1st South Carolina Infantry, NA. Higginson may have doubted the diagnosis of toxicohaemia as it had only been advanced by doctors for ten years.
68. TWH to John Greenleaf Whittier, October 10, 1864, in *Letters of Whittier*, ed. Albree, 150–151; TWH to LSH, April 20, 1864, TWH to MCH, April 4, 1864, TWH Journal, March 16, 1864, in *War Journal*, ed. Looby, 207, 365–367; *Cleveland Morning Leader*, June 10, 1864.
69. *Portland Daily Press*, November 3, 1864; Ralph Waldo Emerson to TWH, July 18, 1864, Higginson Papers, Huntington Library; Martha Smith, *Open Me Carefully: Emily Dickinson's Intimate Letters to Susan Huntington Dickinson* (New York, 1998), 65; Aife Murray, *Maid as Muse: How Servants Changed Emily Dickinson's Life and Language* (Durham, 2010), 182; ED to TWH, June 1864, in *Letters of Dickinson*, ed. Johnson, 431.
70. Taylor, *Reminiscences*, 32; MTH, *Story of His Life*, 251; Brattleboro *Vermont Phoenix*, June 24, 1864.
71. TWH, Regimental Description Book, November 1864, 1st South Carolina Infantry, NA; LSH, Vermont, U.S. Vital Records, 1720–1908, p. 1056; Vermont, U.S. Wills and Probate Records, vol. 26, 1870–1872; vols. 27–28, 1872–1877; vol. 29, 1877–1880; TWH Diary, November 15, 1864, Higginson Papers, HLH.
72. TWH to MCH, April 4, 1864, in *War Journal*, ed. Looby, 365; TWH to Ralph Waldo Emerson, July 6, 1864, Higginson Papers, Huntington Library; Beaufort *Free South*, November 19, 1864; *Cleveland Morning Leader*, August 23, November 2, 1864, January 25, March 28, 1865; Wilmington *Delaware State Journal*, September 8, 1865; Pomeroy (OH) *Weekly Telegraph*, March 2, 1865; *Cass County* (MI) *Republican*, February 18, 1864; *Jeffersonian* (OH) *Democrat*, October 21, 1864; Rutland (VT) *Weekly Herald*, November 9, 1865; *Lansing State Republican*, July 6, 1864; *Columbia Democrat and Bloomsburg* (PA) *General Advertiser*, October 1, 1864.
73. American Freedmen's Inquiry Commission, *Preliminary Report Touching the Condition and Management of Emancipated Refugees* (New York, 1863), 11, 14; TWH Journal, January 20, 1864, in *War Journal*, ed. Looby, 183; Rose, *Rehearsal for Reconstruction*, 290.
74. TWH Journal, April 17, 1864, in *War Journal*, ed. Looby, 217; TWH to William Fessenden, February 18, 1864, Higginson Papers, NYHS.
75. Charles Sumner to TWH, December 12, 1863, June 22, 1864, in *Letters of Sumner*, ed. Palmer, 2: 212–213, 245–246; W. Scott Poole, "Memory and the Abolitionist Heritage: Thomas Wentworth Higginson and the Uncertain Meaning of the Civil War," *Civil War History* 51 (2005): 214; Wheeling *Daily Intelligencer*, January 8, 1864; Wheeling *Daily Register*, January 8, December 13, 1864; Indianapolis *Indiana Daily Sentinel*, January 11, 1864; *Journal of the Senate*, December 12, 1864, 38th Cong., 2nd Sess., 21, 59.
76. *New Orleans Tribune*, August 23, October 19, 1864; *Liberator*, May 13, 1864; TWH to James Garfield, February 14, 1869, Garfield Papers, LC.
77. TWH Journal, January 20, 1864, *War Journal*, ed. Looby, 183–184; "A Song of War," *Cleveland Leader*, July 22, 1865.

Chapter 9

1. TWH to MCH, July 14, 1863, in *War Journal*, ed. Looby, 296; TWH Diary, February 5, 1866, Higginson Papers, HLH. On Civil War veterans and posttraumatic stress disorder, see Diane Miller Sommerville, *Aberration of the Mind: Suicide and Suffering in the Civil War–Era South* (Chapel Hill, 2018), and Paul Cimbala, *Veterans North and South: The Transition from Soldier to Civilian after the American Civil War* (Santa Barbara, 2015).
2. TWH to ECS, May 2, 1866, in *Selected Papers*, ed. Gordon, 1: 578.
3. Wineapple, *White Heat*, 262; TWH Diary, January 6, 1866, April 17, 1866, Higginson Papers, HLH.
4. MTH, *Story of His Life*, 255–256, 276.
5. TWH Diary, April 10–18, 1865, Higginson Papers, HLH.
6. ED to TWH, January 1866, in *Letters of Dickinson*, ed. Johnson, 2: 423–426; TWH Diary, March 31, April 14, 1866, March 1, 1870, Higginson Papers, HLH.
7. Warren (OH) *Western Reserve Chronicle*, January 1, 1868; Fremont (OH) *Weekly Journal*, March 29, 1867; Brookville *Indiana American*, February 1, 1867; Wheeling (WV) *Daily Intelligencer*, April 30, 1867; Delaware (OH) *Gazette*, May 3, 1867; *Atlantic Monthly* 19 (February 1867), (April 1867), (May 1867); TWH Diary, January 1, February 18, 1866, Higginson Papers, HLH.

8. *Fremont* (OH) *Journal*, October 26, 1866; TWH Diary, December 31, 1866, Higginson Papers, HLH; TWH, Federal Census, 1870, National Archives.
9. TWH Diary, December 22, 1877, TWH to ASH and SLH, August 31, October 22, 1867, Higginson Papers, HLH.
10. *New York Herald*, June 2, 1866; TWH to ASH and SLH, June 3, 1966, TWH Diary, May 31, 1866, Higginson Papers, HLH.
11. TWH to Gerrit Smith, March 27, 1867, Smith Papers, Syracuse University; Brenda Wineapple, *The Impeachers: The Trial of Andrew Johnson and the Dream of a Just Nation* (New York, 2019), 67–68; Harrold, *American Abolitionism*, 175; *New-York Tribune*, September 18, 1866.
12. *Atlantic Monthly* 19 (March 1867), (June 1867), (August 1867); *Portland* (ME) *Daily Press*, January 31, February 23, 1867; Warren *Western Reserve Chronicle*, March 6, 1867; *Hillsborough Highland Weekly News*, May 23, 1867; *Emporia* (KS) *News*, May 31, 1867; *Fremont* (OH) *Weekly Journal*, May 24, 1867; *Evansville* (IN) *Journal*, July 27, 1867; *Charleston Daily News*, March 14, 1867.
13. TWH Diary, May 7, May 9, 1867, Higginson Papers, HLH; *New-York Tribune*, May 7, 1867; *New York Herald*, May 8, 1867; Richmond *Daily Dispatch*, May 9, 1867; Columbia *Daily Phoenix*, May 11, 1867.
14. McKivigan, *Forgotten Firebrand*, 120–121; *Watertown* (WI) *Republican*, January 10, 1872; *Chicago Tribune*, March 29, 1870; St. Albans *Vermont Daily Transcript*, October 2, 1868; TWH to ASH, November 27, December 9, 1867, Higginson Papers, HLH. According to CPI Online Inflation Calculator, $100 in 1870 equals $2,183.74 today.
15. *New-York Tribune*, May 11, 1870; *New York Herald*, November 11, 1869; *Boston Journal*, November 14, 1870; TWH Diary, May 10, 1870, THW to ASH, January 19, 1868, Higginson Papers, HLH.
16. *Toledo Index*, June 11, 1870; *Rutland* (VT) *Weekly Herald*, May 11, 1871; *Portland Daily Press*, September 22, 1871; undated *Philadelphia Commonwealth* clipping, TWH Diary, June 23, 1874, Higginson Papers, HLH.
17. *New-York Tribune*, July 27, 1869, January 29, 1870; TWH Diary, January 27, 1870, Higginson Papers, HLH; TWH to Charles Allen, February 23, 1869, Higginson Papers, BPL.
18. TWH Diary, January 15–16, 22–23, 27, 1868, Higginson Papers, HLH; *New York Herald*, December 1, 1865.
19. Wineapple, *The Impeachers*, 373; Charles Sumner to TWH, April 11, 1868, in *Selected Letters*, ed. Palmer, 2: 423–424; *Carson* (NV) *Daily Appeal*, June 9, 1868; *Hancock* (OH) *Jeffersonian*, January 31, 1868; TWH Diary, October 26, 1868, Higginson Papers, HLH.
20. *Wheeling Daily Intelligencer*, June 15, 1870; *New-York Tribune*, June 7, 1870; Honolulu *Pacific Commercial Advertiser*, November 20, 1869; TWH to MCH, January 9, 1869, TWH to ASH, January 10, 1869, unidentified newspaper clipping, TWH Diary, February 26, 1874, Higginson Papers, HLH.
21. MTH, *Story of His Life*, 253.
22. TWH, *Cheerful Yesterdays*, 193; TWH to Francis Bird, November 23, 1866, Higginson Papers, NYHS; unidentified newspaper clipping, TWH Diary, April 13, 1870, and Diary, April 6, August 6, 1866, Higginson Papers, HLH.
23. *Newport Mercury*, April 18, 1874; TWH Diary, March 23, April 15, 1874, Higginson Papers, HLH.
24. New York *Friend of Progress*, February 1, 1865; Memphis *Public Ledger*, June 6, 1868.
25. *Urbana Union*, November 20, 1867, June 2, 1869; *Portland Daily Press*, November 18, 1867, January 25, 1868; Columbia *Daily Phoenix*, June 7, 1868; Rutland (VT) *Weekly Herald*, June 8, 1871; *Charleston Daily News*, June 2, 1869; *Philadelphia Evening Telegraph*, May 28, 1869.
26. *New-York Tribune*, January 22, January 31, June 3, 1870; *Toledo* (OH) *Index*, April 23, 1870; *Boston Journal*, December 22, 1873; TWH Diary, January 12, 1873, May 24, October 29, 1874.
27. TWH, "A Plea for Culture," *Atlantic Monthly* 19 (1867): 30–31; *Portland Daily Press*, December 18, 1866; *Holt County* (MO) *Sentinel*, January 4, 1867; ED to TWH, July 1867, in *Letters of Dickinson*, ed. Johnson, 2: 323.
28. TWH, *Malbone: An Oldport Romance* (Boston, 1869), 9, 50; TWH to ASH and SLH, September 30, 1868, Higginson Papers, HLH.
29. TWH Diary, November 8, 1868, TWH to James Fields, October 3, 1868, Higginson Papers, HLH.
30. *Tamas County* (IA) *Republican*, June 3, 1869; *Green-Mountain* (VT) *Freeman*, December 16, 1868; *Plymouth* (IN) *Democrat*, January 21, 1869; *Evansville* (IN) *Journal*, January 22, 1869;

Philadelphia Evening Telegraph, May 21, 1869; TWH Diary, November 3, 1869, Higginson Papers, HLH.
31. *Middlebury* (VT) *Register*, September 21, 1869; *Columbia* (SC) *Phoenix*, November 4, 1869; *Wheeling* (WV) *Register*, October 12, 1869; TWH Diary, November 3, 1869, Higginson Papers, HLH; *Marshall County* (IN) *Republican*, December 8, 1870; *Mineral Point* (WI) *Tribune*, December 8, 1870; TWH to James Fields, February 4, 1868, Higginson Papers, HLH.
32. *Delaware* (OH) *Gazette*, July 16, 1869; TWH to ASH, November 17, 1867, Higginson Papers, HLH. On the formation of the Radical Club, see Stirling, *Abby Kelley*, 362; Faulkner, *Lucretia Mott*, 202; Stewart, *Phillips*, 313.
33. *New-York Tribune*, May 24, 1870; *Springfield Republican*, March 21, 1870; Philadelphia *Evening Telegraph*, January 5, 1870.
34. Unidentified newspaper clipping, TWH Diary, January 17, 1871, Higginson Papers, HLH; *Chicago Tribune*, May 29, 1871; *New-York Tribune*, March 24, October 20, 1870.
35. TWH to "Sarah," January 26, 1869, Higginson Papers, HLH; *New-York Tribune*, December 23, 1870; "Sappho," *Atlantic Monthly* 27 (1871). The essay has attracted a good amount of modern scholarly attention; see, for example, Gloria Duclos, "Thomas Wentworth Higginson's Sappho," *New England Quarterly* 57 (1984): 403–411.
36. Ron Powers, *Mark Twain: A Life* (New York, 2005), 378; TWH to "dear Friend," February 24, 1874, TWH Diary, February 19, 1874, Higginson Papers, HLH.
37. TWH to ECS, May 2, December 22, 1866, in *Selected Papers*, ed. Gordon, 1: 578, 2: 10; Edwin Mead, "Thomas Wentworth Higginson," *New England Magazine* 45 (1911): 407; Sally McMillen, *Seneca Falls and the Origins of the Women's Rights Movement* (New York, 2009), 162.
38. Mayer, *All on Fire*, 612; Faye Dudden, *Fighting Chance: The Struggle over Woman Suffrage and Black Suffrage in Reconstruction America* (New York, 2011), 95–96; *Evansville* (IN) *Journal*, October 9, 1867; Raleigh *Tri-Weekly Standard*, October 8, 1867; *Yorkville* (SC) *Enquirer*, November 21, 1867.
39. ECS to TWH, January 13, 1868, in *Selected Papers*, ed. Gordon, 2: 127.
40. Griffith, *In Her Own Right*, 132; *New-York Tribune*, May 14, 1868; Columbus *Daily Ohio Statesman*, May 15, 1868; Susan B. Anthony to TWH, May 20, 1868, in *Selected Papers*, ed. Gordon, 2: 141; TWH to Harriet Beecher Stowe, October 11, 1868, Higginson Papers, Stowe Center.
41. *Wyandot* (OH) *Pioneer*, December 3, 1868; *Cambria* (PA) *Freeman*, August 6, 1868; *Ashtabula* (OH) *Weekly Telegraph*, October 31, 1868; *New York Herald*, November 22, 27, 1868; *Burlington Weekly Free Press*, November 27, 1868; *Vermont Watchman and State Journal*, November 11, 1868; *Wheeling Daily Intelligencer*, November 19, 1868; TWH to Harriet Beecher Stowe, October 11, 1868, Higginson Papers, Stowe Center; Dudden, *Fighting Chance,* 163; TWH Diary, November 12, 18–23, Higginson Papers, HLH.
42. *Emporia News*, October 29, 1869; *New York Herald*, October 23, 1869; Lucy Stone and TWH to Isabella Hooker, August 5, 1869, Higginson Papers, Stowe Center; ECS to Paulina Davis, August 12, 1869, and "The Cleveland Convention," October 28, 1869, in *Selected Papers*, ed. Gordon, 2: 256, 276–277.
43. *Gold Hill* (NV) *Daily News*, November 26, 1869; McMillen, *Seneca Falls*, 177; "Remarks by Susan B. Anthony," November 25, 1869, in *Selected Papers*, ed. Gordon, 2: 284; Griffith, *In Her Own Right*, 138; *Dodgeville* (WI) *Chronicle*, December 3, 1869; *Weekly Oskaloosa* (IA) *Herald*, December 23, 1869; Jackson *Weekly Clarion*, December 16, 1869.
44. *Portland* (ME) *Daily Press*, January 11, 1870; *Rutland* (VT) *Weekly Herald*, March 10, 1870; *Hancock* (OH) *Jeffersonian*, December 3, 1869; Louisiana *Planters' Banner*, December 29, 1869; *New-York Tribune*, January 3, 1870; *Bellows Falls Times*, February 4, 1870; *Philadelphia Evening Telegraph*, December 3, 1870.
45. Faulkner, *Mott*, 204–205; Robertson, *Pillsbury*, 155; *New-York Tribune*, January 6, April 7, 1870; Lucretia Mott to Martha Wright, December 5, 1869, April 7, 1870, in *Letters of Mott*, ed. Palmer, 427, 439; Griffith, *In Her Own Right*, 142; TWH Diary, April 6, 1870, Higginson Papers, HLH.
46. *New Orleans Republican*, November 30, 1870; McMillen, *Stone*, 197; "Remarks by Susan B. Anthony," November 23, 1870, in *Selected Papers*, ed. Gordon, 2: 377; TWH Diary, November 23, 1870, Higginson Papers, HLH.
47. Washington *Evening Star,* November 12, 1870; *Idaho World*, December 22, 1870; *Chicago Tribune*, November 13, 1870; *Leavenworth Weekly Times*, December 15, 1870; *Nashville Union*

and American, November 20, 1870; *New-York Tribune*, December 2, 1870; ECS to Josephine Griffing, December 1, 1871; Susan B. Anthony to Isabella Hooker, December 2, 1870, Susan B. Anthony to Martha Wright, March 21, 1871, Susan B. Anthony to Lepha Canfield, January 2, 1871, in *Selected Papers*, ed. Gordon, 2: 381–383, 399, 425.

48. *Woman's Journal*, November 4, 1871; Washington *Evening Star*, December 8, 1871; *Daily Kennebec* (ME) *Journal*, December 23, 1871; *New-York Tribune*, August 19, 1872; *Burlington Free Press*, January 28, 1870; *Portland Daily Press*, October 15, 1870; *Middlebury Register*, March 21, 1871; TWH Diary, May 11, 1870, February 24, 1871, April 18, 1871, Higginson Papers, HLH.
49. Van Wyck Brooks, *New England: Indian Summer, 1865–1915* (New York, 1940), 132; ED to TWH, "early 1866," June 9, 1866, in *Letters of Dickinson*, ed. Johnson, 2: 450–452.
50. ED to TWH, June 1869, TWH to ED, June 1869, in *Letters of Dickinson*, ed. Johnson, 2: 460–462.
51. Murray, *Maid as Muse*, 171; ED to TWH, August 16, 1870, TWH to MCH, August 16, 1870, in *Letters of Dickinson*, ed. Johnson, 2: 472–473; TWH Diary, August 16, 1870, TWH to MCH, August 17, 1870, Higginson Papers, HLH.
52. Cynthia Wolff, *Emily Dickinson* (New York, 1986), 7; Wineapple, *White Heat*, 193; TWH Diary, December 3, 1873, Higginson Papers, HLH; ED to TWH, November 1871, January 1874, TWH to ASH, December 9, 1873, TWH to ED, January 1874, in *Letters of Dickinson*, ed. Johnson, 2: 491, 717–520.
53. Butler, *Critical Americans*, 94; TWH to ASH and SLH, May 18, 30, 1872, Higginson Papers, HLH. John Russell, Viscount Amberley, was the son of the former prime minister of the same name.
54. Elizabeth Chase to Matthew Arnold, June 19, 1872, copy, Higginson Papers, HLH.
55. TWH, *Cheerful Yesterdays*, 284.
56. ED to TWH, "late 1872," in *Letters of Dickinson*, ed. Johnson, 2: 611, 423–426; *Woman's Journal*, June 22, 1872; TWH Diary, December 23, 1873, Higginson Papers, HLH.
57. Stephen Higginson, September 27, 1870, Massachusetts Wills and Probate Records, p. 375, and Massachusetts Town and Vital Records, Deerfield, both MHS; Boston *New England Insurance Gazette*, August 1, 1870; *Boston Medical and Surgical Journal*, March 14, 1872; *Highland* (OH) *Weekly News*, May 11, 1871; TWH Diary, August 12–15, 1870, Higginson Papers, HLH.
58. TWH Diary, March 11, 1872, Higginson Papers, HLH; ED to TWH, March 1872, in *Letters of Dickinson*, ed. Johnson, 2: 494.
59. TWH Diary, August 27–31, 1875, TWH to ASH, November 12, 30, 1875, Higginson Papers, HLH.
60. ED to TWH, October 1876, ED to MCH, December 1876, TWH to ASH, December 28, 1876, ED to MCH, August 1876, ED to MCH, Spring 1877, ED to TWH, early 1877, in *Letters of Dickinson*, ed. Johnson, 2: 561, 566, 569–570, 573, 579.
61. *Nashville Union and American*, June 7, 1872; TWH Diary, November 2, 1872, Higginson Papers, HLH; TWH to John Greenleaf Whittier, September 30, 1872, in *Letters of Whittier*, ed. Pickard, 277–278.
62. *Woman's Journal*, July 29, 1876; *Chicago Daily Tribune*, April 29, 1877; *Rock Island Argus*, April 28, 1877; *Memphis Public Ledger*, April 28, 1877; James Russell Lowell to TWH, June 16, 1877, Higginson Papers, Huntington Library.
63. TWH Diary, September 5, 1877, Higginson Papers, HLH; ED to TWH, June 1877, September 1877 (three that month), Autumn 1877, in *Letters of Dickinson*, ed. Johnson, 2: 583, 590–592, 594.

Chapter 10

1. TWH Diary, September 6–8, 10, 15, 1877, Higginson Papers, HLH.
2. MTH, *Story of His Life*, 363; TWH, *Army Life*, 363; TWH to ASH, October 26, 1877, TWH Diary, February 22, 1787, Higginson Papers, HLH; Michigan *True Northerner*, January 18, 1878.
3. TWH, *Cheerful Yesterdays*, 283–284, 298–299; MTH, *Story of His Life*, 340; TWH to ASH, June 13, 1878, Higginson Papers, HLH. On the conference, see Frederick Wines, *Report on the International Prison Congress, Held at Stockholm, Sweden* (Springfield, 1879).
4. ED to TWH, June 1878, in *Letters of Dickinson*, ed. Johnson, 2: 611; MTH, *Story of His Life*, 292; *Clariton* (MO) *Courier*, April 5, 1879; Wineapple, *White Heat*, 226.
5. *Arkansas Ladies' Journal*, August 16, 1884; Peter Thatcher, Federal Census, 1870, NA; MTH, *Seashore and Prairie* (Boston, 1877), 5–6, 13, 142–147; TWH to Ellen Conway, January 31, November 4, 1878, Conway Papers, Columbia University.

6. TWH to Ellen Conway, November 4, 1878, TWH to Ellen Garrison, December 6, 1878, both in Conway Papers, Columbia University.
7. ED to TWH, December 1878, in *Letters of Dickinson*, ed. Johnson, 2: 627; TWH, *Malbone*, 149. Edelstein, *Strange Enthusiasm*, 336, writes, without documentation, that the marriage "shocked some of his acquaintances because the new Mrs. Higginson looked younger than twenty."
8. TWH, Marriage, February 6, 1879, Records of Marriage, MHS; John Greenleaf Whittier to TWH, February 12, 1879, Higginson Papers, Huntington Library; ED to TWH, February 1879, in *Letters of Dickinson*, ed. Johnson, 2: 635; TWH Diary, February 6–7, 1879, Higginson Papers, HLH.
9. TWH to ASH, April 17, 1879, Higginson Papers, HLH.
10. TWH Diary, March 20, December 16, 22, 1879, Higginson Papers, HLH; Hélène Quanquin, *Men in the American Women's Rights Movement, 1830–1890* (New York, 2021), 150. In the United States in the 1870s, the average age for women to give birth for the first time was twenty-three. See Michael Haines, "The Population of the United States, 1790–1920," *National Bureau of Economic Research* 12 (1994).
11. MTH, *Story of His Life*, 294–295; Louisa W. Higginson, January 24, 1880, Massachusetts, U.S. Birth Records, 1840–1910, MHS.
12. MTH, *Story of His Life*, 295; ED to TWH, "about 1881," in *Letters of Dickinson*, ed. Johnson, 2: 735; Louisa W. Higginson, March 18, 1880, U.S. Federal Census Mortality Schedules, 1850–1885, NA.
13. MTH, *Story of His Life*, 298; TWH to ASH, December 8, 1881, July 7, 1882, June 30, 1883, January 25, 1883, Higginson Papers, HLH.
14. TWH to Ellen Conway, December 15, 1883, Conway Papers, Columbia; *Memphis Daily Appeal*, December 27, 1885; *Daily Yellowstone Journal*, February 4, 1885.
15. MTH, *Story of His Life*, 298; TWH Diary, February 27–28, September 16, 1879, Higginson Papers, HLH; *Cincinnati Daily Star*, November 25, 1879.
16. TWH, *Cheerful Yesterdays*, 344; House Bills 11, 173, 205, in *Journal of the House of Representatives of the Commonwealth of Massachusetts* (Boston, 1980).
17. *Helena Weekly Herald*, April 15, 1880; *Yorkville* (SC) *Enquirer*, April 22, 1880; *St. Johnsbury* (VT) *Caledonian*, January 23, 1880.
18. Samuel Clemens to William Dean Howells, May 18, 1880, Samuel Clemens to James Osgood, November 26, 1880, Twain Papers, University of California at Berkeley.
19. House Bills 118, 211, 295, in *Journal of the House*, 18, 29, 34, 58, 90, 102, 119; *St. Paul Daily Globe*, February 22, 1884.
20. Thomas Aldrich to TWH, October 5, November 10, 1885, Higginson Papers, Huntington; TWH to ASH, December 31, 1880, Higginson Papers, HLH; *Sacramento Daily Record-Union*, August 14, 1880; *Belmont* (OH) *Chronicle*, December 25, 1879; *Memphis Daily Appeal*, November 18, 1879; *Helena Weekly Herald*, October 23, 1879; *Middlebury* (VT) *Register*, August 7, 1885.
21. TWH to ASH, December 31, 1880, Higginson Papers, HLH; *New-York Tribune*, March 12, 1881; *Memphis Daily Appeal*, May 12, 1881; *Baltimore County Union*, May 14, 1991; *Savannah Morning News*, May 14, 1881.
22. TWH to James Blaine, May 7, 1881, Blaine Papers, LC; *Richmond Daily Dispatch*, May 13, 1881; *Westminster* (MD) *Democratic Advocate*, May 14, 1881. The speech is reprinted in *A Just and Lasting Peace: A Documentary History of Reconstruction*, ed. John David Smith (New York, 2013), 517.
23. *Just and Lasting Peace*, ed. Smith, 523.
24. Washington *National Republican*, May 12, 1881; *Chicago Daily Tribune*, May 12, 1881; *Memphis Daily Appeal*, May 11, 1881; *Newbury* (SC) *Herald*, May 18, 1881; TWH, *Army Life*, 64.
25. TWH, *Cheerful Yesterdays*, 186; Washington *National Republican*, February 5, 1875.
26. TWH, *Young Folks' History of the United States* (Boston, 1875), 264–265, 286, 305–306, 324. In *Teaching White Supremacy: America's Democratic Ordeal and the Forging of Our National Identity* (New York, 2022), 135, Donald Yacovone notes that Higginson's book "broke the textbook mold" with its nonracist approach.
27. *Springfield Republican*, March 3, 1875; *Portland Daily Press*, April 28, 1875; Yacovone, *Teaching White Supremacy*, 135; Idaho City *Semi-Weekly Herald*, November 27, 1883.
28. TWH Diary, February 2, 1885, Higginson Papers, HLH; TWH, "First Americans," "Visit of the Vikings," "Spanish Discoverers," "French Voyageurs," all in *Harper's Monthly* 64 (1882–1883); *Indianapolis Journal*, February 19, 1883; *New-York Tribune*, February 28, 1883. *Travelers and Outlaws: Episodes in American History* appeared in 1889.

29. *Jamesville* (NJ) *Record*, March 17, 1883; *Salt Lake Herald*, May 20, 1883; *Ellsworth* (ME) *American*, July 19, 1883; *Helena Weekly Herald*, January 3, 1884; *Belmont* (OH) *Chronicle*, January 24, 1884; *Jackson* (OH) *Standard*, January 31, 1884.
30. TWH, *A Larger History of the United States to the Close of President Jackson's Administration* (New York, 1886), vi, 356, 453; *Sacramento Daily Record-Union*, October 31, 1885; *Portland* (ME) *Daily Press*, November 2, 1885; *Richmond Dispatch*, October 18, 1885.
31. *Bismarck Tribune*, May 2, 1884; *Iowa County Democrat*, May 2, 1884; *Delaware Gazette and State Journal*, May 22, 1884.
32. TWH to James Garfield, January 12, 1881, Garfield Papers, LC.
33. *Sacramento Daily Record-Union*, June 14, 1884; *St. Paul Daily Globe*, June 14, 1884; *Savannah Morning News*, June 9, 1884; *Wheeling Register*, June 11, 1884; *Westminster* (MD) *Democratic Advocate*, June 14, 1884; *Alexandria Gazette*, June 14, 1884.
34. *Indianapolis Journal*, June 17, 1884; *Watertown* (WI) *Republican*, June 25, 1844; *New-York Tribune*, June 18, 1884; *Breckinridge* (KY) *News*, June 25, 1884; *Wilmington Gazette*, June 12, 1884.
35. Idaho City *Semi-Weekly World*, June 27, 1884; Washington *National Tribune*, July 3, 1884; *Portland* (ME) *Daily Press*, July 23, 1884; *Savannah Morning News*, July 23, 1884; *Crawford* (MI) *Avalanche*, August 21, 1884; *Salt Lake Herald*, July 23, 1884; *Westminster* (MD) *Democratic Advocate*, July 26, 1884; *Wheeling Register*, July 24, 1884.
36. *Helena Weekly Herald*, August 7, 1884; *Indianapolis Journal*, July 29, 1884.
37. *Woman's Journal*, August 16, 1884; *Portland* (ME) *Daily Press*, August 12, 1884; Richard Welch, *The Presidencies of Grover Cleveland* (Lawrence, 1988), 38. The relationship between Cleveland and Halpin was surely far worse than Higginson imagined. See Charles Lachman, *A Secret Life: The Lies and Scandals of President Grover Cleveland* (New York, 2011).
38. *Portland* (ME) *Daily Press*, August 12, 1884; *Indianapolis Journal*, August 14, 1884; *Woman's Journal*, August 2, 16, September 20, October 25, 1884.
39. *Vermont Phoenix*, September 5, 1884; *St. Paul Daily Globe*, September 17, October 29, 1884; *Delaware Gazette and State Journal*, October 9, 1884; *Salt Lake Herald*, October 29, 1884; TWH to MTH, October 28, 1884, TWH to Peter Thatcher, October 30, 1884, Higginson Papers, HLH.
40. TWH to MTH, October 28, 1884, Higginson Papers, HLH.
41. *Vermont Phoenix*, October 31, 1884; TWH to Grover Cleveland, July 18, 1885, Cleveland Papers, LC; Thomas Aldrich to TWH, December 13, 1884, Higginson Papers, Huntington; TWH, "Wendell Phillips," *Nation*, February 7, 1884; TWH, "Palmer's Odyssey," *Atlantic Monthly* 53 (1884); TWH to ASH, April 14, 1886, Higginson Papers, HLH.
42. McMillen, *Stone*, 227; *Indianapolis Journal*, November 16, December 4, 1884, June 30, 1885; Boston *Woman's Journal*, January 3, 1885; George Robinson to TWH, July 29, 1884, Higginson Papers, HLH.
43. TWH to MCH, December 12, 1863, in *War Journal*, ed. Looby, 335; *New York Times*, August 10, 1884; Crofts, *Secession Crisis Enigma*, 197–202.
44. *St. Paul Daily Globe*, April 19, 1884; *Maysville* (KY) *Daily Evening Bulletin*, February 5, 1884; TWH, "Wendell Phillips," *Nation*, February 7, 1884.
45. TWH to unknown, 1886, Higginson Papers, HLH; MTH, *Story of His Life*, 313; Wineapple, *White Heat*, 263–265; Patrick Keane, *Emily Dickinson's Approving God: Divine Design and the Problem of Suffering* (Columbia, 2008), 204.
46. TWH, *The Monarch of Dreams* (Boston, 1887), 10–14.
47. TWH, *Monarch*, 44–52.
48. TWH to ASH, November 22, December 7, 1886, Higginson Papers, HLH.
49. TWH to Edmund Stedman, October 24, 1887, in *Letters and Journals*, ed. MTH, 335; *Wheeling Daily Intelligencer*, March 21, 1887; *Portland Daily Press*, January 29, 1887; New Haven *Morning Journal and Courier*, February 25, 1887; Chicago *Universalist*, July 9, 1887. For an example of the *Atlantic*'s declining to accept Higginson's writings "on the price which you have named," see Thomas Aldrich to TWH, July 9, 1885, Higginson Papers, Huntington.
50. Sacramento *Daily Record Union*, September 25, 1888; *Waterbury Evening Democrat*, September 25, 1888; TWH to ASH, June 11, September 26, 1888, Higginson Papers, HLH.
51. *Mower County* (MN) *Transcript*, October 3, 1888; *Wilmington Evening Journal*, October 8, 1888; *Washington Critic*, September 26, 1888.
52. *Portland Daily Press*, October 17, 1888.

53. *Lexington* (MO) *Intelligencer*, October 27, 1888; *Barton County* (KS) *Democrat*, November 1, 1888; *Salt Lake Herald*, October 26, 1888; *St. Johnsbury* (VT) *Caledonian*, October 11, 1888; *Marietta* (GA) *Journal*, November 1, 1888.
54. "Extract of a Speech at Lexington," October 23, 1888, in Higginson Club of Cambridge, circular, November 3, 1888; TWH to ASH, November 7, 1888, Higginson Papers, HLH.
55. Indianapolis *Indiana State Sentinel*, October 31, 1888; Washington *Evening Star*, November 6, 1888; *New-York Tribune*, November 7, 9, 1888; *St. Johnsbury* (VT) *Caledonian*, November 8, 1888; *Clarksville* (TN) *Evening Chronicle*, November 8, 1888; TWH to ASH, November 7, 1888, Higginson Papers, HLH. On Hayden's 1886 totals, see New York *Sun*, November 4, 1886.
56. TWH to ASH, November 7, 1888, Higginson Papers, HLH.

Chapter 11

1. *Providence News*, February 13, 1900; TWH to Kate Coe, August 23, 1889, Higginson Papers, Stowe Center; TWH to ASH, January 28, 1890, Higginson Papers, HLH.
2. *Wheeling Daily Intelligencer*, July 18, 1890; *St. Paul Daily Globe*, July 25, 1890; *Portland Daily Press*, June 19, 1893.
3. *Cape Girardeau* (MO) *Democrat*, January 23, 1897; TWH to ASH, December 1, 1891, Higginson Papers, HLH.
4. Connie Ann Kirk, *Emily Dickinson: A Biography* (Westport, 2004), 132; Wineapple, *White Heat*, 280–283; MTH, *Story of His Life*, 368.
5. Wineapple, *White Heat*, 285; Virginia Jackson, *Emily Dickinson's Misery: A Theory of Lyric Reading* (Princeton, 2005), 16; TWH, "Emily Dickinson's Letters," *Atlantic Monthly* 68 (1891); TWH and Mabel Todd, eds., *Poems, by Emily Dickinson* (Boston, 1890).
6. *Providence News*, December 24, 1891; TWH to Mabel Todd, November 12, 1890, February 9, 1891, in *Letters and Journals*, ed. MTH, 331.
7. John Picker, "'Red War Is My Song': Whitman, Higginson, and Civil War Music," in *Walt Whitman and Modern Music: War, Desire, and the Trials of Nationhood*, ed. Lawrence Kramer (New York, 2000), 1–2; TWH, "Women and Men: War Pensions for Women," *Harper's Bazar* 20 (1887): 162.
8. TWH, *The New Landscape: Poems and Translations* (New York, 1889); TWH Diary, May 2, 1900, Higginson Papers, HLH; *New-York Tribune*, May 8, 1889, December 18, 1893; TWH and MTH, *Such as They Are: Poems* (Boston, 1893).
9. TWH to Kate Coe, June 8, 1889, Higginson Papers, Stowe Center; TWH to ASH, January 20, 1891, February 25, 1892, TWH Higginson Diary, March 12, June 1, 1900, Higginson Papers, HLH; Washington *National Tribune*, November 12, 1891; TWH, *Massachusetts in the Army and Navy during the War, 1861–1865*, 2 vols. (Boston, 1895–1896).
10. *Portland Daily Press*, February 8, 1895; W. Scott Poole, "Memory and the Abolitionist Heritage: Thomas Wentworth Higginson and the Uncertain Meaning of the Civil War," *Civil War History* 51 (2005): 203; Newport News *Daily Press*, July 21, 1909.
11. *St. Johnsbury* (VT) *Caledonian*, January 31, 1900; *Indianapolis Journal*, January 1, 1894; *St. Paul Daily Globe*, December 17, 1893.
12. TWH Diary, February 10, 28, April 8, June 8, July 30, November 4, 12, 1896, February 3, 1897, Higginson Papers, HLH; *Atlantic Monthly*, November–December 1896, January–May 1897; Worcester *Morning Daily Spy*, February 28, 1898; TWH, *Cheerful Yesterdays*, 230, 262–263, 285.
13. *Mower County* (MN) *Transcript*, October 28, 1896; *Salt Lake Herald*, May 27, 1897; Belfast (ME) *Republican Journal*, December 10, 1896; Henry James, The *American Essays of Henry James*, ed. Leon Edel (Princeton, 1990), 239; Alan Gribben, *Mark Twain's Library: A Reconstruction* (Boston, 1980), 1: 313. I am grateful to Ann Ryan for the Twain citation.
14. *Iron County* (MO) *Register*, April 18, 1889.
15. *Vermont Phoenix*, November 18, 1892, May 11, 1894; Anna S. Higginson, Massachusetts Death Records, 1841–1915, p. 428, MHS; MTH, *Story of His Life*, 381; *Portland Daily Press*, October 22, 1894.
16. *Portland Daily Press*, September 7, 1895; *Sacramento Record-Union*, September 7, 1895; *St. Paul Globe*, March 13, 1898.
17. San Francisco *Morning Call*, December 9, 1893; *Somerset* (ME) *Reporter*, November 9, 1893; *Vermont Phoenix*, October 27, 1893. On Blackwell's probable infidelity, see Faulkner, *Unfaithful*, 125.

18. MTH, *Story of His Life*, 381, 373; *Perth Amboy Evening News*, July 30, 1907; TWH Diary, October 21, 1896, February 16, 1897, July 9, 1900, Higginson Papers, HLH.
19. Washington *Evening Star*, October 17, 1892; *Dalles* (OR) *Times-Mountaineer*, January 28, 1893; TWH Diary, July 10, 1896, Higginson Papers, HLH.
20. *Los Angeles Herald*, May 26, 1894; *Jersey City News*, August 14, 1894; Westminster (MN) *Democratic Advocate*, March 23, 1895. Thomas's departure from his Methodist congregation was discussed in the *Los Angeles Herald*, January 27, 1903.
21. Little Rock *Woman's Chronicle*, January 31, 1891; *Daily Kennebec* (ME) *Journal*, December 11, 1907; *Providence News*, July 7, 1892; TWH, *Concerning All of Us* (New York, 1892), 200–202.
22. *Providence News*, May 2, 1893; *Portland Daily Press*, May 10, 1893; *Savannah Morning News*, May 29, 1894; *Mower County* (MN) *Transcript*, October 30, 1895; *Marble Hill* (MO) *Press*, March 12, 1896; Glenn Valley *Dakota Chief*, April 2, 1896.
23. MTH, *Story of His Life*, 382; Washington *Morning Times*, December 22, 1895; *Portland Daily Press*, December 27, 1895; TWH Diary, January 13, February 26, March 1, 19, April 1, 16, 1896, Higginson Papers, HLH.
24. TWH Diary, May 27, October 30, December 22, 1896, November 22, December 7, 1897, Higginson Papers, HLH.
25. *St. Paul Globe*, May 16, 1897; *Orleans* (VT) *Country Monitor*, June 7, 1897; Edward Atkinson to John Murray Forbes, December 10, 1896, Atkinson Letterbooks, MHS (I am grateful to Thomas Brown for this citation); TWH Diary, January 25, 1902, Higginson Papers, HLH.
26. *Bourbon* (KY) *News*, September 10, 1897; TWH Diary, May 3, June 1, 22, 1897, Higginson Papers, HLH; MTH, *Story of His Life*, 347–348.
27. MTH, *Story of His Life*, 303; TWH Diary, June 27, July 3, 22, 24, October 15, 24, November 1, 9, December 22, 1897, Higginson Papers, HLH.
28. TWH Diary, March 9, May 4, 7, 1898, Higginson Papers, HLH.
29. Nebraska City *Conservative*, March 23, 1899; Phoenix *Arizona Republican*, October 21, 1900.
30. TWH Diary, February 14, 1900; *Lamar* (CO) *Register*, March 14, 1900; Garnett *Kansas Agitator*, March 16, 1900; *Topeka State Journal*, February 16, 1900; Duluth *Labor World*, January 5, 1901.
31. Poole, "Memory and the Abolitionist Heritage," 216; Douglas Shand-Tucci, *The Crimson Letter: Harvard, Homosexuality, and the Shaping of American Culture* (New York, 2003), 43; *Phillipsburg* (KS) *Herald*, October 25, 1900.
32. *Rock Island* (IL) *Argus*, August 30, 1900; Raleigh *News and Observer*, September 20, 1900; *Jamesburg* (NJ) *Record*, September 22, 1900; TWH to William Jennings Bryan, November 27, 1901, Higginson Papers, HLH.
33. TWH, Federal Census, 1900, p. 305, NA; TWH, passport, March 5, 1901, Higginson Papers, HLH.
34. TWH to unknown, March 23, April 16, 1901, in *Letters and Journals*, ed. MTH, 306–316; TWH Diary, May 24, August 1, 1901, TWH to "Lizzie," July 1, 1901, Higginson Papers, HLH; *New-York Tribune*, September 21, 1901.
35. TWH Diary, July 25, August 27, September 3, 5, December 22, 1905, Higginson Papers, HLH; James Barney and Margaret Higginson, September 2, 1905, New Hampshire Marriage and Divorce Records, 1659–1947, New Hampshire Bureau of Vital Records, Concord, New Hampshire. Nancy Young, Smith College archivist, informs me there is no record that Margaret ever attended that institution (or fro Vassar, Radcliffe, or Mount Holyoke), but she donated her autograph book and small collection of her personal letters, many of them from Julia Ward Howe, to Smith, despite living at the opposite end of the state.
36. MTH, *Story of His Life*, 394–395; Margaret Barney, New Hampshire Marriage and Divorce Records, New England Historical Genealogical Society; New Hampshire Bureau of Vital Records, Concord, New Hampshire.
37. TWH, *A Thanksgiving Sermon: Preached in Newburyport, November 30, 1848* (Boston, 1848), 4–5; *Santa Fe Daily New Mexican*, October 31, 1892; *New-York Tribune*, May 9, 1900; New York *Sun*, October 29, 1905; TWH, "The Aristocracy of the Dollar," *Atlantic Monthly* (1904): 506–513.
38. *New York Sun*, June 23, 1912; *Durango* (CO) *Semi-Weekly Herald*, August 3, 1908; Lewistown *Montana News*, November 14, 1907; TWH Diary, February 6, 1909, Higginson Papers, HLH.
39. TWH, "The Future Life," *Harper's Bazar* (May 1909); TWH, "Old Newport Days," *Outlook* (April 1909); TWH, "White Slaves in Africa," *North American Review* (July 1909); TWH Diary, April 27, 1909, Higginson Papers, HLH.

40. Charleston (WV) *Advocate*, May 18, 1911; TWH Diary, May 17, 1906, Higginson Papers, HLH; TWH, Federal Census, 1910, NA; TWH to John Heise, April 14, 1911, Higginson Papers, Stowe Center.
41. *Palestine* (TX) *Daily Herald*, December 22, 1909, December 22, 1910; *Bisbee* (AZ) *Daily Review*, December 23, 1909.
42. MTH, *Story of His Life*, 399; TWH Diary, February 8, March 7, 29, April 21, 23, 29, May 9, 1911. TWH, Certificate of Death, May 9, 1911, p. 402, MHS, lists cause of death as "Senility," but both New York and Boston were in the midst of a typhoid fever epidemic, and a vaccine was developed only in his death year of 1911.
43. *Harvard Crimson*, May 12, 1911; *Washington Bee*, May 27, 1911; New York *Sun*, May 13, 1911; *Topeka State Journal*, May 12, 1911; *Norwich* (CT) *Bulletin*, May 15, 1911; *Omaha Daily Bee*, May 13, 1911.
44. St. Paul *Minnesotské Noviny*, May 18, 1911; Skagway *Daily Alaskan*, May 10, 1911; *Washington Times*, May 10, 1911; *Detroit Times*, May 10, 1911; Iowa *Plain Dealer*, May 12, 1911; *Mahoning* (OH) *Dispatch*, May 12, 1911; Minneapolis *Irish Standard*, May 13, 1911; *Willmar* (MN) *Tribune*, May 17, 1911; Iowa *Evening-Times Republican*, May 19, 1911; Washington *Evening Star*, July 1, 1911.
45. New York *Sun*, May 20, 1911; Iowa *Daily Gate City*, June 8, 1911; *Journal of Education*, May 25, 1911; Pierre *Weekly Free Press*, June 8, 1911; *Brattleboro Reformer*, May 12, 1911; Pendleton *East Oregonian*, May 13, 1911; *Washington Times*, May 10, 1911.
46. Phoenix *Arizona Republican*, October 17, 1911; *Fargo Forum and Daily Republican*, March 21, 1914; Wilmington *Evening Journal*, May 5, 1914. The title of this chapter is taken from the final pages of *Story of His Life*.
47. Cambridge City Directory, 1921, p. 547, MHS; Phoenix *Arizona Republican*, April 10, 1917; *Oroville* (WA) *Weekly Gazette*, June 23, 1922; *New York Herald*, December 15, 1921; MTH, 1940 Federal Census, NA; MTH, New York, U.S. arriving passengers, May 21, 1926, NA; *Boston Globe*, January 12, 1941; Wentworth Higginson Barney, 1940–1950 Federal Census, NA.
48. Annapolis *Evening Capital and Maryland Gazette*, June 7, 1920; Washington *Evening Star*, May 3, 1942, March 14, 1951; Everett (WA) *Labor Journal*, May 12, 1922.
49. David Brion Davis, "Slavery and the Post World War II Historians," *Daedalus* 103 (1974): 1–5; Merton Dillon, "The Abolitionists: A Decade of Historiography, 1959–1969," *Journal of Southern History* 35 (1969): 500–511; Robert Levine, *The Lives of Frederick Douglass* (Cambridge, 2016), 16. On the rival publishing histories of Du Bois and Mitchell, see my *Wars of Reconstruction: The Brief, Violent History of America's Most Progressive Era* (New York, 2014), 336–338.
50. Frederick Douglass, *Narrative of the Life of Frederick Douglass*, ed. Benjamin Quarles (Cambridge, 1960); John Thomas, *The Liberator: William Lloyd Garrison, A Biography* (Boston, 1963); Washington *Evening Star*, March 31, September 9, October 29, 1963.
51. TWH, *Cheerful Yesterdays*, 362–364.

Index

For the benefit of digital users, indexed terms that span two pages (e.g., 52–53) may, on occasion, appear on only one of those pages.

Figures are indicated by an italic *f* following the page number.

Abbott, James, 154
abolitionists, 1–4, 5, 6–8, 9–10, 36–37, 38, 40, 45, 48, 50–51, 54, 55–56, 57–59, 68, 70–71, 85–86, 88, 89–91, 94–95, 96–97, 104–5, 107–8, 111–12, 114–18, 120, 129, 130–31, 136, 137, 143–44, 147, 149, 152, 158–59, 161, 182–83, 194, 209–10, 220–21, 233, 234, 250
    disunion faction, 38–39, 40–41, 47–48, 58, 69, 105–6, 109–10
    hostility to, 45–46, 47–48, 74, 82, 87–88, 144, 159, 295
    pacifism of, 39–40, 104–5, 116
    physical force, 5, 79–80, 130–31, 133, 151, 153, 164–65, 176, 287
    and politics, 58–59, 64–65, 107, 108, 110, 131, 145–46, 155–56, 176
    See also antislavery
Adam, Hannah, 26
Adam, William, 26
Adams, Charles Francis, Jr., 163, 174–75, 255–56, 262, 263–64, 271–72, 281, 284, 286, 288–89, 292–93
Adams, Charles Francis, Sr., 50, 51–52, 61, 64, 107, 110–11
Adams, John Quincy, 28, 50, 154–55
Addams, Jane, 281
African Methodist Episcopal Churches and Schools, 226, 279–80
Aguinaldo, Emilio, 286
Alberti, Edwin, 185–86, 191–92, 194–95
Alcott, Amos Bronson, 54–55, 76, 230, 231
Alcott, Louisa May, 267–68
Aldrich, Thomas, 266–67, 269–70
American Anti-Slavery Society, 221, 274
American Equal Rights Association, 233–34, 235–36. *See also* National Woman Suffrage Association
American Freedmen's Inquiry Commission, 213–14, 220

American Party, 86
American Revolution, 16–17, 257–58
Andrew, John A., 80–81, 86–87, 151–52, 156, 161, 162–63, 166–67, 170–71, 173, 184–85, 190, 205–6, 220, 222–23
Andrew, John F., 271–72
Andrews, Caroline, 171
Anthony, Susan B., 72, 73, 74, 75, 90, 96, 101, 128, 234–35, 237, 239, 282–83
    disagreements with TWH, 234, 235–36, 237–39
Antietam, Battle of, 170
Anti-Slavery Bugle, 59, 128
antislavery, 7–8, 39–40, 48, 52, 57, 60–61, 64–65, 66–67, 70–71, 75, 76, 81, 85–87, 101, 105, 109, 110–11, 115–16, 120, 129–30, 132–33, 137, 145–46, 156, 158–59, 162–63, 172–73, 182–83, 223–24, 264, 293
    influences on TWH, 22–23, 38–39, 42
    meetings, 47–48, 58, 63–64, 68, 241–42 (*see also* abolitionists)
Army Life in a Black Regiment, 9–10, 229–30, 278, 295–96
Articles of Confederation, 13–14
Atlantic Club, 86, 131
Atlantic Monthly, 4, 8–9, 70, 86, 128, 131, 154, 163, 167, 170, 176, 178, 193, 203, 213, 257, 276
Austen, Jane, 228–29
Azores, 93–94

Bacon, John, 65
Bailey, John, 161–62
Baker, Lowell, 81–82
Bancroft, George, 260–61
Banks, Nathaniel, 271–73
Barbauld. Anna, 20
Barney, James, 289
Barney, Margaret Dellinger, 289
Barney, Wentworth Higginson, 289, 294

Barnum, P. T., 74
Barnum, William, 224
Batchelder, James, 78–79, 80, 99, 176–77
Battery Wagner, South Carolina, 205, 209–11, 259–60
Beaufort, South Carolina, 166–67, 172–74, 178–79, 181–85, 187, 188, 192–93, 196, 202–3, 204, 205, 206, 209, 210, 212, 220–21, 247–48, 258
   January 1 ceremony, 181–82
Beecher, Henry Ward, 103–4, 144, 233–34, 236, 238–39, 264, 266, 267–68
Bell, John, 154–55
Benét, Stephen Vincent, 140
Bennett, James Gordon, 128, 144
Bibb, Henry, 163–64
Bird, Francis William, 107–8, 111–12
Birney, James G., 102–3
Black activism, 5–6, 7, 80, 90, 107–8, 110, 118, 125–26, 128, 279–80
Blackwell, Alice Stone, 267
Black codes, 220–21
Blackwell, Antoinette Brown, 128
Blackwell, Emily, 282–83
Blackwell, Henry, 88–89, 90–91, 234, 280–81
Blackwell, Samuel, 137
Blaine, James G., 263–65, 266, 271
Blair, Montgomery, 137
Boston, Massachusetts, 5–6, 8–9, 11, 13–15, 16–17, 23–24, 31, 35, 38, 54, 59–60, 65–67, 71, 76, 79–80, 83–84, 86–88, 89, 93, 94, 97, 101, 103–4, 107, 109–10, 112, 115–16, 122–23, 126–27, 130, 137, 141–42, 145, 151, 155, 161, 173, 178, 184–85, 208–9, 220, 223–24, 227–28, 234–35, 239–40, 244, 247–48, 262, 267–68, 278, 279–80, 281, 283, 285, 289, 291
   Faneuil Hall, 58–78, 104, 130–31, 217
   Melodeon, 68–69, 87, 127
   Tremont Temple, 90, 143–44, 159, 231, 266, 282–83
Boston Lyceum Bureau, 221–22
Boston University, 283
Boston Vigilance Committee, 65–66, 76, 81–82, 137
Botts, Lawson, 147–48
Botts, Mary Mildred, 86–87
Botts, Seth, 86–87
Bowdich, Nathanial, 21
Bowdich, William Ingersol, 137
Bradwell, James, 236
Breckinridge, John C., 154–55
Briggs, Dean LeBaron, 285–86
Brisbane, William Henry, 181–82

Brontë, Emily, 268
Brooks, Preston, 94
Brown, Alpheus, 60, 62–63
Brown, Anne, 145
Brown, Antoinette Louisa, 68
Brown, Ellen, 141
Brown, John, 1–2, 104, 114, 118–22, 136–46, 154, 161–62, 164, 170, 177, 205–6, 251, 259–60
   attempts to rescue, 146–48, 182–83
   evolving plans of, 113, 118, 122–24, 131–34, 192–93
   Harpers Ferry raid, 134–35, 151
   in Kansas, 6, 100, 112–17
Brown, John, Jr., 161–62
Brown, Martha, 141
Brown, Mary Ann, 140, 141–42, 150
Brown, Oliver, 141
Brown, Salmon, 141, 146–47, 161
Brown, Sarah, 141
Brown, William Wells, 6–7, 49, 52
Browning, Elizabeth Barrett, 54–55
Bryan, William Jennings, 281, 287–88
Bryon, George Gordon, 43
Buchanan, James, 40–41, 102–3, 104–6, 108, 111, 118, 138, 156–57
Bull Run Creek, Battle of, 163, 165–66, 203–4, 269
Burns, Anthony, 5–6, 76–80, 81–82, 264–65, 279–80
Burnside, Ambrose, 178–79
Businessmen and merchants, 46–47, 49, 52–54, 55–56, 63–64, 93, 243, 295
Butler, Benjamin, 137, 166, 167, 170–71
Butman, Aso O., 7, 65, 76, 81–83
Butman, Sarah, 83

Cabot, Edward, 17
Calhoun, John C., 70, 259–60
Calhoun, John C., Jr., 209–10
Calvinism, 3–4, 11–13, 52–54, 116
Cambridge, Massachusetts, 11, 16, 17–19, 22, 23, 25–26, 27–28, 36–37, 38, 41–42, 43, 46, 48, 178, 223, 253–55, 264, 266, 267, 285–86
   First Parish Church, 292–93
   TWH's home in, 248–50, 251–52, 294
Cameron, Simon, 167
Camp Saxton, 179, 195–96, 203
Canada, 16–17, 65–66, 68–69, 87, 89, 120–22, 123, 133–34, 139–40, 152–53, 184–85, 281, 285
Carnegie, Andrew, 286, 292–93
Carpenter, J. Estlin, 282
Cass, Lewis, 64–65

Catholicism, 4, 11–12, 41, 48–49, 86, 225–26
Century Club (Boston), 242, 286–87
Century Magazine, 278–79, 283, 284
Chamberlain, Joshua, 255–56
Channing, Margaret "Greta," 91–92, 97, 152–53, 166–67, 173, 178
Channing, Walter, 35, 91
Channing, William Ellery, 72–73, 79, 80
Channing, William Henry, 46–47, 74
Chapman, Maria Weston, 5, 39
Charleston, South Carolina, 41–42, 163–64, 186–88, 195, 203, 205, 206, 208, 209–10, 226, 258
Chase, Elizabeth, 242
Chase, Salmon, 213–14, 224
Chatfield, John, 205
Cheerful Yesterdays, 34, 36, 278–79, 288
Cheney, Nathan, 146–47
Chicago, Illinois, 95, 97, 121, 150, 151, 221–22, 231, 263, 269–70, 282
Child, Lydia Maria, 38–39, 99–100, 144, 159, 163–64, 236–37
Chilton, Samuel, 138, 147–48
Christians, 36–37, 38, 40–41, 43–45, 49–50, 64, 79–80, 115–16, 194–95. *See also individual denominations*
Churchill, Winston, 281
Civil Rights Act, 223–24, 225–26
Clarke, James Freeman, 38, 46
Clay, Henry, 28, 58–59
Clemens, Olivia, 232
Clemens, Samuel, 2, 232, 248, 256, 279, 281
Cleveland, Frances Folsom, 266–67
Cleveland, Grover, 263, 264–65, 266–67, 271–73, 281
  scandal, 265, 267, 280–81
Clifton, Jack, 188, 192, 216
Coffin, Levi, 257
Compromise of 1850, 58–59, 75
Confederate States of America, 184–85, 196–98, 204, 205–6, 278, 293
  Confederate military, 158, 165–66, 170–71, 173–74, 178–79, 187, 188–95, 196, 198–200, 201–3, 205, 206–8, 209–10, 220–21, 259–60, 276–77
Confiscation Acts, 165–66
Congress, U.S., 13–15, 28, 45, 50, 51, 56, 57–58, 60, 62–63, 94–95, 111–12, 118, 156, 158–59, 165–66, 170–71, 223–24, 225–26, 233–34, 239, 257–58, 270–71, 273, 285–86
  and Black soldiers, 214–15
Connecticut, 13, 182–83, 194–95, 200–3, 205, 206–7, 224, 232, 277–78, 294

Constitution, U.S., 40–41, 50, 63–64, 70, 105–6, 107–8, 109–10, 112–13, 161, 271
  fugitive slave clause in, 62, 66–67
  proslavery aspects of, 49, 69–70, 90
  and women, 235–36
Constitutional Union Party, 270
Conway, Ellen, 250
Conway, Moncure Daniel, 250
Craft, Helen, 66
Craft, William, 66
Crothers, S. M., 292–93
Curtis, Andrew, 162
Curtis, George Williams, 237
Curzon, Margaret, 57
Curzon, Mary, 57, 67–68
Cutler, Ebenezer, 116–17

Dall, Caroline Wells, 128
Dame, Hannah, 211–12
Dana, Charles, 122, 263
Dana, Richard Henry, Jr., 5–6, 80–81
Darrow, Clarence, 291
Darwin, Charles, 242, 248
Davis, Garrett, 176–77, 178
Davis, Jefferson, 196–98, 205–6, 263–64
Davis, John, 21
Davis, Paulina, 235–36
Democratic Party, 7, 51, 58, 60, 69, 79, 90, 98–99, 100–1, 102, 109, 136, 137, 145–46, 154–55, 159, 166, 259, 260, 271–72, 287–88
  antislavery faction in, 62–63, 64, 111
  popular sovereignty, 75, 123–24
  racism and proslavery faction in, 75, 104–5, 118, 132–33, 151, 194–95, 199–200, 213, 245
  TWH's conversion to, 262, 263–67, 270–72, 287–88, 293–94
Department of the South, 174–75, 181–83, 195, 205, 206
Devons, Charles, 59
Dewey, George, 285–86
Dickinson, Anna, 213
Dickinson, Emily, 2, 5, 7–8, 9–10, 168–70, 172, 200, 212, 228, 242–43, 244–46, 250, 252, 275–76, 294
  contacts TWH, 168
  death of, 268–69
  meetings with TWH, 239–41, 248–49
  sends poems to TWH, 172, 218f, 240
Dickinson, Lavinia Norcross, 276
Disunion movement, 40–41, 47–48, 58, 69–70, 88, 90, 95, 96–97, 105–9, 110–13, 114, 151, 157, 161, 162–63, 176, 196–98

Dolliver, William, 13
Douglas, Stephen A., 75, 123–24, 154–55
Douglass, Frederick, 1–2, 6–7, 50, 52, 60–61, 68, 74, 79–80, 83–84, 85–86, 108–9, 110, 113, 118–19, 128, 130, 135, 138, 141, 184–85, 221–22, 224, 234–35, 237–38, 271–72, 293, 295–96
Douglass, Lewis, 204, 284
Dow, Neal, 71–72
Dred Scott decision, 108, 110, 111, 114, 137
Du Bois, W. E. B., 295
Dunbar, Paul Lawrence, 291–92
Duncan, James Henry, 51–52, 58–60, 62–63
DuPont, Samuel, 195, 196
Dutton, William, 81–82

Eaton, Abby, 91–92, 152–53
Election of 1848, 45–46, 50–54
Election of 1850, 56
Election of 1856, 102–5
Election of 1860, 154–57
Election of 1872, 245
Election of 1884, 263–67
Election of 1888, 271
Eliot, Charles, 263, 264, 281, 292–93
Emancipation and proclamations, 38–39, 68–69, 87–88, 165–66, 167, 176, 190
  Beaufort ceremony and, 181–82
Embargo Act, 14–15
Emerson, Ralph Waldo, 5–6, 34, 49, 86
Everett, Edward, 33–34

Factories and mills, 27, 48–49
Female Anti-Slavery Society (Boston), 52
Fessenden, William Pitt, 214, 224
Field, Kate, 124
Fields, James, 229–30, 239–40, 259
51st Massachusetts Infantry Regiment, 171–72
Finegan, Joseph, 198–99, 201, 202
Finney, Charles Grandison, 125–26
First Religious Society (Newburyport), 45–46, 49, 57–58, 67
1st South Carolina Infantry Regiment, 2–3, 6, 7, 9–10, 172–76, 178–215
Fitzhugh, George, 70
Florida, 174–75, 184–86, 190, 191–92, 203–4, 205, 247–48
  TWH's invasion of, 195–203
Folsom, Abby, 143–44
Forbes, Hugh, 105–6, 121–23
Ford, Chandler, 85–86
Fort Sumter, 158, 161, 184–85, 205, 215
Forten, Charlotte, 193–94, 217–19, 231

Foster, Abby Kelley, 54–55, 67–68, 71–72, 74–75, 108, 130, 133, 231, 236
Foster, Daniel, 116–17
Foster, David, 67–68
Foster, Dwight, 34, 171–72
Foster, John, 171–72
Foster, Stephen, 81–82, 105, 131, 132–33, 156, 236
Fowler, J. D., 145–46
Fowler, James, 172–73, 179–82
Frederickson, George, 5
Free Blacks, 58, 74, 83–84, 102, 163–64, 184–85, 215
Free labor, 49–50, 57–58
  slavery versus, 62, 87–88
Free soil movement, Free Soil Party, 2, 5–6, 48, 50–52, 54, 56, 57–63, 64–66, 67, 68, 69, 70, 75, 76, 82, 83–84, 87–88, 94–95, 97–99, 102–3, 106–8, 110–11, 115–16, 117, 118, 136, 140, 154–55, 156, 187, 211–12, 264
free wage labor, 28–29, 70, 72–73
Freeman, Elizabeth, 14
Freeman, Watson, 78f, 81
Frémont, John C., 102–3, 106
French, Mansfield, 181–82
Frothingham, Octavius, 227, 230
fugitive slaves, 14, 39–41, 52, 58–59, 62, 65–66, 67–68, 76, 79–80, 81, 86–87, 89, 100, 112, 116, 118, 123, 159, 170
  Act of 1793, 58–59, 66–67, 96–97
  Act of 1850, 57–59, 60, 62–64, 65–66, 69, 81, 83, 85–86, 87–88, 95, 104–5, 108–9, 111, 159–61, 176–77, 271–72
  See also runaways
Fuller, Margaret, 231, 232
Fuller, Richard, 91–92

Gabriel, 118, 170
Gage, Frances, 128
Gannett, William Channing, 92
Garfield, James A., 215, 256, 258, 263
Garnett, Henry Highland, 6–7
Garrison, William Lloyd, 1–2, 5, 7–8, 17–18, 22–23, 38–41, 51, 52, 54–55, 58–59, 60–61, 64–66, 69–70, 72, 74–75, 79–80, 81, 86–87, 96, 105–6, 108, 109–12, 115–16, 120, 125–26, 127–28, 136, 140, 143–44, 145, 156, 161, 162–63, 224, 231, 233–34, 236–37, 257, 259–60, 274, 293, 295–96
  disagreements with TWH, 40, 68–69, 76, 130–31, 132–33, 155
  pacifism of, 39–40, 66, 87–88, 105–6, 171
Garrison, William Lloyd, Jr., 271–72, 279–80, 281, 282–83

Geary, John, 97–99, 101–2, 104–5, 187
Georgia, 66–67, 68, 174–75, 184–86, 187–88, 192, 195, 196, 223–24
Giddings, Joshua, 68, 110–11, 125–26
Gillmore, Quincy Adams, 206, 207, 210
Gilman, Charlotte Perkins, 291
Goethe, Johann Wolfgang von, 34
Gompers, Samuel, 286
Grand Army of the Republic (GAR), 222–23
Grant, Ulysses, 224–25, 245, 255–56
Great Britain, 66, 88, 138, 154, 241–42, 248, 267, 284–85, 288–89, 294
Greeley, Horace, 67–68, 80, 101, 103–4, 134–35, 165, 193, 220–21, 223–24, 234–35, 237, 245, 261–62
Grimes, Leonard, 66–67
Grimké, Archibald, 295

Hale, John, 69, 83
Hallett, Benjamin, 81, 83
Hallowell, Edward "Ned," 204–5
Hallowell, Norwood Penrose "Pen," 158–59, 170–71, 263–64, 292–93
Hallowell, William, 294
Halpin, Maria, 265
Hamilton, Alexander, 261
Hamilton, Robert, 203–4
Hamilton-Gordon, John, 285
Hampton, Wade III, 258
Harlan, John Marshall, 251
Harper, Joseph W., 264
Harper's Bazar, 276–77, 278–79, 280–81, 283, 291
Harpers Ferry, Virginia, 6–7, 114, 134–35, 136, 138, 139, 140, 141, 144–45, 146–48, 151, 154, 159, 164–65, 220, 236, 251
Harrison, Benjamin, 281
Harrison, William Henry, 32
Harvard College, 5–6, 9, 11, 13–14, 16, 18*f*, 18–19, 21–22, 23–24, 25, 26, 27–28, 31–32, 33–34, 35, 36, 37, 48, 59, 107–8, 123–24, 228, 239, 248–49, 260–61, 262, 263, 275, 278, 281, 285–86, 291–93
    Divinity School, 41–42, 44*f*, 46–47, 67, 124–25, 154, 170, 172, 204, 223, 225
    Law School, 81
Hawks, Esther Hill, 209
Hawthorne, Nathaniel, 212, 261–62, 269–70
Hayden, Edward, 270, 272–73
Hayden, Lewis, 7, 65–66, 76–78, 80, 81, 83–84, 279–80
Hayes, Lucy Webb, 251
Hayes, Rutherford B., 245

Hazlett, Albert, 140, 145, 147–48, 149–50, 151
Hegel, George, 41
Hendricks, Thomas, 264–65
Higginson, Ann Herbert, 12, 13
Higginson, Ann Storrow, 9
Higginson, Edward Cabot (TWH's brother), 17
Higginson, Edward Cabot (TWH's brother, the second of that name), 17, 21, 243
Higginson, Elizabeth (TWH's half-sister), 16
Higginson, Elizabeth (TWH's half-sister, the second of that name), 16, 17–18, 28
Higginson, Elizabeth Cabot, 13–14
Higginson, Francis, 3–4, 11–13
Higginson, Francis John, 17–20, 22, 34–35, 38–39
Higginson, Francis Lee (TWH's nephew), 204, 205
Higginson, James, 15
Higginson, John, 12, 13, 17
Higginson, John, Jr., 13
Higginson, Louisa Storrow, 9, 16–17, 33, 34–36, 41, 46, 60, 67, 97–98, 107, 173–74, 179, 196–98, 201, 208–9, 226, 228–29, 252
    death of, 212–13
    marriage of, 17, 18–19, 22
    as mother, 11, 19–21, 22–23, 27–28, 29–30
Higginson, Louisa (TWH's niece), 80–81
Higginson, Louisa Wentworth (TWH's daughter), 252
Higginson, Margaret Waldo (TWH's daughter), 9, 252–53, 266–67, 269, 273, 274, 275, 277–78, 284–85, 288–89, 291, 292–93, 294
Higginson, Martha Sewall Salisbury, 11, 16
Higginson, Mary Channing, 3–4, 9, 35–36, 41–42, 43–45, 46, 49, 50–51, 57–48, 67–68, 73–74, 85–86, 88–89, 91–92, 95, 103–4, 150, 166–67, 170–72, 178, 181, 196–98, 201, 208–9, 239, 240–41
    caustic nature of, 46, 241
    death of, 245–46, 247–49, 251–52, 268–69
    health issues of, 46, 47–48, 80–81, 91, 92–93, 97, 125–26, 166, 203, 208, 211–12, 216–17, 219–20, 244–45
Higginson, Mary Lee (TWH's sister), 17–18
Higginson, Mary "Minnie" Thatcher, 9, 43, 249–50, 251, 252, 253–55, 266–67, 270, 272, 273, 274, 275, 280, 281, 283, 284–85, 289, 292–93, 294
    birth of children, 252–53
    death of, 294
    publications of, 249–50, 277, 293–94
Higginson, Samuel Thatcher, 17–18, 19–20, 41–42
    death of, 34–35

Higginson, Stephen (TWH's father), 9, 13–14, 16–17, 19
  death of, 22
  financial problems, 18–19, 21
  TWH's disdain for, 16
Higginson, Stephen (TWH's half-brother), 16
Higginson, Stephen (TWH's brother), 17, 20, 22, 80–81
Higginson, Stephen (TWH's great-grandfather), 13–14
Higginson, Stephen, Jr. (TWH's grandfather), 14, 15–16
Higginson, Susan Channing, 17–18
Higginson, Susan Louisa, 9, 17–18, 217, 220, 228–29, 244–45, 248–49
Higginson, Thomas Wentworth, birth and childhood, 11, 20–23
  and abolitionism, 22–23, 38–40, 50–51, 58, 59–60, 68, 69, 96–97, 105, 131
  as army officer, 166–67, 171–77, 178–211
  courtships, 31–32, 35–36, 43–45, 249–50
  death of, 1, 292–93 (see also specific book and magazine titles)
  education, 20, 23–28, 31, 36–38, 41, 43–45
  educational reform, 225–26, 228, 255, 259, 283
  as father, 252–53, 289
  foreign languages, 24, 31, 34, 41, 228, 232, 275
  freedom of religion, 4, 48–49, 86, 225–26, 227–28, 282
  and fugitive slaves, 65–67, 76–80, 83–84, 86–87
  Higginson, Waldo, 17–18, 19–20, 22, 34–35, 46, 48, 51–52, 59–61, 178, 217, 241–42, 244, 273, 280
  illnesses, 208–9, 274–75, 283–84, 291–92
  marriages of, 43–46, 251
  in Massachusetts legislature, 253–55, 256–57
  ministries, 43–48, 49–50, 52–54, 55–56, 67
  physical fitness, 1–2, 4, 33–34, 37, 40, 43, 57–58, 128, 163, 211, 287
  political candidacies of, 60–63, 270–73
  publications, 9–10, 52, 59–60, 163–65, 170, 221, 228–30, 257, 259–62, 268–69, 276, 277, 278–79
  socialism and anti-imperialism, 274, 286–87, 291
  as teacher, 31, 33–34, 40
  temperance and anti-tobacco, 71, 74, 163, 227–28, 256–57
  travels of, 27, 28–29, 241–43, 248, 284–85, 288–89
  and women's rights, 54–55, 67, 71–73, 74–75, 90, 128–30, 221, 234–39, 256–57, 267, 282, 283
Hildreth, John, 283, 292
Hinton, Richard, 147–48
Hoar, George Frisbie, 81–82
Hobart, Garret, 287
Holmes, Oliver Wendell, Jr., 158–59, 170–71
Holmes, Oliver Wendell, Sr., 11, 49, 86, 131, 211–12, 293
Hooker, Isabella Beecher, 236
Houghton Mifflin Publishers, 275–76, 278–79, 293–94
Howe, Julia Ward, 7–8, 227, 230, 232, 236–37, 267–68, 278, 282–83
Howe, Samuel Gridley, 115–16, 137, 162
Howells, William Dean, 256, 291–92
Hoyt, George, 138, 147
Hugo, Victor, 179, 248
Hunter, Andrew, 138
Hunter, David, 174–75, 182–83, 184, 185, 195, 198, 200–1, 202, 203, 205–6
Hurlbert, Katharine Parker Tracy, 267
Hurlbut, Stephen, 222–23
Hurlbut, William Henry, 41–43, 46, 48, 123–24, 222–23, 267, 268–69, 280
Huxley, Thomas Henry, 248

Inter-Collegiate Socialist Society, 291
Islamic faith, 41, 64

Jabir, Johari, 9–10
Jackson, Helen Hunt, 217, 275–76
Jackson, Jonathan, 13–14
Jackson, Thomas J., 146
Jacksonville, Florida, 195–96, 198–204, 210–11, 247–48, 258
  capture of, 196–98
James, Henry, 8–9
Jefferson, Thomas, 14–15, 260–61
Jewish faith, 41, 227
Jewitt, John, 70
Johnson, Andrew, 176–77, 220–21, 222–23, 224, 256, 259–60
Johnson, Samuel, 37–38, 43–45, 46, 48, 49–50

Kanada, Swani Vive, 282
Kansas, 5, 76, 85–86, 95, 96–97, 101–5, 108–9, 114–19, 121–22, 148, 187
  "Bleeding" Kansas, 6, 88, 94, 130, 137, 141, 154
  TWH's travels in, 5, 97–101, 112–13, 161, 166–67, 270, 278

INDEX 337

Kansas-Nebraska Act, 75, 100–1, 110, 123–24
Kant, Immanuel, 41
Keats, John, 168–69
Keith, Reuel, 17–18, 22–23, 28
Keller, Helen, 281
Kempton, William, 14–15
Kennedy, William Sloane, 276–77
Kentucky, 28, 49, 58–59, 102–3, 108–9, 148, 176–77, 263–64, 284–85
Knapp, Charles, 51–52, 58–59, 62–63
Kropotkin, Peter, 285

Ladies' Home Journal, 278–79, 283
Lane, James Henry, 100–1, 104–5, 107–8
Larger History of the United States to the Close of President Jackson's Administration, 261–62
Laud, William, 11–12
Lawrence, Kansas, 95, 99–100, 102–4, 118, 123, 154
LeBarnes, John, 147, 148, 149–50, 151
Lecompton, Kansas, 5, 99, 118
Lee, Robert E., 135
Liberator, 7–8, 22–23, 38–40, 60–61, 64–66, 71–72, 75, 86–87, 93, 95, 105–6, 109–10, 115–16, 155, 161
Liberty Bell, The, 5, 39, 52
Liberty Party, 2, 39–41, 50–51, 59–61, 64–66, 88, 101, 102–3, 130–31, 133, 145–46, 154–55, 156, 264
Lincoln, Abraham, 1–2, 136, 154–55, 156, 157, 158, 161–62, 170, 174–75, 176–77, 181, 182–83, 184–85, 195, 198, 205–6, 212–14, 215, 220–21, 259–60, 262, 286
Livermore, Mary, 236–37
Livermore, Thomas, 284
Lodge, Henry Cabot, 284
Loguen, Jermain Wesley, 85–86
London, Great Britain, 124, 241–42, 248, 267, 284–85
London, Jack, 291
Long, John Davis, 257–58
Longfellow, Henry Wadsworth, 24–25, 54–55, 86, 131, 249–50, 252, 293
Longfellow, Samuel, 37–38, 67, 230, 251
Lovell, John, 97
Lowell, James Russell, 3–4, 49, 73, 128–29, 131, 245, 293
Lowndes, James, 187
Loyal Legion (Massachusetts), 278
Lyceum circuit, 8–9, 49, 56, 58, 62, 221–22
Lynch, Bridget, 57

Madison, James, 13–14
Mahan, Alfred, 286–88

Maine, 71, 90, 92–93, 137, 138, 148, 152–53, 181–82, 193–95, 200–3, 210–11, 214, 223, 224, 228, 249–50, 252–53, 255–56, 263, 265, 280, 282–83
Malbone: An Oldport Romance, 228–29, 240–41, 250, 259, 267, 268–69
Mann, Horace, 62–63, 145, 259–60
Mann, Mary, 145
Marmion, Nicholas, 251
Martin, J. Sella, 145, 159
Martin, Oramel, 93–94
Martineau, Harriet, 38–39, 52
Maryland, 108–9, 123, 136, 138, 142, 170, 251
Mason, James Murray, 58–59, 151–53
Massachusetts, 11, 14, 50–52, 56, 59, 62, 64, 65, 66–67, 71, 79–80, 81, 85, 87, 88, 94–95, 101, 104, 107–8, 116–17, 128, 148, 152, 153–54, 158, 161, 166–67, 171–72, 173–74, 208–9, 213–14, 239, 249–50, 256–57, 262, 266–67, 280, 285–86
Massachusetts Anti-Slavery Society, 77–78
Massachusetts Historical Society, 163–64, 277–78
Massachusetts State Kansas Committee, 114, 115
May, Samuel, 63–64, 76, 137, 145
May, Samuel Joseph, 85–86, 109–10, 156
Mayo, A. D., 85–86
McCormick, Abner, 200
McDowell, Irvin, 165–66
McKim, James, 146–47
McKinley, William, 259, 281, 286–87
Merriam, Francis Jackson, 205–6
Mexican War, 45–46, 49
Military Reconstruction Act, 233–34
Militia Acts, 214
Missouri Compromise, 75
Mitchell, Margaret, 295
Monroe, James, 170
Montgomery, James, 148–50, 161, 182–83, 195–98, 200–1, 202, 203–4, 205, 206, 209–10
Moore, Miles, 101
Mott, Lucretia, 72–73, 74, 75, 90–91, 101, 227, 230, 236, 237

Nast, Thomas, 260–61
National Woman Suffrage Association, 235–36, 237
Nell, William C., 125–26, 163–64
New England, 4, 8–9, 16, 22–23, 24–25, 33–34, 37, 39, 45–46, 48, 49, 52–55, 57–58, 63–64, 68, 73, 83–84, 87–88, 93, 94–95, 96–97, 102–3, 108–9, 111, 115–16, 123, 131, 143–44, 157, 159, 167, 172, 178, 199–200, 209, 213, 219, 221, 227–28, 239–40, 249–50, 256, 262–63, 266, 281, 293

New England Anti-Slavery Society, 147–48
New England Emigrant Aid Company, 116–17
New England Historical Society, 284
New England Woman Suffrage League, 283
New Jersey, 102–3, 105–6, 150, 226
New Mexico, 57–59
New Orleans, Louisiana, 63–64, 74–75, 82, 170–71, 220–21
New York, New York, 14, 22, 63–64, 71–72, 74, 90–91, 97, 110, 111–12, 118–19, 121–22, 124, 126–27, 128, 130–31, 147, 173, 181–82, 185, 194, 208–9, 221–23, 234, 237, 239, 263, 264, 266, 267
New York Anti-Slavery Society, 130–31
New York State, 68, 76, 90, 116, 117, 120, 124–25, 135, 138, 156, 227–28, 258, 263, 266–67, 272–73, 287
Newburyport, Massachusetts, 4, 43–49, 50–51, 54–55, 57, 58, 59, 63–64, 71, 171
Newport, Rhode Island, 211–12, 216, 219, 225–26, 228–29, 232, 241–42, 245, 247, 248–50
Newton, Edward, 15
Niles, Thomas, 275–76
North American Review, 41, 86, 257, 291
North Elba, New York, 118–19, 123, 140, 141–43, 145, 150

Olmsted, Frederick Law, 103–4
Ormsby, Ella, 286–87
Osceola, 261–62
Osgood, James, 256

Palfrey, John Gorham, 64
Palmer, George, 266–67
Paris, France, 248, 285, 288–89
Parker, Francis, 24–26, 28–29, 42
Parker, Theodore, 4, 5, 6, 36–37, 38, 59, 67–69, 74, 83
Parkman, Francis, 257
Parsons, William, 190, 191
Parton, James, 260–62
Peirce, Benjamin, 24–25
Pennsylvania, 69–70, 98–99, 102, 105–6, 134, 147–48, 154, 156–57, 162, 194, 203, 204, 213, 262
Perkins, Samuel, 15, 38–39
Perkins, Stephen Higginson, 33–34, 35
Personal liberty laws, 87, 151, 159
Philadelphia, 13–14, 28, 70–71, 75, 87–88, 90, 120, 146–47, 181–82, 193–94, 198–99, 222–23, 224, 236–37, 251, 264
Phillips, Wendell, 17–18, 38, 51, 59, 68, 72–73, 74, 77–78, 81, 83

Pierce, Edward, 202
Pierce, Franklin, 69, 81, 83
Pillsbury, Parker, 7–8, 52, 68–69, 125–26, 132–33, 154–55, 233–34, 237
planters, 38–39, 63–64, 83–84, 96, 116, 131, 206. *See also* slaveholders
Port Royal, South Carolina, 166–67, 173, 174–75, 177, 187–88, 193–94, 203, 206
Porter, John, 45–46
Post, Amy Kirby, 125–26
Potter, James, 65
Pratt, Caleb, 103–4
Pratt, Elvira, 117
Prescott, Harriet, 48–49
Proslavery thought, 6, 32, 64–65, 69–70, 85, 90, 95, 101–2, 104–5, 115–16, 118, 130–31, 148, 151, 173, 202, 209–10
Purvis, Robert, 6–7, 110
Putman, Caroline, 260
Pyle, Howard, 261

Quakers, 48, 59–60, 69–70, 72–73, 147–48, 178–79, 226
Quarles, Benjamin, 6–7
Quincy, Josiah, 23–24, 107–8

Racism and segregation, 86, 99, 102, 109, 111, 159, 185, 186–87, 194–95, 202, 205, 209–10, 213–14, 225–26, 229–30
Radical Club (Boston), 2–3, 230–31, 232, 239–40
Randolph, William, 205
Rantoul, Robert, 64
Reconstruction, 220–22, 233–34, 259–60, 262, 274, 295
Redpath, James, 97–98, 108, 116–17, 132, 136, 137–38, 146–47, 148–49, 153, 221–22
Reed, William, 198–99
Reid, Marion, 43–45, 283
Remond, Charles Lenox, 68–69, 110, 128, 145
Republican Party, 6–7, 80, 89–90, 94–95, 100–1, 102, 104–12, 116, 122, 132–33, 136, 140, 144–46, 151, 154–55, 156–57, 159, 171, 176, 182–83, 194–95, 199–200, 209–10, 220–21, 224, 245, 253–55, 259–60, 262, 263–65, 266–67, 270–72, 286–89, 293
Reynold, David, 6
Rhode Island, 21, 211–12, 225–26, 235–36, 239, 258, 268–69, 283
Richmond, Virginia, 28–29, 130–31, 165–66, 170, 178–79, 194–95, 247–48, 261–62
Richter, Jean Paul, 41
Rivers, Prince, 181–82, 185, 186, 187, 213–14, 222–23, 245, 257–58

Roberts Brothers Publishers, 275–76, 277
Robertson, Stacey, 7–8
Robinson, Charles, 98–99
Rogers, Seth, 105, 178–79, 182, 187, 191–94, 208, 209, 222–23
Rome (Italy), 123–24, 288–89
Roosevelt, Theodore, 287
Rose, Ernestine, 75
Round Table Club (Boston), 267, 278
Ruffin, Edmund, 146
runaway slaves, 7, 14, 52, 58–59, 62, 65, 67–68, 83–84, 86–87, 109, 118, 120–21, 131, 133–34, 154, 159, 165–66, 172–73, 174–75, 192–93, 195, 204, 206. *See also* fugitive slaves
Rust, John, 200–1, 202–3
Rutherford, William, 149

Salem, Massachusetts, 11–14, 16, 38–39, 67
Sanborn, Franklin, 97–98, 102–3, 112–13, 114–17, 119, 120–23, 132, 133–34, 137–40, 147, 151–53, 236, 292–93
Sand, George (Amantine Aurore Lucile Dupin), 232
Sargent, John Turner, 230, 232
Sargent, Mary, 230
Saxton, Rufus, 10, 166–67, 172–76, 178–83, 187–88, 190–91, 192–93, 194, 195–96, 198–99, 203, 210–11, 213–14, 259–60, 295–96
Sayles, Lita Barney, 265
Schiller, Friedrich, 34, 41
Schurz, Carl, 264, 271–72
Secession, 109, 111–12, 146, 157, 158–59, 161–63, 247–48
Seneca Falls, New York, 128, 156–57
Sennott, George, 137, 142
Sewall, Samuel, 38–39, 77–78
Seward, William Henry, 68, 106–7, 122, 145–46, 152, 154–55, 159, 162–63
Seymour, Truman, 202
Shakespeare, William, 48–49, 179, 207, 241–42
Shaw, Francis, 210
Shaw, Robert Gould, 162, 176–77, 184, 204–5, 258, 259–60, 279–80, 284
Shaw, Sarah, 159, 162, 284
Sheffield, William, 225–26
Sims, Thomas, 65–67, 68–69, 76, 81–82
Sinclair, Upton, 291
slave power theory, 6–7, 50, 54, 57–59, 66–67, 69–71, 83–84, 108–9, 110, 153, 156
slaveholders, 3–4, 40–41, 45–46, 49, 54, 58, 82, 87–88, 102–3, 105–6, 107, 109–11, 122, 133, 138, 142, 151, 155, 156, 161, 163, 179. *See also* planters
slavery, 1–2, 3–4, 6–7, 14, 22–23, 28–29, 32, 38–41, 46–47, 48, 49, 50, 51, 54, 57–59, 62, 63–64, 65, 68, 69, 70, 72, 75, 79–80, 83–84, 85, 87, 94–95, 96–97, 101–3, 107–8, 109, 112, 118, 130, 145–46, 154–55, 161, 162–63, 164, 165–66, 167, 170, 176, 177, 184–85, 196–98, 211–12, 233, 259–60, 261–62
Smalls, Robert, 173–74, 210, 213–14
Smith, Gerrit, 4, 51, 68, 88, 103, 104, 105–6, 109–10, 114, 116, 119, 120, 121, 122–23, 132, 133, 134, 138–39, 140, 145–46, 152–53, 154–56, 220–21, 233–34, 237
Smith, James Joyner, 179
Smith, Thomas, 14
Smith-Miller, Elizabeth, 282–83
South Atlantic Blockading Squadron, 277–78
South Carolina, 2–3, 6, 9–10, 42, 73–74, 88, 94, 101, 158–59, 164, 166–67, 172–75, 178, 181–83, 184–85, 194–95, 205, 212, 213–14, 215, 216, 222–24, 226, 229–30, 245, 257–58, 259–60, 278–79
South Edisto River, South Carolina, 206–7, 213, 216, 221
Spain, 154–55, 288–89
Spanish-American War, 285–86
Spencer, Herbert, 248
Spiritualism, 13, 124–28, 226–27
Spooner, Lysander, 118, 131
Sprague, Augustus, 171–72
Sprague, Peleg, 85
Spring, Rebecca Buffum, 147–48
St. Louis, Missouri, 95, 96, 101, 110, 116–17, 247–48, 255–56
St. Mary's River, South Carolina, 185–86, 187–88, 191–92, 194, 195–96, 213
Stanton, Edwin, 194, 195, 198
Stanton, Elizabeth Cady, 2, 128, 137–57, 162–63, 216, 221–22, 233–39
Stanton, Henry, 156–57, 162–63
Stearns, George Luther, 116–17, 120–21, 122–23, 156, 162, 220–21
Steedman, Charles, 186–87, 200–1, 208–9
Stevens, Aaron Dwight, 140, 145, 147–48, 149–51
Stevens, Thaddeus, 194–95, 214
Stickley, Daniel, 137
Stockholm Prison Congress, 247–48
Stone, Lucy, 9, 71–72, 73–75, 83, 90–91, 92–93, 96, 101, 128–29, 145, 156, 221, 234, 235–37, 239, 257, 279–81
  disagreement with TWH, 266–67
  and marriage protest, 88–90, 237–39

Story, Joseph, 26, 28
Story, William, 26
Storrow, Ann "Anna," 16–17, 21
Storrow, Anne "Nancy," 9, 21, 22, 27–28, 35–36, 43–45, 46, 228–29, 280
Storrow, Thomas, 16–17
Stowe, Harriet Beecher, 17–18, 67–68, 125–26, 163, 164–65, 234, 236, 247–48, 291–92
Stowell, Martin, 76–78, 79–80, 81–82, 83, 85–86, 97
Strong, Charles, 124
Strong, John, 209
Stuart, Henry Middleton, 185
Sullivan, Anne, 281
Sumner, Charles, 50–51, 54–55, 62–63, 64–65, 86–87, 107, 156, 165, 176–77, 213–15, 220–21, 224–25, 234, 259–60
  attack on, 94, 106, 130
Sutton, Robert, 181–82, 185–86, 187–88, 190–93, 205–6, 213–14, 258
Syracuse, New York, 76, 85–86, 109–10, 118–19

Taney, Roger, 108, 110
Tappan, Lewis, 102–3
Tappan, Samuel, 102–3
Tariff Reform League, 262, 273
Taylor, Susie King, 196, 201, 202, 212
Taylor, Zachary, 45–46, 50, 51–52
temperance, 49, 70–72, 74–75, 85–86, 93, 110–11, 182, 204–5, 208, 210, 224, 227–28, 256–57, 296
Tennyson, Alfred, 43
Texas, 32, 50, 63–64, 292
Thatcher, Francis, 294
Thatcher, Peter, 249–50, 251, 280
Thayer, Eli, 94–95, 97, 98–99, 103–5, 153
Thirteenth Amendment, 7–8, 216, 220–21, 233
Thomas, Hiram, 282
Thompson, Corbin, 96–97, 101
Thompson, Henry, 141
Thompson, Ruth, 145
Thoreau, Henry David, 2, 4, 58, 139, 167–68
Tidd, Charles, 148–49, 154
Tocqueville, Alexis de, 73
Todd, Mabel Loomis, 275–76
Toombs, Robert, 194–95
Towne, Laura, 181–82, 210–11
Train, George Francis, 234, 236
transcendentalism, 4, 13, 34, 36–37, 49, 54–55, 116, 126–27
Travelers and Outlaws: Episodes in American History, 260–61

Trowbridge, Charles, 188, 209–10
Trumbull, Lyman, 176–77, 224
Tubman, Harriet, 9–10, 123, 130, 132–33, 206
Turner, Henry McNeal, 223–24
Turner, Nat, 8–9, 118, 163–65, 170
Tyler, John, 32

Underwood, Francis, 70
Unitarianism, 3–4, 5–6, 36–37, 41, 42, 63–64, 72–73, 115–16, 125–26, 127, 226, 227–28, 230, 282, 292–93
United States Army, 134–35, 161, 166, 176, 187–88, 198, 206
United States Colored Troops (USCT), 194–95, 211, 221, 222–23, 284

Van Buren, Martin, 50, 69
Van Horne, Mahlon, 226
Vermont, 17–18, 34–35, 97, 103, 104, 165, 171–72, 178, 223, 227, 236–37, 239, 244, 280
Very, Jones, 24–25
Vesey, Denmark, 7, 8–9, 118, 163–64, 165, 170
Vigilance committees, 59, 65–66, 76, 81–82
Villard, Oswald, 5
Virginia, 6, 17–18, 22–23, 28, 32, 70, 76, 79, 90, 101, 108–9, 114, 118–19, 120, 122, 133–35, 137–38, 139–40, 141–42, 146, 147–48, 152, 154, 161, 164–66, 170–71, 178–79, 192–93, 260
Virginia Military Academy, 146
Voting rights, 50–51, 73, 102, 224–25, 233–34, 256, 258, 281

Wade, Benjamin, 233–34
Walker, Arnold, 107–8
Walker, Quok, 14
Walker, William, 97–98, 187
War Department, U.S., 100–1, 161, 166, 174–75, 182–83, 192–93, 194, 195–96, 205, 211, 214–15
War of 1812, 15
Warren, G. F., 148–49
Warren, William, 283
Washburne, William, 255–56
Washington, Booker T., 292–93
Wasson, David, 231
Wayland, H. W., 144–45
Webb, Richard, 54
Webster, Daniel, 49, 63–64
Weld, Stephen, 31, 33–34, 37
Wells, H. G., 285
Wells, Kate Gannett, 250
Wells, William, 17–18, 23

West Virginia, 229–30, 251
Weston, Anne Warren, 54–55
Whig Party, 3–4, 45–46, 49, 50, 51–52, 54, 55–56, 58–61, 62–65, 105–6, 154–55, 262
   Conscience Whigs, 61
Whitman, Walt, 168–69, 276–77, 278–79
Whittier, John Greenleaf, 48, 59–60, 61, 64
Wightman, Joseph, 159
Willis, Nathaniel, 124–25
Wilmot Proviso, 62
Wilson, Henry, 68–69
Wilson, Rufus, 278
Wilson, Woodrow, 10
Winehouse, Brenda, 5
Wines, Frederick, 247–48
Winthrop, John, 12–13
Wise, Henry, 137–38, 141–42, 143, 146–48
Women's Club (Boston), 244

Woman's Journal, 236–39, 265, 267, 270
   TWH's resignation from, 265, 267, 280–81
women's rights, 1–2, 3–4, 7–8, 39–40, 45, 54–55, 71–72, 73, 74–75, 90, 92–93, 97, 101, 109, 128, 130–31, 134, 141, 143–44, 216, 221, 227, 230, 233–37, 241–43, 259, 274, 282–83, 293, 296
Woods, John, 272–73
Woodward, W. E., 295
Worcester, Massachusetts, 7, 67–68, 70–71, 76, 79–83, 86, 89, 92–93, 94–95, 97, 105, 108, 109–11, 116–17, 118–20, 132, 136, 140, 143–44, 149, 151, 153–54, 158, 166, 171–72, 178, 211–12, 225–26, 282–83
Worcester County Kansas Committee, 115
Wright, Elizur, 7–8

Young Folks' History of the United States, 213, 259, 260–62, 269–70, 282